Advanced Deep Learning with Python

Design and implement advanced next-generation AI solutions
using TensorFlow and PyTorch

Ivan Vasilev

BIRMINGHAM - MUMBAI

Advanced Deep Learning with Python

Commissioning Editor: Pravin Dhandre
Acquisition Editor: Devika Battike
Content Development Editor: Nathanya Dias
Senior Editor: Ayaan Hoda
Technical Editor: Manikandan Kurup
Copy Editor: Safis Editing
Project Coordinator: Aishwarya Mohan
Proofreader: Safis Editing
Indexer: Tejal Daruwale Soni
Production Designer: Nilesh Mohite

First published: December 2019

Production reference: 1111219

Published by Packt Publishing Ltd.
Livery Place
35 Livery Street
Birmingham
B3 2PB, UK.

ISBN 978-1-78995-617-7

www.packt.com

`Packt.com`

Subscribe to our online digital library for full access to over 7,000 books and videos, as well as industry leading tools to help you plan your personal development and advance your career. For more information, please visit our website.

Why subscribe?

- Spend less time learning and more time coding with practical eBooks and Videos from over 4,000 industry professionals

- Improve your learning with Skill Plans built especially for you

- Get a free eBook or video every month

- Fully searchable for easy access to vital information

- Copy and paste, print, and bookmark content

Did you know that Packt offers eBook versions of every book published, with PDF and ePub files available? You can upgrade to the eBook version at `www.packt.com` and as a print book customer, you are entitled to a discount on the eBook copy. Get in touch with us at `customercare@packtpub.com` for more details.

At `www.packt.com`, you can also read a collection of free technical articles, sign up for a range of free newsletters, and receive exclusive discounts and offers on Packt books and eBooks.

Contributors

About the author

Ivan Vasilev started working on the first open source Java deep learning library with GPU support in 2013. The library was acquired by a German company, where he continued to develop it. He has also worked as a machine learning engineer and researcher in the area of medical image classification and segmentation with deep neural networks. Since 2017, he has been focusing on financial machine learning. He is working on a Python-based platform that provides the infrastructure to rapidly experiment with different machine learning algorithms for algorithmic trading. Ivan holds an MSc degree in artificial intelligence from the University of Sofia, St. Kliment Ohridski.

About the reviewer

Saibal Dutta has been working as an analytical consultant in SAS Research and Development. He is also pursuing a PhD in data mining and machine learning from IIT, Kharagpur. He holds an M.Tech in electronics and communication from the National Institute of Technology, Rourkela. He has worked at TATA communications, Pune, and HCL Technologies Limited, Noida, as a consultant. In his 7 years of consulting experience, he has been associated with global players including IKEA (in Sweden) and Pearson (in the US). His passion for entrepreneurship led him to create his own start-up in the field of data analytics. His areas of expertise include data mining, artificial intelligence, machine learning, image processing, and business consultation.

Packt is searching for authors like you

If you're interested in becoming an author for Packt, please visit `authors.packtpub.com` and apply today. We have worked with thousands of developers and tech professionals, just like you, to help them share their insight with the global tech community. You can make a general application, apply for a specific hot topic that we are recruiting an author for, or submit your own idea.

Table of Contents

Preface

This book is a collection of newly evolved deep learning models, methodologies, and implementations based on the areas of their application. In the first section of the book, you will learn about the building blocks of deep learning and the math behind **neural networks** (**NNs**). In the second section, you'll focus on **convolutional neural networks** (**CNNs**) and their advanced applications in **computer vision** (**CV**). You'll learn to apply the most popular CNN architectures in object detection and image segmentation. Finally, you'll discuss variational autoencoders and generative adversarial networks.

In the third section, you'll focus on natural language and sequence processing. You'll use NNs to extract sophisticated vector representations of words. You'll discuss various types of recurrent networks, such as **long short-term memory** (**LSTM**) and **gated recurrent unit** (GRU). Finally, you'll cover the attention mechanism to process sequential data without the help of recurrent networks. In the final section, you'll learn how to use graph NNs to process structured data. You'll cover meta-learning, which allows you to train an NN with fewer training samples. And finally, you'll learn how to apply deep learning in autonomous vehicles.

By the end of this book, you'll have gained mastery of the key concepts associated with deep learning and evolutionary approaches to monitoring and managing deep learning models.

Who this book is for

This book is for data scientists, deep learning engineers and researchers, and AI developers who want to master deep learning and want to build innovative and unique deep learning projects of their own. This book will also appeal to those who are looking to get well-versed with advanced use cases and the methodologies adopted in the deep learning domain using real-world examples. Basic conceptual understanding of deep learning and a working knowledge of Python is assumed.

What this book covers

Chapter 1, *The Nuts and Bolts of Neural Networks*, will briefly introduce what deep learning is and then discuss the mathematical underpinnings of NNs. This chapter will discuss NNs as mathematical models. More specifically, we'll focus on vectors, matrices, and differential calculus. We'll also discuss some gradient descent variations, such as Momentum, Adam, and Adadelta, in depth. We will also discuss how to deal with imbalanced datasets.

Chapter 2, *Understanding Convolutional Networks*, will provide a short description of CNNs. We'll discuss CNNs and their applications in CV

Chapter 3, *Advanced Convolutional Networks*, will discuss some advanced and widely used NN architectures, including VGG, ResNet, MobileNets, GoogleNet, Inception, Xception, and DenseNets. We'll also implement ResNet and Xception/MobileNets using PyTorch.

Chapter 4, *Object Detection and Image Segmentation*, will discuss two important vision tasks: object detection and image segmentation. We'll provide implementations for both of them.

Chapter 5, *Generative Models*, will begin the discussion about generative models. In particular, we'll talk about generative adversarial networks and neural style transfer. The particular style transfer will be implemented later.

Chapter 6, *Language Modeling*, will introduce word and character-level language models. We'll also talk about word vectors (word2vec, Glove, and fastText) and we'll use Gensim to implement them. We'll also walk through the highly technical and complex process of preparing text data for machine learning applications such as topic modeling and sentiment modeling with the help of the **Natural Language ToolKit's** (**NLTK**) text processing techniques.

Chapter 7, *Understanding Recurrent Networks*, will discuss the basic recurrent networks, LSTM, and GRU cells. We'll provide a detailed explanation and pure Python implementations for all of the networks.

Chapter 8, *Sequence-to-Sequence Models and Attention*, will discuss sequence models and the attention mechanism, including bidirectional LSTMs, and a new architecture called transformer with encoders and decoders.

Chapter 9, *Emerging Neural Network Designs*, will discuss graph NNs and NNs with memory, such as **Neural Turing Machines** (**NTM**), differentiable neural computers, and MANN.

Chapter 10, *Meta Learning*, will discuss meta learning—the way to teach algorithms how to learn. We'll also try to improve upon deep learning algorithms by giving them the ability to learn more information using less training samples.

Chapter 11, *Deep Learning for Autonomous Vehicles*, will explore the applications of deep learning in autonomous vehicles. We'll discuss how to use deep networks to help the vehicle make sense of its surrounding environment.

To get the most out of this book

To get the most out of this book, you should be familiar with Python and have some knowledge of machine learning. The book includes short introductions to the major types of NNs, but it will help if you are already familiar with the basics of NNs.

Download the example code files

You can download the example code files for this book from your account at www.packt.com. If you purchased this book elsewhere, you can visit www.packtpub.com/support and register to have the files emailed directly to you.

You can download the code files by following these steps:

1. Log in or register at www.packt.com.
2. Select the **Support** tab.
3. Click on **Code Downloads**.
4. Enter the name of the book in the **Search** box and follow the onscreen instructions.

Once the file is downloaded, please make sure that you unzip or extract the folder using the latest version of:

- WinRAR/7-Zip for Windows
- Zipeg/iZip/UnRarX for Mac
- 7-Zip/PeaZip for Linux

The code bundle for the book is also hosted on GitHub at https://github.com/PacktPublishing/Advanced-Deep-Learning-with-Python. In case there's an update to the code, it will be updated on the existing GitHub repository.

We also have other code bundles from our rich catalog of books and videos available at https://github.com/PacktPublishing/. Check them out!

Download the color images

We also provide a PDF file that has color images of the screenshots/diagrams used in this book. You can download it here: `http://www.packtpub.com/sites/default/files/downloads/9781789956177_ColorImages.pdf`.

Conventions used

There are a number of text conventions used throughout this book.

`CodeInText`: Indicates code words in text, database table names, folder names, filenames, file extensions, pathnames, dummy URLs, user input, and Twitter handles. Here is an example: "Build the full GAN model by including the `generator`, `discriminator`, and the `combined` network."

A block of code is set as follows:

```
import matplotlib.pyplot as plt
from matplotlib.markers import MarkerStyle
import numpy as np
import tensorflow as tf
from tensorflow.keras import backend as K
from tensorflow.keras.layers import Lambda, Input, Dense
```

Bold: Indicates a new term, an important word, or words that you see onscreen. For example, words in menus or dialog boxes appear in the text like this. Here is an example: "The collection of all possible outcomes (events) of an experiment is called, **sample space**."

 Warnings or important notes appear like this.

 Tips and tricks appear like this.

Get in touch

Feedback from our readers is always welcome.

General feedback: If you have questions about any aspect of this book, mention the book title in the subject of your message and email us at customercare@packtpub.com.

Errata: Although we have taken every care to ensure the accuracy of our content, mistakes do happen. If you have found a mistake in this book, we would be grateful if you would report this to us. Please visit www.packtpub.com/support/errata, selecting your book, clicking on the Errata Submission Form link, and entering the details.

Piracy: If you come across any illegal copies of our works in any form on the Internet, we would be grateful if you would provide us with the location address or website name. Please contact us at copyright@packt.com with a link to the material.

If you are interested in becoming an author: If there is a topic that you have expertise in and you are interested in either writing or contributing to a book, please visit authors.packtpub.com.

Reviews

Please leave a review. Once you have read and used this book, why not leave a review on the site that you purchased it from? Potential readers can then see and use your unbiased opinion to make purchase decisions, we at Packt can understand what you think about our products, and our authors can see your feedback on their book. Thank you!

For more information about Packt, please visit packt.com.

Section 1: Core Concepts

This section will discuss some core **Deep Learning** (**DL**) concepts: what exactly DL is, the mathematical underpinnings of DL algorithms, and the libraries and tools that make it possible to develop DL algorithms rapidly.

This section contains the following chapter:

- Chapter 1, *The Nuts and Bolts of Neural Networks*

1
The Nuts and Bolts of Neural Networks

In this chapter, we'll discuss some of the intricacies of neural networks (**NNs**)—the cornerstone of **deep learning** (**DL**). We'll talk about their mathematical apparatus, structure, and training. Our main goal is to provide you with a systematic understanding of NNs. Often, we approach them from a computer science perspective—as a machine learning (**ML**) algorithm (or even a special entity) composed of a number of different steps/components. We gain our intuition by thinking in terms of neurons, layers, and so on (at least I did this when I first learned about this field). This is a perfectly valid way to do things and we can still do impressive things at this level of understanding. Perhaps this is not the correct approach, though.

NNs have solid mathematical foundations and if we approach them from this point of view, we'll be able to define and understand them in a more fundamental and elegant way. Therefore, in this chapter, we'll try to underscore the analogy between NNs from mathematical and computer science points of view. If you are already familiar with these topics, you can skip this chapter. Still, I hope that you'll find some interesting bits you didn't know about already (we'll do our best to keep this chapter interesting!).

In this chapter, we will cover the following topics:

- The mathematical apparatus of NNs
- A short introduction to NNs
- Training NNs

The mathematical apparatus of NNs

In the next few sections, we'll discuss the mathematical branches related to NNs. Once we've done this, we'll connect them to NNs themselves.

Linear algebra

Linear algebra deals with linear equations such as $a_1 x_1 + a_2 x_2 + \ldots + a_n x_n + b = 0$ and linear transformations (or linear functions) and their representations, such as matrices and vectors.

Linear algebra identifies the following mathematical objects:

- **Scalars**: A single number.
- **Vectors**: A one-dimensional array of numbers (or components). Each component of the array has an index. In literature, we will see vectors denoted either with a superscript arrow ($\vec{x}$) or in bold (**x**). The following is an example of a vector:

$$\mathbf{x} = \vec{x} = \begin{bmatrix} x_1 \\ x_2 \\ \vdots \\ x_n \end{bmatrix}$$

Throughout this book, we'll mostly use the bold (**x**) graph notations. But in some instances, we'll use formulas from different sources and we'll try to retain their original notation.

We can visually represent an n-dimensional vector as the coordinates of a point in an n-dimensional Euclidean space, $\mathbb{R}^n$ (equivalent to a coordinate system). In this case, the vector is referred to as Euclidean and each vector component represents the coordinate along the corresponding axis, as shown in the following diagram:

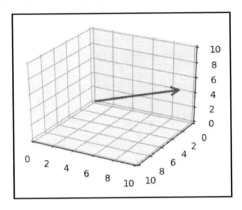

Vector representation in $\mathbb{R}^3$ space

However, the Euclidean vector is more than just a point and we can also represent it with the following two properties:

- **Magnitude** (or **length**) is a generalization of the Pythagorean theorem for an *n*-dimensional space:

$$|\mathbf{x}| = \sqrt{x_1^2 + x_2^2 + \ldots + x_n^2}$$

- **Direction** is the angle of the vector along each axis of the vector space.

- **Matrices**: This is a two-dimensional array of numbers. Each element is identified by two indices (row and column). A matrix is usually denoted with a bold capital letter; for example, **A**. Each matrix element is denoted with the small matrix letter and a subscript index; for example, a_{ij}. Let's look at an example of the matrix notation in the following formula:

$$\mathbf{A} = \begin{bmatrix} a_{11} & a_{12} & \cdots & a_{1n} \\ a_{21} & a_{22} & \cdots & a_{2n} \\ \vdots & \vdots & \ddots & \vdots \\ a_{m1} & a_{m2} & \cdots & a_{mn} \end{bmatrix}$$

We can represent a vector as a single-column *n×1* matrix (referred to as a column matrix) or a single -ow *1×n* matrix (referred to as a row matrix).

- **Tensors**: Before we explain them, we have to start with a disclaimer. Tensors originally come from mathematics and physics, where they have existed long before we started using them in ML. The tensor definition in these fields differs from the ML one. For the purposes of this book, we'll only consider tensors in the ML context. Here, a tensor is a multi-dimensional array with the following properties:

  - **Rank**: Indicates the number of array dimensions. For example, a tensor of rank 2 is a matrix, a tensor of rank 1 is a vector, and a tensor of rank 0 is a scalar. However, the tensor has no limit on the number of dimensions. Indeed, some types of NNs use tensors of rank 4.
  - **Shape**: The size of each dimension.
  - **The data type** of the tensor elements. These can vary between libraries, but typically include 16-, 32-, and 64-bit float and 8-, 16-, 32-, and 64-bit integers.

Contemporary DL libraries such as TensorFlow and PyTorch use tensors as their main data structure.

> You can find a thorough discussion on the nature of tensors here: https:/
> /stats.stackexchange.com/questions/198061/why-the-sudden-
> fascination-with-tensors. You can also check the TensorFlow (https:/
> /www.tensorflow.org/guide/tensors) and PyTorch (https://pytorch.
> org/docs/stable/tensors.html) tensor definitions.

Now that we've introduced the types of objects in linear algebra, in the next section, we'll discuss some operations that can be applied to them.

Vector and matrix operations

In this section, we'll discuss the vector and matrix operations that are relevant to NNs. Let's start:

- **Vector addition** is the operation of adding two or more vectors together into an output vector sum. The output is another vector and is computed with the following formula:

$$\mathbf{a} + \mathbf{b} = [a_1 + b_1, a_2 + b_2, \ldots, a_n + b_n]$$

- The **dot (or scalar) product** takes two vectors and outputs a scalar value. We can compute the dot product with the following formula:

$$\mathbf{a} \cdot \mathbf{b} = |\mathbf{a}|\,|\mathbf{b}|\cos\theta$$

Here, $|a|$ and $|b|$ are the vector magnitudes and θ is the angle between the two vectors. Let's assume that the two vectors are n-dimensional and that their components are a_1, b_1, a_2, b_2, and so on. Here, the preceding formula is equivalent to the following:

$$\mathbf{a} \cdot \mathbf{b} = a_1 b_1 + a_2 b_2 + \ldots + a_n b_n$$

The dot product of two two-dimensional vectors, **a** and **b**, is illustrated in the following diagram:

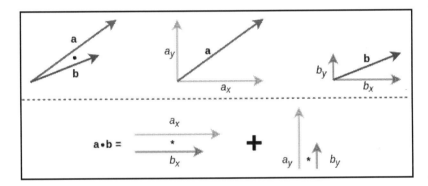

The dot product of vectors. Top: vector components: Bottom: dot product of the two vectors

The dot product acts as a kind of similarity measure between the two vectors—if the angle θ between the two vectors is small (the vectors have similar directions), then their dot product will be higher because of $\cos\theta$.

Following this idea, we can define a **cosine similarity** between two vectors as follows:

$$\cos\theta = \frac{\mathbf{a} \cdot \mathbf{b}}{|\mathbf{a}|\,|\mathbf{b}|}$$

- The **cross (or vector) product** takes two vectors and outputs another vector, which is perpendicular to both initial vectors. We can compute the magnitude of the cross product output vector with the following formula:

$$\mathbf{a} \times \mathbf{b} = |\mathbf{a}|\,|\mathbf{b}|\sin\theta$$

The following diagram shows an example of a cross product between two two-dimensional vectors:

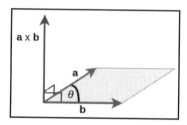

Cross product of two two-dimensional vectors

As we mentioned previously, the output vector is perpendicular to the input vectors, which also means that the vector is normal to the plane containing them. The magnitude of the output vector is equal to the area of the parallelogram with the vectors **a** and **b** for sides (denoted in the preceding diagram).

We can also define a vector through **vector space**, which is a collection of objects (in our case, vectors) that can be added together and multiplied by a scalar value. The vector space will allow us to define a **linear transformation** as a function, f, which can transform each vector (point) of vector space, V, into a vector (point) of another vector space, $W: f: V \mapsto W$. f has to satisfy the following requirements for any two vectors, $\mathbf{u}, \mathbf{v} \in V$:

- Additivity: $f(\mathbf{u} + \mathbf{v}) = f(\mathbf{u}) + f(\mathbf{v})$
- Homogeneity: $f(c\mathbf{u}) = cf(\mathbf{u})$, where c is a scalar

- **Matrix transpose**: Here, we flip the matrix along its main diagonal (the main diagonal is the collection of matrix elements, a_{ij}, where $i = j$). The transpose operation is denoted with superscript, т. To clarify, the cell a_{ij} of $\mathbf{A}^\mathsf{T}$ is equal to the cell a_{ji} of $\mathbf{A}$:

$$[\mathbf{A}^\mathsf{T}]_{ij} = \mathbf{A}_{ji}$$

The transpose of an $m \times n$ matrix is an $n \times m$ matrix. The following are a few transpose examples:

$$\mathbf{A} = \begin{bmatrix} a_{11} & a_{12} & a_{13} \\ a_{21} & a_{22} & a_{23} \\ a_{31} & a_{32} & a_{33} \end{bmatrix} \Rightarrow \mathbf{A}^\mathsf{T} = \begin{bmatrix} a_{11} & a_{21} & a_{31} \\ a_{12} & a_{22} & a_{32} \\ a_{13} & a_{23} & a_{33} \end{bmatrix}$$

$$\mathbf{A} = \begin{bmatrix} a_{11} & a_{12} & a_{13} \\ a_{21} & a_{22} & a_{23} \end{bmatrix} \Rightarrow \mathbf{A}^\mathsf{T} = \begin{bmatrix} a_{11} & a_{21} \\ a_{12} & a_{22} \\ a_{13} & a_{23} \end{bmatrix}$$

$$\mathbf{A} = \begin{bmatrix} a_{11} & a_{12} & a_{13} \end{bmatrix} \Rightarrow \mathbf{A}^\mathsf{T} = \begin{bmatrix} a_{11} \\ a_{12} \\ a_{13} \end{bmatrix}$$

- **Matrix-scalar multiplication** is the multiplication of a matrix by a scalar value. In the following example, y is a scalar:

$$\mathbf{A}y = \begin{bmatrix} a_{11} & a_{12} \\ a_{21} & a_{22} \end{bmatrix} y = \begin{bmatrix} a_{11} * y & a_{12} * y \\ a_{21} * y & a_{22} * y \end{bmatrix}$$

- **Matrix-matrix addition** is the element-wise addition of one matrix with another. For this operation, both matrices must have the same size. The following is an example:

$$\mathbf{A} + \mathbf{B} = \begin{bmatrix} a_{11} & a_{12} \\ a_{21} & a_{22} \end{bmatrix} + \begin{bmatrix} b_{11} & b_{12} \\ b_{21} & b_{22} \end{bmatrix} = \begin{bmatrix} a_{11} + b_{11} & a_{12} + b_{12} \\ a_{21} + b_{21} & a_{22} + b_{22} \end{bmatrix}$$

- **Matrix-vector multiplication** is the multiplication of a matrix by a vector. For this operation to be valid, the number of matrix columns must be equal to the vector length. The result of multiplying the $m \times n$ matrix and an n-dimensional vector is an m-dimensional vector. The following is an example:

$$\mathbf{A}x = \begin{bmatrix} a_{11} & a_{12} \\ a_{21} & a_{22} \\ a_{31} & a_{32} \end{bmatrix} \begin{bmatrix} x_1 \\ x_2 \end{bmatrix} = \begin{bmatrix} a_{11}x_1 + a_{12}x_2 \\ a_{21}x_1 + a_{22}x_2 \\ a_{31}x_1 + a_{32}x_2 \end{bmatrix}$$

$$\begin{bmatrix} a_{11} & a_{12} \end{bmatrix} \begin{bmatrix} x_1 \\ x_2 \end{bmatrix} = \begin{bmatrix} a_{11}x_1 + a_{12}x_2 \end{bmatrix}$$

We can think of each row of the matrix as a separate *n*-dimensional vector. Here, each element of the output vector is the dot product between the corresponding matrix row and **x**. The following is a numerical example:

$$\mathbf{Ax} = \begin{bmatrix} 1 & 2 \\ 3 & 4 \end{bmatrix} \begin{bmatrix} 5 \\ 6 \end{bmatrix} = \begin{bmatrix} 1*5+2*6 \\ 3*5+4*6 \end{bmatrix} = \begin{bmatrix} 17 \\ 39 \end{bmatrix}$$

- **Matrix multiplication** is the multiplication of one matrix with another. To be valid, the number of columns of the first matrix has to be equal to the number of rows of the second (this is a non-commutative operation). We can think of this operation as multiple matrix-vector multiplications, where each column of the second matrix is one vector. The result of an *m*×*n* matrix multiplied by an *n*×*p* matrix is an *m*×*p* matrix. The following is an example:

$$\mathbf{AB} = \begin{bmatrix} a_{11} & a_{12} & a_{13} \\ a_{21} & a_{22} & a_{23} \end{bmatrix} \begin{bmatrix} b_{11} & b_{12} \\ b_{21} & b_{22} \\ b_{31} & b_{32} \end{bmatrix} = \begin{bmatrix} a_{11}b_{11}+a_{12}b_{21}+a_{13}b_{31} & a_{11}b_{12}+a_{12}b_{22}+a_{13}b_{32} \\ a_{21}b_{11}+a_{22}b_{21}+a_{23}b_{31} & a_{21}b_{12}+a_{22}b_{22}+a_{23}b_{32} \end{bmatrix}$$

$$\mathbf{AB} = \begin{bmatrix} 1 & 2 & 3 \\ 4 & 5 & 6 \end{bmatrix} \begin{bmatrix} 1 & 2 \\ 3 & 4 \\ 5 & 6 \end{bmatrix} = \begin{bmatrix} 1+6+15 & 2+8+18 \\ 4+15+30 & 8+20+36 \end{bmatrix} = \begin{bmatrix} 22 & 28 \\ 49 & 64 \end{bmatrix}$$

If we consider two vectors as row matrices, we can represent a vector dot product as matrix multiplication, that is, $\mathbf{a} \cdot \mathbf{b} = \mathbf{ab}^\mathsf{T}$.

This concludes our introduction to linear algebra. In the next section, we'll introduce the probability theory.

Introduction to probability

In this section, we'll discuss some of the aspects of probability and statistics that are relevant to NNs.

Let's start by introducing the concept of a **statistical experiment**, which has the following properties:

- Consists of multiple independent trials.
- The outcome of each trial is non-deterministic; that is, it's determined by chance.
- It has more than one possible outcome. These outcomes are known as **events** (we'll also discuss events in the context of sets in the following section).
- All the possible outcomes of the experiment are known in advance.

One example of a statistical experiment is a coin toss, which has two possible outcomes—heads or tails. Another example is a dice throw with six possible outcomes: 1, 2, 3, 4, 5, and 6.

We'll define **probability** as the likelihood that some event, **e**, would occur and we'll denote it with **P(e)**. The probability is a number in the range of [0, 1], where 0 indicates that the event cannot occur and 1 indicates that it will always occur. If *P(e) = 0.5*, there is a 50-50 chance the event would occur, and so on.

There are two ways we can approach probability:

- **Theoretical**: The event we're interested in compared to the total number of possible events. All the events are equally as likely:

$$P(e) = \frac{\text{number of successful outcomes}}{\text{total number of outcomes}}$$

  To understand this, let's use the coin toss example with two possible outcomes. The theoretical probability of each possible outcome is P(heads) = P(tails) = 1/2. The theoretical probability for each of the sides of a dice throw would be 1/6.

- **Empirical**: This is the number of times an event we're interested in occurs compared to the total number of trials:

$$P(e) = \frac{\text{number of times } e \text{ occurs}}{\text{total number of trials}}$$

  The result of the experiment may show that the events aren't equally likely. For example, let's say that we toss a coin 100 times and that we observe heads 56 times. Here, the empirical probability for heads is P(heads) = 56 / 100 = 0.56. The higher the number of trials, the more accurate the calculated probability is (this is known as the law of large numbers).

In the next section, we'll discuss probability in the context of sets.

Probability and sets

The collection of all possible outcomes (events) of an experiment is called, **sample space**. We can think of the sample space as a mathematical **set**. It is usually denoted with a capital letter and we can list all the set outcomes with {} (the same as Python sets). For example, the sample space of coin toss events is $S_c = \{\text{heads, tails}\}$, while for dice rows it's $S_d = \{1, 2, 3, 4, 5, 6\}$. A single outcome of the set (for example, heads) is called a **sample point**. An **event** is an outcome (sample point) or a combination of outcomes (subset) of the sample space. An example of a combined event is for the dice to land on an even number, that is, {2, 4, 6}.

Let's assume that we have a sample space $S = \{1, 2, 3, 4, 5\}$ and two subsets (events) $A = \{1, 2, 3\}$ and $B = \{3, 4, 5\}$. Here, we can do the following operations with them:

- **Intersection**: The result is a new set that contains only the elements found in both sets:

$$A \cap B = \{3\}$$

Sets whose intersections are empty sets {} are **disjoint**.

- **Complement**: The result is a new set that contains all the elements of the sample space that aren't included in a given set:

$$A' = \{4, 5\} \quad B' = \{1, 2\}$$

- **Union:** The result is a new set that contains the elements that can be found in either set:

$$A \cup B = \{1, 2, 3, 4, 5\}$$

The following Venn diagrams illustrate these different set relationships:

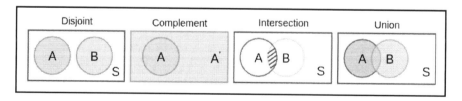

Venn diagrams of the possible set relationships

We can transfer the set properties to events and their probabilities. We'll assume that the events are **independent**—the occurrence of one event doesn't affect the probability of the occurrence of another. For example, the outcomes of the different coin tosses are independent of one another. That being said, let's learn how to translate the set operations in the events domain:

- The intersection of two events is a subset of the outcomes, contained in both events. The probability of the intersection is called **joint probability** and is computed via the following formula:

$$P(A \cap B) = P(A) * P(B)$$

  Let's say that we want to compute the probability of a card being red (either hearts or diamonds) and a Jack. The probability for red is *P(red) = 26/52 = 1/2*. The probability for getting a Jack is *P(Jack) = 4/52 = 1/13*. Therefore, the joint probability is *P(red, Jack) = (1/2) * (1/13) = 1/26*. In this example, we assumed that the two events are independent. However, the two events occur at the same time (we draw a single card). Had they occurred successively, for example, two card draws, where one is a Jack and the other is red, we would enter the realm of conditional probability. This joint probability is also denoted as P(A, B) or P(AB).

  The probability of the occurrence of a single event P(A) is also known as **marginal probability** (as opposed to joint probability).

- Two events are disjoint (or **mutually exclusive**) if they don't share any outcomes. That is, their respective sample space subsets are disjoint. For example, the events of odd or even dice rows are disjoint. The following is true for the probability of disjoint events:
    - The joint probability of disjoint events (the probability for these events to occur simultaneously) is P(A∩B) = 0.
    - The sum of the probabilities of disjoint events is $\sum P(\text{disjoint events}) \leq 1$.

- If the subsets of multiple events contain the whole sample space between themselves, they are **jointly exhaustive**. Events A and B from the preceding example are jointly exhaustive because, together, they fill up the whole sample space (1 through 5). The following is true for the probability of jointly exhaustive events:

$$\sum P(\text{jointly exhaustive events}) = 1$$

If we only have two events that are disjoint and jointly exhaustive at the same time, the events are **complement**. For example, odd and even dice throw events are complement.

- We'll refer to outcomes coming from either A or B (not necessarily in both) as the union of A and B. The probability of this union is as follows:

$$P(A \cup B) = P(A) + P(B) - P(A \cap B)$$

So far, we've discussed independent events. In the next section, we'll focus on dependent ones.

Conditional probability and the Bayes rule

If the occurrence of event A changes the probability of the occurrence of event B, where A occurs before B, then the two are dependent. To illustrate this concept, let's imagine that we draw multiple cards sequentially from the deck. When the deck is full, the probability to draw hearts is *P(hearts) = 13/52 = 0.25*. But once we've drawn the first card, the probability to pick hearts on the second turn changes. Now, we only have 51 cards and one less heart. We'll call the probability of the second draw conditional probability and we'll denote it with P(B|A). This is the probability of event B (second draw), given that event A has occurred (first draw). To continue with our example, the probability of picking hearts on the second draw becomes $P(hearts_2 | hearts_1) = 12/51 = 0.235$.

Next, we can extend the joint probability formula (introduced in the preceding section) in terms of dependent events. The formula is as follows:

$$P(A \cap B) = P(A)\, P(B|A)$$

However, the preceding equation is just a special case for two events. We can extend this further for multiple events, $A_1, A_2, ..., A_n$. This new generic formula is known as the chain rule of probability:

$$P(A_n \cap ... \cap A_1) = P(A_n | A_{n-1} \cap ... \cap A_1) \cdot P(A_{n-1} \cap ... \cap A_1)$$

For example, the chain rule for three events is as follows:

$$P(A_3 \cap A_2 \cap A_1) = P(A_3 | A_2 \cap A_1) \cdot P(A_2 \cap A_1)$$
$$= P(A_3 | A_2 \cap A_1) \cdot P(A_2 | A_1) \cdot P(A_1)$$

We can also derive the formula for the conditional probability itself:

$$P(B|A) = \frac{P(A \cap B)}{P(A)}$$

This formula makes sense for the following reasons:

- **P(A ∩ B)** states that we're interested in the occurrences of B, given that A has already occurred. In other words, we're interested in the joint occurrence of the events, hence the joint probability.
- **P(A)** states that we're interested only in the subset of outcomes when event A has occurred. We already know that A has occurred and therefore we restrict our observations to these outcomes.

The following holds true for dependent events:

$$P(A \cap B) = P(A)\,P(B|A)$$
$$P(A \cap B) = P(B)\,P(A|B)$$

Using this equation, we can replace the value of P(A∩B) in the conditional probability formula to come up with the following:

$$P(A \cap B) = P(A)\,P(B|A) = P(B)\,P(A|B) \quad \Leftrightarrow \quad P(B|A) = \frac{P(A \cap B)}{P(A)} = \frac{P(B)\,P(A|B)}{P(A)}$$

The preceding formula gives us the ability to compute the conditional probability, P(B|A), if we know the opposite conditional probability, P(B|A). This equation is known as the **Bayes rule** and is frequently used in ML. In the context of Bayesian statistics, P(A) and P(B|A) are known as prior and posterior probability, respectively.

The Bayes rule can be illustrated in the realm of medical testing. Let's say that we want to determine whether a patient has a particular disease or not. We conduct a medical test, which comes out positive. But this doesn't necessarily mean that the patient has the disease. Most tests have a reliability value, which is the percentage chance of the test being positive when administered on people with a particular disease. Using this information, we'll apply the Bayes rule to compute the actual probability of the patient having the disease, given that the test is positive. We get the following:

$$P(\text{has disease}|\text{test}=positive) = \frac{P(\text{has disease})\,P(\text{test}=positive|\text{has disease})}{P(\text{test}=positive)}$$

Here, *P(has disease)* is the general probability of the disease without any prior conditions. Think of this as the probability of the disease in the general population.

Next, let's make some assumptions about the disease and the test's accuracy:

- The test is 98% reliable, that is, if the test is positive, it will also be positive in 98% of cases: *P(test=positive | has disease)* = 0.98.
- Only 2% of the people under 50 have this kind of disease: *P(has disease)* = 0.02.
- The test that's administered on people under 50 is positive only for 3.9% of the population: *P(test=positive)* = 0.039.

We can ask the following question: if a test is 98% accurate for cancer and if a 45-year-old person took the test, which turned out to be positive, what is the probability that they may have the disease? Using the preceding formula, we can calculate the following:

$$P(\text{has disease}|\text{test}=positive) = \frac{P(\text{has disease})\,P(\text{test}=positive|\text{has disease})}{P(\text{test}=positive)} = \frac{0.02 * 0.98}{0.039} = 0.5$$

In the next section, we'll go beyond probabilities and we'll discuss random variables and probability distributions.

Random variables and probability distributions

In statistics, we define a variable as an attribute that describes a given entity. The value of the attribute can vary between entities. For example, we can describe the height of a person with a variable, which would differ for different people. But let's say that we take the height measurement of the same person multiple times. We can expect to obtain slightly different values each time due to some random factors, such as the person's pose or inaccuracy in our own measurements. Therefore, the value of the variable height would differ, despite the fact that we are measuring the same thing. To account for these changes, we'll introduce random variables. These are variables whose values are determined by some random event. Unlike regular variables, a random variable can take multiple values and each of these values is associated with some probability.

There are two types of random variables:

- **Discrete**, which can take distinct separate values. For example, the number of goals in a football match is a discrete variable.

- **Continuous**, which can take any value within a given interval. For example, a height measurement is a continuous variable.

Random variables are denoted with capital letters and the probability of a certain value *x* for random variable *X* is denoted with either *P(X = x)* or *p(x)*. The collection of probabilities for each possible value of a random variable is called the **probability distribution**. Depending on the variable type, we have two types of probability distributions:

- **Probability mass function (PMF)** for discrete variables. The following is an example of a PMF. The *x* axis shows the possible values and the *y* axis shows the probability for each value:

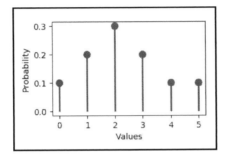

An example of a PMF

The PMF is only defined for the possible values of the random variable. All the values of a PMF are non-negative and their sum is 1. That is, the events of the PMF are mutually exclusive and jointly exhaustive. We'll denote PMF with P(X), where X is the random variable.

- **Probability density function (PDF)** for continuous variables. Unlike PMF, the PDF is uninterrupted (defined for every possible value) in the interval between two values, thereby reflecting the nature of the continuous variable. The following is an example of a PDF:

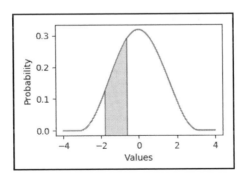

An example of a PDF

In the PDF, the probability is computed for a value interval and is given by the surface area under the curve, enclosed by that interval (this is the marked area in the preceding diagram). The total area under the curve is 1. We'll denote PDF with f_X, where X is the random variable.

Next, let's focus on some of the properties of random variables:

- The **mean** (or **expected value**) is the expected outcome of an experiment over many observations. We'll denote it with μ or $\mathbb{E}$. For a discrete variable, the mean is the weighted sum of all possible values, multiplied by their probabilities:

$$\mu_X = \mathbb{E}(X) = x_1 P(X = x_1) + x_2 P(X = x_2) + \ldots + x_n P(X = x_n) = \sum_{i=1}^{n} x_i P(X = x_i)$$

Let's use the preceding discrete variable example as an example, where we defined a random variable with six possible values (0, 1, 2, 3, 4, 5) and their respective probabilities (0.1, 0.2, 0.3, 0.2, 0.1, 0.1). Here, the mean is $\mu = 0*0.1 + 1*0.2 + 2*0.3 + 3*0.2 + 4*0.1 + 5*0.1 = 2.3$.

The mean for a continuous variable is defined as follows:

$$\mu_X = \mathbb{E}(X) = \int_{-\infty}^{\infty} x f_X(x) dx$$

While with a discrete variable we can think of the PMF as a lookup table, the PDF may be more complex (an actual function or equation), which is why there's different notation between the two. We won't go into further details about the mean of continuous variables.

- **Variance** is defined as the expected value of the squared deviation from the mean, μ, of a random variable:

$$\mathrm{Var}(X) = \mathbb{E}([X - \mu]^2)$$

In other words, the variance measures how the values of a random variable differ from its mean value.

The variance of a discrete random variable is as follows:

$$\mathrm{Var}(X) = \sum_{i=1}^{n} (x_i - \mu)^2 P(X = x_i)$$

Let's use the preceding example, where we calculated the mean value to be 2.3. The new variance would be $Var(X) = (0 - 2.3)^2 * 0 + (1 - 2.3)^2 * 1 + ... + (5 - 2.3)^2 * 5 = 2.01$.

The variance of a continuous variable is defined as follows:

$$\mathrm{Var}(X) = \int_{-\infty}^{\infty} (x - \mu)^2 f_X(x) dx$$

- The **standard deviation** measures the degree to which the values of the random variable differ from the expected value. If this definition sounds similar to variance, it's because it is. In fact, the formula for standard deviation is as follows:

$$\sigma_X = \sqrt{\mathrm{Var}(X)}$$

We can also define the variance in terms of standard deviation:

$$\mathrm{Var}(X) = \sigma_X^2$$

The difference between standard deviation and variance is that the standard deviation is expressed in the same units as the mean value, while the variance uses squared units.

In this section, we defined what a probability distribution is. Next, let's discuss different types of probability distributions.

Probability distributions

We'll start with the **binomial distribution** for discrete variables in binomial experiments. A binomial experiment has only two possible outcomes: success or failure. It also satisfies the following requirements:

- Each trial is independent of the others.
- The probability of success is always the same.

An example of a binomial experiment is the coin toss experiment.

Now, let's assume that the experiment consists of *n* trials. *x* of them are successful, while the probability of success at each trial is *p*. The formula for a binomial PMF of variable X (not to be confused with *x*) is as follows:

$$P(X) = \frac{n!}{x!(n-x)!} p^x (1-p)^{n-x}$$

Here, $n!/(x!(n-x)!)$ is the binomial coefficient. This is the number of combinations of *x* successful trials, which we can select from the *n* total trials. If *n=1*, then we have a special case of binomial distribution called **Bernoulli distribution**.

Next, let's discuss the normal (or Gaussian) distribution for continuous variables, which closely approximates many natural processes. The normal distribution is defined with the following exponential PDF formula, known as normal equation (one of the most popular notations):

$$f(x|\mu, \sigma^2) = N(\mu, \sigma^2) = \frac{1}{\sqrt{2\pi\sigma^2}} e^{-\frac{(x-\mu)^2}{2\sigma^2}}$$

$$= \frac{1}{\sqrt{2\pi\sigma^2}} e^{-\frac{1}{2}\left(\frac{x-\mu}{\sigma}\right)^2}$$

Here, *x* is the value of the random variable, μ is the mean, σ is the standard deviation, and σ^2 is the variance. The preceding equation produces a bell-shaped curve, which is shown in the following diagram:

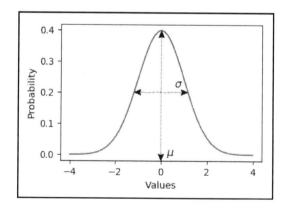

Normal distribution

Let's discuss some of the properties of the normal distribution, in no particular order:

- The curve is symmetric along its center, which is also the maximum value.
- The shape and location of the curve are fully described by the mean and standard deviation, where we have the following:
    - The center of the curve (and its maximum value) is equal to the mean. That is, the mean determines the location of the curve along the x axis.
    - The width of the curve is determined by the standard deviation.

In the following diagram, we can see examples of normal distributions with different μ and σ values:

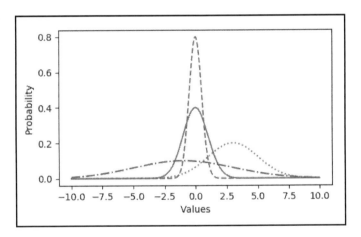

Examples of normal distributions with different μ and σ values

- The normal distribution approaches 0 toward +/- infinity, but it never becomes 0. Therefore, a random variable under normal distribution can have any value (albeit some values with a tiny probability).
- The surface area under the curve is equal to 1, which is ensured by the constant, $1/\sqrt{2\pi\sigma^2}$, being before the exponent.
- $\dfrac{x-\mu}{\sigma}$ (located in the exponent) is called the standard score (or z-score). A standardized normal variable has a mean of 0 and a standard deviation of 1. Once transformed, the random variable participates in the equation in its standardized form.

In the next section, we'll introduce the multidisciplinary field of information theory, which will help us use probability theory in the context of NNs.

Information theory

Information theory attempts to determine the amount of information an event has. The amount of information is guided by the following principles:

- The higher the probability of an event, the less informative the event is considered. Conversely, if the probability is lower, the event carries more informational content. For example, the outcome of a coin flip (with a probability of 1/2) provides less information than the outcome of a dice throw (with a probability of 1/6).
- The information that's carried by independent events is the sum of their individual information contents. For example, two dice rows that come up on the same side of the dice (let's say, 4) are twice as informative as the individual rows.

We'll define the amount of information (or self-information) of event x as follows:

$$I(x) = -\log P(x)$$

Here, *log* is the natural logarithm. For example, if the probability of event is $P(x) = 0.8$, then $I(x) = 0.22$. Alternatively, if $P(x) = 0.2$, then $I(x) = 1.61$. We can see that the event information content is opposite to the event probability. The amount of self-information $I(x)$ is measured in natural units of information (**nat**). We can also compute $I(x)$ with a base 2 logarithm $I(x) = -\log_2(P(x))$, in which case we measure it in bits. There is no principal difference between the two versions. For the purposes of this book, we'll stick with the natural logarithm version.

Let's discuss why we use logarithm in the preceding formula, even though a negative probability would also satisfy the reciprocity between self-information and probability. The main reason is the product and division rules of logarithms:

$$\log(x_1 x_2) = \log(x_1) + \log(x_2)$$
$$\log(x_1/x_2) = \log(x_1) - \log(x_2)$$

Here, x_1 and x_2 are scalar values. Without going into too much detail, note that these properties allow us to easily minimize the error function during network training.

So far, we've defined the information content of a single outcome. But what about other outcomes? To measure them, we have to measure the amount of information over the probability distribution of the random variable. Let's denote it with I(X), where X is a random discrete variable (we'll focus on discrete variables here). Recall that, in the *Random variables and probability distributions* section, we defined the mean (or expected value) of a discrete random variable as the weighted sum of all possible values, multiplied by their probabilities. We'll do something similar here, but we'll multiply the information content of each event by the probability of that event.

This measure is called Shannon entropy (or just entropy) and is defined as follows:

$$H(X) = \mathbb{E}(\mathrm{I}(X)) = \sum_{i=1}^{n} P(X = x_i)\mathrm{I}(X = x_n) = -\sum_{i=1}^{n} P(X = x_i) \log P(X = x_i)$$

Here, x_i represents the discrete variable values. Events with higher probabilities will carry more weight compared to low-probability ones. We can think of entropy as the expected (mean) amount of information about the events (outcomes) of the probability distribution. To understand this, let's try to compute the entropy of the familiar coin toss experiment. We'll calculate two examples:

- First, let's assume that *P(heads) = P(tails) = 0.5*. In this case, the entropy is as follows:

$$H(X) = -P(\text{heads}) \log(P(\text{heads})) - P(\text{tails}) \log(P(\text{tails})) = -0.5 * (-0.69) - 0.5 * (-0.69) = 0.7$$

- Next, let's assume that, for some reason, the outcomes are not equally likely and that the probability distribution is *P(heads) = 0.2 and P(tails) = 0.8*. The entropy is as follows:

$$H(X) = -P(\text{heads}) \log(P(\text{heads})) - P(\text{tails}) \log(P(\text{tails})) = -0.2 * (-1.62) - 0.8 * (-0.22) = 0.5$$

We can see that the entropy is highest when the outcomes are equally likely and decreases when one outcome becomes prevalent. In a sense, we can think of entropy as a measurement of uncertainty or chaos. The following diagram shows a graph of the entropy **H(X)** over a binary event (such as the coin toss), depending on the probability distribution of the two outcomes:

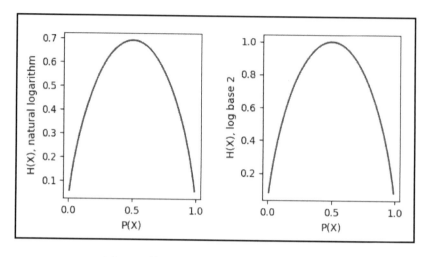

Left: entropy with natural logarithm: right: entropy with base 2 logarithm

Next, let's imagine that we have a discrete random variable, *X*, and two different probability distributions over it. This is usually the scenario where a NN produces some output probability distribution $Q(X)$ and we compare it to a target distribution, $P(X)$, during training. We can measure the difference between these two distributions with **cross-entropy**, which is defined as follows:

$$H(P, Q) = - \sum_{i=1}^{n} P(X = x_i) \log Q(X = x_i)$$

For example, let's calculate the cross entropy between the two probability distributions of the preceding coin toss scenario. We have predicted distribution *Q(heads) = 0.2, Q(tails) = 0.8* and the target (or true) distribution *P(heads) = 0.5, P(tails) = 0.5*. The cross entropy is as follows:

$$H(P, Q) = -P(\text{heads}) * \log(Q(\text{heads})) - P(\text{tails}) * \log(Q(\text{tails})) = -0.5 * (-1.61) - 0.5 * (-0.22) = 0.915$$

Another measure of the difference between two probability distributions is the
Kullback–Leibler divergence (KL divergence):

$$D_{KL}(P||Q) = \sum_{i=1}^{n} P(X = x_i) \log \frac{P(X = x_i)}{Q(X = x_i)}$$

$$= \sum_{i=1}^{n} P(X = x_i)[\log P(X = x_i) - \log Q(X = x_i)]$$

$$= \sum_{i=1}^{n} [P(X = x_i) \log P(X = x_i) - P(X = x_i) \log Q(X = x_i)]$$

$$= H(P, Q) - H(P)$$

The product rule of logarithms helped us to transform the first-row formula into a more
intuitive form on the second row. It is easier to see that the KL divergence measures the
difference between the target and predicted log probabilities. If we derive the equation
further, we can also see the relationship between the entropy, cross-entropy, and KL
divergence.

The KL divergence of the coin toss example scenario is as follows:

$$D_{KL}(P||Q) = P(\text{heads}) * [\log(P(\text{heads})) - Q(\text{heads})] + P(\text{tails}) * [\log(P(\text{tails})) - Q(\text{tails})]$$
$$= 0.5(\log(0.5) - \log(0.2)) + 0.5(\log(0.5) - \log(0.8)) = 0.22$$

In the next section, we'll discuss the field of differential calculus, which will help us with
training NNs.

Differential calculus

In ML, we are often interested in how to approximate some target function by adjusting the
parameters of ML algorithms. If we think of the ML algorithm itself as a mathematical
function (which is the case for NNs), we would like to know how the output of that
function changes when we change some of its parameters (weights). Thankfully,
differential calculus deals with the rate of change of a function with respect to a variable
that the function depends on. The following is a (very) short introduction to derivatives.

Let's say that we have a function, *f(x)*, with a single parameter, *x*, which has the following graph:

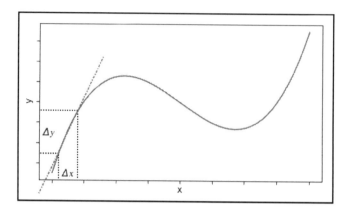

The graph of *f(x)* and the slope (red dot-dashed line)

We can get a relative idea of how *f(x)* changes with respect to *x* at any value of *x* by calculating the slope of the function at that point. If the slope is positive, the function increases. Conversely, if it's negative, it decreases. We can calculate the slope with the following equation:

$$\text{slope} = \frac{\Delta y}{\Delta x} = \frac{f(x + \Delta x) - f(x)}{\Delta x}$$

The idea here is simple—we calculate the difference between two values of *f* at *x* and *x+Δx*: $\Delta y = f(x + \Delta x) - f(x)$. Then, we calculate the ratio between *Δy* and *Δx* to get the slope. But if *Δx* is too big, the measurement won't be very accurate, because the part of the function graph enclosed between *x* and *x+Δx* may change drastically. We can use a smaller *Δx* to minimize this error; here, we can focus on a smaller part of the graph. If *Δx* approaches 0, we can assume that the slope reflects a single point of the graph. In this case, we call the slope the **first derivative** of *f(x)*. We can express this in mathematical terms via the following equation:

$$f'(x) = \frac{dy}{dx} = \lim_{\Delta x \to 0} \frac{f(x + \Delta x) - f(x)}{\Delta x}$$

Here, $f'(x)$ and dy/dx are Lagrange's and Leibniz's notations for derivatives, respectively. $\lim_{\Delta x \to 0}$ is the mathematical concept of the limit—we can think of it as Δx approaches 0. The process of finding the derivative of f is called **differentiation**. The following diagram shows slopes at different values of x:

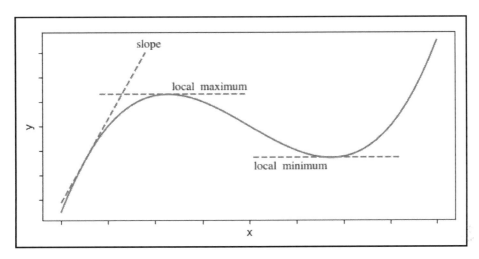

We can see that the slopes at the **local minimum** and **local maximum** of f are 0—at these points (known as saddle points), f neither increases nor decreases as we change x.

Next, let's assume that we have a function of multiple parameters, $f(x_1, x_2, \ldots, x_n)$. The derivative of f with respect to any of the parameters, x_i, is called a partial derivative and is denoted by $\partial f / \partial x$. When computing the partial derivative, we assume that all the other parameters, $x_j \neq x_i$, are constants. We'll denote the partial derivatives of the components of a vector with $\nabla = (\frac{\partial}{\partial x_1}, \ldots, \frac{\partial}{\partial x_n})$.

Finally, let's mention some useful rules for differentiation:

- **Chain rule**: Let's say that f and g are some functions and $h(x) = f(g(x))$. Here, the derivative of f with respect to x for any x is as follows:

$$h'(x) = f'(g(x))g'(x)$$

or

$$\frac{dh}{dx} = \frac{d}{dx}[f(g(x))] = \frac{d}{dg(x)}[f(g(x))] \cdot \frac{d}{dx}[g(x)]$$

- **Sum rule**: Let's say that f and g are some functions and $h(x) = f(x) + g(x)$. The sum rule states the following:

$$h'(x) = (f(x) + g(x))' = f'(x) + g'(x)$$

- **Common functions**:
  - $x' = 1$
  - $(ax)' = a$, where a is scalar
  - $a' = 0$, where a is scalar
  - $x^2 = 2x$
  - $(e^x)' = e^x$

The mathematical apparatus of NNs and NNs themselves form a sort of knowledge hierarchy. If we think of implementing a NN as building a house, then the mathematical apparatus is like mixing concrete. We can learn how to mix the concrete independently of how to build a house. In fact, we can mix concrete for a variety of purposes other than the specific goal of building a house. However, we need to know how to mix concrete before building the house. To continue with our analogy, now that we know how to mix concrete (mathematical apparatus), we'll focus on actually building the house (NNs).

A short introduction to NNs

A NN is a function (let's denote it with f) that tries to approximate another target function, g. We can describe this relationship with the following equation:

$$g(x) \approx f_\theta(x)$$

Here, x is the input data and θ are the NN parameters (weights). The goal is to find such θ parameters with the best approximate, g. This generic definition applies for both regression (approximating the exact value of g) and classification (assigning the input to one of multiple possible classes) tasks. Alternatively, the NN function can be denoted as $f(x; \theta)$.

We'll start our discussion from the smallest building block of the NN—the neuron.

Neurons

The preceding definition is a bird's-eye view of a NN. Now, let's discuss the basic building blocks of a NN, namely the neurons (or **units**). Units are mathematical functions that can be defined as follows:

$$y = f(\sum_{i=1}^{n} x_i w_i + b)$$

Here, we have the following:

- y is the unit output (single value).
- f is the non-linear differentiable activation function. The activation function is the source of non-linearity in a NN—if the NN was entirely linear, it would only be able to approximate other linear functions.
- The argument of the activation function is the weighted sum (with weights w_i) of all the unit inputs x_i (n total inputs) and the bias weight b. The inputs x_i can be either the data input values or outputs of other units.

Alternatively, we can substitute x_i and w_i with their vector representations, where $\mathbf{x} = (x_1, x_2, \ldots, x_n)$ and $\mathbf{w} = (w_1, w_2, \ldots, w_n)$. Here, the formula will use the dot product of the two vectors:

$$y = f(\mathbf{x} \cdot \mathbf{w} + b)$$

The following diagram (left) shows a unit:

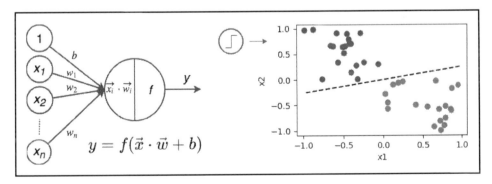

Left: A unit and its equivalent formula: right: A geometric representation of a perceptron.

The input vector **x** will be perpendicular to the weight vector **w** if **x• w = 0**. Therefore, all vectors **x** where **x• w = 0** define a hyperplane in the vector space $\mathbb{R}^n$, where n is the dimension of x. In the case of two-dimensional input (x_1, x_2), we can represent the hyperplane as a line. This could be illustrated with the perceptron (or binary classifier)—a unit with a **threshold** activation function $f(a) = \begin{cases} 1 \text{ if } a \geq 0 \\ 0 \text{ if } a < 0 \end{cases}$ that classifies its input in one of the two classes. The geometric representation of the perceptron with two inputs (x_1, x_2) is a line (or decision boundary) separating the two classes (to the right in the preceding diagram). This imposes a serious limitation on the neuron because it cannot classify linearly inseparable problems—even simple ones such as XOR.

A unit with an identity activation function $(f(x) = x)$ is equivalent to multiple linear regression, while a unit with a sigmoid activation function is equivalent to logistic regression.

Next, let's learn how to organize the neurons in layers.

Layers as operations

The next level in the NN organizational structure is the layers of units, where we combine the scalar outputs of multiple units in a single output vector. The units in a layer are not connected to each other. This organizational structure makes sense for the following reasons:

- We can generalize multivariate regression to a layer, as opposed to only linear or logistic regression for a single unit. In other words, we can approximate multiple values with a layer as opposed to a single value with a unit. This happens in the case of classification output, where each output unit represents the probability the input belongs to a certain class.
- A unit can convey limited information because its output is a scalar. By combining the unit outputs, instead of a single activation, we can now consider the vector in its entirety. In this way, we can convey a lot more information, not only because the vector has multiple values, but also because the relative ratios between them carry additional meaning.
- Because the units in a layer have no connections to each other, we can parallelize the computation of their outputs (thereby increasing the computational speed). This ability is one of the major reasons for the success of DL in recent years.

In classical NNs (that is, NNs before DL, when they were just one of many ML algorithms), the primary type of layer is the **fully connected** (**FC**) layer. In this layer, every unit receives weighted input from all the components of the input vector, **x**. Let's assume that the size of the input vector is m and that the FC layer has n units and an activation function f, which is the same for all the units. Each of the n units will have m weights: one for each of the m inputs. The following is a formula we can use for the output of a single unit j of an FC layer. It's the same as the formula we defined in the *Neurons* section, but we'll include the unit index here:

$$y_j = f(\sum_{i=1}^{m} x_i w_{ij} + b_j)$$

Here, w_{ij} is the weight between the j-th layer unit and the i-th input component. We can represent the weights connecting the input vector to the units as an $m{\times}n$ matrix **W**. Each matrix column represents the weight vector of all the inputs to one layer unit. In this case, the output vector of the layer is the result of matrix-vector multiplication. However, we can also combine multiple input samples, $\mathbf{x}_i$, in an input matrix (or **batch**) **X**, which will be passed through the layer simultaneously. In this case, we have matrix-matrix multiplication and the layer output is also a matrix. The following diagram shows an example of an FC layer, as well as its equivalent formulas in the batch and single sample scenarios:

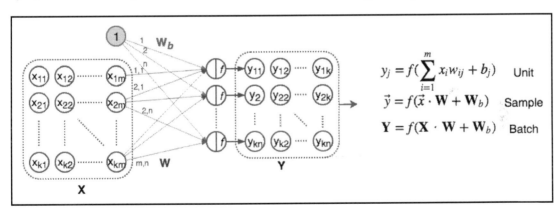

An FC layer with vector/matrix inputs and outputs and its equivalent formulas

We have explicitly separated the bias and input weight matrices, but in practice, the underlying implementation may use a shared weight matrix and append an additional row of 1s to the input data.

Contemporary DL is not limited to FC layers. We have many other types, such as convolutional, pooling, and so on. Some of the layers have trainable weights (FC, convolutional), while others don't (pooling). We can also use the terms functions or operations interchangeably with the layer. For example, in TensorFlow and PyTorch, the FC layer we just described is a combination of two sequential operations. First, we perform the weighted sum of the weights and inputs and then we feed the result as an input to the activation function operation. In practice (that is, when working with DL libraries), the basic building block of a NN is not the unit but an operation that takes one or more tensors as input and outputs one or more tensors:

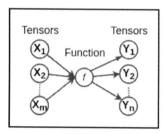

A function with input and output tensors

Next, let's discuss how to combine the layer operations in a NN.

NNs

In the *Neurons* section, we demonstrated that a neuron (also valid for a layer) can only classify linearly separable classes. To overcome this limitation, we have to combine multiple layers in a NN. We'll define the NN as a directed graph of operations (or layers). The graph nodes are the operations, and the edges between them determine the data flow. If two operations are connected, then the output tensor of the first will serve as input to the second, which is determined by the edge direction. A NN can have multiple inputs and outputs—the input nodes only have outgoing edges, while the outputs only have incoming edges.

Based on this definition, we can identify two main types of NNs:

- **Feed-forward**, which are represented by **acyclic** graphs.
- **Recurrent (RNN)**, which are represented by **cyclic** graphs. The recurrence is temporal; the loop connection in the graph propagates the output of an operation at moment *t-1* and feeds it back into the network at the next moment, *t*. The RNN maintains an internal state, which represents a kind of summary of all the previous network inputs. This summary, along with the latest input, is fed to the RNN. The network produces some output but also updates its internal state and waits for the next input value. In this way, the RNN can take inputs with variable lengths, such as text sequences or time series.

The following is an example of the two types of networks:

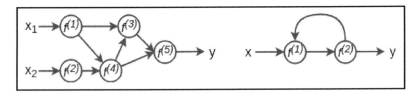

Left: Feed-forward network: Right: Recurrent network

Let's assume that, when an operation receives input from more than one operation, we use the element-wise sum to combine the multiple input tensors. Then, we can represent the NN as a series of nested functions/operations. We'll denote a NN operation with $f^{(i)}(x)$, where *i* is some index that helps us differentiate between multiple operations. For example, the equivalent formula for the feed-forward network on the left is as follows:

$$f_\theta^{(ff)}(x) = f^{(5)}\left(f^{(3)}\left(f^{(1)}(x_1) + f^{(4)}\left(f^{(1)}(x_1) + f^{(2)}(x_2)\right)\right) + f^{(4)}\left(f^{(1)}(x_1) + f^{(2)}(x_2)\right)\right)$$

The formula for the RNN on the right is as follows:

$$f_\theta^{(rnn)}(x_t) = f^{(2)}\left(f^{(1)}\left(x_t + f^{(2)}(x_{t-1})\right)\right)$$

We'll also denote the parameters (weights) of an operation with the same index as the operation itself. Let's take an FC network layer with index *l*, which takes its input from a previous layer with index *l-1*. The following are the layer formulas for a single unit and vector/matrix layer representations with layer indexes:

$$y_j^{(l)} = f^{(i)}\left(\sum_{i=1}^{m} y_i^{(l-1)} w_{i,j}^{(l)} + b_j^{(l)}\right)$$

$$\mathbf{y}^{(l)} = f^{(l)}\left(\mathbf{y}^{(l-1)} \cdot \mathbf{W}^{(l)} + \mathbf{W}_b^{(l)}\right)$$

$$\mathbf{Y}^{(l)} = f^{(l)}\left(\mathbf{Y}^{(l-1)} \cdot \mathbf{W}^{(l)} + \mathbf{W}_b^{(l)}\right)$$

Now that we're familiar with the full NN architecture, let's discuss the different types of activation functions.

Activation functions

Let's discuss the different types of activation functions, starting with the classics:

- **Sigmoid**: Its output is bounded between 0 and 1 and can be interpreted stochastically as the probability of the neuron activating. Because of these properties, the sigmoid was the most popular activation function for a long time. However, it also has some less desirable properties (more on that later), which led to its decline in popularity. The following diagram shows the sigmoid formula, its derivative, and their graphs (the derivative will be useful when we discuss backpropagation):

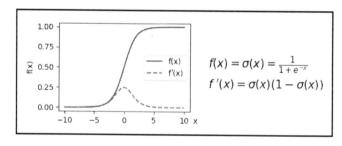

Sigmoid activation function

- **Hyperbolic tangent** (**tanh**): The name speaks for itself. The principal difference with the sigmoid is that the tanh is in the (-1, 1) range. The following diagram shows the tanh formula, its derivative, and their graphs:

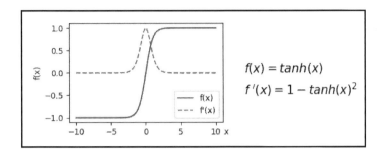

The hyperbolic tangent activation function

Next, let's focus on the new kids on the block—the *LU (**LU** stands for **linear unit**) family of functions. We'll start with the rectified linear unit (**ReLU**), which was first successfully used in 2011 (*Deep Sparse Rectifier Neural Networks*, http://proceedings.mlr.press/v15/glorot11a/glorot11a.pdf). The following diagram shows the ReLU formula, its derivative, and their graphs:

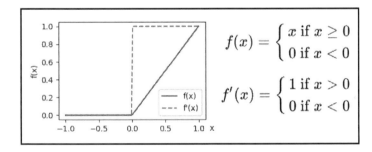

ReLU activation function

As we can see, the ReLU repeats its input when **x > 0** and stays at 0 otherwise. This activation has several important advantages over sigmoid and tanh:

- Its derivative helps prevent vanishing gradients (more on that in the *Weights initialization* section). Strictly speaking, the derivative ReLU at value 0 is undefined, which makes the ReLU only semi-differentiable (more information about this can be found at https://en.wikipedia.org/wiki/Semi-differentiability). But in practice, it works well enough.

- It's idempotent—if we pass a value through an arbitrary number of ReLU activations, it will not change; for example, *ReLU(2) = 2, ReLU(ReLU(2)) = 2*, and so on. This is not the case for a sigmoid, where the value is *squashed* on each pass: $\sigma(\sigma(2)) = 0.707$. The following is an example of the activation of three consecutive sigmoid activations:

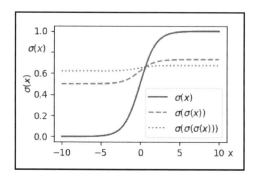

Consecutive sigmoid activations "squash" the data

The idempotence of ReLU makes it theoretically possible to create networks with more layers compared to the sigmoid.

- It creates sparse activations—let's assume that the weights of the network are initialized randomly through normal distribution. Here, there is a 0.5 chance that the input for each ReLU unit is < 0. Therefore, the output of about half of all activations will also be 0. The sparse activations have a number of advantages, which we can roughly summarize as the Occam's razor in the context of NNs—it's better to achieve the same result with a simpler data representation than a complex one.
- It's faster to compute in both the forward and backward passes.

However, during training, the network weights can be updated in such a way that some of the ReLU units in a layer will always receive inputs smaller than 0, which in turn will cause them to permanently output 0 as well. This phenomenon is known as **dying** ReLUs. To solve this, a number of ReLU modifications have been proposed. The following is a non-exhaustive list:

- **Leaky ReLU**: When the input is larger than 0, leaky ReLU repeats its input in the same way as the regular ReLU does. However, when **x < 0**, the leaky ReLU outputs x multiplied by some constant α *(0 < α < 1)*, instead of 0. The following diagram shows the leaky ReLU formula, its derivative, and their graphs for α=0.2:

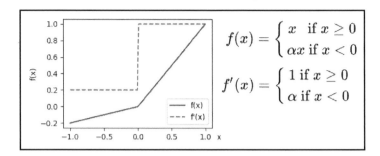

Leaky ReLU activation function

- **Parametric ReLU (PReLU**, *Delving Deep into Rectifiers: Surpassing Human-Level Performance on ImageNet Classification*, `https://arxiv.org/abs/1502.01852`): This activation is the same as the leaky ReLU, but the parameter α is tunable and is adjusted during training.
- **Exponential linear units (ELU**, *Fast and Accurate Deep Network Learning by Exponential Linear Units (ELUs)*, `https://arxiv.org/abs/1511.07289`): When the input is larger than 0, ELU repeats its input in the same way as ReLU does. However, when $x < 0$, the ELU output becomes $f(x) = \alpha(e^x - 1)$, where α is a tunable parameter. The following diagram shows the ELU formula, its derivative, and their graphs for α=0.2:

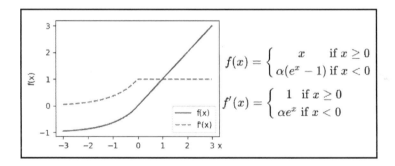

ELU activation function

- **Scaled exponential linear units** (**SELU**, *Self-Normalizing Neural Networks*, https://arxiv.org/abs/1706.02515): This activation is similar to ELU, except that the output (both smaller and larger than 0) is scaled with an additional training parameter, λ. The SELU is part of a larger concept called self-normalizing NNs (SNNs), which is described in the source paper. The following is the SELU formula:

$$f(x) = \lambda \begin{cases} x & \text{if } x \geq 0 \\ \alpha(e^x - 1) & \text{if } x < 0 \end{cases}$$

Finally, we'll mention the **softmax**, which is the activation function of the output layer in classification problems. Let's assume that the output of the final network layer is a vector, $z = (z_1, z_2, \ldots, z_n)$, where each of the n components represents the probability that the input data belongs to one of n possible classes. Here, the softmax output for each of the vector components is as follows:

$$f(z_i) = \frac{\exp(z_i)}{\sum_{j=1}^{n} \exp(z_j)}$$

The denominator in this formula acts as a normalizer. The softmax output has some important properties:

- Every value $f(z_i)$ is in the [0, 1] range.
- The total sum of values of z is equal to 1: $\sum_j f(z_j) = 1$
- An added bonus (in fact, obligatory) is that the function is differentiable.

In other words, we can interpret the softmax output as a probability distribution of a discrete random variable. However, it also has one more subtle property. Before we normalize the data, we transform each vector component exponentially with e^{z_i}. Let's imagine that two of the vector components are $z_1 = 1$ and $z_2 = 2$. Here, we would have $exp(1) = 2.7$ and $exp(2) = 7.39$. As we can see, the ratios between the components before and after the transformation are very different—0.5 and 0.36. In effect, the softmax increases the probability of the higher scores compared to lower ones.

In the next section, we'll shift our attention from the building blocks of the NN and focus on its entirety instead. More specifically, we'll demonstrate how NNs can approximate any function.

The universal approximation theorem

The universal approximation theorem was first proved in 1989 for a NN with sigmoid activation functions and then in 1991 for NNs with arbitrary non-linear activation functions. It states that any continuous function on compact subsets of $\mathbb{R}^n$ can be approximated to an arbitrary degree of accuracy by a feedforward NN with at least one hidden layer with a finite number of units and a non-linear activation. Although a NN with a single hidden layer won't perform well in many tasks, the theorem still tells us that there are no theoretical insurmountable limitations in terms of NNs. The formal proof of the theorem is too complex to be explained here, but we'll attempt to provide an intuitive explanation using some basic mathematics.

> The idea for the following example was inspired by Michael A. Nielsen's book *Neural Networks and Deep Learning* (http://neuralnetworksanddeeplearning.com/).

We'll implement a NN that approximates the boxcar function (shown on the right in the following diagram), which is a simple type of step function. Since a series of step functions can approximate any continuous function on a compact subset of R, this will give us an idea of why the universal approximation theorem holds:

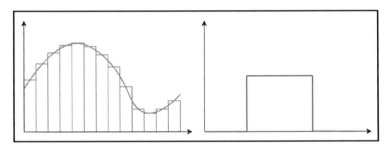

The diagram on the left depicts continuous function approximation with a series of step functions, while the diagram on the right illustrates a single boxcar step function.

To understand how this approximation works, we'll start with a single unit with a single scalar input x and sigmoid activation. The following is a visualization of the unit and its equivalent formula:

$$f(x) = \frac{1}{1 + exp(-(wx + b))}$$

In the following diagrams, we can see the graph of the formula for different values of *b* and *w* for inputs in the range of [-10: 10]:

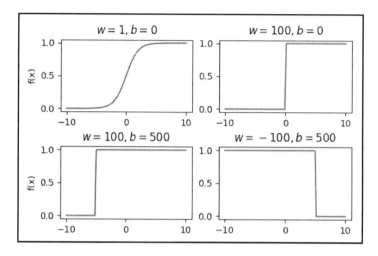

The neuron output based on different values of *w* and *b*. The network input *x* is represented on the x axis.

Upon closer inspection of the formula and the graph, we can see that the steepness of the sigmoid function is determined by the weight, *w*. Also, the translation of the function along the *x* axis is determined by the formula $t = -b/w$. Let's discuss the different scenarios in the preceding diagram:

- The top-left graph shows the regular sigmoid.
- The top-right graph demonstrates that a large weight *w* amplifies the input *x* to a point, where the unit output resembles threshold activation.
- The bottom-left graph shows how the bias *b* translates the unit activation along the *x* axis.
- The bottom-right graph shows that we can simultaneously reverse the activation with negative weight *w* and translate the activation along the *x* axis with the bias *b*.

We can intuitively see that the preceding graphs contain all the ingredients of the box function. We can combine the different scenarios with the help of a NN with one hidden layer, which contains two of the aforementioned units. The following diagram shows the network architecture, along with the weights and biases of the units, as well as the box function that's produced by the network:

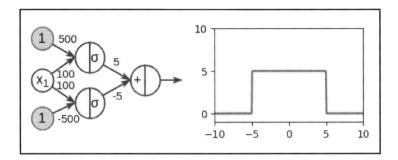

Here's how it works:

- First, the top unit activates for the upper step of the function and stays active.
- The bottom unit activates afterward for the bottom step of the function and stays active. The outputs of the hidden units cancel each other out because of the weights in the output layer, which are the same but with opposite signs.
- The weights of the output layer determine the height of the boxcar rectangle.

The output of this network isn't 0, but only in the (-5, 5) interval. Therefore, we can approximate additional boxes by adding more units to the hidden layer in a similar manner.

Now that we're familiar with the structure of a NN, let's focus on the training process.

Training NNs

In this section, we'll define training a NN as the process of adjusting its parameters (weights) θ in a way that minimizes the cost function $J(\theta)$. The cost function is some performance measurement over a training set that consists of multiple samples, represented as vectors. Each vector has an associated label (supervised learning). Most commonly, the cost function measures the difference between the network output and the label.

We'll start this section with a short recap of the gradient descent optimization algorithm. If you're already familiar with it, you can skip this.

Gradient descent

For the purposes of this section, we'll use a NN with a single regression output and **mean square error** (**MSE**) cost function, which is defined as follows:

$$J(\theta) = \frac{1}{2n} \sum_{i=1}^{n} (f_\theta(\mathbf{x}^{(i)}) - t^{(i)})^2$$

Here, we have the following:

- $f_\theta(\mathbf{x}^{(i)})$ is the output of the NN.
- n is the total number of samples in the training set.
- $\mathbf{x}^{(i)}$ are the vectors for the training samples, where the superscript i indicates the i-th sample of the dataset. We use superscript because $\mathbf{x}^{(i)}$ is a vector and the subscript is reserved for each of the vector components. For example, $x_j^{(i)}$ is the j-th component of the i-th training sample.
- $t^{(i)}$ is the label associated with sample $\mathbf{x}^{(i)}$.

We shouldn't confuse the (i) superscript index of the i-th training sample with the (l) superscript, which represents the layer index of the NN. We'll only use the (i) sample index notation in the *Gradient descent* and *Cost functions* sections, and elsewhere we'll use the (l) notation for the layer index.

First, gradient descent computes the derivative (gradient) of $J(\theta)$ with respect to all the network weights. The gradient gives us an indication of how $J(\theta)$ changes with respect to every weight. Then, the algorithm uses this information to update the weights in a way that will minimize $J(\theta)$ in future occurrences of the same input/target pairs. The goal is to gradually reach the global minimum of the cost function. The following is a visualization of gradient descent for MSE and a NN with a single weight:

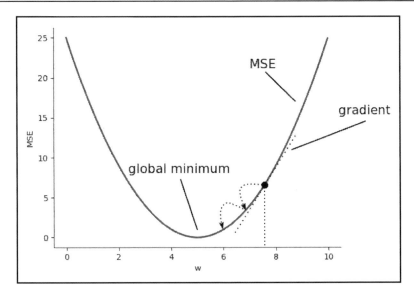

A visualization of gradient descent for MSE

Let's go over the step-by-step execution of gradient descent:

1. Initialize the network weights θ with random values.
2. Repeat until the cost function falls below a certain threshold:
    1. Forward pass: compute the MSE $J(\theta)$ cost function for all the samples of the training set using the preceding formula.
    2. Backward pass: compute the derivative of $J(\theta)$ with respect to all the network weights using the chain rule:

$$\frac{\partial J(\theta)}{\partial \theta_j} = \frac{\partial \frac{1}{2n} \sum_i^n (f_\theta(\mathbf{x}^{(i)}) - t^{(i)})^2}{\partial \theta_j} = \frac{1}{2n} \sum_i^n \frac{\partial (f_\theta(\mathbf{x}^{(i)}) - t^{(i)})^2}{\partial \theta_j} = \frac{1}{n} \sum_i^n \frac{\partial f_\theta(\mathbf{x}^{(i)})}{\partial \theta_j} [f_\theta(\mathbf{x}^{(i)}) - t^{(i)}]$$

 Let's analyze the derivative $\partial J(\theta)/\partial \theta_j$. J is a function of θ_j by being a function of the network output. Therefore, it is also a function of the NN function itself, that is, $J(f(\theta))$. Then, by following the chain rule, we get
$$\frac{\partial J(\theta)}{\partial \theta_j} = \frac{\partial J(f(\theta))}{\partial \theta_j} = \frac{\partial J(f(\theta))}{\partial f(\theta)} \frac{\partial f(\theta)}{\partial \theta_j}.$$

3. Use these derivatives to update each of the network weights:

$$\theta_j \rightarrow \theta_j - \eta \frac{\partial J(\theta)}{\partial \theta_j} = \theta_j - \eta \frac{1}{n} \sum_{i}^{n} \frac{\partial f_\theta(\mathbf{x}^{(i)})}{\partial \theta_j} [f_\theta(\mathbf{x}^{(i)}) - t^{(i)}]$$

Here, η is the learning rate.

Gradient descent updates the weights by accumulating the error across all the training samples. In practice, we would use two of its modifications:

- **Stochastic (or online) gradient descent (SGD)** updates the weights after every training sample.
- **Mini-batch gradient descent** accumulates the error for every n samples (one mini-batch) and performs one weight update.

Next, let's discuss the different cost functions we can use with SGD.

Cost functions

Besides MSE, there are also a few other loss functions that are commonly used in regression problems. The following is a non-exhaustive list:

- **Mean absolute error (MAE)** is the mean of the absolute differences (not squared) between the network output and the target. The following is the MAE graph and formula:

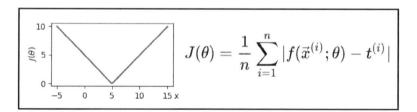

$$J(\theta) = \frac{1}{n} \sum_{i=1}^{n} |f(\vec{x}^{(i)}; \theta) - t^{(i)}|$$

One advantage of MAE over MSE is that it deals with outlier samples better. With MSE, if the difference of a sample is $f_\theta(\mathbf{x}^{(i)}) - t^{(i)} > 1$, it increases exponentially (because of the square). We'll get an outsized weight of this sample compared to the others, which may skew the results. With MAE, the difference is not exponential and this issue is less pronounced.

On the other hand, the MAE gradient will have the same value until we reach the minimum, where it will become 0 immediately. This makes it harder for the algorithm to anticipate how close the cost function minimum is. Compare this to MSE, where the slope gradually decreases as we get close to the cost minimum. This makes MSE easier to optimize. In conclusion, unless the training data is corrupted with outliers, it is usually recommended to use MSE over MAE.

- **Huber loss** attempts to fix the problems of both MAE and MSE by combining their properties. In short, when the absolute difference between the output and the target data falls below the value of a fixed parameter, δ, the Huber loss behaves like MSE. Conversely, when the difference is greater than δ, it resembles MAE. In this way, it is less sensitive to outliers (when the difference is big) and at the same time, the minimum of the function is properly differentiable. The following is the Huber loss graph for three values of δ and its formula for a single training sample, which reflects its dualistic nature:

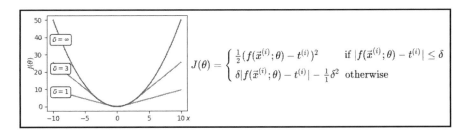

$$J(\theta) = \begin{cases} \frac{1}{2}(f(\vec{x}^{(i)};\theta) - t^{(i)})^2 & \text{if } |f(\vec{x}^{(i)};\theta) - t^{(i)}| \le \delta \\ \delta|f(\vec{x}^{(i)};\theta) - t^{(i)}| - \frac{1}{1}\delta^2 & \text{otherwise} \end{cases}$$

Huber loss

Next, let's focus on cost functions for classification problems. The following is a non-exhaustive list:

- **Cross-entropy** loss: We have our work cut out for us here as we already defined cross-entropy in the *Information theory* section. This loss is usually applied over the output of a softmax function. The two work very well together. First, the softmax converts the network output into a probability distribution. Then, cross-entropy measures the difference between the network output (Q) and the true distribution (P), which is provided as a training label. Another nice property is that the derivative of $H(P, Q_{softmax})$ is quite straightforward (although the computation isn't):

$$H'(P, Q_{\text{softmax}}) = Q_{\text{softmax}}(x^{(i)}) - P(t^{(i)})$$

Here, $x^{(i)}/t^{(i)}$ is the *i*-th input/label training pair.

- **KL Divergence** loss: Like cross-entropy loss, we already did the grunt work in the *Information theory* section, where we derived the relationship between KL divergence and cross-entropy loss. From their relationship, we can state that if we use either of the two as a loss function, we implicitly use the other one as well.

> Sometimes, we may encounter the terms loss function and cost function being used interchangeably. It is usually accepted that they differ slightly. We'll refer to the loss function as the difference between the network output and target data for a **single** sample of the training set. The cost function is the same thing but is averaged (or summed) over multiple samples (batch) of the training set.

Now that we have looked at different cost functions, let's focus on propagating the error gradient through the network with backpropagation.

Backpropagation

In this section, we'll discuss how to update the network weights in order to minimize the cost function. As we demonstrated in the *Gradient descent* section, this means finding the derivative of the cost function $J(\theta)$ with respect to each network weight. We already took a step in this direction with the help of the chain rule:

$$\frac{\partial J(\theta)}{\partial \theta_j} = \frac{\partial J(f(\theta))}{\partial \theta_j} = \frac{\partial J(f(\theta))}{\partial f(\theta)} \frac{\partial f(\theta)}{\partial \theta_j}$$

Here, $f(\theta)$ is the network output and θ_j is the j-th network weight. In this section, we'll push the envelope further and we'll learn how to derive the NN function itself for all the network weights (hint: chain rule). We'll do this by propagating the error gradient backward through the network (hence the name). Let's start with a few assumptions:

- For the sake of simplicity, we'll work with a sequential feed-forward NN. Sequential means that each layer takes input from the preceding layer and sends its output to the following layer.
- We'll define w_{ij} as the weight between the i-th neuron of layer l and the j-th neuron of layer $l+1$. In other words, we use subscripts i and j, where the element with subscript i belongs to the preceding layer, which is the layer containing the element with subscript j. In a multi-layer network, l and $l+1$ can be any two consecutive layers, including input, hidden, and output layers.

- We'll denote the output of the *i*-th unit of layer l with $y_i^{(l)}$ and the output of the *j*-th unit of layer l+1 with $y_j^{(l+1)}$.
- We'll denote the input to the activation function (that is, the weighted sum of the inputs before activation) of unit *j* of layer *l* with $a_j^{(l)}$.

The following diagram shows all the notations we introduced:

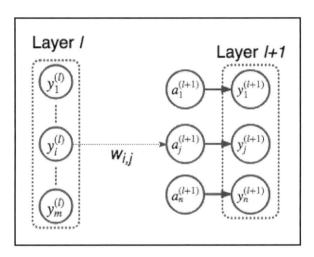

Here, layer l represents the input, layer l+1 represents the output, and w_{ij} connects the y_i activation in layer l to the inputs of the j-th neuron of layer l+1

Armed with this great knowledge, let's get down to business:

1. First, we'll assume that *l* and *l+1* are the second-to-last and the last (output) network layers, respectively. Knowing this, the derivative of J with respect to w_{ij} is as follows:

$$\frac{\partial J}{\partial w_{i,j}} = \frac{\partial J}{\partial y_j^{(l+1)}} \frac{\partial y_j^{(l+1)}}{\partial a_j^{(l+1)}} \frac{\partial a_j^{(l+1)}}{\partial w_{i,j}}$$

2. Let's focus on $\partial a_j^{(l+1)}/\partial w_{i,j}$. Here, we compute the partial derivative of the weighted sum of the output of layer l with respect to one of the weights, w_{ij}. As we discussed in the *Differential calculus* section, in partial derivatives, we'll consider all the function parameters except w_{ij} constants. When we derive $a_j^{(l+1)}$, they all become 0 and we're only left with $\partial(y_i^{(l)} w_{i,j})/\partial w_{i,j} = y_i^{(l)}$. Therefore, we get the following:

$$\frac{\partial a_j^{(l+1)}}{\partial w_{i,j}} = y_i^{(l)}$$

3. The formula from point 1 holds for any two consecutive hidden layers, l and $l+1$, of the network. We know that $\partial(y_i^{(l)} w_{i,j})/\partial w_{i,j} = y_i^{(l)}$, and we also know that $\partial y_j^{(l+1)}/\partial a_j^{(l+1)}$ is the derivative of the activation function, which we can calculate (see the *Activation functions* section). All we need to do is calculate the derivative $\partial J/\partial y_j^{(l+1)}$ (recall that, here, *l+1* is some hidden layer). Let's note that this is the derivative of the error with respect to the activation function in layer *l+1*. We can now calculate all the derivatives, starting from the last layer and moving backward, because the following apply:

   - We can calculate this derivative for the last layer.
   - We have a formula that allows us to calculate the derivative for one layer, assuming that we can calculate the derivative for the next.

4. With these points in mind, we get the following equation by applying the chain rule:

$$\frac{\partial J}{\partial y_i^{(l)}} = \sum_j \frac{\partial J}{\partial y_j^{(l+1)}} \frac{\partial y_j^{(l+1)}}{\partial y_i^{(l)}} = \sum_j \frac{\partial J}{\partial y_j^{(l+1)}} \frac{\partial y_j^{(l+1)}}{\partial a_j^{(l+1)}} \frac{\partial a_j^{(l+1)}}{\partial y_i^{(l)}}$$

The sum over j reflects the fact that, in the feedforward part of the network, the output $y_i^{(l)}$ is fed to all the neurons in layer *l+1*. Therefore, they all contribute to $y_i^{(l)}$ when the error is propagated backward.

Once again, we can calculate $\partial y_j^{(i+1)}/\partial a_j^{(i+1)}$. Following the same logic that we followed in *step 3*, we can compute that $\partial a_j^{(l+1)}/\partial y_i^{(l)} = w_{i,j}$. Therefore, once we know that $\partial J/\partial y_j^{(l+1)}$, we can calculate $\partial J/\partial y_i^{(l)}$. Since we can calculate $\partial J/\partial y_j^{(l+1)}$ for the last layer, we can move backward and calculate $\partial J/\partial y_i^{(l)}$ for any layer, and therefore $\partial J/\partial w_{i,j}$ for any layer.

5. To summarize, let's say we have a sequence of layers where the following applies:

$$y_i \rightarrow y_j \rightarrow y_k$$

Here, we have the following fundamental equations:

$$\frac{\partial J}{\partial w_{i,j}} = \frac{\partial J}{\partial y_j^{(l+1)}} \frac{\partial y_j^{(l+1)}}{\partial a_j^{(l+1)}} \frac{\partial a_j^{(l+1)}}{\partial w_{i,j}}$$

$$\frac{\partial J}{\partial y_i^{(l)}} = \sum_j \frac{\partial J}{\partial y_j^{(l+1)}} \frac{\partial y_j^{(l+1)}}{\partial y_i^{(l)}} = \sum_j \frac{\partial J}{\partial y_j^{(l+1)}} \frac{\partial y_j^{(l+1)}}{\partial a_j^{(l+1)}} \frac{\partial a_j^{(l+1)}}{\partial y_i^{(l)}}$$

By using these two equations, we can calculate the derivatives for the cost with respect to each layer.

6. If we set $\delta_j^{(l+1)} = \frac{\partial J}{\partial y_j^{(l+1)}} \frac{\partial y_j^{(l+1)}}{\partial a_j^{(l+1)}}$, then $\delta_j^{(l+1)}$ represents the variation in cost with respect to the activation value, and we can think of $\delta_j^{(l+1)}$ as the error at neuron $y_j^{(l+1)}$. We can rewrite these equations as follows:

$$\frac{\partial J}{\partial y_i^{(l)}} = \sum_j \frac{\partial J}{\partial y_j^{(l+1)}} \frac{\partial y_j^{(l+1)}}{\partial y_i^{(l)}} = \sum_j \frac{\partial J}{\partial y_j^{(l+1)}} \frac{\partial y_j^{(l+1)}}{\partial a_j^{(l+1)}} \frac{\partial a_j^{(l+1)}}{\partial y_i^{(l)}} = \sum_j \delta_j^{(l+1)} w_{ij}$$

Following this, we can write the following equation:

$$\delta_i^{(l)} = \left(\sum_j \delta_j^{(l+1)} w_{ij}\right) \frac{\partial y_i^{(l)}}{\partial a_i^{(l)}}$$

These two equations provide us with an alternative view of backpropagation since there is a variation in cost with respect to the activation value. They provide us with a way to calculate the variation for any layer *l* once we know the variation for the following layer, *l+1*.

7. We can combine these equations to show the following:

$$\frac{\partial J}{\partial w_{i,j}} = \delta_j^{(l+1)} \frac{\partial a_j^{(l+1)}}{\partial w_{i,j}} = \delta_j^{(l+1)} y_i^{(l)}$$

8. The updated rule for the weights of each layer is given by the following equation:

$$w_{i,j} \rightarrow w_{i,j} - \eta \delta_j^{(l+1)} y_i^{(l)}$$

Now that we're familiar with backpropagation, let's discuss another component of the training process: weight initialization.

Weight initialization

One key component of training deep networks is the random weight initialization. This matters because some activation functions, such as sigmoid and ReLU, produce meaningful outputs and gradients if their inputs are within a certain range.

A famous example is the vanishing gradient problem. To understand it, let's take an FC layer with sigmoid activation (this example is also valid for tanh). We saw the sigmoid's graph (blue) and its derivative (green) in the *Activation functions* section. If the weighted sum of the inputs falls roughly outside the (-5, 5) range, the sigmoid activation will be effectively 0 or 1. In essence, it saturates. This is visible during the backward pass where we derive the sigmoid (the formula is $\sigma' = \sigma(1 - \sigma)$). We can see that the derivative is larger than 0 within the same (-5, 5) range of the input. Therefore, whatever error we try to propagate back to the previous layers, it will vanish if the activation doesn't fall within this range (hence the name).

Besides the tight meaningful range of the sigmoid derivative, let's note that, even under the best conditions, its maximum value is 0.25. When we propagate the gradient through the sigmoid derivative, it will be four times smaller at best once it passes through. Because of this, the gradient may vanish in just a few layers, even if we don't fall outside the desired range. This is one of the major disadvantages of sigmoid over the *LU family of functions, where the gradient is 1 in most cases.

One way to solve this problem is to use *LU activations. But even so, it still makes sense to use better weight initialization since it can speed up the training process. One popular technique is the Xavier/Glorot initializer (often found under either of the two names: http://proceedings.mlr.press/v9/glorot10a/glorot10a.pdf). In short, this technique takes the number of input and output connections of the unit into account. There are two variations:

- **Xavier uniform initializer**, which draws samples from a uniform distribution in the range [-a, a]. The parameter, a, is defined as follows:

$$a = \sqrt{\frac{6}{n_{\text{in}} + n_{\text{out}}}}$$

  Here, n_{in} and n_{out} are the number of inputs and outputs, respectively (that is, the number of units that send their output to the current unit and the number of units the current unit sends its output to).

- **Xavier normal initializer**, which draws samples from a normal distribution (see the *Probability distributions* section) with a mean of 0 and variance as follows:

$$\text{Var}(w_{ij}) = \frac{2}{n_{\text{in}} + n_{\text{out}}}$$

The Xavier/Glorot initialization is recommended for sigmoid or tanh activations functions. The paper *Delving Deep into Rectifiers: Surpassing Human-Level Performance on ImageNet Classification* (https://arxiv.org/abs/1502.01852) proposes a similar technique that's better suited for ReLU activations. Again, there are two variations:

- **He uniform initializer**, which draws samples from a uniform distribution in the range [-a, a]. The parameter, a, is defined as follows:

$$a = \sqrt{\frac{6}{n_{\text{in}}}}$$

- **He normal initializer**, which draws samples from a normal distribution with a mean of 0 and variance as follows:

$$\mathrm{Var}(w_{ij}) = \frac{2}{n_{\mathrm{in}}}$$

The ReLU output is always 0 when the input is negative. If we assume that the initial inputs of the ReLU units are centered around 0, half of them will produce 0 outputs. The He initializer compensates this by increasing the variance twice, compared to the Xavier initialization.

In the next section, we'll discuss some improvements in the weight update rule over the standard SGD.

SGD improvements

We'll start with **momentum**, which extends vanilla SGD by adjusting the current weight update with the values of the previous weight updates. That is, if the weight update at step *t-1* was big, it will also increase the weight update of step *t*. We can explain momentum with an analogy. Think of the loss function surface as the surface of a hill. Now, imagine that we are holding a ball at the top of the hill (maximum). If we drop the ball, thanks to the Earth's gravity, it will start rolling toward the bottom of the hill (minimum). The more distance it travels, the more its speed will increase. In other words, it will gain momentum (hence the name of the optimization).

Now, let's look at how to implement momentum in the weight update rule. Recall the update rule that we introduced in the *Gradient descent* section, that is, $\theta_j \rightarrow \theta_j - \eta \partial J(\theta)/\partial \theta_j$. Let's assume that we are at step *t* of the training process:

1. First, we'll calculate the current weight update value v_t by also including the **velocity** of the previous update v_{t-1}:

$$v_t \rightarrow \mu v_{t-1} - \eta \partial J(\theta)/\partial \theta_j$$

   Here, μ is a hyperparameter in the [0:1] range called the momentum rate. v_t is initialized as 0 during the first iteration.

2. Then, we perform the actual weight update:

$$\theta_j \rightarrow \theta_j + v_t$$

An improvement over the basic momentum is the **Nesterov momentum**. It relies on the observation that the momentum from step *t-1* may not reflect the conditions at step *t*. For example, let's say that the gradient at *t-1* is steep and therefore the momentum is high. However, after the *t-1* weight update, we actually reach the cost function minimum and require only a minor weight update at *t*. Despite that, we'll still get the large momentum from *t-1*, which may lead the adjusted weight to jump over the minimum. Nesterov momentum proposes a change in the way we compute the velocity of the weight update. We'll calculate v_t based on the gradient of the cost function that's computed by the potential future value of the weight θ_j. The following is the updated velocity formula:

$$v_t \rightarrow \mu v_{t-1} - \eta \partial J(\theta; \theta_j + \mu v_{t-1})/\partial \theta_j$$

If the momentum at *t-1* is incorrect with respect to *t*, the modified gradient will compensate for this error in the same update step.

Next, let's discuss the Adam adaptive learning rate algorithm (*Adam: A Method for Stochastic Optimization*, `https://arxiv.org/abs/1412.6980`). It calculates individual and adaptive learning rates for every weight based on previous weight updates (momentum). Let's see how that works:

1. First, we need to compute the first moment (or mean) and the second moment (or variance) of the gradient:

$$m_t \rightarrow \beta_1 m_{t-1} + (1 - \beta_1)\frac{\partial J(\theta)}{\partial \theta_j}$$

$$v_t \rightarrow \beta_2 v_{t-1} + (1 - \beta_2)(\frac{\partial J(\theta)}{\partial \theta_j})^2$$

Here, β_1 and β_2 are hyperparameters with default values of 0.9 and 0.999, respectively. m_t and v_t act as moving-average values of the gradient, somewhat similar to momentum. They are initialized with 0 during the first iteration.

2. Since m_t and v_t start as 0, they will have a bias toward 0 in the initial phase of the training. For example, let's say that, at $t=1$, $\beta 1 = 0.9$ and $\partial J(\theta)/\partial\theta_j = 10$. Here, $m1 = 0.9 * 0 + (1 - 0.9) * 10 = 1$, which is a lot less than the actual gradient of 10. To compensate for this bias, we'll compute the bias-corrected versions of m_t and v_t:

$$\hat{m}_t \rightarrow \frac{m_t}{1 - \beta_1^t}$$

$$\hat{v}_t \rightarrow \frac{v_t}{1 - \beta_2^t}$$

3. Finally, we need to perform the weight update using the following formula:

$$\theta_j \rightarrow \theta_j - \eta\frac{\hat{m}_t}{\sqrt{\hat{v}_t + \epsilon}}$$

Here, η is the learning rate and ϵ is some small value to prevent division by 0.

Summary

We started this chapter with a tutorial on the mathematical apparatus that forms the foundation of NNs. Then, we recapped on NNs and their architecture. Along the way, we tried to explicitly connect the mathematical concepts with the various components of the NNs. We paid special attention to the various types of activation functions. Finally, we took a comprehensive look at the NN training process. We discussed gradient descent, cost functions, backpropagation, weights initialization, and SGD optimization techniques.

In the next chapter, we'll discuss the intricacies of convolutional networks and their applications in the computer vision domain.

Section 2: Computer Vision 2

This section will discuss **Deep Learning** (**DL**) applications in the computer vision domain. We'll talk about convolutional networks, object detection and image segmentation, generative models (GANs), and neural style transfer.

This section contains the following chapters:

- Chapter 2, *Understanding Convolutional Networks*
- Chapter 3, *Advanced Convolutional Networks*
- Chapter 4, *Object Detection and Image Segmentation*
- Chapter 5, *Generative Models*

Understanding Convolutional Networks

In this chapter, we'll discuss **Convolutional Neural Networks** (**CNNs**) and their applications in **Computer Vision** (**CV**). CNNs started the modern deep learning revolution. They are at the base of virtually all recent CV advancements, including **Generative Adversarial Networks** (**GANs**), object detection, image segmentation, neural style transfer, and much more. For this reason, we believe CNNs deserve an in-depth look that's beyond our basic understanding of them.

To do this, we'll start with a short recap of the CNN building blocks, that is, the convolutional and pooling layers. We'll discuss the various types of convolutions in use today since they are reflected in a large number of CNN applications. We'll also learn how to visualize the internal state of CNNs. Then, we'll focus on regularization techniques and implement a transfer learning example.

This chapter will cover the following topics:

- Understanding CNNs
- Introducing transfer learning

Understanding CNNs

In Chapter 1, *The Nuts and Bolts of Neural Networks*, we discussed that many NN operations have solid mathematical foundations, and convolutions are no exception. Let's start by defining the mathematical convolution:

$$s(t) = (f * g)(t) = \int_{-\infty}^{\infty} f(\tau)g(t - \tau) \, d\tau$$

Here, we have the following:

- The convolution operation is denoted with *.
- *f* and *g* are two functions with a common parameter, *t*.
- The result of the convolution is a third function, *s(t)* (not just a single value).

The convolution of *f* and *g* at value *t* is the integral of the product of *f(t)* and the reversed (mirrored) and shifted value of *g(t-τ)*, where *t-τ* represents the shift. That is, for a single value of *f* at time *t*, we shift *g* in the range $(t - \infty, t + \infty)$ and we compute the product *f(t)g(t-τ)* continuously because of the integral. The integral (and hence the convolution) is equivalent to the area under the curve of the product of the two functions.

This is best illustrated in the following diagram:

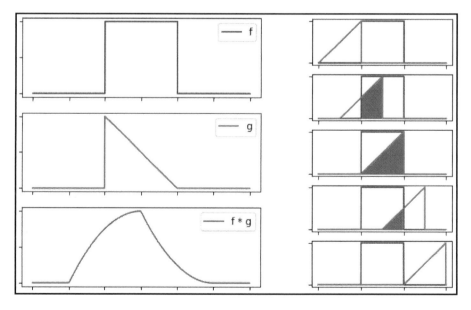

Left: a convolution. where *g* is shifted and reversed: right: a step-by-step illustration of a convolution operation

In the convolution operation, g is shifted and reversed in order to preserve the operation's commutative property. In the context of CNNs, we can ignore this property and we can implement it without reversing g. In this case, the operation is called cross-correlation. These two terms are used interchangeably.

We can define the convolution for discrete (integer) values of t with the following formula (which is very similar to the continuous case):

$$s(t) = (f * g)(t) = \sum_{\tau=-\infty}^{\infty} f(\tau)g(t - \tau)$$

We can also generalize it to the convolution of functions with two shared input parameters, i and j:

$$s(i, j) = (f * g)(i, j) = \sum_{m=-\infty}^{\infty} \sum_{n=-\infty}^{\infty} f(i, j)g(i - m, j - n)$$

We can derive the formula in a similar manner for three parameters.

In CNNs, the function f is the input of the convolution operation (also referred to as the convolutional layer). Depending on the number of input dimensions, we have 1D, 2D, or 3D convolutions. A time series input is a 1D vector, an image input is a 2D matrix, and a 3D point cloud is a 3D tensor. The function g, on the other hand, is called a kernel (or filter). It has the same number of dimensions as the input data and it is defined by a set of learnable weights. For example, a filter of size n for a 2D convolution is an $n \times n$ matrix. The following diagram illustrates a 2D convolution with a 2×2 filter applied over a single 3×3 slice:

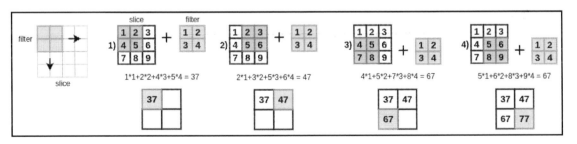

2D convolution with a 2×2 filter applied over a single 3×3 slice

The convolution works as follows:

1. We slide the filter along all of the dimensions of the input tensor.
2. At every input position, we multiply each filter weight by its corresponding input tensor cell at the given location. The input cells, which contribute to a single output cell, are called **receptive fields**. We sum all of these values to produce the value of a single output cell.

Unlike fully-connected layers, where each output unit gathers information from all of the inputs, the activation of a convolution output cell is determined by the inputs in its receptive field. This principle works best for hierarchically structured data such as images. For example, neighboring pixels form meaningful shapes and objects, but a pixel at one end of the image is unlikely to have a relationship with a pixel at another end. Using a fully-connected layer to connect all of the input pixels with each output unit is like asking the network to find a needle in a haystack. It has no way of knowing whether an input pixel is in the receptive field of the output unit or not.

The filter highlights some particular features in the receptive field. The output of the operation is a tensor (known as a feature map), which marks the locations where the feature is detected. Since we apply the same filter throughout the input tensor, the convolution is translation invariant; that is, it can detect the same features, regardless of their location on the image. However, the convolution is neither rotation invariant (it is not guaranteed to detect a feature if it's rotated), nor scale invariant (it is not guaranteed to detect the same artifact in different scales).

In the following diagram, we can see examples of 1D and 3D convolutions (we've already introduced an example of a 2D convolution):

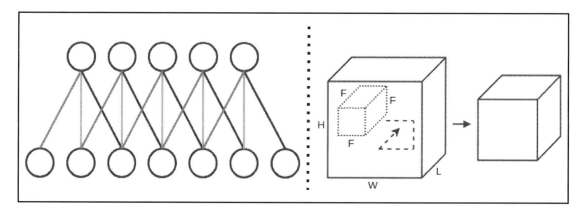

1D convolution: The filter (denoted with multicolored lines) slides over a single axis: 3D convolution: The filter (denoted with dashed lines) slides over three axes

The CNN convolution can have multiple filters, highlighting different features, which results in multiple output feature maps (one for each filter). It can also gather input from multiple feature maps, for example, the output of a previous convolution. The combination of feature maps (input or output) is called a volume. In this context, we can also refer to the feature maps as slices. Although the two terms refer to the same thing, we can think of the slice as part of the volume, whereas the feature map highlights its role as, well, a feature map.

As we mentioned earlier in this section, each volume (as well as the filter) is represented by a tensor. For example, a red, green, and blue (RGB) image is represented by a 3D tensor of three 2D slices (one slice per color channel). But in the context of CNNs, we add one more dimension for the sample index in the mini-batch. Here, a 1D convolution would have 3D input and output tensors. Their axes can be in either *NCW* or *NWC* order, where *N* is the index of the sample in the mini-batch, *C* is the index of the depth slice in the volume, and *W* is the vector size of each sample. In the same way, a 2D convolution will be represented by *NCHW* or *NHWC* tensors, where *H* and *W* are the height and width of the slices. A 3D convolution will have an *NCLHW* or *NLHWC* order, where *L* stands for the depth of the slice.

We use 2D convolutions to work with RGB images. However, we may consider the three colors an additional dimension, hence making the RGB image 3D. Why didn't we use 3D convolutions, then? The reason for this is that, even though we can think of the input as 3D, the output is still a 2D grid. Had we used 3D convolution, the output would also be 3D, which doesn't carry any meaning in the case of 2D images.

Let's say we have *n* input and *m* output slices. In this case, we'll apply *m* filters across the set of *n* input slices. Each filter will generate a unique output slice that highlights the feature that was detected by the filter (*n* to *m* relationship).

Depending on the relationship of the input and output slice, we get cross-channel and depth-wise convolutions, as illustrated in the following diagram:

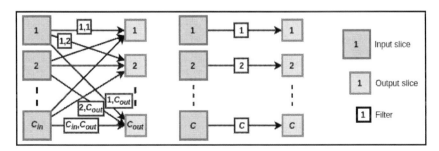

Left: cross-channel convolution: right: depthwise convolution

Let's discuss their properties:

- **Cross-channel convolutions**: One output slice receives input from all of the input slices (*n*-to-one relationship). With multiple output slices, the relationship becomes *n*-to-*m*. In other words, each input slice contributes to the output of each output slice. Each pair of input/output slices uses a separate filter slice that's unique to that pair. Let's denote the size of the filter (equal width and height) with *F*, the depth of the input volume with C_{in}, and the depth of the output volume with C_{out}. With this, we can compute the total number of weights, *W*, in a 2D convolution with the following equation:

$$W = (C_{in} * F^2 + 1) * C_{out}$$

  Here, +1 represents the bias weight for each filter. Let's say we have three slices and want to apply four 5×5 filters to them. If we did this, the convolution filter would have a total of *(3*5*5 + 1) * 4 = 304* weights, four output slices (output volume with a depth of 4), and one bias per slice. The filter for each output slice will have three 5×5 filter patches for each of the three input slices and one bias for a total of 3*5*5 + 1 = 76 weights.

- **Depthwise convolutions**: Each output slice receives input from a single input slice. It's a kind of reversal of the previous case. In its most simple form, we apply a filter over a single input slice to produce a single output slice. In this case, the input and output volumes have the same depth, that is, *C*. We can also specify a **channel multiplier** (an integer, *m*), where we apply *m* filters over a single output slice to produce *m* output slices. This is a case of a one-to-*m* relationship. In this case, the total number of output slices is *n * m*. We can compute the number of weights, *W*, in a 2D depthwise convolution with the following formula:

$$W = (C * F^2 + C) * m$$

  Here, *m* is the channel multiplier and +*C* represents the biases of each output slice.

The convolution operation is also described by two other parameters:

- **Stride** is the number of positions that we slide the filter over on the input slice on each step. By default, the stride is 1. If it's larger than 1, then we call it a **stride convolution**. The largest stride increases the receptive field of the output neurons. With stride 2, the size of the output slice will be roughly four times smaller than the input. In other words, one output neuron will cover the area, which is four times larger, compared to a stride 1 convolution. The neurons in the following layers will gradually capture input from the larger regions of the input image.
- **Padding** the edges of the input slice with rows and columns of zeros before the convolution operation. The most common way to use padding is to produce output with the same dimensions as the input. The newly padded zeros will participate in the convolution operation with the slice, but they won't affect the result.

Knowing the input dimensions and the filter size, we can compute the dimensions of the output slices. Let's say the size of the input slice is I (equal height and width), the size of the filter is F, the stride is S, and the padding is P. Here, the size, O, of the output slice is given by the following equation:

$$O = \frac{I + 2P - F}{S} + 1$$

Besides stride convolutions, we can also use **pooling** operations to increase the receptive field of the deeper neurons and reduce the size of the future slices. The pooling splits the input slice into a grid, where each grid cell represents a receptive field of a number of neurons (just like it does with the convolution). Then, a pooling operation is applied over each cell of the grid. Similar to convolution, pooling is described by the stride, S, and the size of the receptive field, F. If the size of input slice is I, then the formula for the output size of the pooling is as follows:

$$O = \frac{I - F}{S} + 1$$

In practice, only two combinations are used. The first is a 2×2 receptive field with stride 2, while the second is a 3×3 receptive field with stride 2 (overlapping). The most common pooling operations are as follows:

- **Max pooling**: This propagates the maximum value of the input values of the receptive field.

- **Average pooling**: This propagates the average value of the inputs in the receptive field.
- **Global Average Pooling (GAP)**: This is the same as average pooling, but the pooling region has the same size as the feature map, *I×I*. GAP performs an extreme type of dimensionality reduction: the output is a single scalar, which represents the average value of the whole feature map.

Typically, we would alternate one or more convolutional layers with one pooling (or stride convolution) layer. In this way, the convolutional layers can detect features at every level of the receptive field size because the aggregated receptive field size of deeper layers is larger than the ones at the beginning of the network. The deeper layers also have more filters (hence, a higher volume depth) compared to the initial ones. The feature detector at the beginning of the network works on a small receptive field. It can only detect a limited number of features, such as edges or lines, that are shared among all classes.

On the other hand, a deeper layer would detect more complex and numerous features. For example, if we have multiple classes, such as cars, trees, or people, each would have its own set of features, such as tires, doors, leaves, and faces. This would require more feature detectors. The output of the final convolution (or pooling) is "translated" to the target labels by adding one or more fully connected layers.

Now that we have had an overview of convolutions, pooling operations, and CNNs, in the next section, we'll focus on different types of convolution operations.

Types of convolutions

So far, we've discussed the most common type of convolution. In the upcoming sections, we'll talk about a few of its variations.

Transposed convolutions

In the convolutional operations we've discussed so far, the output dimensions are either equal or smaller than the input dimensions. In contrast, transposed convolutions (first proposed in *Deconvolutional Networks* by Matthew D. Zeiler, Dilip Krishnan, Graham W. Taylor, and Rob Fergus: `https://www.matthewzeiler.com/mattzeiler/deconvolutionalnetworks.pdf`) allow us to upsample the input data (their output is larger than the input). This operation is also known as **deconvolution**, **fractionally strided convolution**, or **sub-pixel convolution**. These names can sometimes lead to confusion. To clarify things, note that the transposed convolution is, in fact, a regular convolution with a slightly modified input slice or convolutional filter.

For the longer explanation, we'll start with a 1D regular convolution over a single input and output slice:

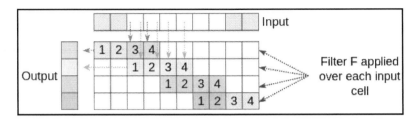

1D regular convolution

It uses a filter with a size of 4, stride 2, and padding 2 (denoted with gray in the preceding diagram). The input is a vector of size 6 and the output is a vector of size 4. The filter, a vector **f** = [1, 2, 3, 4], is always the same, but it's denoted with different colors for each position we apply it to. The respective output cells are denoted with the same color. The arrows show which input cells contribute to one output cell.

 The example that is being discussed in this section is inspired by the paper; *Is the deconvolution layer the same as a convolutional layer?* (https://arxiv.org/abs/1609.07009).

Next, we'll discuss the same example (1D, single input and output slices, filter of size 4, padding 2, and stride 2), but for transposed convolution. The following diagram shows two ways we can implement it:

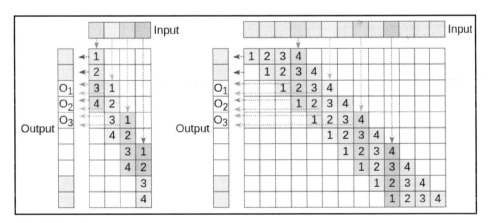

Left: A convolution with stride 2. applied with the transposed filter **f**. The 2 pixels at the beginning and the end of the output are cropped: right: A convolution with stride 0.5. applied over input data. padded with subpixels. The input is filled with 0-valued pixels (gray).

Let's discuss them in detail:

- In the first case, we have a regular convolution with stride 2 and a filter represented as transposed row matrix (equivalent to column matrix) with size 4: $\mathbf{f}^\mathsf{T} = [1, 2, 3, 4]^\mathsf{T}$ (shown in the preceding diagram, left). Note that the stride is applied over the output layer as opposed to the regular convolution, where we stride over the input. By setting the stride larger than 1, we can increase the output size, compared to the input. Here, the size of the input slice is I, the size of the filter is F, the stride is S, and the input padding is P. Due to this, the size, O, of the output slice of a transposed convolution is given by the following formula:

$$O = S(I - 1) + F - 2P$$

In this scenario, an input of size 4 produces an output of size $2*(4 - 1) + 4 - 2*2 = 6$. We also crop the two cells at the beginning and the end of the output vector because they only gather input from a single input cell.

- In the second case, the input is filled with imaginary 0-valued subpixels between the existing ones (shown in the preceding diagram, right). This is where the name subpixel convolution comes from. Think of it as padding but within the image itself and not only along the borders. Once the input has been transformed in this way, a regular convolution is applied.

Let's compare the two output cells, o_1 and o_3, in both scenarios. As shown in the preceding diagram, in either case, o_1 receives input from the first and the second input cells and o_3 receives input from the second and third cells. In fact, the only difference between these two cases is the index of the weight, which participates in the computation. However, the weights are learned during training and, because of this, the index is not important. Therefore, the two operations are equivalent.

Next, let's take a look at a 2D transposed convolution from a subpixel point of view (the input is at the bottom). As with the 1D case, we insert 0-valued pixels and padding in the input slice to achieve upsampling:

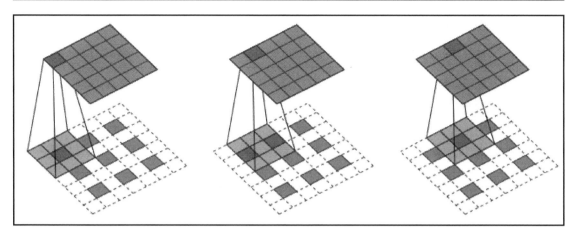

The first three steps of a 2D transpose convolution with padding 1 and stride 2: Source: https://github.com/vdumoulin/conv_arithmetic. https://arxiv.org/abs/1603.07285

The backpropagation operation of a regular convolution is a transposed convolution.

1×1 convolutions

A 1×1 (or pointwise) convolution is a special case of convolution where each dimension of the convolution filter is of size 1 (1×1 in 2D convolutions and 1×1×1 in 3D). At first, this doesn't make sense—a 1×1 filter doesn't increase the receptive field size of the output neurons. The result of such a convolution would be pointwise scaling. But it can be useful in another way—we can use them to change the depth between the input and output volumes.

To understand this, let's recall that, in general, we have an input volume with a depth of D slices and M filters for M output slices. Each output slice is generated by applying a unique filter over all of the input slices. If we use a 1×1 filter and $D \mathrel{!=} M$, we'll have output slices of the same size, but with different volume depths. At the same time, we won't change the receptive field size between the input and output. The most common use case is to reduce the output volume, or $D > M$ (dimension reduction), nicknamed the "bottleneck" layer.

Depth-wise separable convolutions

An output slice in a cross-channel convolution receives input from all of the input slices using a single filter. The filter tries to learn features in a 3D space, where two of the dimensions are spatial (the height and width of the slice) and the third is the channel. Therefore, the filter maps both spatial and cross-channel correlations.

Depthwise separable convolutions (**DSC**, *Xception: Deep Learning with Depthwise Separable Convolutions*, https://arxiv.org/abs/1610.02357) can completely decouple cross-channel and spatial correlations. A DSC combines two operations: a depthwise convolution and a 1×1 convolution. In a depthwise convolution, a single input slice produces a single output slice, so it only maps spatial (and not cross-channel) correlations. With 1×1 convolutions, we have the opposite. The following diagram represents the DSC:

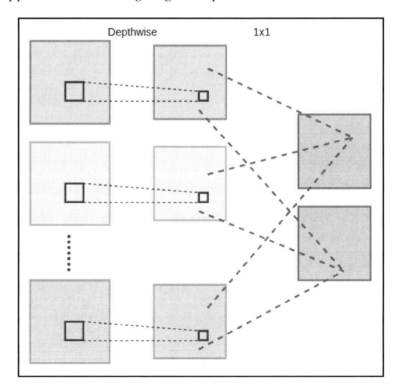

A depthwise separable convolution

The DSC is usually implemented without non-linearity after the first (depthwise) operation.

Let's compare the standard and depthwise separable convolutions. Imagine that we have 32 input and output channels and a filter with a size of 3×3. In a standard convolution, one output slice is the result of applying one filter for each of the 32 input slices for a total of *32 * 3 * 3 = 288* weights (excluding bias). In a comparable depthwise convolution, the filter has only *3 * 3 = 9* weights and the filter for the 1×1 convolution has *32 * 1 * 1 = 32* weights. The total number of weights is *32 + 9 = 41*. Therefore, the depthwise separable convolution is faster and more memory-efficient compared to the standard one.

Dilated convolutions

Recall the discrete convolution formula we introduced at the beginning of the *A quick recap of CNNs* section. To explain dilated convolutions (*Multi-Scale Context Aggregation by Dilated Convolutions*, https://arxiv.org/abs/1511.07122), let's start with the following formula:

$$s(t) = (f *_l g)(t) = \sum_{\tau=-\infty}^{\infty} f(\tau)g(t - l\tau)$$

We'll denote the dilated convolution with $*_l$, where l is a positive integer value called the dilation factor. The key is the way we apply the filter over the input. Instead of applying the $n \times n$ filter over the $n \times n$ receptive field, we apply the same filter sparsely over a receptive field of size $(n*l-1) \times (n*l-1)$. We still multiply each filter weight by one input slice cell, but these cells are at a distance of l away from each other. The regular convolution is a special case of dilated convolution with $l=1$. This is best illustrated with the following diagram:

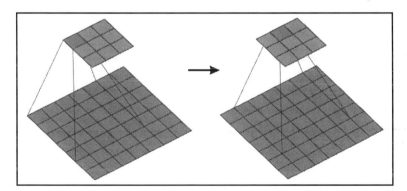

A dilated convolution with a dilation factor of l=2: Here, the first two steps of the operation are displayed. The bottom layer is the input while the top layer is the output.
Source: https://github.com/vdumoulin/conv_arithmetic

Dilated convolutions can increase the receptive field size exponentially without losing resolution or coverage. We can also increase the receptive field with stride convolutions or pooling but at the cost of resolution and/or coverage. To understand this, let's imagine that we have a stride convolution with stride $s>1$. In this case, the output slice is s times smaller than the input (loss of resolution). If we increase $s>n$ further (n is the size of either the pooling or convolutional kernel), we get loss of coverage because some of the areas of the input slice will not participate in the output at all. Additionally, dilated convolutions don't increase the computation and memory costs because the filter uses the same number of weights as the regular convolution.

Improving the efficiency of CNNs

One of the main reasons for the advances in recent **Deep Learning** (**DL**) is its ability to run **Neural Networks** (**NNs**) very fast. This is in large part because of the good match between the nature of NN algorithms and the specifics of **Graphical Processing Units** (**GPUs**). In Chapter 1, *The Nuts and Bolts of Neural Networks*, we underscored the importance of matrix multiplication in NNs. As a testament to this, it is possible to transform the convolution into a matrix multiplication as well. Matrix multiplication is embarrassingly parallel (trust me, this is a term—you can Google it!). The computation of each output cell is not related to the computation of any other output cell. Therefore, we can compute all of the outputs in parallel.

Not coincidentally, GPUs are well suited for highly parallel operations like this. On the one hand, a GPU has a high number of computational cores compared to a **Central Processing Unit** (**CPU**). Even though a GPU core is faster than a CPU one, we can still compute a lot more output cells in parallel. But what's even more important is that GPUs are optimized for memory bandwidth, while CPUs are optimized for latency. This means that a CPU can fetch small chunks of memory very quickly but will be slow when it comes to fetching large chunks. The GPU does the opposite. Because of this, in tasks such as large matrix multiplication for NNs, the GPU has an advantage.

Besides hardware specifics, we can optimize CNNs on the algorithmic side as well. The majority of computational time in a CNN is devoted to the convolutions themselves. Although the implementation of the convolution is straightforward enough, in practice, there are more efficient algorithms to achieve the same result. Although contemporary DL libraries such as TensorFlow or PyTorch shield the developer from such details, in this book, we are aiming for a deeper (pun intended) understanding of DL.

Because of this, in the next section, we'll discuss two of the most popular fast convolution algorithms.

Convolution as matrix multiplication

In this section, we'll describe the algorithm that we use to transform convolutions into matrix multiplication, just like how it's implemented in the cuDNN library (*cuDNN: Efficient Primitives for Deep Learning*, https://arxiv.org/abs/1410.0759). To understand this, let's assume that we perform a cross-channel 2D convolution over an RGB input image. Let's look at the following table for the parameters of the convolution:

Parameter	Notation	Value
Mini-batch size	N	1
Input feature maps (volume depth)	C	3 (one for each RGB channel)
Input image height	H	4
Input image width	W	4
Output feature maps (volume depth)	K	2
Filter height	R	2
Filter width	S	2
Output feature map height	P	2 (based on the input/filter sizes)
Output feature map width	Q	2 (based on the input/filter sizes)

For the sake of simplicity, we'll assume we have zero padding and stride 1. We'll denote the input tensor with D and the convolution filter tensor with F. The matrix convolution works in the following way:

1. We unfold the tensors, D and F, into the $D \to \mathbf{D}_m$ and $F \to \mathbf{F}_m$ matrices, respectively.
2. Then, we multiply the matrices to get the output matrix, $\mathbf{O}_m = \mathbf{D}_m \cdot \mathbf{F}_m$.

We discussed matrix multiplication in `Chapter 1`, *The Nuts and Bolts of Neural Networks*. Now, let's focus on the way we can unfold the tensors in matrices. The following diagram shows how to do this:

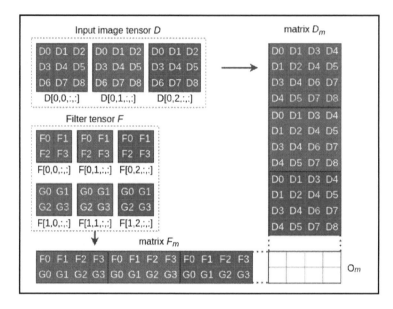

Convolution as matrix multiplication: Inspired by https://arxiv.org/abs/1410.0759

Each feature map has a different color (R, G, B). In the regular convolution, the filter has a square shape and we apply it over a square input region. In the transformation, we unfold each possible square region of *D* into one column of $\mathbf{D}_m$. Then, we unfold each square component of *F* into one row of $\mathbf{F}_m$. In this way, the input and filter data for each output cell is situated in a single column/row of the matrices $\mathbf{D}_m$ and $\mathbf{F}_m$. This makes it possible to compute the output value as a matrix multiplication. The dimensions of the transformed input/filter/output are as follows:

- $\dim(\mathbf{D}_m) = CRS \times NPQ = 12 \times 4$
- $\dim(\mathbf{F}_m) = K \times CRS = 2 \times 12$
- $\dim(\mathbf{O}_m) = K \times NPQ = 2 \times 4$

To understand this transformation, let's learn how to compute the first output cell with the regular convolution algorithm:

$$O[0,0,0,0] = D[0,0,0,0] * F[0,0,0,0] + D[0,0,0,1] * F[0,0,0,1] + D[0,0,1,0] * F[0,0,1,0] + D[0,0,1,1] * F[0,0,1,1]$$
$$+ D[0,1,0,0] * F[0,1,0,0] + D[0,1,0,1] * F[0,1,0,1] + D[0,1,1,0] * F[0,1,1,0] + D[0,1,1,1] * F[0,1,1,1]$$
$$+ D[0,2,0,0] * F[0,2,0,0] + D[0,2,0,1] * F[0,2,0,1] + D[0,2,1,0] * F[0,2,1,0] + D[0,2,1,1] * F[0,2,1,1]$$

Next, let's observe the same formula, but this time, in matrix multiplication form:

$$\mathbf{O}_m[0,0] = \mathbf{D}_m[0,0] * \mathbf{F}_m[0,0] + \mathbf{D}_m[1,0] * \mathbf{F}_m[0,1] + \mathbf{D}_m[2,0] * \mathbf{F}_m[0,2] + \mathbf{D}_m[3,0] * \mathbf{F}_m[0,3]$$
$$+ \mathbf{D}_m[4,0] * \mathbf{F}_m[0,4] + \mathbf{D}_m[5,0] * \mathbf{F}_m[0,5] + \mathbf{D}_m[6,0] * \mathbf{F}_m[0,6] + \mathbf{D}_m[7,0] * \mathbf{F}_m[0,7]$$
$$+ \mathbf{D}_m[8,0] * \mathbf{F}_m[0,8] + \mathbf{D}_m[9,0] * \mathbf{F}_m[0,9] + \mathbf{D}_m[10,0] * \mathbf{F}_m[0,10] + \mathbf{D}_m[11,0] * \mathbf{F}_m[0,11]$$

If we compare the components of the two equations, we'll see that they are exactly the same. That is, $D[0,0,0,0] = \mathbf{D}_m[0,0]$, $F[0,0,0,0] = \mathbf{F}_m[0,0]$, $D[0,0,0,1] = \mathbf{D}_m[0,1]$, $F[0,0,0,1] = \mathbf{F}_m[0,1]$, and so on. We can do the same for the rest of the output cells. Therefore, the output of the two approaches is the same.

One disadvantage of the matrix convolution is increased memory usage. In the preceding diagram, we can see that some of the input elements are duplicated multiple times (up to RS = 4 times, like D4).

Winograd convolutions

The Winograd algorithm (*Fast Algorithms for Convolutional Neural Networks*, https://arxiv. org/abs/1509.09308) can provide 2 or 3× speedup compared to the direct convolution. To explain this, we'll use the same notations that we used in the *Convolution as matrix multiplication* section but with a 3×3 (*R=S=3*) filter. We'll also assume that the input slices are bigger than 4×4 (*H>4, W>4*).

Here's how to compute Winograd convolutions:

1. Divide the input image into 4×4 tiles that overlap with stride 2, as shown in the following diagram:

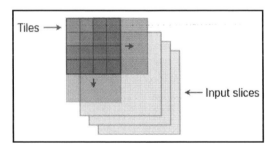

The input is split into tiles

The tile size can vary, but for the sake of simplicity, we'll only focus on 4×4 tiles.

2. Transform each tile using the following two matrix multiplications:

$$\mathbf{D}_t = (\mathbf{B}\mathbf{D})\mathbf{B}^\mathsf{T}$$

$$
\begin{bmatrix} \circ & \circ & \circ & \circ \\ \circ & \circ & \circ & \circ \\ \circ & \circ & \circ & \circ \\ \circ & \circ & \circ & \circ \end{bmatrix}
=
\left(\begin{bmatrix} 1 & 0 & -1 & 0 \\ 0 & 1 & 1 & 0 \\ 0 & -1 & 1 & 0 \\ 0 & 1 & 0 & -1 \end{bmatrix} \bullet \begin{bmatrix} \cdot & \cdot & \cdot & \cdot \\ \cdot & \cdot & \cdot & \cdot \\ \cdot & \cdot & \cdot & \cdot \\ \cdot & \cdot & \cdot & \cdot \end{bmatrix} \right) \bullet \begin{bmatrix} 1 & 0 & -1 & 0 \\ 0 & 1 & 1 & 0 \\ 0 & -1 & 1 & 0 \\ 0 & 1 & 0 & -1 \end{bmatrix}^\mathsf{T}
$$

In the preceding formula, the matrix **D** is the input slice (the one with circle values) while **B** is a special matrix, which results from the specifics of the Winograd algorithm (you can find more information about them in the paper linked at the beginning of this section).

3. Transform the filter using the following two matrix multiplications:

$$\mathbf{F}_t = (\mathbf{G}\mathbf{F})\mathbf{G}^\mathsf{T}$$

$$
\begin{bmatrix} \times & \times & \times & \times \\ \times & \times & \times & \times \\ \times & \times & \times & \times \\ \times & \times & \times & \times \end{bmatrix}
=
\left(\begin{bmatrix} 1 & 0 & 0 \\ 1/2 & 1/2 & 1/2 \\ 1/2 & -1/2 & 1/2 \\ 0 & 0 & 1 \end{bmatrix} \bullet \begin{bmatrix} \cdot & \cdot & \cdot \\ \cdot & \cdot & \cdot \\ \cdot & \cdot & \cdot \end{bmatrix} \right) \bullet \begin{bmatrix} 1 & 0 & 0 \\ 1/2 & 1/2 & 1/2 \\ 1/2 & -1/2 & 1/2 \\ 0 & 0 & 1 \end{bmatrix}^\mathsf{T}
$$

In the preceding formula, the matrix **F** (the one with dot values) is the 3×3 convolution filter between one input and one output slice. **G** and its $\mathbf{G}^\mathsf{T}$ transpose, , are, again, special matrices, which result from the specifics of the Winograd algorithm. Note that the transformed filter matrix, $\mathbf{F}_t$, has the same dimensions as the input tile, $\mathbf{D}_t$.

4. Compute the transformed output as an **element-wise** multiplication (the $\odot$ symbol) of the transformed input and filter:

$$\mathbf{O}_t = \mathbf{F}_t \odot \mathbf{D}_t$$

$$
\begin{bmatrix} \otimes & \otimes & \otimes & \otimes \\ \otimes & \otimes & \otimes & \otimes \\ \otimes & \otimes & \otimes & \otimes \\ \otimes & \otimes & \otimes & \otimes \end{bmatrix}
=
\begin{bmatrix} \times & \times & \times & \times \\ \times & \times & \times & \times \\ \times & \times & \times & \times \\ \times & \times & \times & \times \end{bmatrix} \odot \begin{bmatrix} \circ & \circ & \circ & \circ \\ \circ & \circ & \circ & \circ \\ \circ & \circ & \circ & \circ \\ \circ & \circ & \circ & \circ \end{bmatrix}
$$

5. Transform the output back into its original form:

$$\mathbf{O} = (\mathbf{AO}_t)\mathbf{A}^\mathsf{T}$$

$$\begin{bmatrix} \cdot & \cdot \\ \cdot & \cdot \end{bmatrix} = \left(\begin{bmatrix} 1 & 1 & 1 & 0 \\ 0 & 1 & -1 & -1 \end{bmatrix} \bullet \begin{bmatrix} \otimes & \otimes & \otimes & \otimes \\ \otimes & \otimes & \otimes & \otimes \\ \otimes & \otimes & \otimes & \otimes \\ \otimes & \otimes & \otimes & \otimes \end{bmatrix} \right) \bullet \begin{bmatrix} 1 & 1 & 1 & 0 \\ 0 & 1 & -1 & -1 \end{bmatrix}^\mathsf{T}$$

A is a transformation matrix, which makes it possible to transform $\mathbf{O}_t \rightarrow \mathbf{O}$ back into the form, which would have resulted from a direct convolution. As shown in the preceding formula and in the following diagram, the Winograd convolution allows us to compute 2×2 output tile simultaneously (four output cells):

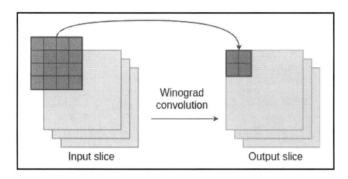

The Winograd convolution allows us to compute four output cells simultaneously

At first glance, it seems that the Winograd algorithm performs a lot more operations than direct convolution. So, how is it faster, then? To find out, let's focus on the $\mathbf{D} \rightarrow \mathbf{D}_t$ transformation. The key here is that we have to perform $\mathbf{D} \rightarrow \mathbf{D}_t$ only once and then $\mathbf{D}_t$ can participate in the outputs of all K (following the notation) output slices. Therefore, $\mathbf{D} \rightarrow \mathbf{D}_t$ is amortized among all of the outputs and it doesn't affect the performance as much. Next, let's take a look at the $\mathbf{F} \rightarrow \mathbf{F}_t$ transformation. This one is even better because, once we compute $\mathbf{F}_t$, we can apply it $N \times P \times Q$ times (across all of the cells of the output slice and all of the images in the batch). Therefore, the performance penalty for this transformation is negligible. Similarly, the output transformation $\mathbf{O}_t \rightarrow \mathbf{O}$ is amortized over the number of input channels C.

Finally, we'll discuss the element-wise multiplication, $\mathbf{O}_t = \mathbf{F}_t \odot \mathbf{D}_t$, which is applied $P \times Q$ times across all of the cells of the output slice and takes the bulk of the computational time. It consists of 16 scalar multiply operations and allows us to compute 2×2 output tile, which results in four multiplications for one output cell. Let's compare this with the direct convolution, where we have to perform *3*3=9* scalar multiplications (each filter element is multiplied by each receptive field input cell) for a single output. Therefore, the Winograd convolution requires *9/4 = 2.25* fewer operations.

 The Winograd convolution has the most benefits when working with smaller filter sizes (for example, 3×3). Convolutions with larger filters (for example, 11×11) can be efficiently implemented with Fast Fourier Transform (FFT) convolutions, which are beyond the scope of this book.

In the next section, we'll try to understand the inner workings of CNNs by visualizing their internal state.

Visualizing CNNs

One of the criticisms of NNs is that their results aren't interpretable. It's common to think of a NN as a black box whose internal logic is hidden from us. This could be a serious problem. On the one hand, it's less likely we trust an algorithm that works in a way we don't understand, while on the other hand, it's hard to improve the accuracy of CNNs if we don't know how they work. Because of this, in the upcoming sections, we'll discuss two methods of visualizing the internal layers of a CNN, both of which will help us to gain insight into the way they learn.

Guided backpropagation

Guided backpropagation (*Striving for Simplicity: The All Convolutional Net*, https://arxiv.org/abs/1412.6806) allows us to visualize the features that are learned by a single unit of one layer of a CNN. The following diagram shows how the algorithm works:

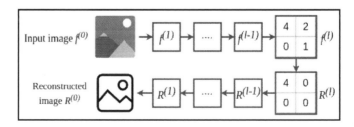

Guided backpropagation visualization: Inspired by https://arxiv.org/abs/1412.6806.

Here is the step-by-step execution:

1. First, we start with a regular CNN (for example, AlexNet, VGG, and so on) with ReLU activations.

2. Then, we feed the network with a single image $f^{(0)}$ and propagate it forward until we get to the layer, *l*, we're interested in. This could be any network layer—hidden or output, convolutional or fully-connected.

3. Set all but one activation of the output tensor $f^{(l)}$ of that layer to 0. For example, if we're interested in the output layer of a classification network, we'll select the unit with maximum activation (equivalent to the predicted class) and we'll set its value to 1. All of the other units will be set to 0. By doing this, we can isolate the unit in question and see which parts of the input image impact it the most.

4. Finally, we propagate the activation value of the selected unit backward until we reach the input layer and the reconstructed image $R^{(0)}$. The backward pass is very similar to the regular backpropagation (but not the same), that is, we still use transposed convolution as the backward operation of the forward convolution. In this case, though, we are interested in its image restoration properties rather than error propagation. Because of this, we aren't limited by the requirement to propagate the first derivative (gradient) and we can modify the signal in a way that will improve the visualization.

To understand the backward pass, we'll use an example convolution with a single 3×3 input and output slices. Let's assume that we're using a 1×1 filter with a single weight equal to 1 (we repeat the input). The following diagram shows this convolution, as well as three different ways to implement the backward pass:

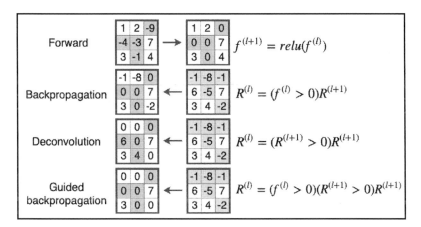

Convolution and the three different ways to reconstruct the image: Inspired by https://arxiv.org/abs/1412.6806.

Let's discuss these three different ways to implement the backward pass in detail:

- **Regular backpropagation**: The backward signal is preconditioned on the input image since it also depends on the forward activations (`Chapter 1`, *The Nuts and Bolts of Neural Networks*, in the *Backpropagation* section). Our network uses a ReLU activation function, so the signal will only pass through the units that had positive activations in the forward pass.
- **Deconvolutional network** (*deconvnet*, `https://arxiv.org/abs/1311.2901`): The backward signal of layer *l* depends only on the backward signal of layer *l+1*. A deconvnet will only route the positive values of *l+1* to *l*, regardless of what the forward activations are. Theoretically, the signal is not preconditioned on the input image at all. In this case, the deconvnet tries to restore the image based on its internal knowledge and the image class. However, this is not entirely true—if the network contains max-pooling layers, the deconvnet will store the so-called **switches** for each pooling layer. Each switch represents a map of the units with max activations of the forward pass. This map determines how to route the signal through the backward pass (you can read more about this in the source paper).
- **Guided backpropagation**: This is a combination of deconvnet and regular backprop. It will only route signals that have positive forward activations in *l* and positive backward activations in *l+1*. This adds additional guidance signal (hence the name) from the higher layers to the regular backprop. In essence, this step prevents negative gradients from flowing through the backward pass. The rationale is that the units that act as suppressors of our starting unit will be blocked and the reconstructed image will be free of their influence. Guided backpropagation performs so well that it doesn't need to use deconvnet switches and instead routes the signal to all the units in each pooling region.

The following screenshot shows a reconstructed image that was generated using guided backpropagation and AlexNet:

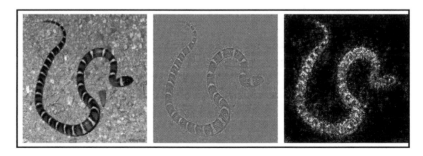

From left to right: original image. color reconstruction. and grayscale reconstruction using guided backpropagation on AlexNet: these images were generated using https://github.com/utkuozbulak/pytorch-cnn-visualizations.

Gradient-weighted class activation mapping

To understand gradient-weighted class activation mapping (*Grad-CAM: Visual Explanations from Deep Networks via Gradient-Based Localization*, `https://arxiv.org/abs/1610.02391`), let's quote the source paper itself:

> *"Grad-CAM uses the gradients of any target concept (say, the logits for 'dog' or even a caption) flowing into the final convolutional layer to produce a coarse localization map highlighting the important regions in the image for predicting the concept."*

The following screenshot shows the Grad-CAM algorithm:

(a) Original Image (b) Guided Backprop 'Cat' (c) Grad-CAM 'Cat' (d) Guided Grad-CAM 'Cat'

(g) Original Image (h) Guided Backprop 'Dog' (i) Grad-CAM 'Dog' (j) Guided Grad-CAM 'Dog'

Grad-CAM schema: Source: https://arxiv.org/abs/1610.02391

Now, let's look at how it works:

1. First, you start with a classification CNN model (for example, VGG).
2. Then, you feed the CNN with a single image and propagate it to the output layer.
3. Like we did in guided backpropagation, we take the output unit with maximum activation (equivalent to the predicted class c), set its value to 1, and set all of the other outputs to 0. In other words, create a one-hot encoded vector, y^c, of the prediction.

4. Next, compute the gradient of y^c with respect to the feature maps, A^k, of the final convolutional layer, $\partial y^c / \partial A_{ij}^k$, using backpropagation. i and j are the cell coordinates in the feature map.

5. Then, compute the scalar weight, α_k^c, which measures the "importance" of feature map k for the predicted class, c:

$$\alpha_k^c = \overbrace{\frac{1}{Z} \sum_i \sum_j}^{\text{Global average pooling}} \underbrace{\frac{\partial y^c}{\partial A_{ij}^k}}_{\text{gradients}}$$

6. Finally, compute a weighted combination between the scalar weights and the forward activation feature maps of the final convolutional layer and follow this with a ReLU:

$$L_{\text{Grad-CAM}}^c = ReLU \underbrace{\left(\sum_k \alpha_k^c A^k \right)}_{\text{linear combination}}$$

Note that we multiply the scalar importance weight, α_k^c, by the tensor feature map, A^k. The result is a heatmap with the same dimensions as the feature map (14×14 in the case of VGG and AlexNet). It will highlight the areas of the feature map with the highest importance to class c. The ReLU discards the negative activations because we're only interested in the features that increase y^c. We can upsample this heatmap back to the size of the input image and then superimpose it on it, as shown in the following screenshot:

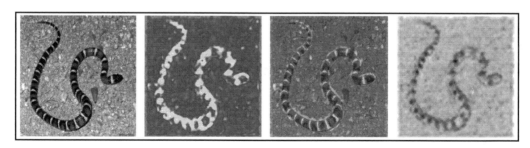

Left to right: input image: upsampled heat-map: heat-map superimosed on the input (RGB): grayscale heat-map. The images were generated using https://github.com/utkuozbulak/pytorch-cnn-visualizations.

One problem with Grad-CAM is upsampling the heatmap from 14×14 to 224×224 because it doesn't provide a fine-grained perspective of the important features for each class. To mitigate this problem, the authors of the paper proposed a combination of Grad-CAM and guided backpropagation (displayed in the Grad-CAM schema at the beginning of this section). We take the upsampled heatmap and combine it with the guided backprop visualization with element-wise multiplication. The input image contains two objects: a dog and a cat. Therefore, we can run Grad-CAM with both classes (the two rows of the diagram). This example shows how different classes detect different relevant features in the same image.

In the next section, we'll discuss how to optimize CNNs with the help of regularization.

CNN regularization

As we discussed in `Chapter 1`, *The Nuts and Bolts of Neural Networks*, a NN can approximate any function. But with great power comes great responsibility. The NN may learn to approximate the noise of the target function rather than its useful components. For example, imagine that we are training a NN to classify whether an image contains a car or not, but for some reason, the training set contains mostly red cars. It may turn out that the NN will associate the color red with the car, rather than its shape. Now, if the network sees a green car in inference mode, it may not recognize it as such because the color doesn't match. This problem is referred to as overfitting and it is central in machine learning (and even more so in deep networks). In this section, we'll discuss several ways to prevent it. Such techniques are collectively known as **regularization**.

In the context of NNs, these regularization techniques usually impose some artificial limitations or obstacles on the training process to prevent the network from approximating the target function too closely. They try to guide the network to learn generic rather than specific approximation of the target function in the hope that this representation will generalize well on previously unseen examples of the test dataset. You may already be familiar with many of these techniques, so we'll keep it short:

- **Input feature scaling**: $x = \frac{x - x_{min}}{x_{max} - x_{min}}$. This operation scales all of the inputs in the [0, 1] range. For example, a pixel with intensity 125 would have a scaled value of $\frac{125 - 0}{250 - 0} = 0.5$. Feature scaling is fast and easy to implement.

- **Input standard score**: $x = \frac{x-\mu}{\sigma}$. Here, μ and σ are the mean and standard deviation of all of the training data. They are usually computed separately for each input dimension. For example, in an RGB image, we would compute the mean μ and σ for each channel. We should note that μ and σ have to be computed on the training data and then applied to the test data. Alternatively, we can compute μ and σ per sample if it's not practical to compute them over the entire dataset.

- **Data augmentation**: This is where we artificially increase the size of the training set by applying random modifications (rotation, skew, scaling, and so on) on the training samples before feeding them to the network.

- **L2 regularization** (or **weight decay**): Here, we add a special regularization term to the cost function. Let's assume that we're using MSE (Chapter 1, *The Nuts and Bolts of NNs*, *Gradient descent* section). Here, the MSE + L2 regularization formula is as follows:

$$J(\theta) = \frac{1}{2n} \sum_{i=1}^{n} (f(\mathbf{x}^{(i)}; \theta) - t^{(i)})^2 + \lambda \overbrace{\frac{1}{2n} \sum_{j=1}^{k} w_j^2}^{L_2 \text{ regularization}}$$

$$\underbrace{\qquad\qquad\qquad\qquad}_{\text{MSE}}$$

Here, w_j is one of k total network weights and λ is the weight decay coefficient. The rationale is that if the network weights, w_j, are large, then the cost function will also increase. In effect, weight decay penalizes large weights (hence the name). This prevents the network from relying too heavily on a few features associated with these weights. There is less chance of overfitting when the network is forced to work with multiple features. In practical terms, when we compute the derivative of the weight decay cost function (the preceding formula) with respect to each weight and then propagate it to the weights themselves, the weight update rule changes from $w \to w - \eta \nabla(J(w))$ to $w \to w - \eta(\nabla(J(w)) - \lambda w)$.

- **Dropout**: Here, we randomly and periodically remove some of the neurons (along with their input and output connections) from the network. During a training mini-batch, each neuron has a probability, p, of being stochastically dropped. This is to ensure that no neuron ends up relying too much on other neurons and "learns" something useful for the network instead.

- **Batch Normalization** (**BN**, *Batch Normalization: Accelerating Deep Network Training by Reducing Internal Covariate Shift*, https://arxiv.org/abs/1502.03167): This is a way to apply data processing, similar to the standard score, for the hidden layers of the network. It normalizes the outputs of the hidden layer for each mini-batch (hence the name) in a way that maintains its mean activation value close to 0 and its standard deviation close to 1. Let's say $D = \{\mathbf{x}_1, \ldots, \mathbf{x}_n\}$ is a mini-batch of size n. Each sample of D is a vector, $\mathbf{x}_i$, and $x_i^{(k)}$ is a cell with an index k of that vector. For the sake of clarity, we'll omit the (k) superscript in the following formulas; that is, we'll write x_i, but we'll mean $x_i^{(k)}$. We can compute BN for each activation, k, over the whole minibatch in the following way:

  1. $\mu_D = \dfrac{1}{n} \sum_{i=1}^{n} x_i$: This is the mini-batch mean. We compute μ separately for each location, k, over all samples.

  2. $\sigma_D = \dfrac{1}{n} \sum_{i=1}^{n} (x_i - \mu_D)^2$: This is the mini-batch standard deviation. We compute σ separately for each location, k, over all samples.

  3. $\hat{x}_i = \dfrac{x_i - \mu_D}{\sqrt{\sigma_D^2 + \epsilon}}$: We normalize each sample. ε is a constant that's added for numerical stability.

  4. $y_i = \gamma \hat{x}_i + \beta = \mathrm{BN}_{\gamma,\beta}(x_i)$: γ and β are learnable parameters and we compute them over each location, k ($\gamma^{(k)}$ and $\beta^{(k)}$), over all of the samples of the mini-batch (the same applies for μ and σ). In convolutional layers, each sample, x, is a tensor with multiple feature maps. To preserve the convolutional property, we compute μ and σ per location over all of the samples, but we use the same μ and σ in the matching locations across all of the feature maps. On the other hand, we compute γ and β per feature map, rather than per location.

This section concludes our analysis of the structure and inner workings of CNNs. At this point, we would normally proceed with some sort of CNN coding example. But in this book, we want to do things a little differently. Therefore, we won't implement a plain old feed-forward CNN, which you may have already done before. Instead, in the next section, you will be introduced to the technique of transfer learning—a way to use pretrained CNN models for new tasks. But don't worry—we'll still implement a CNN from scratch. We'll do this in `Chapter 3`, *Advanced Convolutional Networks*. In this way, we'll be able to create a more complex network architecture using our knowledge from that chapter.

Introducing transfer learning

Let's say that we want to train a model on a task that doesn't have readily available labeled training data like ImageNet does. Labeling training samples could be expensive, time-consuming, and error-prone. So, what does a humble engineer do when they want to solve a real ML problem with limited resources? Enter **Transfer Learning** (**TL**).

TL is the process of applying an existing trained ML model to a new, but related, problem. For example, we can take a network trained on ImageNet and repurpose it to classify grocery store items. Alternatively, we could use a driving simulator game to train a neural network to drive a simulated car and then use the network to drive a real car (but don't try this at home!). TL is a general ML concept that's applicable to all ML algorithms, but in this context, we'll talk about CNNs. Here's how it works.

We start with an existing pretrained network. The most common scenario is to take a pretrained network from ImageNet, but it could be any dataset. TensorFlow and PyTorch both have popular ImageNet pretrained neural architectures that we can use. Alternatively, we can train our own network with a dataset of our choice.

The fully-connected layers at the end of a CNN act as translators between the network's language (the abstract feature representations learned during training) and our language, which is the class of each sample. You can think of TL as a translation into another language. We start with the network's features, which is the output of the last convolutional or pooling layer. Then, we translate them into a different set of classes of the new task. We can do this by removing the last fully-connected layer (or all the fully-connected layers) of an existing pretrained network and replacing it with another layer, which represents the classes of the new problem.

Let's look at the TL scenario shown in the following diagram:

In TL. we can replace the fully-connected layer(s) of a pretrained net and repurpose it/them for a new problem

However, we cannot do this mechanically and expect the new network to work because we still have to train the new layer with data related to the new task. Here, we have two options:

- **Use the original part of the network as a feature extractor and only train the new layer(s)**: In this scenario, we feed the network a training batch of the new data and propagate it forward to see the network's output. This part works just like regular training would. But in the backward pass, we lock the weights of the original network and only update the weights of the new layers. This is the recommended way to do things when we have limited training data for the new problem. By locking most of the network weights, we prevent overfitting on the new data.
- **Fine-tune the whole network**: In this scenario, we'll train the whole network and not just the newly added layers at the end. It is possible to update all of the network weights, but we can also lock some of the weights in the first layers. The idea here is that the initial layers detect general features—not related to a specific task—and it makes sense to reuse them. On the other hand, the deeper layers may detect task-specific features and it would be better to update them. We can use this method when we have more training data and don't need to worry about overfitting.

Implementing transfer learning with PyTorch

Now that we know what TL is, let's look at whether it works in practice. In this section, we'll apply an advanced ImageNet pretrained network on the CIFAR-10 images with **PyTorch 1.3.1** and the `torchvision` 0.4.2 package. We'll use both types of TL. It's preferable to run this example on a GPU.

 This example is partially based on `https://github.com/pytorch/tutorials/blob/master/beginner_source/transfer_learning_tutorial.py`.

Let's get started:

1. Do the following imports:

```
import torch
import torch.nn as nn
import torch.optim as optim
import torchvision
from torchvision import models, transforms
```

2. Define `batch_size` for convenience:

```
batch_size = 50
```

3. Define the training dataset. We have to consider a few things:
    - The CIFAR-10 images are 32×32, while the ImageNet network expects 224×224 input. Since we are using an ImageNet-based network, we'll upsample the 32×32 CIFAR images to 224×224.
    - Standardize the CIFAR-10 data using the ImageNet mean and standard deviation since this is what the network expects.
    - We'll also add some data augmentation in the form of random horizontal or vertical flips:

```
# training data
train_data_transform = transforms.Compose([
    transforms.Resize(224),
    transforms.RandomHorizontalFlip(),
    transforms.RandomVerticalFlip(),
    transforms.ToTensor(),
    transforms.Normalize((0.4914, 0.4821, 0.4465), (0.2470,
    0.2435, 0.2616))
])
```

```
train_set = torchvision.datasets.CIFAR10(root='./data',
                                train=True, download=True,
                                transform=train_data_transform)

train_loader = torch.utils.data.DataLoader(train_set,
                                batch_size=batch_size,
                                shuffle=True, num_workers=2)
```

4. Follow the same steps with the validation/test data, but this time without augmentation:

```
val_data_transform = transforms.Compose([
    transforms.Resize(224),
    transforms.ToTensor(),
    transforms.Normalize((0.4914, 0.4821, 0.4465), (0.2470, 0.2435,
    0.2616))
])

val_set = torchvision.datasets.CIFAR10(root='./data',
                                train=False, download=True,
                                transform=val_data_transform)

val_order = torch.utils.data.DataLoader(val_set,
                                batch_size=batch_size,
                                shuffle=False, num_workers=2)
```

5. Choose `device`, preferably a GPU with a fallback on CPU:

```
device = torch.device("cuda:0" if torch.cuda.is_available() else
"cpu")
```

6. Define the training of the model. Unlike TensorFlow, in PyTorch, we have to iterate over the training data manually. This method iterates once over the whole training set (one epoch) and applies the optimizer after each forward pass:

```
def train_model(model, loss_function, optimizer, data_loader):
    # set model to training mode
    model.train()

    current_loss = 0.0
    current_acc = 0

    # iterate over the training data
    for i, (inputs, labels) in enumerate(data_loader):
        # send the input/labels to the GPU
        inputs = inputs.to(device)
        labels = labels.to(device)
```

```
                        # zero the parameter gradients
                        optimizer.zero_grad()

                        with torch.set_grad_enabled(True):
                            # forward
                            outputs = model(inputs)
                            _, predictions = torch.max(outputs, 1)
                            loss = loss_function(outputs, labels)

                            # backward
                            loss.backward()
                            optimizer.step()

                        # statistics
                        current_loss += loss.item() * inputs.size(0)
                        current_acc += torch.sum(predictions == labels.data)

                    total_loss = current_loss / len(data_loader.dataset)
                    total_acc = current_acc.double() / len(data_loader.dataset)

                    print('Train Loss: {:.4f}; Accuracy: {:.4f}'.format(total_loss,
                    total_acc))
```

7. Define the testing/validation of the model. This is very similar to the training phase, but we will skip the backpropagation part:

```
            def test_model(model, loss_function, data_loader):
                # set model in evaluation mode
                model.eval()

                current_loss = 0.0
                current_acc = 0

                # iterate over  the validation data
                for i, (inputs, labels) in enumerate(data_loader):
                    # send the input/labels to the GPU
                    inputs = inputs.to(device)
                    labels = labels.to(device)

                    # forward
                    with torch.set_grad_enabled(False):
                        outputs = model(inputs)
                        _, predictions = torch.max(outputs, 1)
                        loss = loss_function(outputs, labels)

                    # statistics
                    current_loss += loss.item() * inputs.size(0)
                    current_acc += torch.sum(predictions == labels.data)
```

```
total_loss = current_loss / len(data_loader.dataset)
total_acc = current_acc.double() / len(data_loader.dataset)

print('Test Loss: {:.4f}; Accuracy: {:.4f}'.format(total_loss,
total_acc))

return total_loss, total_acc
```

8. Define the first TL scenario, where we use the pretrained network as a feature
   extractor:

   - We'll use a popular network known as ResNet-18. We'll talk about this
     in detail in the *Advanced network architectures* section. PyTorch will
     automatically download the pretrained weights.
   - Replace the last network layer with a new layer with 10 outputs (one
     for each CIFAR-10 class).
   - Exclude the existing network layers from the backward pass and only
     pass the newly added fully-connected layer to the Adam optimizer.
   - Run the training for `epochs` and evaluate the network accuracy after
     each epoch.
   - Plot the test accuracy with the help of the `plot_accuracy` function. Its
     definition is trivial and you can find it in this book's code repository.

The following is the `tl_feature_extractor` function, which implements all of
this:

```
def tl_feature_extractor(epochs=5):
    # load the pretrained model
    model = torchvision.models.resnet18(pretrained=True)

    # exclude existing parameters from backward pass
    # for performance
    for param in model.parameters():
        param.requires_grad = False

    # newly constructed layers have requires_grad=True by default
    num_features = model.fc.in_features
    model.fc = nn.Linear(num_features, 10)

    # transfer to GPU (if available)
    model = model.to(device)

    loss_function = nn.CrossEntropyLoss()

    # only parameters of the final layer are being optimized
    optimizer = optim.Adam(model.fc.parameters())
```

```
# train
test_acc = list()  # collect accuracy for plotting
for epoch in range(epochs):
    print('Epoch {}/{}'.format(epoch + 1, epochs))

    train_model(model, loss_function, optimizer, train_loader)
    _, acc = test_model(model, loss_function, val_order)
    test_acc.append(acc)

plot_accuracy(test_acc)
```

9. Implement the fine-tuning approach. This function is similar to `tl_feature_extractor`, but here, we're training the whole network:

```
def tl_fine_tuning(epochs=5):
    # load the pretrained model
    model = models.resnet18(pretrained=True)

    # replace the last layer
    num_features = model.fc.in_features
    model.fc = nn.Linear(num_features, 10)

    # transfer the model to the GPU
    model = model.to(device)

    # loss function
    loss_function = nn.CrossEntropyLoss()

    # We'll optimize all parameters
    optimizer = optim.Adam(model.parameters())

    # train
    test_acc = list()  # collect accuracy for plotting
    for epoch in range(epochs):
        print('Epoch {}/{}'.format(epoch + 1, epochs))

        train_model(model, loss_function, optimizer, train_loader)
        _, acc = test_model(model, loss_function, val_order)
        test_acc.append(acc)

    plot_accuracy(test_acc)
```

10. Finally, we can run the whole thing in one of two ways:
    - Call `tl_fine_tuning()` to use the fine-tuning TL approach for five epochs.
    - Call `tl_feature_extractor()` to train the network with the feature extractor approach for five epochs.

This is the accuracy of the networks after five epochs for the two scenarios:

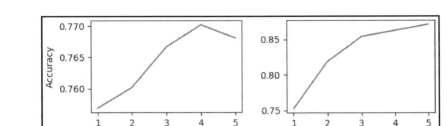

Left: Feature extraction TL accuracy: right: Fine-tuning TL accuracy

Due to the large size of the chosen `ResNet18` pretrained model, the network starts to overfit in the feature extraction scenario.

Transfer learning with TensorFlow 2.0

In this section, we'll implement the two transfer learning scenarios again, but this time using **TensorFlow 2.0.0 (TF)**. In this way, we can compare the two libraries. Instead of `ResNet18`, we'll use the `ResNet50V2` architecture (more on that in the Chapter 3, *Advanced Convolutional Networks*). In addition to TF, this example also requires the TF Datasets 1.3.0 package (`https://www.tensorflow.org/datasets`), a collection of various popular ML datasets.

This example is partially based on `https://github.com/tensorflow/docs/blob/master/site/en/tutorials/images/transfer_learning.ipynb`.

With that, let's get started:

1. As usual, first, we need to do the imports:

```
import matplotlib.pyplot as plt
import tensorflow as tf
import tensorflow_datasets as tfds
```

2. Then, we'll define the mini-batch and input images sizes (the image size is determined by the network architecture):

```
IMG_SIZE = 224
BATCH_SIZE = 50
```

3. Next, we'll load the CIFAR-10 dataset with the help of TF datasets. The `repeat()` method allows us to reuse the dataset for multiple epochs:

```
data, metadata = tfds.load('cifar10', with_info=True,
as_supervised=True)
raw_train, raw_test = data['train'].repeat(), data['test'].repeat()
```

4. Then, we'll define the `train_format_sample` and `test_format_sample` functions, which will transform the input images into suitable CNN inputs. These functions play the same roles that the `transforms.Compose` object plays, which we defined in the *Implementing transfer learning with PyTorch* section. The input is transformed as follows:
   - The images are resized to 96×96, which is the expected network input size.
   - Each image is standardized by transforming its values so that it's in the (-1; 1) interval.
   - The labels are transformed for one-hot encoding.
   - The training images are randomly flipped horizontally and vertically.

Let's look at the actual implementation:

```
def train_format_sample(image, label):
    """Transform data for training"""
    image = tf.cast(image, tf.float32)
    image = tf.image.resize(image, (IMG_SIZE, IMG_SIZE))
    image = (image / 127.5) - 1
    image = tf.image.random_flip_left_right(image)
    image = tf.image.random_flip_up_down(image)

    label = tf.one_hot(label,
metadata.features['label'].num_classes)

    return image, label


def test_format_sample(image, label):
    """Transform data for testing"""
    image = tf.cast(image, tf.float32)
    image = tf.image.resize(image, (IMG_SIZE, IMG_SIZE))
    image = (image / 127.5) - 1

    label = tf.one_hot(label,
metadata.features['label'].num_classes)

    return image, label
```

5. Next is some boilerplate code that assigns these transformers to the train/test datasets and splits them into mini-batches:

```
# assign transformers to raw data
train_data = raw_train.map(train_format_sample)
test_data = raw_test.map(test_format_sample)

# extract batches from the training set
train_batches = train_data.shuffle(1000).batch(BATCH_SIZE)
test_batches = test_data.batch(BATCH_SIZE)
```

6. Then, we need to define the feature extraction model:
   - We'll use Keras for the pretrained network and model definition since it is an integral part of TF 2.0.
   - We load the `ResNet50V2` pretrained net, excluding the final fully-connected layers.
   - Then, we call `base_model.trainable = False`, which *freezes* all of the network weights and prevents them from training.
   - Finally, we add a `GlobalAveragePooling2D` operation, followed by a new and trainable fully-connected trainable layer at the end of the network.

The following code implements this:

```
def build_fe_model():
    # create the pretrained part of the network, excluding FC
    layers
    base_model =
tf.keras.applications.ResNet50V2(input_shape=(IMG_SIZE,
    IMG_SIZE, 3), include_top=False, weights='imagenet')

    # exclude all model layers from training
    base_model.trainable = False

    # create new model as a combination of the pretrained net
    # and one fully connected layer at the top
    return tf.keras.Sequential([
        base_model,
        tf.keras.layers.GlobalAveragePooling2D(),
        tf.keras.layers.Dense(
            metadata.features['label'].num_classes,
            activation='softmax')
    ])
```

7. Next, we'll define the fine-tuning model. The only difference it has from the feature extraction is that we only freeze some of the bottom pretrained network layers (as opposed to all of them). The following is the implementation:

```python
def build_ft_model():
    # create the pretrained part of the network, excluding FC
    layers
    base_model =
tf.keras.applications.ResNet50V2(input_shape=(IMG_SIZE,
        IMG_SIZE, 3), include_top=False, weights='imagenet')

    # Fine tune from this layer onwards
    fine_tune_at = 100

    # Freeze all the layers before the `fine_tune_at` layer
    for layer in base_model.layers[:fine_tune_at]:
        layer.trainable = False

    # create new model as a combination of the pretrained net
    # and one fully connected layer at the top
    return tf.keras.Sequential([
        base_model,
        tf.keras.layers.GlobalAveragePooling2D(),
        tf.keras.layers.Dense(
            metadata.features['label'].num_classes,
            activation='softmax')
    ])
```

8. Finally, we'll implement the `train_model` function, which trains and evaluates the models that are created by either the `build_fe_model` or `build_ft_model` function:

```python
def train_model(model, epochs=5):
    # configure the model for training
    model.compile(optimizer=tf.keras.optimizers.Adam(lr=0.0001),
                  loss='categorical_crossentropy',
                  metrics=['accuracy'])

    # train the model
    history = model.fit(train_batches,
                        epochs=epochs,
steps_per_epoch=metadata.splits['train'].num_examples //
BATCH_SIZE,
                        validation_data=test_batches,
validation_steps=metadata.splits['test'].num_examples //
BATCH_SIZE,
                        workers=4)
```

```
# plot accuracy
test_acc = history.history['val_accuracy']

plt.figure()
plt.plot(test_acc)
plt.xticks(
    [i for i in range(0, len(test_acc))],
    [i + 1 for i in range(0, len(test_acc))])
plt.ylabel('Accuracy')
plt.xlabel('Epoch')
plt.show()
```

9. We can run either the feature extraction or fine-tuning TL using the following
   code:

   - `train_model(build_ft_model())`
   - `train_model(build_fe_model())`

TF will automatically use the machine GPU if one is available; otherwise, it will revert to
the CPU. The following diagram shows the accuracy of the networks after five epochs for
the two scenarios:

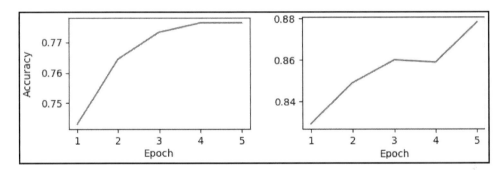

Left: Feature extraction TL: right: Fine-tuning TL

Summary

We started this chapter with a quick recap of CNNs and discussed transposed, depthwise separable, and dilated convolutions. Next, we talked about improving the performance of CNNs by representing the convolution as a matrix multiplication or with the Winograd convolution algorithm. Then, we focused on visualizing CNNs with the help of guided backpropagation and Grad-CAM. Next, we discussed the most popular regularization techniques. Finally, we learned about transfer learning and implemented the same TL task with both PyTorch and TF as a way to compare the two libraries.

In the next chapter, we'll discuss some of the most popular advanced CNN architectures.

3
Advanced Convolutional Networks

In Chapter 2, *Understanding Convolutional Networks*, we discussed the building blocks of **convolutional neural networks (CNNs)** and some of their properties. In this chapter, we'll go a step further and talk about some of the most popular CNN architectures. These networks usually combine multiple primitive convolution and/or pooling operations in a novel building block that serves as a base for a complex architecture. This allows us to build very deep (and sometimes wide) networks with high representational power that perform well on complex tasks such as ImageNet classification, image segmentation, speech recognition, and so on. Many of these models were first released as participants in the ImageNet challenge, which they usually won. To simplify our task, we'll discuss all architecture within the context of image classification. We'll still discuss more complex tasks, but we'll do it in Chapter 4, *Object Detection and Image Segmentation*.

This chapter will cover the following topics:

- Introducing AlexNet
- An introduction to Visual Geometry Group
- Understanding residual networks
- Understanding Inception networks
- Introducing Xception
- Introducing MobileNet
- An introduction to DenseNets
- The workings of neural architecture search
- Introducing capsule networks

Introducing AlexNet

The first model we'll discuss is the winner of the 2012 **ImageNet Large Scale Visual Recognition Challenge** (ILSVRC, or simply ImageNet). It's nicknamed AlexNet (*ImageNet Classification with Deep Convolutional Neural Networks*, `https://papers.nips.cc/paper/` `4824-imagenet-classification-with-deep-convolutional-neural-networks.pdf`), after one of its authors, Alex Krizhevsky. Although this model is rarely used nowadays, it's an important milestone in contemporary deep learning.

The following diagram shows the network architecture:

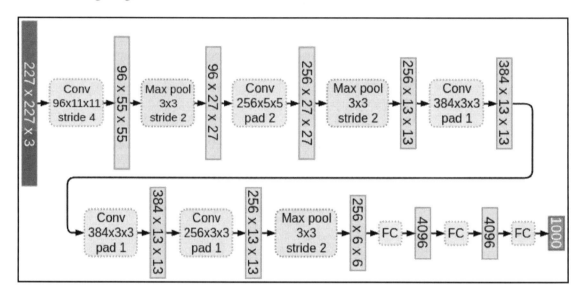

The AlexNet architecture. The original model was split in two. so it can fit on the memory of two GPUs

The model has five cross-correlated convolutional layers, three overlapping max pooling layers, three fully connected layers, and ReLU activations. The output is a 1,000-way softmax (one for each ImageNet class). The first and second convolutional layers use local response normalization—a type of normalization, somewhat similar to batch normalization. The fully connected layers have a dropout rate of 0.5. To prevent overfitting, the network was trained using random 227×227 crops of the 256×256 input images. The network achieves top-1 and top-5 test set error rates of 37.5% and 17.0%.

In the next section, we'll discuss an NN architecture that was introduced by Oxford's Visual Geometry Group in 2014, when it became a runner-up in the ImageNet challenge of that year.

An introduction to Visual Geometry Group

The next architecture we're going to discuss is **Visual Geometry Group (VGG)** (from Oxford's Visual Geometry Group, *Very Deep Convolutional Networks for Large-Scale Image Recognition*, https://arxiv.org/abs/1409.1556). The VGG family of networks remains popular today and is often used as a benchmark against newer architectures. Prior to VGG (for example, LeNet-5: http://yann.lecun.com/exdb/lenet/ and AlexNet), the initial convolutional layers of a network used filters with large receptive fields, such as 11×11. Additionally, the networks usually had alternating single convolutional and pooling layers. The authors of the paper observed that a convolutional layer with a large filter size can be replaced with a stack of two or more convolutional layers with smaller filters (factorized convolution). For example, we can replace one 5×5 layer with a stack of two 3×3 layers, or a 7×7 layer with a stack of three 3×3 layers.

This structure has several advantages, as follows:

- The neurons of the last of the stacked layers have the equivalent receptive field size of a single layer with a large filter.
- The number of weights and operations of stacked layers is smaller, compared to a single layer with a large filter size. Let's assume we want to replace one 5×5 layer with two 3×3 layers. Let's also assume that all layers have an equal number of input and output channels (slices), M. The total number of weights (excluding biases) of the 5×5 layer is $5*5*M*M = 25*M^2$. On the other hand, the total weights of a single 3×3 layer is $3*3*M*M = 9*M^2$, and simply $2*(3*3*M*M) = 18*M^2$ for two layers, which makes this arrangement 28% more efficient (18/25 = 0.72). The efficiency will increase further with larger filters.
- Stacking multiple layers makes the decision function more discriminative.

The VGG networks consist of multiple blocks of two, three, or four stacked convolutional layers combined with a max pooling layer. We can see the two most popular variants, **VGG16** and **VGG19**, in the following table:

VGG16	VGG19
conv 3x3, 64	conv 3x3, 64
conv 3x3, 64	conv 3x3, 64
max pool	
conv 3x3, 128	conv 3x3, 128
conv 3x3, 128	conv 3x3, 128
max pool	
conv 3x3, 256	conv 3x3, 256
conv 3x3, 256	conv 3x3, 256
conv 3x3, 256	conv 3x3, 256
	conv 3x3, 256
max pool	
conv 3x3, 512	conv 3x3, 512
conv 3x3, 512	conv 3x3, 512
conv 3x3, 512	conv 3x3, 512
	conv 3x3, 512
max pool	
conv 3x3, 512	conv 3x3, 512
conv 3x3, 512	conv 3x3, 512
conv 3x3, 512	conv 3x3, 512
	conv 3x3, 512
max pool	
fc-4096	
fc-4096	
fc-1000	
softmax	

Architecture of the VGG16 and VGG19 networks. named after the number of weighted layers in each network

As the depth of the VGG network increases, so does the width (the number of filters) in the convolutional layers. We have multiple pairs of cross-channel convolutions with a volume depth of 128/256/512 connected to other layers with the same depth. In addition, we also have two 4,096-unit fully connected layers, followed by a 1000-unit fully connected layer and a softmax (one for each ImageNet class). Because of this, the VGG networks have a large number of parameters (weights), which makes them memory-inefficient, as well as computationally expensive. Still, this is a popular and straightforward network architecture, which has been further improved by the addition of batch normalization.

In the next section, we'll use VGG as an example of how to load pretrained network models with TensorFlow and PyTorch.

VGG with PyTorch and TensorFlow

Both PyTorch and TensorFlow have pretrained VGG models. Let's see how to use them.

Keras is an official part of TensorFlow 2, therefore, we'll use it to load the model:

```
import tensorflow as tf

# VGG16
vgg16 = tf.keras.applications.vgg16.VGG16(include_top=True,
                                          weights='imagenet',
                                          input_tensor=None,
                                          input_shape=None,
                                          pooling=None,
                                          classes=1000)

# VGG19
vgg19 = tf.keras.applications.vgg19.VGG19(include_top=True,
                                          weights='imagenet',
                                          input_tensor=None,
                                          input_shape=None,
                                          pooling=None,
                                          classes=1000)
```

By setting the `weights='imagenet'` parameter, the network will be loaded with pretrained ImageNet weights (they will be downloaded automatically). You can set `include_top` to `False`, which will exclude the fully connected layers for a transfer learning scenario. In this case, you can also use an arbitrary input size by setting a tuple value to `input_shape`—the convolutional layers will automatically scale to match the desired input shape. This is possible because the convolution filter is shared along the whole feature map. Therefore, we can use the same filter on feature maps with different sizes.

We'll continue with PyTorch, where you can choose whether you want to use a pretrained model (again, with automatic download):

```
import torchvision.models as models
model = models.vgg16(pretrained=True)
```

You can try other pretrained models, using the same procedures we described. To avoid repetition, we won't include the same code examples for the other architectures in this section.

In the next section, we'll discuss one of the most popular CNN architectures, which was released after VGG.

Understanding residual networks

Residual networks (**ResNets**, *Deep Residual Learning for Image Recognition*, https://arxiv. org/abs/1512.03385) were released in 2015, when they won all five categories of the ImageNet challenge that year. In Chapter 1, *The Nuts and Bolts of Neural Networks*, we mentioned that the layers of a neural network are not restricted to sequential order, but form a graph instead. This is the first architecture we'll learn, which takes advantage of this flexibility. This is also the first network architecture that has successfully trained a network with a depth of more than 100 layers.

Thanks to better weight initializations, new activation functions, as well as normalization layers, it's now possible to train deep networks. But, the authors of the paper conducted some experiments and observed that a network with 56 layers had higher training and testing errors compared to a network with 20 layers. They argue that this should not be the case. In theory, we can take a shallow network and stack identity layers (these are layers whose output just repeats the input) on top of it to produce a deeper network that behaves in exactly the same way as the shallow one. Yet, their experiments have been unable to match the performance of the shallow network.

To solve this problem, they proposed a network constructed of residual blocks. A residual block consists of two or three sequential convolutional layers and a separate parallel identity (repeater) shortcut connection, which connects the input of the first layer and the output of the last one. We can see three types of residual blocks in the following screenshot:

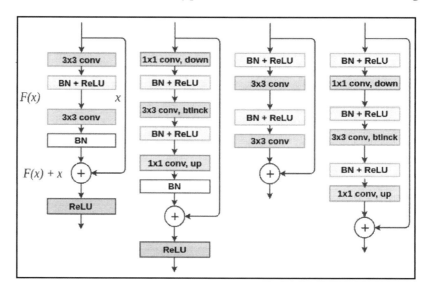

From left to right: original residual block: original bottleneck residual block: pre-activation residual block: pre-activation bottleneck residual block

Each block has two parallel paths. The left-hand path is similar to the other networks we've seen, and consists of sequential convolutional layers + batch normalization. The right path contains the identity shortcut connection (also known as the skip connection). The two paths are merged via an element-wise sum. That is, the left and right tensors have the same shape and an element of the first tensor is added to the element in the same position in the second tensor. The output is a single tensor with the same shape as the input. In effect, we propagate forward the features learned by the block, but also the original unmodified signal. In this way, we can get closer to the original scenario, as described by the authors. The network can decide to skip some of the convolutional layers thanks to the skip connections, in effect reducing its own depth. The residual blocks use padding in such a way that the input and the output of the block have the same dimensions. Thanks to this, we can stack any number of blocks for a network with an arbitrary depth.

And now, let's see how the blocks in the diagram differ:

- The first block contains two 3×3 convolutional layers. This is the original residual block, but if the layers are wide, stacking multiple blocks becomes computationally expensive.
- The second block is equivalent to the first, but it uses the so-called bottleneck layer. First, we use a 1×1 convolution to downsample the input volume depth (we discussed this in `Chapter 2`, *Understanding Convolutional Networks*). Then, we apply a 3×3 (bottleneck) convolution to the reduced input. Finally, we expand the output back to the desired depth with another 1×1 convolution. This layer is less computationally expensive than the first.
- The third block is the latest revision of the idea, published in 2016 by the same authors (*Identity Mappings in Deep Residual Networks*, `https://arxiv.org/abs/1603.05027`). It uses pre-activations, and the batch normalization and the activation function come before the convolutional layer. This may seem strange at first, but thanks to this design, the skip connection path can run uninterrupted throughout the network. This is contrary to the other residual blocks, where at least one activation function is on the path of the skip connection. A combination of stacked residual blocks still has the layers in the right order.
- The fourth block is the bottleneck version of the third layer. It follows the same principle as the bottleneck residual layer v1.

In the following table, we can see the family of networks proposed by the authors of the paper:

output size	18-layer		34-layer		50-layer		101-layer		152-layer	
112x112	7x7 conv, stride 2									
56x56	3x3 max pool, stride 2									
	3x3, 64 3x3, 64	x2	3x3, 64 3x3, 64	x3	1x1, 64 3x3, 64 1x1, 256	x3	1x1, 64 3x3, 64 1x1, 256	x3	1x1, 64 3x3, 64 1x1, 256	x3
28x28	3x3, 128 3x3, 128	x2	3x3, 128 3x3, 128	x4	1x1, 128 3x3, 128 1x1, 512	x4	1x1, 128 3x3, 128 1x1, 512	x4	1x1, 128 3x3, 128 1x1, 512	x8
14x14	3x3, 256 3x3, 256	x2	3x3, 256 3x3, 256	x6	1x1, 256 3x3, 256 1x1, 1024	x6	1x1, 256 3x3, 256 1x1, 1024	x23	1x1, 256 3x3, 256 1x1, 1024	x36
7x7	3x3, 512 3x3, 512	x2	3x3, 512 3x3, 512	x3	1x1, 512 3x3, 512 1x1, 2048	x3	1x1, 512 3x3, 512 1x1, 2048	x3	1x1, 512 3x3, 512 1x1, 2048	x3
1x1	average pool, 1000-d fc, softmax									

The family of the most popular residual networks. The residual blocks are represented by rounded rectangles

Some of their properties are as follows:

- They start with a 7x7 convolutional layer with stride 2, followed by 3x3 max-pooling. This layer also serves as a downsampling step—the rest of the network starts with a much smaller slice of 56x56, compared to 224x224 of the input.
- Downsampling in the rest of the network is implemented with a modified residual block with stride 2.
- Average pooling downsamples the output after all residual blocks and before the 1,000-unit fully connected softmax layer.

The ResNet family of networks is popular not only because of their accuracy, but also because of their relative simplicity and the versatility of the residual blocks. As we mentioned, the input and output shape of the residual block can be the same due to the padding. We can stack residual blocks in different configurations to solve various problems with wide-ranging training set sizes and input dimensions. Because of this universality, we'll implement an example of ResNet in the next section.

Implementing residual blocks

In this section, we'll implement a pre-activation ResNet to classify the CIFAR-10 images using PyTorch 1.3.1 and `torchvision` 0.4.2. Let's start:

1. As usual, we'll start with the imports. Note that we'll use the shorthand F for the PyTorch functional module (`https://pytorch.org/docs/stable/nn.html#torch-nn-functional`):

```python
import matplotlib.pyplot as plt
import torch
import torch.nn as nn
import torch.nn.functional as F
import torch.optim as optim
import torchvision
from torchvision import transforms
```

2. Next, let's define the pre-activation regular (non-bottleneck) residual block. We'll implement it as `nn.Module`—the base class for all neural network modules. Let's start with the class definition and the __init__ method:

```python
class PreActivationBlock(nn.Module):
    expansion = 1
    def __init__(self, in_slices, slices, stride=1):
        super(PreActivationBlock, self).__init__()

        self.bn_1 = nn.BatchNorm2d(in_slices)
                            out_channels=slices,kernel_size=3,
                            stride=stride, padding=1,
                            bias=False)

        self.bn_2 = nn.BatchNorm2d(slices)
        self.conv_2 = nn.Conv2d(in_channels=slices,
                            out_channels=slices,kernel_size=3,
                            stride=1, padding=1,
                            bias=False)

        # if the input/output dimensions differ use convolution for
        the shortcut
        if stride != 1 or in_slices != self.expansion * slices:
            self.shortcut = nn.Sequential(
                nn.Conv2d(in_channels=in_slices,
                        out_channels=self.expansion * slices,
                        kernel_size=1,
                        stride=stride,
                        bias=False)
            )
```

We will define only the learnable block components in the __init__ method—these include the convolution and batch normalization operations. Also, note the way we implement the shortcut connection. If the input dimensions are the same as the output dimensions, we can directly use the input tensor as the shortcut. However, if the dimensions differ, we have to transform the input with the help of a 1×1 convolution with the same stride and output channels as the one in the main path. The dimensions may differ either by height/width (stride != 1) or by depth (in_slices != self.expansion * slices). self.expansion is a hyper-parameter, which was included in the original ResNet implementation. It allows us to expand the output depth of the residual block.

3. The actual data propagation is implemented in the forward method (please mind the indentation, as it's a member of PreActivationBlock):

```
def forward(self, x):
    out = F.relu(self.bn_1(x))

    # reuse bn+relu in downsampling layers
    shortcut = self.shortcut(out) if hasattr(self, 'shortcut')
    else x

    out = self.conv_1(out)

    out = F.relu(self.bn_2(out))
    out = self.conv_2(out)

    out += shortcut

    return out
```

We use the functional F.relu for the activation function, as it doesn't have learnable parameters. Then, if the shortcut connection is a convolution and not an identity (that is, the input/output dimensions of the block differ), we'll reuse F.relu(self.bn_1(x)) to add non-linearity and batch normalization to the shortcut. Otherwise, we'll just repeat the input.

4. Then, let's implement the bottleneck version of the residual block. We'll use the same blueprint as in the non-bottleneck implementation. We'll start with the class definition and the __init__ method:

```
class PreActivationBottleneckBlock(nn.Module):
    expansion = 4
    def __init__(self, in_slices, slices, stride=1):
        super(PreActivationBottleneckBlock, self).__init__()
```

```
self.bn_1 = nn.BatchNorm2d(in_slices)
self.conv_1 = nn.Conv2d(in_channels=in_slices,
                        out_channels=slices, kernel_size=1,
                        bias=False)

self.bn_2 = nn.BatchNorm2d(slices)
self.conv_2 = nn.Conv2d(in_channels=slices,
                        out_channels=slices, kernel_size=3,
                        stride=stride, padding=1,
                        bias=False)

self.bn_3 = nn.BatchNorm2d(slices)
self.conv_3 = nn.Conv2d(in_channels=slices,
                        out_channels=self.expansion *
                        slices,
                        kernel_size=1,
                        bias=False)

# if the input/output dimensions differ use convolution for
the shortcut
if stride != 1 or in_slices != self.expansion * slices:
    self.shortcut = nn.Sequential(
        nn.Conv2d(in_channels=in_slices,
                  out_channels=self.expansion * slices,
                  kernel_size=1, stride=stride,
                  bias=False)
    )
```

The `expansion` parameter is 4 after the original implementation. The `self.conv_1` convolution operation represents the 1×1 downsampling bottleneck connection, `self.conv_2` is the actual convolution, and `self.conv_3` is the upsampling 1×1 convolution. The shortcut mechanism follows the same logic as in `PreActivationBlock`.

5. Next, let's implement the `PreActivationBottleneckBlock.forward` method. Once again, it follows the same logic as the one in `PreActivationBlock`:

```
def forward(self, x):
    out = F.relu(self.bn_1(x))

    #  reuse bn+relu in downsampling layers
    shortcut = self.shortcut(out) if hasattr(self, 'shortcut')
    else x

    out = self.conv_1(out)

    out = F.relu(self.bn_2(out))
```

```
out = self.conv_2(out)

out = F.relu(self.bn_3(out))
out = self.conv_3(out)

out += shortcut

return out
```

6. Next, let's implement the residual network itself. We'll start with the class definition (it inherits nn.Module) and the __init__ method:

```
class PreActivationResNet(nn.Module):
    def __init__(self, block, num_blocks, num_classes=10):
        """
        :param block: type of residual block (regular or
        bottleneck)
        :param num_blocks: a list with 4 integer values.
            Each value reflects the number of residual blocks in
            the group
        :param num_classes: number of output classes
        """

        super(PreActivationResNet, self).__init__()

        self.in_slices = 64

        self.conv_1 = nn.Conv2d(in_channels=3, out_channels=64,
                                kernel_size=3, stride=1, padding=1,
                                bias=False)

        self.layer_1 = self._make_group(block, 64, num_blocks[0],
        stride=1)
        self.layer_2 = self._make_group(block, 128, num_blocks[1],
        stride=2)
        self.layer_3 = self._make_group(block, 256, num_blocks[2],
        stride=2)
        self.layer_4 = self._make_group(block, 512, num_blocks[3],
        stride=2)
        self.linear = nn.Linear(512 * block.expansion, num_classes)
```

The network contains four groups of residual blocks, just like the original implementation. The number of blocks of each group is specified by the num_blocks parameter. The initial convolution uses a 3×3 filter with stride 1, as opposed to a 7×7 with stride 2 of the original implementation. This is because the 32×32 CIFAR-10 images are much smaller than the 224×224 ImageNet ones, and the downsampling is unnecessary.

7. Then, we'll implement the `PreActivationResNet._make_group` method, which creates one residual block group. All blocks in the group have stride 1, except for the first, where `stride` is supplied as a parameter:

```
def _make_group(self, block, slices, num_blocks, stride):
    """Create one residual group"""

    strides = [stride] + [1] * (num_blocks - 1)
    layers = []
    for stride in strides:
        layers.append(block(self.in_slices, slices, stride))
        self.in_slices = slices * block.expansion

    return nn.Sequential(*layers)
```

8. Next, we'll implement the `PreActivationResNet.forward` method, which propagates the data through the network. We can see the downsampling average pooling before the fully connected final layer:

```
def forward(self, x):
    out = self.conv_1(x)
    out = self.layer_1(out)
    out = self.layer_2(out)
    out = self.layer_3(out)
    out = self.layer_4(out)
    out = F.avg_pool2d(out, 4)
    out = out.view(out.size(0), -1)
    out = self.linear(out)

    return out
```

9. Once we're done with the network, we can implement several ResNet configurations. The following is `ResNet34` with 34 convolution layers, grouped in `[3, 4, 6, 3]` non-bottleneck residual blocks:

```
def PreActivationResNet34():
    return PreActivationResNet(block=PreActivationBlock,
                               num_blocks=[3, 4, 6, 3])
```

10. Finally, we can train the network. We'll start by defining the train and test datasets. We won't go into much detail about the implementation, as we've already looked at a similar scenario, in Chapter 2, *Understanding Convolutional Networks*. We'll augment the training set by padding the samples with four pixels, and then we'll take random 32×32 crops out of it. The following is the implementation:

```
# training data transformation
transform_train = transforms.Compose([
    transforms.RandomCrop(32, padding=4),
    transforms.RandomHorizontalFlip(),
    transforms.ToTensor(),
    transforms.Normalize((0.4914, 0.4821, 0.4465), (0.2470, 0.2435,
    0.2616))
])

# training data loader
train_set = torchvision.datasets.CIFAR10(root='./data', train=True,
                                          download=True,
                                          transform=transform_train)

train_loader = torch.utils.data.DataLoader(dataset=train_set,
                                           batch_size=100,
                                           shuffle=True,
                                           num_workers=2)

# test data transformation
transform_test = transforms.Compose([
    transforms.ToTensor(),
    transforms.Normalize((0.4914, 0.4821, 0.4465), (0.2470, 0.2435,
    0.2616))
])

# test data loader
testset = torchvision.datasets.CIFAR10(root='./data', train=False,
                                       download=True,
                                       transform=transform_test)

test_loader = torch.utils.data.DataLoader(dataset=testset,
                                          batch_size=100,
                                          shuffle=False,
                                          num_workers=2)
```

11. Then, we'll instantiate the network model and the training parameters—cross-entropy loss and the Adam optimizer:

```
# load the pretrained model
model = PreActivationResNet34()

# select gpu 0, if available
# otherwise fallback to cpu
device = torch.device("cuda:0" if torch.cuda.is_available() else
"cpu")

# transfer the model to the GPU
model = model.to(device)

# loss function
loss_function = nn.CrossEntropyLoss()

# We'll optimize all parameters
optimizer = optim.Adam(model.parameters())
```

12. We can now train the network for `EPOCHS` epochs. The `train_model`, `test_model`, and `plot_accuracy` functions are the same as the ones we defined in the *Implementing transfer learning with PyTorch* section of `Chapter 2`, *Understanding Convolutional Networks*, and we won't repeat their implementation here. The following is the code:

```
# train
EPOCHS = 15

test_acc = list()  # collect accuracy for plotting
for epoch in range(EPOCHS):
    print('Epoch {}/{}'.format(epoch + 1, EPOCHS))

    train_model(model, loss_function, optimizer, train_loader)
    _, acc = test_model(model, loss_function, test_loader)
    test_acc.append(acc)

plot_accuracy(test_acc)
```

And, in the following graph, we can see the test accuracy in 15 iterations (the training might take a while):

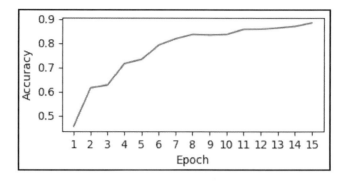

ResNet34 CIFAR accuracy in 15 epochs

 The code in this section is partially based on the pre-activation ResNet implementation in `https://github.com/kuangliu/pytorch-cifar`.

In this section, we discussed the various types of ResNets, and then we implemented one with PyTorch. In the next section, we'll discuss Inception networks—yet another family of networks, which elevate the use of parallel connections to a new level.

Understanding Inception networks

Inception networks (*Going Deeper with Convolutions*, `https://arxiv.org/abs/1409.4842`) were introduced in 2014, when they won the ImageNet challenge of that year (there seems to be a pattern here). Since then, the authors have released multiple improvements (versions) of the architecture.

 Fun fact: the name Inception comes in part from the **We need to go deeper** internet meme, related to the movie *Inception*.

The idea behind Inception networks started from the basic premise that the objects in an image have different scales. A distant object might take up a small region of the image, but the same object, once nearer, might take up the majority of the image. This presents a difficulty for standard CNNs, where the neurons in the different layers have a fixed receptive field size as imposed on the input image. A regular network might be a good detector of objects at a certain scale, but could miss them otherwise. To solve this problem, the authors of the paper proposed a novel architecture: one composed of Inception blocks. An Inception block starts with a common input, and then splits it into different parallel paths (or towers). Each path contains either convolutional layers with a different-sized filter, or a pooling layer. In this way, we apply different receptive fields on the same input data. At the end of the Inception block, the outputs of the different paths are concatenated. In the next few sections, we'll discuss the different variations of Inception networks.

Inception v1

The following diagram shows the first version of the Inception block, part of the GoogLeNet network architecture (https://arxiv.org/abs/1409.4842). GoogLeNet contains nine such Inception blocks:

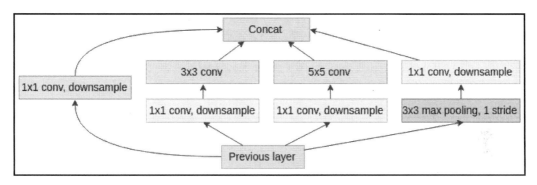

Inception v1 block. inspired by https://arxiv.org/abs/1409.4842

The v1 block has four paths:

- 1×1 convolution, which acts as a kind of repeater to the input
- 1×1 convolution, followed by a 3×3 convolution
- 1×1 convolution, followed by a 5×5 convolution
- 3×3 max pooling with stride 1

The layers in the block use padding in such a way that the input and the output have the same shape (but different depths). The padding is also necessary, because each path would produce an output with a different shape, depending on the filter size. This is valid for all versions of Inception blocks.

The other major innovation of this Inception block is the use of downsampling 1×1 convolutions. They are needed because the output of all paths is concatenated to produce the final output of the block. The result of the concatenation is an output with a quadrupled depth. If another Inception block followed the current one, its output depth would quadruple again. To avoid such exponential growth, the block uses 1×1 convolutions to reduce the depth of each path, which in turn reduces the output depth of the block. This makes it possible to create deeper networks, without running out of resources.

GoogLeNet also utilizes auxiliary classifiers—that is, it has two additional classification outputs (with the same groundtruth labels) at various intermediate layers. During training, the total value of the loss is a weighted sum of the auxiliary losses and the real loss.

Inception v2 and v3

Inception v2 and v3 were released together and propose several improvements over the original Inception block (*Rethinking the Inception Architecture for Computer Vision*, https://arxiv.org/abs/1512.00567). The first is the factorization of the 5×5 convolution in two stacked 3×3 convolutions. We discussed the advantages of this in the *Introduction to Visual Geometry Group* section.

We can see the new Inception block in the following diagram:

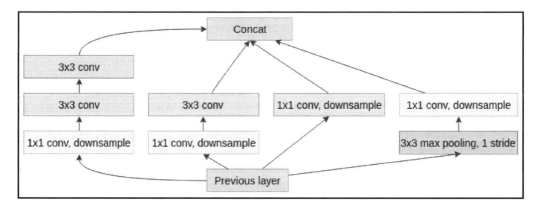

Inception block A. inspired by https://arxiv.org/abs/1512.00567

The next improvement is the factorization of an $n \times n$ convolution in two stacked asymmetrical $1 \times n$ and $n \times 1$ convolutions. For example, we can split a single 3×3 convolution into two 1×3 and 3×1 convolutions, where the 3×1 convolution is applied over the output of the 1×3 convolution. In the first case, the filter size would be 3*3 = 9, while in the second case, we would have a combined size of (3*1) + (1*3) = 3 + 3 = 6, resulting in 33% efficiency, as seen in the following diagram:

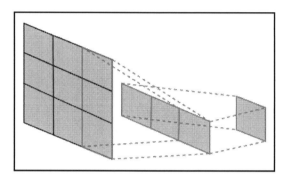

Factorization of a 3×3 convolution in 1×3 and 3×1 convolutions. Inspired by https://arxiv.org/abs/1512.00567

The authors introduced two new blocks, which utilizes factorized convolutions. The first of these blocks (and the second in total) is equivalent of Inception block A:

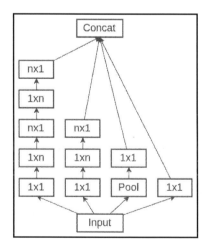

Inception block B. When n=3. it is equivalent to block A. Inspired by https://arxiv.org/abs/1512.00567

The second (third in total) block is similar, but the asymmetrical convolutions are parallel, resulting in a higher output depth (more concatenated paths). The hypothesis here is that the more features (different filters) the network has, the faster it learns (we also discussed the need for more filters in Chapter 2, *Understanding Convolutional Networks*). On the other hand, the wider layers take more memory and computation time. As a compromise, this block is only used in the deeper part of the network, after the other blocks:

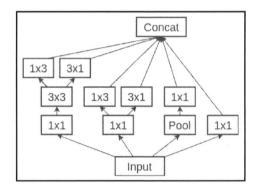

Inception block C. inspired by https://arxiv.org/abs/1512.00567

Using these new blocks, the authors proposed two new Inception networks: v2 and v3. Another major improvement in this version is the use of batch normalization, which was introduced by the same authors.

Inception v4 and Inception-ResNet

In the latest revision of Inception networks, the authors introduced three new streamlined Inception blocks that build upon the idea of the previous versions (*Inception-v4, Inception-ResNet and the Impact of Residual Connections on Learning*, https://arxiv.org/abs/1602.07261). They introduced 7×7 asymmetric factorized convolutions, and average pooling instead of max pooling. More importantly, they created a residual/Inception hybrid network known as Inception-ResNet, where the Inception blocks also include residual connections. We can see the schematic of one such block in the following diagram:

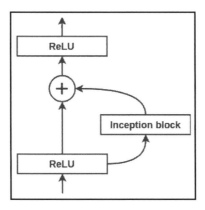

An Inception block with a residual skip connection

In this section, we discussed different types of Inception networks and the different principles used in the various Inception blocks. Next, we'll talk about a newer CNN architecture, which takes the Inception concept to a new depth (or width, as it should be).

Introducing Xception

All Inception blocks so far start by splitting the input into several parallel paths. Each path continues with a dimensionality-reduction 1×1 cross-channel convolution, followed by regular cross-channel convolutions. On one hand, the 1×1 connection maps cross-channel correlations, but not spatial ones (because of the 1×1 filter size). On the other hand, the subsequent cross-channel convolutions map both types of correlations. Let's recall that in Chapter 2, *Understanding Convolutional Networks*, we introduced **depthwise separable convolutions** (**DSC**), which combine the following two operations:

- **A depthwise convolution**: In a depthwise convolution, a single input slice produces a single output slice, therefore it only maps spatial (and not cross-channel) correlations.
- **A 1×1 cross-channel convolution**: With 1×1 convolutions, we have the opposite, that is, they only map cross-channel correlations.

The author of Xception (*Xception: Deep Learning with Depthwise Separable Convolutions*, `https://arxiv.org/abs/1610.02357`) argues that, in fact, we can think of DSC as an extreme (hence the name) version of an Inception block, where each depthwise input/output slice pair represents one parallel path. We have as many parallel paths as the number of input slices. The following diagram shows a simplified Inception block and its transformation to an Xception block:

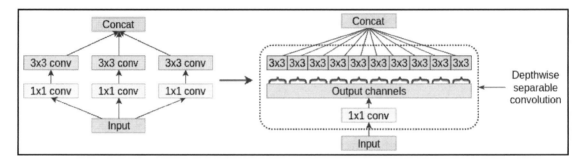

Left: simplified Inception module. Right: Xception block. Inspired by https://arxiv.org/abs/1610.02357

The Xception block and the DSC have two differences:

- In Xception, the 1x1 convolution comes first, instead of last as in DSC. But, these operations are meant to be stacked anyway, and we can assume that the order is of no significance.
- The Xception block uses ReLU activations after each convolution, while the DSC doesn't use non-linearity after the cross-channel convolution. According to the author's experiments, networks with absent non-linearity depthwise convolution converged faster and were more accurate.

The following diagram depicts the architecture of the Xception network:

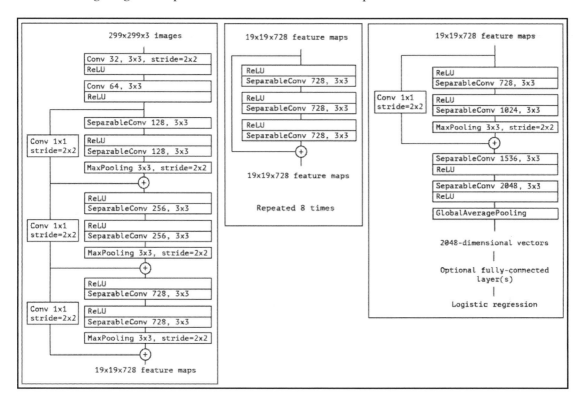

From left to right: Entry flow: Middle flow. repeated eight times: Exit flow. Source: https://arxiv.org/abs/1610.02357

It is built of linearly stacked DSCs and some of its properties are as follows:

- The network contains 36 convolutional layers, structured into 14 modules, all of which have linear residual connections around them, except for the first and last modules. The modules are grouped in three sequential virtual flows—entry, middle, and exit.
- Downsampling with 3×3 max pooling in the entry and exit flows; no downsampling in the middle flow; global average pooling before the fully connected layers.
- All convolutions and DSCs are followed by batch normalization.
- All DSCs have a depth multiplier of 1 (no depth expansion).

This section concludes the series of Inception-based models. In the next section, we'll focus on a special model, which prioritizes a small footprint and computational efficiency.

Introducing MobileNet

In this section, we'll discuss a lightweight CNN model called MobileNet (*MobileNetV2: Inverted Residuals and Linear Bottlenecks*, `https://arxiv.org/abs/1801.04381`). We'll focus on the second revision of this idea (MobileNetV1 was introduced in *MobileNets: Efficient Convolutional Neural Networks for Mobile Vision Applications*, `https://arxiv.org/abs/1704.04861`).

MobileNet is aimed at devices with limited memory and computing power, such as mobile phones (the name kind of gives it away). To reduce its footprint, the network uses DSC, linear bottlenecks, and inverted residuals.

We are already familiar with DSC, so let's discuss the other two:

- **Linear bottlenecks**: To understand this concept, we'll quote the paper:

  "Consider a deep neural network consisting of n layers L_i each of which has an activation tensor of dimensions $h_i \times w_i \times d_i$. Throughout this section we will be discussing the basic properties of these activation tensors, which we will treat as containers of $h_i \times w_i$ "pixels" with d_i dimensions. Informally, for an input set of real images, we say that the set of layer activations (for any layer L_i) forms a "manifold of interest". It has been long assumed that manifolds of interest in neural networks could be embedded in low-dimensional subspaces. In other words, when we look at all individual d-channel pixels of a deep convolutional layer, the information encoded in those values actually lie in some manifold, which can be embedded into a low-dimensional subspace."

  One way to do this is with 1x1 bottleneck convolutions. But, the authors of the paper argue that if this convolution is followed by non-linearity like ReLU, this might lead to a loss of manifold information. If the ReLU input is larger than 0, then the output of this unit is equivalent to the linear transformation of the input. But, if the input is smaller, then the ReLU collapses and the information of that unit is lost. Because of this, MobileNet uses 1x1 bottleneck convolution without non-linear activation.

- **Inverted residuals**: In the *Residual networks* section, we introduced the bottleneck residual block, where the data flow in the non-shortcut path is **input -> 1×1 bottleneck conv -> 3×3 conv -> 1×1 unsampling conv**. In other words, it follows a **wide -> narrow -> wide** data representation. The authors argue that *the bottlenecks actually contain all the necessary information, while an expansion layer acts merely as an implementation detail that accompanies a non-linear transformation of the tensor*. Because of this, they propose having shortcut connections between the bottleneck connections instead.

Based on these properties, the MobileNet model is composed of the following building blocks:

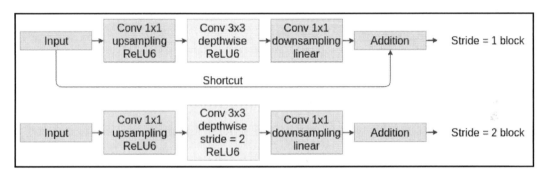

Top: inverted residual block with stride 1. Bottom: stride 2 block

The model uses ReLU6 non-linearity: ReLU6 = min(max(input, 0),6). The maximum activation value is limited to 6—in this way, the non-linearity is more robust in low-precision floating-point computations. That's because 6 can take at most 3 bits, leaving the rest for the floating-point portion of the number.

Besides stride, the blocks are described by an expansion factor, *t*, which determines the expansion ratio of the bottleneck convolution.

The following table shows the relationship between the input and output dimensions of the blocks:

Input	Operator	Output
$h \times w \times k$	1x1 conv2d , ReLU6	$h \times w \times (tk)$
$h \times w \times tk$	3x3 dwise s=s, ReLU6	$\frac{h}{s} \times \frac{w}{s} \times (tk)$
$\frac{h}{s} \times \frac{w}{s} \times tk$	linear 1x1 conv2d	$\frac{h}{s} \times \frac{w}{s} \times k'$

The input and output dimensions relationship. Source: https://arxiv.org/abs/1801.04381

In the preceding table, **h** and **w** are the input height and width, **s** is the stride, and **k** and **k'** are the input and output number of channels.

Finally, here is the full model architecture:

Input	Operator	t	c	n	s
$224^2 \times 3$	conv2d	-	32	1	2
$112^2 \times 32$	bottleneck	1	16	1	1
$112^2 \times 16$	bottleneck	6	24	2	2
$56^2 \times 24$	bottleneck	6	32	3	2
$28^2 \times 32$	bottleneck	6	64	4	2
$14^2 \times 64$	bottleneck	6	96	3	1
$14^2 \times 96$	bottleneck	6	160	3	2
$7^2 \times 160$	bottleneck	6	320	1	1
$7^2 \times 320$	conv2d 1x1	-	1280	1	1
$7^2 \times 1280$	avgpool 7x7	-	-	1	-
$1 \times 1 \times 1280$	conv2d 1x1	-	k	-	

The MobileNetV2 architecture. Source: https://arxiv.org/abs/1801.04381

Each line describes a group of one or more identical blocks, repeated *n* times. All layers in the same group have the same number, **c**, of output channels. The first layer of each sequence has a stride, **s**, and all others use stride 1. All spatial convolutions use 3 × 3 kernels. The expansion factor, **t**, is always applied to the input size, as described in the preceding table.

The next model we'll discuss is a network model with a new type of building block, where all layers are interconnected.

An introduction to DenseNets

DenseNet (*Densely Connected Convolutional Networks*, https://arxiv.org/abs/1608.06993) try to alleviate the vanishing gradient problem and improve feature propagation, while reducing the number of network parameters. We've already seen how ResNets introduce residual blocks with skip connections to solve this. DenseNets take some inspiration from this idea and take it even further with the introduction of dense blocks. A dense block consists of sequential convolutional layers, where any layer has a direct connection to all subsequent layers. In other words, a network layer, *l*, will receive input, $\mathbf{x}_l$, from all preceding network layers:

$$\mathbf{x}_l = H_l([\mathbf{x}_0, \mathbf{x}_1, \ldots, \mathbf{x}_{l-1}])$$

Here, $[\mathbf{x}_0, \mathbf{x}_1, \ldots, \mathbf{x}_{l-1}]$ are the **concatenated** output feature maps of the preceding network layers. This is unlike ResNets, where we combine different layers with the element-wise sum. H_l is a composite function, which defines three types of DenseNet blocks (only two are displayed):

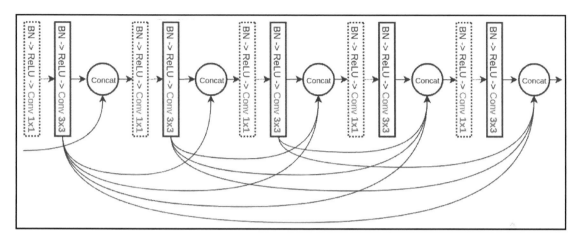

A dense block: the dimensionality-reduction layers (dashed lines) are part of the DenseNet-B architecture. while DenseNet-A doesn't have them. DenseNet-C is not displayed

Let's define them:

- **DenseNet-A**: This is the base block, where H_l consists of batch normalization, followed by activation, and a 3×3 convolution:

$$H_l = BatchNorm \rightarrow ReLU \rightarrow Conv\ 3x3$$

- **DenseNet-B**: The authors also introduced a second type of dense block, DenseNet-B, which applies a dimensionality-reduction 1×1 convolution after each concatenation:

$$H_l = BatchNorm \rightarrow ReLU \rightarrow Bottleneck\ Conv\ 1x1 \rightarrow BatchNorm \rightarrow ReLU \rightarrow Conv\ 3x3$$

- **DenseNet-C**: A further modification, which adds a downsampling 1×1 convolution after each dense block. The combination of B and C is referred to as DenseNet-BC.

A dense block is specified by its number of convolutional layers and the output volume depth of each layer, which is called the **growth rate** in this context. Let's assume that the input of the dense block has a volume depth of k_0 and the output volume depth of each convolutional layer is k. Then, because of the concatenation, the input volume depth for the *l*-th layer will be $k_0+k_x(l-1)$. Although the later layers of a dense block have a large input volume depth (because of the many concatenations), DenseNets can work with growth rate values as low as 12, which reduces the total number of parameters. To understand why this works, let's think of the feature maps as the **collective knowledge** (or global state) of the network. Each layer adds its own k feature maps to this state, and the growth rate determines the amount of information the layer contributes to it. Because of the dense structure, the global state can be accessed from everywhere within the network (hence the term global). In other words, there is no need to replicate it from one layer to the next as in traditional network architectures, which allows us to start with a smaller number of feature maps.

To make concatenation possible, dense blocks use padding in such a way that the height and width of all output slices are the same throughout the block. But because of this, downsampling is not possible within a dense block. Therefore, a dense network consists of multiple sequential dense blocks, separated by downsampling pooling operations.

The authors of the paper have proposed a family of DenseNets, whose overall architecture resembles ResNet:

Layers	Output Size	DenseNet-121	DenseNet-169	DenseNet-201	DenseNet-264
Convolution	112 × 112	7 × 7 conv, stride 2			
Pooling	56 × 56	3 × 3 max pool, stride 2			
Dense Block (1)	56 × 56	[1 × 1 conv; 3 × 3 conv] × 6	[1 × 1 conv; 3 × 3 conv] × 6	[1 × 1 conv; 3 × 3 conv] × 6	[1 × 1 conv; 3 × 3 conv] × 6
Transition Layer (1)	56 × 56	1 × 1 conv			
	28 × 28	2 × 2 average pool, stride 2			
Dense Block (2)	28 × 28	[1 × 1 conv; 3 × 3 conv] × 12	[1 × 1 conv; 3 × 3 conv] × 12	[1 × 1 conv; 3 × 3 conv] × 12	[1 × 1 conv; 3 × 3 conv] × 12
Transition Layer (2)	28 × 28	1 × 1 conv			
	14 × 14	2 × 2 average pool, stride 2			
Dense Block (3)	14 × 14	[1 × 1 conv; 3 × 3 conv] × 24	[1 × 1 conv; 3 × 3 conv] × 32	[1 × 1 conv; 3 × 3 conv] × 48	[1 × 1 conv; 3 × 3 conv] × 64
Transition Layer (3)	14 × 14	1 × 1 conv			
	7 × 7	2 × 2 average pool, stride 2			
Dense Block (4)	7 × 7	[1 × 1 conv; 3 × 3 conv] × 16	[1 × 1 conv; 3 × 3 conv] × 32	[1 × 1 conv; 3 × 3 conv] × 32	[1 × 1 conv; 3 × 3 conv] × 48
Classification Layer	1 × 1	7 × 7 global average pool			
		1000D fully connected, softmax			

The family of DenseNet networks. Source: https://arxiv.org/abs/1608.06993

They have the following properties:

- Start with a 7×7 stride 2 downsampling convolution.
- A further downsampling 3×3 max pooling with stride 2.
- Four groups of DenseNet-B blocks. The family of networks differs by the number of dense blocks within each group.
- Downsampling is handled by a transition layer of a 2×2 pooling operation with stride 2 between the dense groups.
- The transition layer contains a further 1×1 bottleneck convolution to reduce the number of feature maps. The compression ratio of this convolution is specified by a hyper-parameter, θ, where $0 < \theta \leq 1$. If the number of input feature maps is m, then the number of output feature maps is θm.
- The dense blocks end up with a 7×7 global average pooling, followed by a 1,000-unit fully connected softmax layer.

The authors of DenseNet have also released an improved DenseNet model called MSDNet (*Multi-Scale Dense Networks for Resource Efficient Image Classification*, `https://arxiv.org/abs/1703.09844`), which (as the name suggests) uses multi-scale dense blocks.

With DenseNet, we conclude our discussion about conventional CNN architectures. In the next section, we'll discuss whether it's possible to automate the process of finding the optimal NN architecture.

The workings of neural architecture search

The NN models we've discussed so far were designed by their authors. But, what if we could make the computer itself design the NN? Enter **neural architecture search (NAS)**—a technique that automates the design of NNs.

Before we continue, let's see what the network architecture consists of:

- The graph of operations, which represents the network. As we discussed in `Chapter 1`, *The Nuts and bolts of Neural Networks*, the operations include (but are not limited to) convolutions, activation functions, fully connected layers, normalization, and so on.

- The parameters of each operation. For example, the convolution parameters are: type (cross-channel, depthwise, and so on), input dimensions, number of input and output slices, stride, and padding.

This set of architecture parameters are a subset of all hyperparameters of the NN ML algorithm. Other parameters include learning rate, mini-batch size, optimization algorithm (for example, Adam or SGD). Therefore, we can think of NAS as a type of hyperparameter optimization problem (the task of selecting optimal hyperparameters for an ML algorithm). Hyperparameter optimization itself is one of the components of automated machine learning (AutoML). This is a broader process, which aims to automate all steps of an ML solution. An AutoML algorithm will first select the type of algorithm (for example, decision tree or NN) and then it will proceed with the hyperparameter optimization of the selected algorithm. Since our book is focused on NNs, we'll assume that we've already selected the algorithm (how convenient!) and now we want to design our network.

In this section, we'll discuss gradient-based NAS with reinforcement learning (*Neural Architecture Search with Reinforcement Learning*, `https://arxiv.org/abs/1611.01578`). At this point, we won't discuss reinforcement learning, and we'll focus on the algorithm instead. It starts with the premise that we can represent the network definition as a string (a sequence of tokens). Let's assume that we'll generate a sequential CNN, which consists only of convolutions.

Then, part of the string definition will look like this:

$$\ldots; \underbrace{FW_{\text{filter w}}; FH_{\text{filter h}}; SW_{\text{stride w}}; SH_{\text{stride h}}; N_{\text{num filters}}}_{\text{CNN layer definition}}; \underbrace{FW_{\text{filter w}}; FH_{\text{filter h}}; SW_{\text{stride w}}; SH_{\text{stride h}}; N_{\text{num filters}}}_{\text{CNN layer definition}}; \ldots$$

$$\ldots; \underbrace{3;3;2;2;32}_{\text{CNN layer}}; \underbrace{3;3;1;1;64}_{\text{CNN layer}}; \ldots$$

We don't have to specify the layer type, because we only use convolutions. We exclude padding for the sake of simplicity. The subscript text on the first line is included for clarity, but won't be included in the algorithmic version.

We can see the algorithm overview in the following diagram:

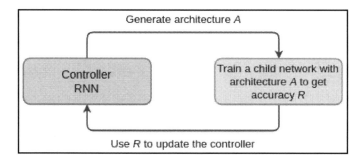

NAS overview. Source: https://arxiv.org/abs/1611.01578

Let's start with the controller. It is an RNN, whose task is to generate new network architectures. Although we haven't yet discussed RNNs (this honor won't come until Chapter 7, *Understanding Recurrent Networks*), we'll try to explain how it works nevertheless. In Chapter 1, *The Nuts and Bolts of Neural Networks*, we mentioned that an RNN maintains an internal state—a summary of all its previous inputs. Based on that internal state and the latest input sample, the network generates a new output, updates its internal state, and waits for the next input.

Here, the controller will generate the string sequence, which describes the network architecture. The controller output is a single token of the sequence. This could be filter height/width, stride width/height, or the number of output filters. The type of token depends on the length of the currently generated architecture. Once we have this token, we feed it back to the RNN controller as input. Then, the network generates the next token of the sequence.

This process is depicted in the following diagram:

Generating a network architecture with the RNN controller. The output token is fed back to the controller as input to generate the next token.
Source: https://arxiv.org/abs/1611.01578

The white vertical squares in the diagram represent the RNN controller, which consists of a two-layer **Long short-term memory** (**LSTM**) cell (along the *y*-axis). Although the diagram shows multiple instances of the RNN (along the *x*-axis), it is in fact the same network; it's just **unfolded** in time, to represent the process of sequence generation. That is, each step along the *x*-axis represents a single token of the network definition. A token prediction at step *t* is carried out by a softmax classifier and then fed as controller input at step *t+1*. We continue this process until the length of the generated network reaches a certain value. Initially, this value is small (a short network), but it gradually increases (a longer network) as the training progresses.

To better understand NAS, let's see a step-by-step execution of the algorithm:

1. The controller generates a new architecture, *A*.
2. It builds and **trains** a new network with said architecture until it converges.
3. It tests the new network on a withheld part of the training set and measures the error, *R*.
4. It uses this error to update the controller parameters, θ_c. As our controller is RNN, this means training the network and adjusting its weights. The model parameters are updated in such a way as to reduce the error, *R*, of the future architectures. This is made possible by a reinforcement learning algorithm called REINFORCE, which is beyond the scope of this section.
5. It repeats these steps until the error, *R*, of the generated network falls below a certain threshold.

The controller can generate network architectures with some restrictions. As we mentioned earlier in this section, the most severe is that the generated network only consists of convolutional layers. To simplify things, each convolutional layer automatically includes batch normalization and ReLU activation. But in theory, the controller could generate more complex architectures with other layers such as pooling or normalization. We could implement this by adding additional controller steps in the architecture sequence for the layer type.

The authors of the paper implemented a technique that allows us to add residual skip connections to the generated architecture. It works with a special type of controller step called an anchor point. The anchor point at layer N has content-based sigmoids. The output of a sigmoid j ($j = 1, 2, 3, ..., N-1$) represents the probability that the current layer has a residual connection to layer j.

The modified controller is depicted in the following diagram:

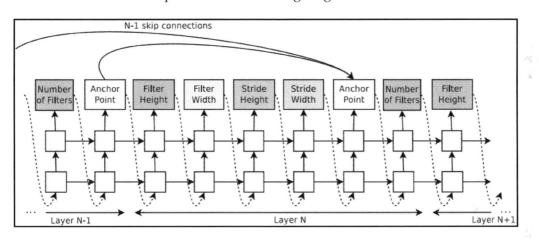

RNN controller with anchor points for the residual connections. Source: https://arxiv.org/abs/1611.01578

If one layer has many input layers, all inputs are concatenated along the channel (depth) dimension. Skip connections could create some issues in the network design:

- The first hidden layer of the network (that is, the one not connected to any other input layer) uses the input image as an input layer.
- At the end of the network, all layer outputs that have not been connected are concatenated in a final hidden state, which is sent to the classifier.
- It may happen that the outputs to be concatenated have different sizes. In that case, the smaller feature maps are padded with zeros to match the size of the bigger ones.

In their experiment, the authors used a controller with a 2-layer LSTM cell with 35 units in each layer. For every convolution, the controller has to select a filter height and width from the values {1, 3, 5, 7}, and a number of filters to be one of {24, 36, 48, 64}. Additionally, they performed 2 sets of experiments—one where the controller was allowed to select strides in {1, 2, 3} and another with a fixed stride of 1.

Once the controller generates an architecture, the new network is trained for 50 epochs on 45,000 images of the CIFAR-10 dataset. The remaining 5,000 images are used for validation. During training, the controller starts with an architecture depth of 6 layers and then increases the depth by 2 layers on every 1,600 iterations. The best performing model has a validation accuracy of 3.65%. It was discovered after 12,800 architectures using 800 GPUs (wow!). The reason for these steep computational requirements is that each new network is trained from scratch just to produce one accuracy value, which can then be used to train the controller. More recently, the new ENAS algorithm (*Efficient Neural Architecture Search via Parameter Sharing*, https://arxiv.org/abs/1802.03268) has made it possible to significantly reduce the computational resources of NAS by sharing the weights among the generated models.

In the next section, we'll discuss a novel type of NN, which tries to overcome some of the limitations of the CNNs we talked about so far.

Introducing capsule networks

Capsule networks (*Dynamic Routing Between Capsules*, https://arxiv.org/abs/1710.09829) were introduced as a way to overcome some of the limitations of standard CNNs. To understand the idea behind capsule networks, we need to understand their limitations first, which we will see in the next section.

The limitations of convolutional networks

Let's start with a quote from professor Hinton himself:

> *"The pooling operation used in convolutional neural networks is a big mistake and the fact that it works so well is a disaster."*

As we mentioned in `Chapter 2`, *Understanding Convolutional Networks*, CNNs are **translation-invariant**. Let's imagine a picture with a face, located in the right half of the picture. Translation invariance means that a CNN is very good at telling us that the picture contains a face, but it cannot tell us whether the face is in the left or right part of the image. The main culprit for this behavior is the pooling layers. Every pooling layer introduces a little translation invariance. For example, the max pooling routes forward the activation of only one of the input neurons, but the subsequent layers don't have any knowledge of which neuron is routed.

By stacking multiple pooling layers, we gradually increase the receptive field size. But, the detected object could be anywhere in the new receptive field, because none of the pooling layers relay such information. Therefore, we also increase the translation invariance. At first, this might seem to be a good thing, because the final labels have to be translation-invariant. But, it poses a problem, as CNNs cannot identify the position of one object relative to another. A CNN would identify both of the following images as a face, because they both contain the components of a face (a nose, mouth, and eyes) regardless of their relative positions to one another.

This is also known as the **Picasso problem**, as demonstrated in the following diagram:

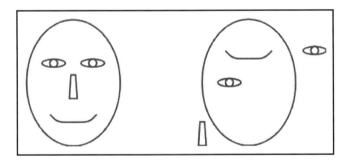

A convolutional network would identify both of these images as a face

But, that's not all. A CNN would be confused even if the face had a different **orientation**, for example, if it was turned upside down. One way to overcome this is with data augmentation (rotation) during training. But, this only shows the limitations of the network. We have to explicitly show the object in different orientations and tell the CNN that this is, in fact, the same object.

So far, we've seen that a CNN discards the translation information (transitional invariance) and doesn't understand the orientation of an object. In computer vision, the combination of translation and orientation is known as the **pose**. The pose is enough to uniquely identify the object's properties in the coordinate system. Let's use computer graphics to illustrate this. A 3D object, say a cube, is entirely defined by its pose and the edge length. The process of transforming the representation of a 3D object into an image on the screen is called rendering. Knowing just its pose and the edge length of the cube, we can render it from any point of view we like.

Therefore, if we can somehow train a network to understand these properties, we won't have to feed it with multiple augmented versions of the same object. A CNN cannot do that, because its internal data representation doesn't contain information about the object's pose (only about its type). In contrast, capsule networks **preserve information** for both the type and the pose of an object. Therefore, they can detect objects that can transform into each other, which is known as **equivariance**. We can also think of this as **reverse graphics**, that is, a reconstruction of the object's properties according to its rendered image.

To solve these problems, the authors of the paper propose a new type of network building block, called a **capsule**, instead of the neuron. Let's discuss it in the next section.

Capsules

The output of a capsule is a vector, compared to the output of a neuron, which is a scalar value. The capsule output vector carries the following meaning:

- The elements of the vector represent the pose and other properties of the object.
- The length of the vector is in the (0, 1) range and represents the probability of detecting the feature at that location. As a reminder, the length of a vector is $|\mathbf{v}| = \sqrt{\sum_{i=1}^{n} v_i^2}$, where v_i are the vector elements.

Let's consider a capsule that detects faces. If we start moving a face across an image, the values of the capsule vector will change to reflect the change in the position. However, its length will always stay the same, because the probability of the face doesn't change with the location.

Capsules are organized in interconnected layers, just like a regular network. The capsules in one layer serve as input to the capsules in the next. And, like a CNN, the shallower layers detect basic features, and the deeper layers combine them in more abstract and complex ones. But now, the capsules also relay positional information, instead of just detected objects. This allows the deeper capsules to analyze not only the presence of features, but also their relationship. For example, a capsule layer may detect a mouth, face, nose, and eyes. The subsequent capsule layer will be able to not only verify the presence of these features, but also whether they have the correct spatial relationship. Only if both conditions are true can the subsequent layer verify that a face is present. This is a high-level overview of capsule networks. Now, let's see how exactly capsules work.

We can see the schematic of a capsule in the following screenshot:

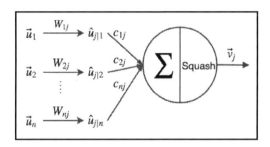

A capsule

Let's analyze it in the following steps:

1. The capsule inputs are the output vectors, $\mathbf{u}_1$, $\mathbf{u}_2$, ... $\mathbf{u}_n$, from the capsules of the previous layer.

2. We multiply each vector, $\mathbf{u}_i$, by its corresponding weight matrix, W_{ij}, to produce **prediction vectors**, $\hat{\mathbf{u}}_{j|i} = W_{ij} \cdot \mathbf{u}_i$. The weight matrices, $\mathbf{W}$, encode spatial and other relationships between the lower-level features, coming from the capsules of the previous layer, and the high-level ones in the current layer. For example, imagine that the capsule in the current layer detects faces and the capsules from the previous layer detect the mouth ($\mathbf{u}_1$), eyes ($\mathbf{u}_2$), and nose ($\mathbf{u}_3$). Then, $\hat{\mathbf{u}}_{j|1} = W_{1j} \cdot \mathbf{u}_1$ is the predicted position of the face, given where the location of the mouth is. In the same way, $\hat{\mathbf{u}}_{j|2} = W_{2j} \cdot \mathbf{u}_2$ predicts the location of the face based on the detected location of the eyes, and $\hat{\mathbf{u}}_{j|3} = W_{3j} \cdot \mathbf{u}_3$ predicts the location of the face based on the location of the nose. If all three lower-level capsule vectors agree on the same location, then the current capsule can be confident that a face is indeed present. We only used location for this example, but the vectors could encode other types of relationships between the features, such as scale and orientation. The weights, $\mathbf{W}$, are learned with backpropagation.

3. Next, we multiply the $\hat{\mathbf{u}}_{j|i}$ vectors by the scalar coupling coefficients, c_{ij}. These coefficients are a separate set of parameters, apart from the weight matrices. They exist between any two capsules, and indicate which high-level capsules will receive input from a lower-level capsule. But, unlike weight matrices, which are adjusted via backpropagation, coupling coefficients are computed on the fly during the forward pass via a process called **dynamic routing**. We'll describe it in the next section.

4. Then, we perform the sum of the weighted input vectors. This step is similar to the weighted sum in neurons, but with vectors:

$$\mathbf{s}_j = \sum_i c_{ij} \hat{\mathbf{u}}_{j|i}$$

5. Finally, we'll compute the output of the capsule, $\mathbf{v}_j$, by squashing the vector, $\mathbf{s}_j$. In this context, squashing means transforming the vector in such a way that its length comes in the (0, 1) range, without changing its direction. As mentioned, the length of the capsule vector represents the probability of the detected feature and squashing it in the (0, 1) range reflects that. To do this, the authors propose a novel formula:

$$\mathbf{v}_j = \frac{|\mathbf{s}_j|^2}{1 + |\mathbf{s}_j|^2} \frac{\mathbf{s}_j}{|\mathbf{s}_j|}$$

Now that we know the structure of the capsules, in the following section, we'll describe the algorithm to compute the coupling coefficients between capsules of different layers. That is, the mechanism by which they relay signals between one another.

Dynamic routing

Let's describe the dynamic routing process to compute the coupling coefficients, c_{ij}, displayed in the following diagram:

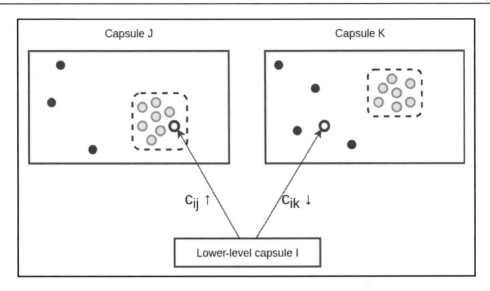

Dynamic routing example. The grouped dots indicate lower-level capsules that agree with each other

We have a lower-level capsule, I, that has to decide whether to send its output to one of two higher-level capsules, J and K. The dark and light dots represent prediction vectors, $\hat{u}_{j|*}$ and $\hat{u}_{k|*}$, which J and K have already received from other lower-level capsules. The arrows from the I capsule to the J and K capsules point to the $\hat{u}_{j|i}$ and $\hat{u}_{k|i}$ prediction vectors from I to J and K. The clustered prediction vectors (lighter dots) indicate lower-level capsules that agree with each other with regard to the high-level feature. For example, if the K capsule describes a face, then the clustered predictions would indicate lower-level features, such as a mouth, nose, and eyes. Conversely, the dispersed (darker) dots indicate disagreement. If the I capsule predicts a vehicle tire, it would disagree with the clustered predictions in K.

However, if the clustered predictions in J represent features such as headlights, windshield, or fenders, then the prediction of I would be in agreement with them. The lower-level capsules have a way of determining whether they fall into the clustered or dispersed group of each higher-level capsule. If they fall into the clustered group, they will increase the corresponding coupling coefficient with that capsule and will route their vector in that direction. Conversely, if they fall into the dispersed group, the coefficient will decrease.

Let's formalize this knowledge with a step-by-step algorithm, introduced by the authors:

1. For all i capsules in the l layer, and j capsules in the $(l + 1)$ layer, we'll initialize $b_{ij} \leftarrow 0$, where b_{ij} is a temporary variable equivalent to c_{ij}. The vector representation of all b_{ij} is $\mathbf{b}_i$. At the start of the algorithm, the i capsule has an equal chance of routing its output to any of the capsules of the $(l + 1)$ layer.

2. Repeat for *r* iterations, where *r* is a parameter:
    1. For all *i* capsules in the *l* layer: $c_i \leftarrow \text{softmax}(b_i)$. The sum of all outgoing coupling coefficients, c_i, of a capsule amounts to 1 (they have a probabilistic nature), hence the softmax.
    2. For all *j* capsules in the *(l + 1)* layer: $s_j \leftarrow \sum_i c_{ij} \hat{u}_{j|i}$. That is, we'll compute all non-squashed output vectors of the *(l + 1)* layer.
    3. For all *j* capsules in the *(l + 1)* layer, we'll compute the squashed vectors: $v_j \leftarrow \text{squash}(s_j)$.
    4. For all *i* capsules in the *l* layer, and *j* capsules in the *(l + 1)* layer: $b_{ij} \leftarrow b_{ij} + \hat{u}_{j|i} \cdot v_j$. Here, $\hat{u}_{j|i} \cdot v_j$ is the dot product of the prediction vector of the low-level *i* capsule and the output vector of the high-level *j* capsule vectors. If the dot product is high, then the *i* capsule is in agreement with the other low-level capsules, which route their output to the *j* capsule, and the coupling coefficient increases.

The authors have recently released an updated dynamic routing algorithm using a clustering technique called expectation-maximization. You can read more about it in the original paper, *Matrix capsules with EM routing* (https://ai.google/research/pubs/pub46653).

The structure of the capsule network

In this section, we'll describe the structure of the capsule network, which the authors used to classify the MNIST dataset. The input of the network is the 28×28 MNIST grayscale images, and the following are the steps:

1. We'll start with a single convolutional layer with 256 9×9 filters, stride 1, and ReLU activation. The shape of the output volume is (256, 20, 20).
2. We have another convolutional layer with 256 9×9 filters and stride 2. The shape of the output volume is (256, 6, 6).
3. Use the output of the layer as a foundation for the first capsule layer, called PrimaryCaps. Take the (256, 6, 6) output volume and split it into 32 separate (8, 6, 6) blocks. That is, each of the 32 blocks contains eight 6×6 slices. Take one activation value with the same coordinates from each slice and combine these values in a vector. For example, we can take activation (3, 7) of slice 1, (3, 7) of slice 2, and so on and combine them in a vector with a length of 8. We'll have 36 of these vectors. Then, we'll **transform** each vector into a capsule for a total of 36 capsules. The shape of the output volume of the PrimaryCaps layer is (32, 8, 6, 6).

4. The second capsule layer is called `DigitCaps`. It contains 10 capsules (1 per digit), whose output is a vector with length 16. The shape of the output volume of the `DigitCaps` layer is (10, 16). During inference, we compute the length of each `DigitCaps` capsule vector. We then take the capsule with the longest vector as the prediction result of the network.

5. During training, the network includes three additional, fully connected layers after `DigitCaps`, the last of which has 784 neurons (28×28). In the forward training pass, the longest capsule vector serves as input to these layers. They try to reconstruct the original image, starting from that vector. Then, the reconstructed image is compared to the original one and the difference serves as additional regularization loss for the backward pass.

Capsule networks are a new and promising approach to computer vision. However, they are not widely adopted yet and don't have an official implementation in any of the deep learning libraries discussed in this book, but you can find multiple third-party implementations.

Summary

In this chapter, we discussed some popular CNN architectures: we started with the classics, AlexNet and VGG. Then, we paid special attention to ResNets, as one of the most well-known network architectures. We also discussed the various incarnations of Inception networks and the Xception and MobileNetV2 models, which are related to them. We also talked about the exciting new ML area of neural architecture search. Finally, we discussed capsule networks—a new type of CV network, which tries to overcome some of the inherent CNN limitations.

We've already seen how to apply these models in Chapter 2, *Understanding Convolutional Networks*, where we employed ResNet and MobileNet in a transfer learning scenario for a classification task. In the next chapter, we'll see how to apply some of them to more complex tasks such as object detection and image segmentation.

4
Object Detection and Image Segmentation

In Chapter 3, *Advanced Convolutional Networks*, we discussed some of the most popular and best performing **convolutional neural network (CNN)** models. To focus on the architecture specifics of each network, we viewed the models in the straightforward context of the classification problem. In the universe of computer vision tasks, classification is fairly straightforward, as it assigns a single label to an image. In this chapter, we'll shift our focus to two more interesting computer vision tasks—object detection and semantic segmentation, while the network architecture will take a backseat. We can say that these tasks are more complex compared to classification, because the model has to obtain a more comprehensive understanding of the image. It has to be able to detect different objects as well as their positions on the image. At the same time, the task complexity allows for more creative solutions. In this chapter, we'll discuss some of them.

This chapter will cover the following topics:

- Introduction to object detection:
  - Approaches to object detection
  - YOLO
  - Faster R-CNN
- Image segmentation:
  - U-Net
  - Mask R-CNN

Introduction to object detection

Object detection is the process of finding object instances of a certain class, such as faces, cars, and trees, in images or videos. Unlike classification, object detection can detect multiple objects as well as their location in the image.

An object detector would return a list of detected objects with the following information for each object:

- The class of the object (person, car, tree, and so on).
- Probability (or confidence score) in the [0, 1] range, which conveys how confident the detector is that the object exists in that location. This is similar to the output of a regular classifier.
- The coordinates of the rectangular region of the image where the object is located. This rectangle is called a **bounding box**.

We can see the typical output of an object-detection algorithm in the following photograph. The object type and confidence score are above each bounding box:

The output of an object detector

Next, let's outline the different approaches to solving an object detection task.

Approaches to object detection

In this section, we'll outline three approaches:

- **Classic sliding window**: Here, we'll use a regular classification network (classifier). This approach can work with any type of classification algorithm, but it's relatively slow and error-prone:
  1. Build an image pyramid: This is a combination of different scales of the same image (see the following photograph). For example, each scaled image can be two times smaller than the previous one. In this way, we'll be able to detect objects regardless of their size in the original image.
  2. Slide the classifier across the whole image: That is, we'll use each location of the image as an input to the classifier, and the result will determine the type of object that is in the location. The bounding box of the location is just the image region that we used as input.
  3. We'll have multiple overlapping bounding boxes for each object: We'll use some heuristics to combine them in a single prediction.

Here is a diagram of the sliding window approach:

Sliding window plus image pyramid object detection

- **Two-stage detection methods**: These methods are very accurate, but relatively slow. As the name suggests, they involve two steps:
    1. A special type of CNN, called a **Region Proposal Network (RPN)**, scans the image and proposes a number of possible bounding boxes, or regions of interest (**RoI**), where objects might be located. However, this network doesn't detect the type of the object, but only whether an object is present in the region.
    2. The regions of interest are sent to the second stage for object classification, which determines the actual object in each bounding box.

- **One-stage (or one-shot) detection methods**: Here, a single CNN produces both the object type and the bounding box. These approaches are usually faster, but less accurate compared to the two-stage methods.

In the next section, we'll introduce the YOLO—an accurate, yet efficient one-stage detection algorithm.

Object detection with YOLOv3

In this section, we'll discuss one of the most popular detection algorithms, called YOLO. The name is an acronym for the popular motto **you only live once**, which reflects the one-stage nature of the algorithm. The authors have released three versions with incremental improvements of the algorithm. We'll only discuss the latest, v3 (for more details, see *YOLOv3: An Incremental Improvement*, https://arxiv.org/abs/1804.02767).

The algorithm starts with the so-called **backbone** network called **Darknet-53** (after the number of convolutional layers). It is trained to classify the ImageNet dataset, just as the networks in Chapter 3, *Advanced Convolutional Networks*. It is fully convolutional (no pooling layers) and uses residual connections.

The following diagram shows the backbone architecture:

	Type	Filters	Size	Output
	Convolutional	32	3 × 3	256 × 256
	Convolutional	64	3 × 3 / 2	128 × 128
1×	Convolutional	32	1 × 1	
	Convolutional	64	3 × 3	
	Residual			128 × 128
	Convolutional	128	3 × 3 / 2	64 × 64
2×	Convolutional	64	1 × 1	
	Convolutional	128	3 × 3	
	Residual			64 × 64
	Convolutional	256	3 × 3 / 2	32 × 32
8×	Convolutional	128	1 × 1	
	Convolutional	256	3 × 3	
	Residual			32 × 32
	Convolutional	512	3 × 3 / 2	16 × 16
8×	Convolutional	256	1 × 1	
	Convolutional	512	3 × 3	
	Residual			16 × 16
	Convolutional	1024	3 × 3 / 2	8 × 8
4×	Convolutional	512	1 × 1	
	Convolutional	1024	3 × 3	
	Residual			8 × 8
	Avgpool		Global	
	Connected		1000	
	Softmax			

The Darknet-53 model (source: https://arxiv.org/abs/1804.02767)

Once the network is trained, it will serve as a base for the following object detection training phase. This is a case of feature extraction transfer learning, which we described in Chapter 2, *Understanding Convolutional Networks*. The fully connected layers of the backbone are replaced with new randomly initialized convolutional and fully connected layers. The new fully connected layers will output the bounding boxes, object classes, and confidence scores of all detected objects in just a single pass.

For example, the bounding boxes in the image of people on the crosswalk at the beginning of this section were generated using a single network pass. YOLOv3 predicts boxes at three different scales. The system extracts features from those scales using a similar concept to feature pyramid networks (for more information, see *Feature Pyramid Networks for Object Detection*, https://arxiv.org/abs/1612.03144). In the detection phase, the network is trained with the common objects in context (*Microsoft COCO: Common Objects in Context*, https://arxiv.org/abs/1405.0312, http://cocodataset.org) object detection dataset.

Next, let's see how YOLO works:

1. Split the image into a grid of $S \times S$ cells (in the following diagram, we can see a 3x3 grid):

    - The network treats the center of each grid cell as the center of the region, where an object might be located.
    - An object might lie entirely within a cell. Then, its bounding box will be smaller than the cell. Alternatively, it can span over multiple cells and the bounding box will be larger. YOLO covers both cases.
    - The algorithm can detect multiple objects in a grid cell with the help of **anchor boxes** (more on that later), but an object is associated with one cell only (a one-to-n relation). That is, if the bounding box of the object covers multiple cells, we'll associate the object with the cell, where the center of the bounding box lies. For example, the two objects in the following diagram span multiple cells, but they are both assigned to the central cell, because their centers lie in it.
    - Some of the cells may contain an object and others might not. We are only interested in the ones that do.

    The following diagram shows a 3x3 cell grid with 2 objects and their bounding boxes (dashed lines). Both objects are associated with the middle cell, because the centers of their bounding boxes lie in that cell:

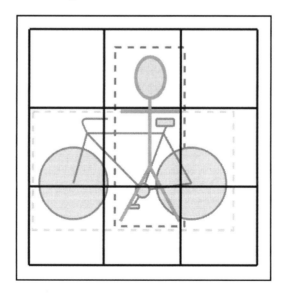

An object detection YOLO example with a 3x3 cell grid and 2 objects

2. The network will output multiple possible detected objects for each grid cell. For example, if the grid is 3×3, then the output will contain 9 possible detected objects. For the sake of clarity, let's discuss the output data (and its corresponding label) for a single grid cell/detected object. It is an array with values, $[b_x, b_y, b_h, b_w, p_c, c_1, c_2, ..., c_n]$, where the values are as follows:

   - b_x, b_y, b_h, b_w describes the object bounding box, if an object exists, then b_x and b_y are the coordinates of the center of the box. They are normalized in the [0, 1] range with respect to the size of the image. That is, if the image is of size 100 x 100 and $b_x = 20$ and $b_y = 50$, their normalized values will be 0.2 and 0.5. Basically, b_h and b_w represent the box height and width. They are normalized with respect to the grid cell. If the bounding box is larger than the cell, its value will be greater than 1. Predicting the box parameters is a regression task.
   - p_c is a confidence score in the [0, 1] range. The labels for the confidence score are either 0 (not present) or 1 (present), making this part of the output a classification task. If an object is not present, we can discard the rest of the array values.
   - $c_1, c_2, ..., c_n$ is a one-hot encoding of the object class. For example, if we have car, person, tree, cat, and dog classes, and the current object is of the cat type, its encoding will be *[0, 0, 0, 1, 0]*. If we have n possible classes, the size of the output array for one cell will be $5 + n$ (9 in our example).

The network output/labels will contain $S \times S$ such arrays. For example, the length of the YOLO output for a 3×3 cell grid and four classes would be $3*3*9 = 81$.

3. Let's address the scenario with multiple objects in the same cell. Thankfully, YOLO proposes an elegant solution to this problem. We'll have multiple candidate boxes (known as **anchor boxes** or priors) with a slightly different shape associated with each cell. In the following diagram, we can see the grid cell (the square, uninterrupted line) and two anchor boxes—vertical and horizontal (the dashed lines). If we have multiple objects in the same cell, we'll associate each object with one of the anchor boxes. Conversely, if an anchor box doesn't have an associated object, it will have a confidence score of zero. This arrangement will also change the network output. We'll have multiple output arrays per grid cell (one output array per anchor box). To extend our previous example, let's assume we have a 3×3 cell grid with 4 classes and 2 anchor boxes per cell. Then, we'll have $3*3*2 = 18$ output bounding boxes and a total output length of $3*3*2*9 = 162$. Because we have a fixed number of cells (*S*×*S*) and a fixed number of anchor boxes per cell, the size of the network output doesn't change with the number of detected objects. Instead, the output will indicate whether an object is present in all possible anchor boxes.

In the following diagram, we can see a grid cell with two anchor boxes:

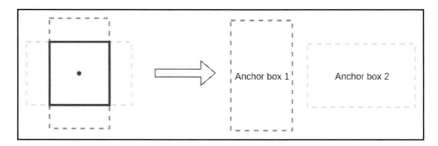

Grid cell (the square. uninterrupted line) with two anchor boxes (the dashed lines)

The only question now is how to choose the proper anchor box for an object during training (during inference, the network will choose by itself). We'll do this with the help of **Intersection over Union (IoU)**. This is just the ratio between the area of the intersection of the object bounding box/anchor box and the area of their union:

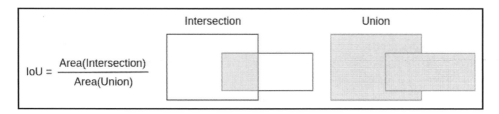

$$IoU = \frac{Area(Intersection)}{Area(Union)}$$

Intersection over Union

We'll compare the bounding box of each object to all anchor boxes, and assign the object to the anchor box with the highest IoU. Since the anchor boxes have varying sizes and shapes, IoU assures that the object will be assigned to the anchor box that most closely resembles its footprint on the image.

4. Now that we (hopefully) know how YOLO works, we can use it for predictions. However, the output of the network might be noisy—that is, the output includes all possible anchor boxes for each cell, regardless of whether an object is present in them. Many of the boxes will overlap and actually predict the same object. We'll get rid of the noise using **non-maximum suppression**. Here's how it works:

1. Discard all bounding boxes with a confidence score of less than or equal to 0.6.
2. From the remaining bounding boxes, pick the one with the highest possible confidence score.
3. Discard any box whose IoU >= 0.5 with the box we selected in the previous step.

If you are worried that the network output/groundtruth data will become too complex or large, don't be. CNNs work well with the ImageNet dataset, which has 1,000 categories, and therefore 1,000 outputs.

For more information about YOLO, check out the original sequence of papers:

- *You Only Look Once: Unified, Real-Time Object Detection* (https://arxiv.org/abs/1506.02640) by Joseph Redmon, Santosh Divvala, Ross Girshick, and Ali Farhadi
- *YOLO9000: Better, Faster, Stronger* (https://arxiv.org/abs/1612.08242) by Joseph Redmon and Ali Farhadi
- *YOLOv3: An Incremental Improvement* (https://arxiv.org/abs/1804.02767) by Joseph Redmon and Ali Farhadi

Now that we've introduced the theory of the YOLO algorithm, in the next section, we'll discuss how to use it in practice.

A code example of YOLOv3 with OpenCV

In this section, we'll demonstrate how to use the YOLOv3 object detector with OpenCV. For this example, you'll need `opencv-python` 4.1.1 or higher, and 250 MB of disk space for the pretrained YOLO network. Let's begin with the following steps:

1. Start with the imports:

```
import os.path

import cv2  # opencv import
import numpy as np
import requests
```

2. Add some boilerplate code that downloads and stores several configuration and data files. We'll start with the YOLOv3 network configuration `yolo_config` and `weights`, and we'll use them to initialize the `net` network. We'll use the YOLO author's GitHub and personal website to do this:

```
# Download YOLO net config file
# We'll it from the YOLO author's github repo
yolo_config = 'yolov3.cfg'
if not os.path.isfile(yolo_config):
    url =
'https://raw.githubusercontent.com/pjreddie/darknet/master/cfg/yolo
v3.cfg'
    r = requests.get(url)
    with open(yolo_config, 'wb') as f:
        f.write(r.content)

# Download YOLO net weights
# We'll it from the YOLO author's website
yolo_weights = 'yolov3.weights'
if not os.path.isfile(yolo_weights):
    url = 'https://pjreddie.com/media/files/yolov3.weights'
    r = requests.get(url)
    with open(yolo_weights, 'wb') as f:
        f.write(r.content)

# load the network
net = cv2.dnn.readNet(yolo_weights, yolo_config)
```

3. Next, we'll download the names of the COCO dataset classes that the network can detect. We'll also load them from the file. The dataset as presented in the COCO paper contains 91 categories. However, the dataset on the website contains only 80. YOLO uses the 80-category version:

```
# Download class names file
# Contains the names of the classes the network can detect
classes_file = 'coco.names'
if not os.path.isfile(classes_file):
    url = \
'https://raw.githubusercontent.com/pjreddie/darknet/master/data/coc
o.names'
    r = requests.get(url)
    with open(classes_file, 'wb') as f:
        f.write(r.content)

# load class names
with open(classes_file, 'r') as f:
    classes = [line.strip() for line in f.readlines()]
```

4. Then, download a test image from Wikipedia. We'll also load the image from the file in the `blob` variable:

```
# Download object detection image
image_file = 'source_1.png'
if not os.path.isfile(image_file):
    url = \
"https://github.com/ivan-vasilev/advanced-deep-learning-with-python
/blob/master/chapter04-detection-segmentation/source_1.png"
    r = requests.get(url)
    with open(image_file, 'wb') as f:
        f.write(r.content)

# read and normalize image
image = cv2.imread(image_file)
blob = cv2.dnn.blobFromImage(image, 1 / 255, (416, 416), (0, 0, 0),
True, crop=False)
```

5. Feed the image to the network and do the inference:

```
# set as input to the net
net.setInput(blob)

# get network output layers
layer_names = net.getLayerNames()
output_layers = [layer_names[i[0] - 1] for i in
net.getUnconnectedOutLayers()]

# inference
# the network outputs multiple lists of anchor boxes,
# one for each detected class
outs = net.forward(output_layers)
```

6. Iterate over the classes and anchor boxes and prepare them for the next step:

```
# extract bounding boxes
class_ids = list()
confidences = list()
boxes = list()

# iterate over all classes
for out in outs:
    # iterate over the anchor boxes for each class
    for detection in out:
        # bounding box
        center_x = int(detection[0] * image.shape[1])
        center_y = int(detection[1] * image.shape[0])
        w, h = int(detection[2] * image.shape[1]), int(detection[3]
* image.shape[0])
        x, y = center_x - w // 2, center_y - h // 2
        boxes.append([x, y, w, h])

        # confidence
        confidences.append(float(detection[4]))

        # class
        class_ids.append(np.argmax(detection[5:]))
```

7. Remove the noise with non-max suppression. You can experiment with different values for `score_threshold` and `nms_threshold` to see how the detected objects change:

```
# non-max suppression
ids = cv2.dnn.NMSBoxes(boxes, confidences, score_threshold=0.75,
nms_threshold=0.5)
```

8. Draw the bounding boxes and their captions on the image:

```
for i in ids:
    i = i[0]
    x, y, w, h = boxes[i]
    class_id = class_ids[i]

    color = colors[class_id]

    cv2.rectangle(img=image,
                  pt1=(round(x), round(y)),
                  pt2=(round(x + w), round(y + h)),
                  color=color,
                  thickness=3)

    cv2.putText(img=image,
                text=f"{classes[class_id]}: {confidences[i]:.2f}",
                org=(x - 10, y - 10),
                fontFace=cv2.FONT_HERSHEY_SIMPLEX,
                fontScale=0.8,
                color=color,
                thickness=2)
```

9. Finally, we can display the detected objects with the following code:

```
cv2.imshow("Object detection", image)
cv2.waitKey()
```

If everything goes alright, this code block will produce the same image that we saw at the beginning of the *Introduction to object detection* section.

This concludes our discussion about YOLO. In the next section, we'll introduce a two-stage object detector called Faster R-CNN (R-CNN stands for Regions with CNN).

Object detection with Faster R-CNN

In this section, we'll discuss a two-stage object detection algorithm called Faster R-CNN (*Faster R-CNN: Towards Real-Time Object Detection with Region Proposal Networks*, https://arxiv.org/abs/1506.01497). It is an evolution of the earlier two-stage detectors Fast R-CNN (https://arxiv.org/abs/1504.08083) and R-CNN (*Rich feature hierarchies for accurate object detection and semantic segmentation*, https://arxiv.org/abs/1311.2524).

We'll start by outlining the general structure of Faster R-CNN, which is displayed in the following diagram:

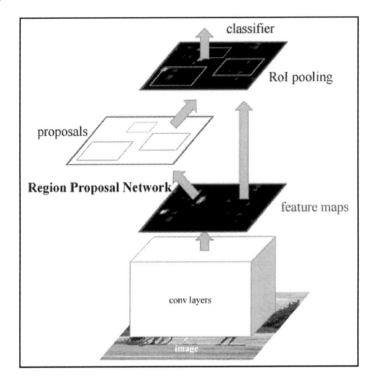

The structure of Faster R-CNN: source: https://arxiv.org/abs/1506.01497

Let's keep that figure in mind while we explain the algorithm. Like YOLO, Faster R-CNN starts with a backbone classification network trained on ImageNet, which serves as a base for the different modules of the model. The authors of the paper experimented with VGG16 and ZF net (*Visualizing and Understanding Convolutional Networks*, https://cs.nyu.edu/~fergus/papers/zeilerECCV2014.pdf) backbones. However, recent implementations use more contemporary architectures such as ResNets. The backbone net serves as a backbone (get it?) to the two other components of the model—the **region proposal network (RPN)** and the detection network. In the next section, we'll discuss the RPN.

Region proposal network

In the first stage, the RPN takes an image (of any size) as input and will output a set of rectangular regions of interest (RoIs), where an object might be located. The RPN itself is created by taking the first p (13 in the case of VGG and 5 for ZF net) convolutional layers of the backbone model (see the preceding diagram). Once the input image is propagated to the last shared convolutional layer, the algorithm takes the feature map of that layer and slides another small net over each location of the feature map. The small net outputs whether an object is present at any of the k anchor boxes over each location (the concept of anchor box is the same as in YOLO). This concept is illustrated on the left-hand side image of the following diagram, which shows a single location of the RPN sliding over a single feature map of the last convolutional layer:

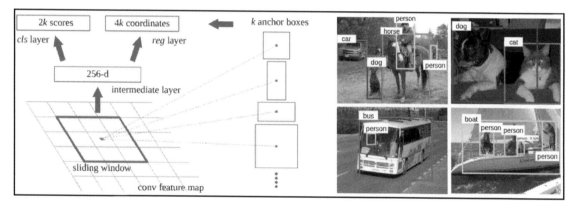

Left: RPN proposals over a single location: Right: example detections using RPN proposals (the labels are artificially enhanced). Source: https://arxiv.org/abs/1506.01497

The small net is fully connected to an $n \times n$ region at the same location over all input feature maps ($n = 3$ according to the paper). For example, if the final convolutional layer has 512 feature maps, then the small net input size at one location is 512 x 3 x 3 = 4,608. Each sliding window is mapped to a lower dimensional (512 for VGG and 256 for ZF net) vector. This vector itself serves as input to the following two parallel fully connected layers:

1. A classification layer with $2k$ units organized into k 2-unit binary softmax outputs. The output of each softmax represents a confidence score of whether an object is located in each of the k anchor boxes. The paper refers to the confidence score as **objectness**, which measures whether the anchor box content belongs to a set of objects versus background. During training, an object is assigned to an anchor box based on the IoU formula in the same way as in YOLO.

2. A regression layer with *4k* units organized into *k* 4-unit RoI coordinates. 2 of the 4 units represent the coordinates of the RoI center in the [0:1] range relative to the whole image. The other two coordinates represent the height and width of the region, relative to the whole image (again, similar to YOLO).

The authors of the paper experimented with three scales and three aspect ratios, resulting in nine possible anchor boxes over each location. The typical HxW size of the final feature map is around 2,400, which results in 2,400*9 = 21,600 anchor boxes.

In theory, we slide the small net over the feature map of the last convolutional layer. However, the small net weights are shared along all locations. Because of this, the sliding can be implemented as a cross-channel convolution. Therefore, the network can produce output for all anchor boxes in a single image pass. This is an improvement over Fast R-CNN, which requires a separate network pass for each anchor box.

The RPN is trained with backpropagation and stochastic gradient descent (what a surprise!). The shared convolutional layers are initialized with the weights of the backbone net and the rest are initialized randomly. The samples of each mini-batch are extracted from a single image, which contains many positive (objects) and negative (background) anchor boxes. The sampling ratio between the two types is 1:1. Each anchor is assigned a binary class label (of being an object or not). There are two kinds of anchors with positive labels: the anchor/anchors with the highest IoU overlap with a groundtruth box or an anchor that has an IoU overlap of higher than 0.7 with any groundtruth box. If the IoU ratio of an anchor is lower than 0.3, the box is assigned a negative label. Anchors that are neither positive nor negative do not participate in the training.

As the RPN has two output layers (classification and regression), the training uses the following composite cost function:

$$L(\{p_i\}, \{t_i\}) = \underbrace{\frac{1}{N_{cls}} \sum_i L_{cls}(p_i, p_i^*)}_{\text{classification cost}} + \underbrace{\lambda \frac{1}{N_{reg}} \sum_i p_i^* L_{reg}(t_i, t_i^*)}_{\text{regression cost}}$$

Let's discuss it in detail:

- *i* is the index of the anchor in the mini-batch.
- p_i is the classification output, which represents the predicted probability of anchor *i* being an object. Note p_i^* is the target data for the same (0 or 1).
- t_i is the regression output vector of size 4, which represents the RoI parameters. As in YOLO, the t_i^* is the target vector for the same.

- L_{cls} is a cross-entropy loss for the classification layer. N_{cls} is a normalization term equal to the mini-batch size.
- L_{reg} is the regression loss. $L_{reg} = R(t_i - t_i^*)$, where R is the mean absolute error (see the *Cost functions* section in `Chapter 1`, *The Nuts and Bolts of Neural Networks*). N_{reg} is a normalization term equal to the total number of anchor locations (around 2,400).

Finally, the classification and regression components of the cost function are combined with the help of the λ parameter. Since $N_{reg} \sim 2400$ and $N_{cls} = 256$, λ is set to 10 to preserve the balance between the two losses.

Detection network

Now that we've discussed the RPN, let's focus on the detection network. To do this, we'll go back to the diagram *The structure of Faster R-CNN* at the beginning of the *Object detection with Faster R-CNN* section. Let's recall that in the first stage, the RPN already generated the RoI coordinates. The detection network is a regular classifier, which determines the type of object (or background) in the current RoI. Both the RPN and the detection net share their first convolutional layers, borrowed from the backbone net. But the detection net also incorporates the proposed regions from the RPN, along with the feature maps of the last shared layer.

But how do we combine the inputs? We can do this with the help of **Region of Interest (RoI)** max pooling, which is the first layer of the second part of the detection network. An example of this operation is displayed in the following diagram:

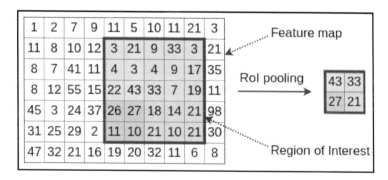

An example of 2×2 RoI max pooling with a 10×7 feature map and a 5×5 region of interest (blue rectangle)

For the sake of simplicity, we'll assume that we have a single *10×7* feature map and a single RoI. As we learned in the *Region proposal network* section, the RoI is defined by its coordinates, width, and height. The operation converts these parameters to actual coordinates on the feature map. In this example, the region size is $h \times w = 5 \times 5$. The RoI max pooling is further defined by its output height, H, and width, W. In this example, $H \times W = 2 \times 2$, but in practice the values could be larger, such as 7×7. The operation splits the $h \times w$ RoI into a grid with $(h / H) \times (w / W)$ subregions.

As we can see from the example, the subregions might have different sizes. Once this is done, each subregion is downsampled to a single output cell by taking the maximum value of that region. In other words, RoI pooling can transform inputs with arbitrary sizes into a fixed-size output window. In this way, the transformed data can propagate through the network in a consistent format.

As we mentioned in the *Object detection with Faster R-CNN* section, the RPN and the detection network share their initial layers. However, they start their life as separate networks. The training alternates between the two in a four-step process:

1. Train the RPN, which is initialized with the ImageNet weights of the backbone net.
2. Train the detection network, using the proposals from the freshly trained RPN from *step 1*. The training also starts with the weights of the ImageNet backbone net. At this point, the two networks don't share weights.
3. Use the detection net shared layers to initialize the weights of the RPN. Then, train the RPN again, but freeze the shared layers and fine-tune the RPN-specific layers only. The two networks share weights now.
4. Train the detection net by freezing the shared layers and fine-tuning the detection-net-specific layers only.

Now that we've introduced Faster R-CNN, in the next section, we'll discuss how to use it in practice with the help of a pretrained PyTorch model.

Implementing Faster R-CNN with PyTorch

In this section, we'll use a pretrained PyTorch Faster R-CNN with a ResNet50 backbone for object detection. This example requires PyTorch 1.3.1, torchvision 0.4.2, and python-opencv 4.1.1:

1. We'll start with the imports:

   ```
   import os.path

   import cv2
   import numpy as np
   import requests
   import torchvision
   import torchvision.transforms as transforms
   ```

2. Next, we'll continue with downloading the input image, and we'll define the class names in the COCO dataset. This step is the same as the one we implemented in the *A code example of YOLOv3 with OpenCV* section. The path to the download image is stored in the `image_file = 'source_2.png'` variable, and the class names are stored in the `classes` list. This implementation uses the full 91 COCO categories.

3. We'll load the pretrained Faster R-CNN model, and we'll set it to evaluation mode:

   ```
   # load the pytorch model
   model =
   torchvision.models.detection.fasterrcnn_resnet50_fpn(pretrained=Tru
   e)

   # set the model in evaluation mode
   model.eval()
   ```

4. Then, we'll read the image file with OpenCV:

   ```
   img = cv2.imread(image_file)
   ```

5. We'll define the PyTorch `transform` sequence, we'll transform the image to a PyTorch compatible tensor, and we'll feed it to the net. The network output is stored in the `output` variable. As we discussed in the *Region Proposal Network* section, `output` contains three components: `boxes` for the bounding box parameters, `classes` for the object class, and `scores` for confidence scores. The model applies NMS internally, and there is no need to do it in the code:

```
transform = transforms.Compose([transforms.ToPILImage(),
transforms.ToTensor()])
nn_input = transform(img)
output = model([nn_input])
```

6. Before we continue with displaying the detected objects, we'll define a set of random colors for each class of the COCO dataset:

```
colors = np.random.uniform(0, 255, size=(len(classes), 3))
```

7. We iterate over each bounding box and draw it on the image:

```
# iterate over the network output for all boxes
for box, box_class, score in
zip(output[0]['boxes'].detach().numpy(),
output[0]['labels'].detach().numpy(),
output[0]['scores'].detach().numpy()):

    # filter the boxes by score
    if score > 0.5:
        # transform bounding box format
        box = [(box[0], box[1]), (box[2], box[3])]

        # select class color
        color = colors[box_class]

        # extract class name
        class_name = classes[box_class]

        # draw the bounding box
        cv2.rectangle(img=img, pt1=box[0], pt2=box[1], color=color,
thickness=2)

        # display the box class label
        cv2.putText(img=img, text=class_name, org=box[0],
                    fontFace=cv2.FONT_HERSHEY_SIMPLEX, fontScale=1,
color=color, thickness=2)
```

Drawing the bounding boxes involves the following steps:

- Filter the boxes with a confidence score of less than 0.5 to prevent noisy detections.
- The bounding `box` parameters (extracted from `output['boxes']`) contain the top-left and bottom-right absolute (pixel) coordinates of the bounding box on the image. They are only transformed in tuples to fit the OpenCV format.
- Extract the class name and the color for the bounding box.
- Draw the bounding box and the class name.

8. Finally, we can display the detection result with the following code:

```
cv2.imshow("Object detection", image)
cv2.waitKey()
```

This code will produce the following result (the passengers on the bus are also detected):

Faster R-CNN object detection

This concludes the section about object detection. To summarize, we discussed two of the most popular detection models—YOLO and Faster R-CNN. In the next section, we'll talk about image segmentation—you can think of it as classification on the pixel level.

Introducing image segmentation

Image segmentation is the process of assigning a class label (such as person, car, or tree) to each pixel of an image. You can think of it as classification, but on a pixel level—instead of classifying the entire image under one label, we'll classify each pixel separately. There are two types of segmentation:

- **Semantic segmentation**: This assigns a class to each pixel, but doesn't differentiate between object instances. For example, the middle image in the following screenshot shows a semantic segmentation mask, where the pixels of each vehicle have the same value. Semantic segmentation can tell us that a pixel is part of a vehicle, but cannot make a distinction between two vehicles.
- **Instance segmentation**: This assigns a class to each pixel and differentiates between object instances. For example, the image on the right in the following screenshot shows an instance segmentation mask, where each vehicle is segmented as a separate object.

The following screenshot shows an example of semantic and instance segmentation:

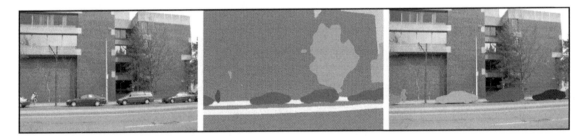

Left: input image: middle: semantic segmentation: right: instance segmentation: source: http://sceneparsing.csail.mit.edu/

To train a segmentation algorithm, we'll need a special type of groundtruth data, where the labels of each image are the segmented version of the image.

The easiest way to segment an image is by using the familiar sliding-window technique, which we described in the *Approaches to object detection* section. That is, we'll use a regular classifier and we'll slide it in either direction with stride 1. After we get the prediction for a location, we'll take the pixel that lies in the middle of the input region and we'll assign it with the predicted class. Predictably, this approach is very slow because of the large number of pixels in an image (even a 1024×1024 image has more than 1 million pixels). Thankfully, there are faster and more accurate algorithms, which we'll discuss in the following sections.

Semantic segmentation with U-Net

The first approach to segmentation we'll discuss is called U-Net (*U-Net: Convolutional Networks for Biomedical Image Segmentation*, `https://arxiv.org/abs/1505.04597`). The name comes from the visualization of the network architecture. U-Net is a type of **fully convolutional network** (**FCN**), called so because it contains only convolutional layers and doesn't have any fully connected layers. An FCN takes the whole image as input, and outputs its segmentation map in a single pass. We can separate an FCN into two virtual components (in reality, this is just a single network):

- The encoder is the first part of the network. It is similar to a regular CNN, without the fully connected layers at the end. The role of the encoder is to learn highly abstract representations of the input image (nothing new here).
- The decoder is the second part of the network. It starts after the encoder and uses it as input. The role of the decoder is to translate these abstract representations into the segmented groundtruth data. To do this, the decoder uses the opposite of the encoder operations. This includes transposed convolutions (the opposite of convolutions) and unpooling (the opposite of pooling).

With that introduction, here is U-Net in all its glory:

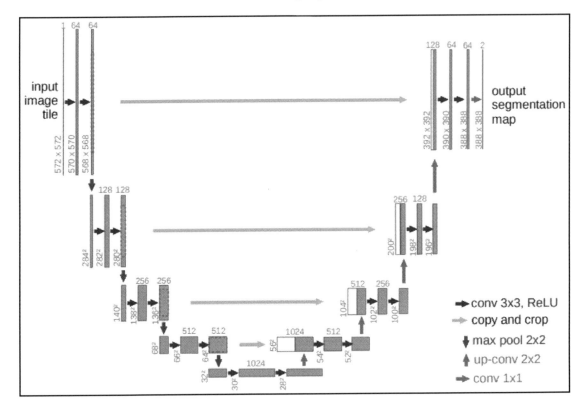

The U-Net architecture: source: https://arxiv.org/abs/1505.04597

Each blue box corresponds to a multichannel feature map. The number of channels is denoted on top of the box, and the feature map size is at the lower-left edge of the box. White boxes represent copied feature maps. The arrows denote the different operations (displayed on the legend as well). The left part of the *U* is the encoder, and the right part is the decoder.

Next, let's segment (get it?) the U-Net modules:

- **Encoder**: the network takes as input a 572×572 RGB image. From there, it continues like a regular CNN with alternating convolutional and max pooling layers. The encoder consists of four blocks of the following layers.
  - Two consecutive cross-channel unpadded 3×3 convolutions with stride 1.
  - A 2×2 max pooling layer.
  - ReLU activations.
  - Each downsampling step doubles the number of feature maps.
  - The final encoder convolution ends with 1,024 28×28 feature maps.
- **Decoder**: This is symmetrical to the encoder. The decoder takes the innermost 28×28 feature maps and simultaneously upsamples and converts them to a 388×388 segmentation map. It contains four upsampling blocks:
  - The upsampling works with 2×2 transposed convolutions with stride 2 (`Chapter 2`, *Understanding Convolutional Networks*), denoted by green vertical arrows.
  - The output of each upsampling step is concatenated with the cropped high-resolution feature maps of the corresponding encoder step (grey horizontal arrows). The cropping is necessary because of the loss of border pixels in every convolution.
  - Each transposed convolution is followed by two regular convolutions to smooth the expanded image.
  - The upsampling steps halve the number of feature maps. The final output uses a 1×1 bottleneck convolution to map the 64-component feature map tensor to the desired number of classes. The authors of the paper have demonstrated the binary segmentation of medical images of cells.
  - The network output is a softmax over each pixel. That is, the output contains as many independent softmax operations as the number of pixels. The softmax output for one pixel determines the pixel class. The U-Net is trained like a regular classification network. However, the cost function is a combination of the cross-entropy losses of the softmax outputs over all pixels.

We can see that because of the valid (unpadded) convolutions of the network, the output segmentation map is smaller than the input image (388 versus 572). However, the output map is not a rescaled version of the input image. Instead, it has a one-to-one scale compared to the input, but only covers the central part of the input tile.

This is illustrated in the following diagram:

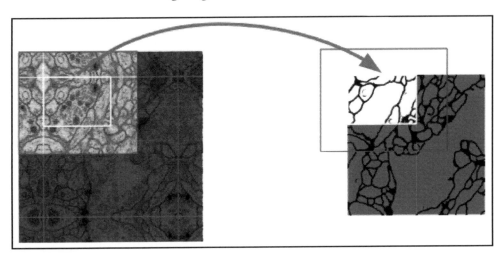

An overlap-tile strategy for segmenting large images: source: https://arxiv.org/abs/1505.04597

The unpadded convolutions are necessary, so the network doesn't produce noisy artifacts at the borders of the segmentation map. This makes it possible to segment images with arbitrary large sizes using the so called overlap-tile strategy. The input image is split in overlapping input tiles, like the one on the left of the preceding diagram. The segmentation map of the small light area in the image on the right requires the large light area (one tile) on the left image as input.

The next input tile overlaps with the previous one in such a way that their segmentation maps cover adjacent areas of the image. To predict the pixels in the border region of the image, the missing context is extrapolated by mirroring the input image. In the next section, we'll discuss Mask R-CNN—a model, which extends Faster R-CNN for instance segmentation.

Instance segmentation with Mask R-CNN

Mask R-CNN (https://arxiv.org/abs/1703.06870) is an extension of Faster R-CNN for instance segmentation. Faster R-CNN has two outputs for each candidate object: bounding box parameters and class labels. In addition to these, Mask R-CNN adds a third output—an FCN that produces a binary segmentation mask for each RoI. The following diagram shows the structure of Mask R-CNN:

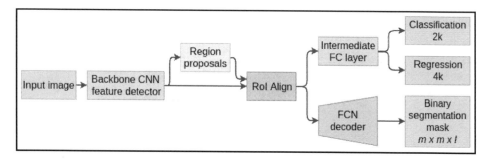

Mask R-CNN

The RPN produces anchors in five scales and three aspect ratios. The segmentation and classification paths both use the RoI predictions of the RPN, but otherwise are independent of each other. The segmentation path produces *I* $m{\times}m$ binary segmentation masks, one for each of the *I* classes. At training or inference, only the mask related to the predicted class of the classification path is considered and the rest are discarded. The class prediction and segmentation are parallel and decoupled—the classification path predicts the class of the segmented object, and the segmentation path determines the mask.

Mask R-CNN replaces the RoI max pooling operation with a more accurate RoI align layer. The RPN outputs the anchor box center, and its height and width as four floating point numbers. Then, the RoI pooling layer translates them to integer feature map cell coordinates (quantization). Additionally, the division of the RoI to $H{\times}W$ bins also involves quantization. The RoI example from the *Object detection with Faster R-CNN* section shows that the bins have different sizes (3×3, 3×2, 2×3, 2×2). These two quantization levels can introduce misalignment between the RoI and the extracted features. The following diagram shows how RoI alignment solves this problem:

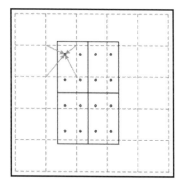

RoI align example: source: https://arxiv.org/abs/1703.06870

The dashed lines represent the feature map cells. The region with solid lines in the middle is a 2×2 RoI overlaid on the feature map. Note that it doesn't match the cells exactly. Instead, it is located according to the RPN prediction without quantization. In the same way, a cell of the RoI (the black dots) doesn't match one particular cell of the feature map. The RoI align operation computes the value of an RoI cell with a bilinear interpolation of its adjacent cells. In this way, RoI align is more accurate than RoI pooling.

At training, an RoI is assigned a positive label if it has IoU with a groundtruth box of at least 0.5, and negative otherwise. The mask target is the intersection between an RoI and its associated groundtruth mask. Only the positive RoIs participate in the segmentation path training.

Implementing Mask R-CNN with PyTorch

In this section, we'll use a pretrained PyTorch Mask R-CNN with a ResNet50 backbone for instance segmentation. This example requires PyTorch 1.1.0, torchvision 0.3.0, and OpenCV 3.4.2. This example is very similar to the one we implemented in the *Implementing Faster R-CNN with PyTorch* section. Because of this, we'll omit some parts of the code to avoid repetition. Let's start:

1. The imports, `classes`, and `image_file` are the same as in the Faster R-CNN example.
2. The first difference between the two examples is that we'll load the Mask R-CNN pretrained model:

```
model =
torchvision.models.detection.maskrcnn_resnet50_fpn(pretrained=True)
model.eval()
```

3. We feed the input image to the network and obtain the `output` variable:

```
# read the image file
img = cv2.imread(image_file)

# transform the input to tensor
transform = transforms.Compose([transforms.ToPILImage(),
transforms.ToTensor()])
nn_input = transform(img)
output = model([nn_input])
```

Besides `boxes`, `classes`, and `scores`, `output` contains an additional `masks` component for the predicted segmentation masks.

4. We iterate over the masks and overlay them on the image. The image and the mask are `numpy` arrays, and we can implement the overlay as a vector operation. We'll display both the bounding boxes and the segmentation masks:

```
# iterate over the network output for all boxes
for mask, box, score in zip(output[0]['masks'].detach().numpy(),
                            output[0]['boxes'].detach().numpy(),
                            output[0]['scores'].detach().numpy()):

    # filter the boxes by score
    if score > 0.5:
        # transform bounding box format
        box = [(box[0], box[1]), (box[2], box[3])]

        # overlay the segmentation mask on the image with random
color
        img[(mask > 0.5).squeeze(), :] = np.random.uniform(0, 255,
size=3)

        # draw the bounding box
        cv2.rectangle(img=img,
                      pt1=box[0],
                      pt2=box[1],
                      color=(255, 255, 255),
                      thickness=2)
```

5. Finally, we can display the segmentation result as follows:

```
cv2.imshow("Object detection", img)
cv2.waitKey()
```

This example will produce the image on the right as follows (the original on the left is for comparison):

Mask R-CNN instance segmentation

We can see that each segmentation mask is defined only within its bounding box, where all values of the segmentation mask are greater than zero. To obtain the actual pixels that belong to the object, we apply the mask only over the pixels, whose segmentation confidence score is greater than 0.5 (this code snippet is part of step 4 of the Mask R-CNN code example):

```
img[(mask > 0.5).squeeze(), :] = np.random.uniform(0, 255, size=3)
```

This concludes the section of the chapter devoted to image segmentation (in fact, it concludes the chapter itself).

Summary

In this chapter, we discussed object detection and image segmentation. We started with the one-shot detection algorithm, YOLO, and then we continued with the two-stage Faster R-CNN algorithm. Next, we discussed the semantic segmentation network architecture, U-Net. Finally, we talked about Mask R-CNN—an extension of Faster R-CNN for instance segmentation.

In the next chapter, we'll explore new types of ML algorithms called generative models. We can use them to generate new content, such as images. Stay tuned—it will be fun!

5
Generative Models

In the previous two chapters (Chapter 4, *Advanced Convolutional Networks*, and Chapter 5, *Object Detection and Image Segmentation*), we focused on supervised computer vision problems, such as classification and object detection. In this chapter, we'll discuss how to create new images with the help of unsupervised neural networks. After all, it's a lot better knowing that you don't need labeled data. More specifically, we'll talk about generative models.

This chapter will cover the following topics:

- Intuition and justification of generative models
- Introduction to **Variational Autoencoders (VAEs)**
- Introduction to **Generative Adversarial Networks (GANs)**
- Types of GAN
- Introducing to artistic style transfer

Intuition and justification of generative models

So far, we've used neural networks as **discriminative models**. This simply means that, given input data, a discriminative model will map it to a certain label (in other words, a classification). A typical example is the classification of MNIST images in 1 of 10 digit classes, where the neural network maps input data features (pixel intensities) to the digit label. We can also say this in another way: a discriminative model gives us the probability of y (class), given x (input). In the case of MNIST, this is the probability of the digit when given the pixel intensities of the image.

On the other hand, a generative model learns how classes are distributed. You can think of it as the opposite of what the discriminative model does. Instead of predicting the class probability, y, given certain input features, it tries to predict the probability of the input features when given a class, $y \sim P(X|Y = y)$. For example, a generative model will be able to create an image of a handwritten digit when given the digit class. Since we only have 10 classes, it will be able to generate just 10 images. However, we've only used this example to illustrate this concept. In reality, the y *class* could be an arbitrary tensor of values, and the model would be able to generate an unlimited number of images with different features. If you don't understand this now, don't worry; we'll look at many examples throughout this chapter.

> Throughout this chapter, we'll denote probability distribution with a lower-case p, rather than the usual upper-case P that we used in the previous chapters. We are doing this to follow the convention that has been established in the context of VAEs and GANs. While writing this book, I couldn't find a definitive reason to use lower-case, but one possible explanation is that P denotes the probability of events, while p denotes the probability of the mass (or density) functions of a random variable.

Two of the most popular ways to use neural networks in a generative way is via VAEs and GANs. In the next section, we'll introduce VAEs.

Introduction to VAEs

To understand VAEs, we need to talk about regular autoencoders. An autoencoder is a feed-forward neural network that tries to reproduce its input. In other words, the target value (label) of an autoencoder is equal to the input data, $y^i = x^i$, where i is the sample index. We can formally say that it tries to learn an identity function, $h_{\mathbf{w},\mathbf{w}'}(\mathbf{x}) = \mathbf{x}$ (a function that repeats its input). Since our labels are just input data, the autoencoder is an unsupervised algorithm.

The following diagram represents an autoencoder:

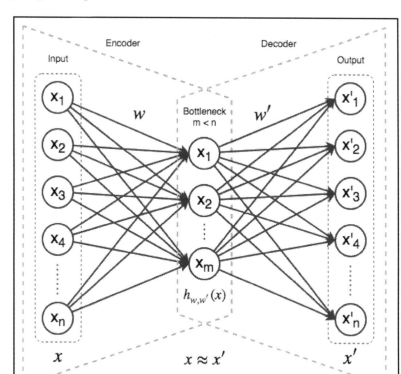

An autoencoder

An autoencoder consists of input, hidden (or bottleneck), and output layers. Similar to U-Net (Chapter 4, *Object Detection and Image Segmentation*), we can think of the autoencoder as a virtual composition of two components:

- **Encoder**: Maps the input data to the network's internal representation. For the sake of simplicity, in this example the encoder is a single, fully connected hidden bottleneck layer. The internal state is just its activation vector. In general, the encoder can have multiple hidden layers, including convolutional ones.
- **Decoder**: Tries to reconstruct the input from the network's internal data representation. The decoder can also have a complex structure that typically mirrors the encoder. While U-Net tries to translate the input image into a target image of some other domain (for example, a segmentation map), the autoencoder simply tries to reconstruct its input.

We can train the autoencoder by minimizing a loss function, which is known as the **reconstruction error**, $J = (\mathbf{x}, \mathbf{x}')$. It measures the distance between the original input and its reconstruction. We can minimize it in the usual way, that is, with gradient descent and backpropagation. Depending on the approach we use, we can use either use **mean square error** (**MSE**) or binary cross-entropy (such as cross-entropy, but with two classes) as reconstruction errors.

At this point, you may be wondering what the point of the autoencoder is since it just repeats its input. However, we aren't interested in the network output, but in its internal data representation (which is also known as representation in the **latent space**). The latent space contains hidden data features that are not directly observed but are inferred by the algorithm instead. The key is that the bottleneck layer has fewer neurons than the input/output ones. There are two main reasons for this:

- Because the network tries to reconstruct its input from a smaller feature space, it learns a compact representation of the data. You can think of this as compression (but not lossless).
- By using fewer neurons, the network is forced to learn only the most important features of the data. To illustrate this concept, let's look at denoising autoencoders, where we intentionally use corrupted input data, but non-corrupted target data during training. For example, if we train a denoising autoencoder to reconstruct MNIST images, we can introduce noise by setting the max intensity (white) to random pixels of the image (as shown in the following screenshot). To minimize the loss with the noiseless target, the autoencoder is forced to look beyond the noise in the input and learn only the important features of the data. However, if the network had more hidden neurons than input, it might overfit on the noise. With the additional constraint of fewer hidden neurons, it can only try to ignore the noise. Once trained, we can use a denoising autoencoder to remove the noise from real images:

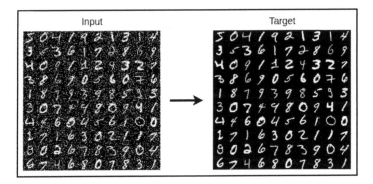

Denoising autoencoder input and target

The encoder maps each input sample to the latent space, where each attribute of the latent representation has a discrete value. This means that an input sample can have only one latent representation. Therefore, the decoder can reconstruct the input in only one possible way. In other words, we can generate a single reconstruction of one input sample. But we don't want this. Instead, we want to generate new images that are different from the original ones. VAEs are one possible solution to this task.

A VAE can describe a latent representation in probabilistic terms. That is, instead of discrete values, we'll have a probability distribution for each latent attribute, making the latent space continuous. This makes it easier for random sampling and interpolation. Let's illustrate this with an example. Imagine that we are trying to encode an image of a vehicle and our latent representation is a vector, $\mathbf{z}$, with n elements (n neurons in the bottleneck layer). Each element represents one vehicle property, such as length, height, and width (as shown in the following diagram).

Say that the average vehicle length is four meters. Instead of the fixed value, the VAE can decode this property as a normal distribution with a mean of 4 (the same applies for the others). Then, the decoder can choose to sample a latent variable from the range of its distribution. For example, it can reconstruct a longer and lower vehicle compared to the input. By doing this, the VAE can generate an unlimited number of modified versions of the input:

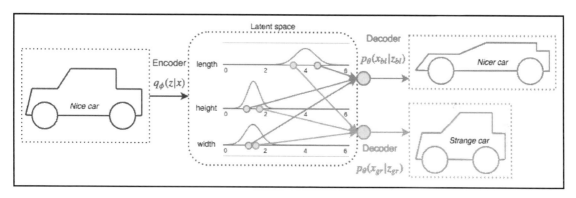

An example of a variational encoder sampling different values from the distribution ranges of the latent variables

Let's formalize this:

- The goal of the encoder is to approximate the real probability distribution, $p(\mathbf{z})$, where $\mathbf{z}$ is the latent space representation. However, it does so indirectly by inferring $p(\mathbf{z})$ from the conditional probability distribution of various samples, $p(\mathbf{z}|\mathbf{x})$, where $\mathbf{x}$ is the input data. In other words, the encoder tries to learn the probability distribution of $\mathbf{z}$, given the input data, $\mathbf{x}$. We'll denote the encoder's approximation of $p(\mathbf{z}|\mathbf{x})$ with $q_\varphi(\mathbf{z}|\mathbf{x})$, where φ are the weights of the network. The encoder output is a probability distribution (for example, Gaussian) over the possible values of $\mathbf{z}$, which could have been generated by $\mathbf{x}$. During training, we continuously update the weights, φ, to bring $q_\varphi(\mathbf{z}|\mathbf{x})$ closer to the real $P(\mathbf{z}|\mathbf{x})$.

- The goal of the decoder is to approximate the real probability distribution, . In other words, the decoder tries to learn the conditional probability distribution of the data, x, given the latent representation, $\mathbf{z}$. We'll denote the decoder's approximation of the real probability distribution with $p_\theta(\mathbf{x}|\mathbf{z})$, where θ is the decoder weights. The process starts by sampling $\mathbf{z}$ stochastically (randomly) from the probability distribution (for example, Gaussian). Then, $\mathbf{z}$ is sent through the decoder, whose output is a probability distribution over the possible corresponding values of x. During training, we continuously update the weights, θ, to bring $p_\theta(\mathbf{x}|\mathbf{z})$ closer to the real $p(\mathbf{x}|\mathbf{z})$.

The VAE uses a special type of loss function with two terms:

$$L(\theta, \varphi; \mathbf{x}) = -D_{KL}(q_\varphi(\mathbf{z}|\mathbf{x})\|p_\theta(\mathbf{z})) + E_{q_\varphi(\mathbf{z}|\mathbf{x})}[\log(p_\theta(\mathbf{x}|\mathbf{z}))]$$

The first is the Kullback-Leibler divergence (Chapter 1, *The Nuts and Bolts of Neural Networks*) between the probability distribution, $q_\varphi(\mathbf{z}|\mathbf{x})$, and the expected probability distribution, $p(\mathbf{z})$. In this context, it measures how much information is lost when we use $q_\varphi(\mathbf{z}|\mathbf{x})$ to represent $p(\mathbf{z})$ (in other words, how close the two distributions are). It encourages the autoencoder to explore different reconstructions. The second is the reconstruction loss, which measures the difference between the original input and its reconstruction. The more they differ, the more it increases. Therefore, it encourages the autoencoder to reconstruct data in a better way.

To implement this, the bottleneck layer won't directly output latent state variables. Instead, it will output two vectors, which describe the **mean** and **variance** of the distribution of each latent variable:

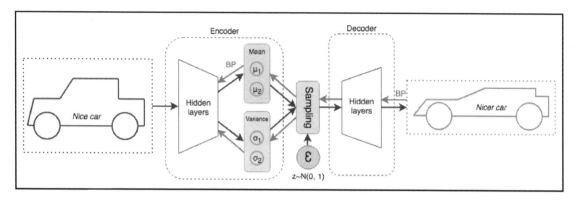

Variational encoder sampling

Once we have the mean and variance distributions, we can sample a state, **z**, from the latent variable distributions and pass it through the decoder for reconstruction. But we can't celebrate yet. This presents us with another problem: backpropagation doesn't work over random processes such as the one we have here. Fortunately, we can solve this with the so-called **reparameterization trick**. First, we'll sample a random vector, ε, with the same dimensions as **z** from a Gaussian distribution (the ε circle in the preceding diagram). Then, we'll shift it by the latent distribution's mean, μ, and scale it by the latent distribution's variance, σ:

$$\mathbf{z} = \mu + \sigma \odot \varepsilon$$

In this way, we'll be able to optimize the mean and variance (red arrows) and we'll omit the random generator from the backward pass. At the same time, the sampled data will have the properties of the original distribution. Now that we've introduced VAEs, we'll learn how to implement one.

Generating new MNIST digits with VAE

In this section, we'll learn how a VAE can generate new digits for the MNIST dataset. We'll use Keras under TF 2.0.0 to do so. We chose MNIST because it will illustrate VAE's generative capabilities well.

The code in this section is partially based on https://github.com/keras-team/keras/blob/master/examples/variational_autoencoder.py.

Let's go through the implementation, step by step:

1. Let's start with the imports. We'll use the Keras module, which is integrated in TF:

```
import matplotlib.pyplot as plt
from matplotlib.markers import MarkerStyle
import numpy as np
import tensorflow as tf
from tensorflow.keras import backend as K
from tensorflow.keras.layers import Lambda, Input, Dense
from tensorflow.keras.losses import binary_crossentropy
from tensorflow.keras.models import Model
```

2. Now, we will instantiate the MNIST dataset. Recall that in Chapter 2, *Understanding Convolutional Networks*, we implemented a transfer learning example with TF/Keras, where we used the tensorflow_datasets module to load the CIFAR-10 dataset. In this example, we'll use the keras.datasets module to load MNIST, which also works:

```
(x_train, y_train), (x_test, y_test) =
tf.keras.datasets.mnist.load_data()

image_size = x_train.shape[1] * x_train.shape[1]
x_train = np.reshape(x_train, [-1, image_size])
x_test = np.reshape(x_test, [-1, image_size])
x_train = x_train.astype('float32') / 255
x_test = x_test.astype('float32') / 255
```

3. Next, we'll implement the build_vae function, which will build the VAE:
   - We'll have separate access to the encoder, decoder, and the full network. The function will return them as a tuple.
   - The bottleneck layer will have only 2 neurons (that is, we'll have only 2 latent variables). In this way, we'll be able to display the latent distribution as a 2D plot.
   - The encoder/decoder will contain a single intermediate (hidden) fully-connected layer with 512 neurons. This is not a convolutional network.
   - We'll use cross-entropy reconstruction loss and KL divergence.

The following shows how this is implemented globally:

```
def build_vae(intermediate_dim=512, latent_dim=2):
    # encoder first
    inputs = Input(shape=(image_size,), name='encoder_input')
```

```
x = Dense(intermediate_dim, activation='relu')(inputs)

# latent mean and variance
z_mean = Dense(latent_dim, name='z_mean')(x)
z_log_var = Dense(latent_dim, name='z_log_var')(x)

# Reparameterization trick for random sampling
# Note the use of the Lambda layer
# At runtime, it will call the sampling function
z = Lambda(sampling, output_shape=(latent_dim,),
name='z')([z_mean, z_log_var])

# full encoder encoder model
encoder = Model(inputs, [z_mean, z_log_var, z], name='encoder')
encoder.summary()

# decoder
latent_inputs = Input(shape=(latent_dim,), name='z_sampling')
x = Dense(intermediate_dim, activation='relu')(latent_inputs)
outputs = Dense(image_size, activation='sigmoid')(x)

# full decoder model
decoder = Model(latent_inputs, outputs, name='decoder')
decoder.summary()

# VAE model
outputs = decoder(encoder(inputs)[2])
vae = Model(inputs, outputs, name='vae')

# Loss function
# we start with the reconstruction loss
reconstruction_loss = binary_crossentropy(inputs, outputs) *
image_size

# next is the KL divergence
kl_loss = 1 + z_log_var - K.square(z_mean) - K.exp(z_log_var)
kl_loss = K.sum(kl_loss, axis=-1)
kl_loss *= -0.5

# we combine them in a total loss
vae_loss = K.mean(reconstruction_loss + kl_loss)
vae.add_loss(vae_loss)

return encoder, decoder, vae
```

4. Immediately tied to the network definition is the `sampling` function, which implements a random sampling of latent vectors z from the Gaussian unit (this is the reparameterization trick we introduced in the *Introduction to VAEs* section):

```
def sampling(args: tuple):
    """
    :param args: (tensor, tensor) mean and log of variance of
    q(z|x)
    """

    # unpack the input tuple
    z_mean, z_log_var = args

    # mini-batch size
    mb_size = K.shape(z_mean)[0]

    # latent space size
    dim = K.int_shape(z_mean)[1]

    # random normal vector with mean=0 and std=1.0
    epsilon = K.random_normal(shape=(mb_size, dim))

    return z_mean + K.exp(0.5 * z_log_var) * epsilon
```

5. Now, we need to implement the `plot_latent_distribution` function. It collects the latent representations of all the images in the test set and displays them over a 2D plot. We can do this because our network has only two latent variables (for the two axes of the plot). Note that to implement this we only need the `encoder`:

```
def plot_latent_distribution(encoder, x_test, y_test,
batch_size=128):
    z_mean, _, _ = encoder.predict(x_test, batch_size=batch_size)
    plt.figure(figsize=(6, 6))

    markers = ('o', 'x', '^', '<', '>', '*', 'h', 'H', 'D', 'd',
    'P', 'X', '8', 's', 'p')

    for i in np.unique(y_test):
        plt.scatter(z_mean[y_test == i, 0], z_mean[y_test == i, 1],
                            marker=MarkerStyle(markers[i],
                            fillstyle='none'),
                            edgecolors='black')

    plt.xlabel("z[0]")
    plt.ylabel("z[1]")
    plt.show()
```

6. Next, we will implement the `plot_generated_images` function. It will sample n*n vectors, z, in a [-4, 4] range for each of the two latent variables. Next, it will generate images based on the sampled vectors and display them in a 2D grid. Note that to do this we only need the `decoder`:

```
def plot_generated_images(decoder):
    # display a nxn 2D manifold of digits
    n = 15
    digit_size = 28

    figure = np.zeros((digit_size * n, digit_size * n))
    # linearly spaced coordinates corresponding to the 2D plot
    # of digit classes in the latent space
    grid_x = np.linspace(-4, 4, n)
    grid_y = np.linspace(-4, 4, n)[::-1]

    # start sampling z1 and z2 in the ranges grid_x and grid_y
    for i, yi in enumerate(grid_y):
        for j, xi in enumerate(grid_x):
            z_sample = np.array([[xi, yi]])
            x_decoded = decoder.predict(z_sample)
            digit = x_decoded[0].reshape(digit_size, digit_size)
            slice_i = slice(i * digit_size, (i + 1) * digit_size)
            slice_j = slice(j * digit_size, (j + 1) * digit_size)
            figure[slice_i, slice_j] = digit

    # plot the results
    plt.figure(figsize=(6, 5))
    start_range = digit_size // 2
    end_range = n * digit_size + start_range + 1
    pixel_range = np.arange(start_range, end_range, digit_size)
    sample_range_x = np.round(grid_x, 1)
    sample_range_y = np.round(grid_y, 1)
    plt.xticks(pixel_range, sample_range_x)
    plt.yticks(pixel_range, sample_range_y)
    plt.xlabel("z[0]")
    plt.ylabel("z[1]")
    plt.imshow(figure, cmap='Greys_r')
    plt.show()
```

7. Now, run the entirety of the code. We'll use the Adam optimizer (introduced in Chapter 1, *The Nuts and Bolts of Neural Networks*) to train the network for 50 epochs:

```
if __name__ == '__main__':
    encoder, decoder, vae = build_vae()
```

```
vae.compile(optimizer='adam')
vae.summary()

vae.fit(x_train,
        epochs=50,
        batch_size=128,
        validation_data=(x_test, None))

plot_latent_distribution(encoder, x_test, y_test,
                                    batch_size=128)

plot_generated_images(decoder)
```

8. If everything goes to plan, once the training is over, we'll see the latent distribution for each digit class for all the test images. The left and bottom axes represent the z_1 and z_2 latent variables. Different marker shapes represent different digit classes:

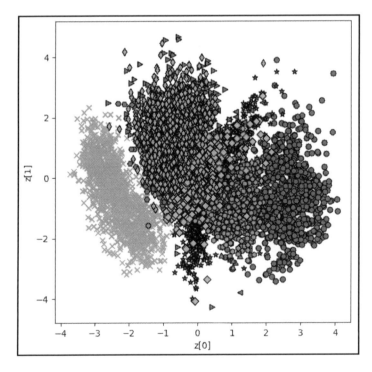

The latent distributions of the MNIST test images

9. Next, we'll look at the images that were generated by `plot_generated_images`. The axes represent the particular latent distribution, `z`, that was used for each image:

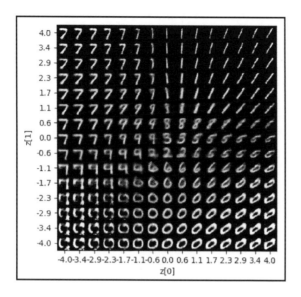

Images generated by the VAE

This concludes our description of VAEs. In the next section, we'll discuss GANs—arguably the most popular family of generative models.

Introduction to GANs

In this section, we'll talk about arguably the most popular generative model today: the GAN framework. It was first introduced in 2014 in the landmark paper *Generative Adversarial Nets* (`http://papers.nips.cc/paper/5423-generative-adversarial-nets.pdf`). The GAN framework can work with any type of data, but its most popular application by far is to generate images, and we'll discuss them in this context only. Let's see how it works:

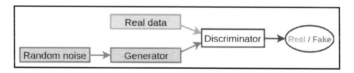

A GAN system

A GAN is a system of two components (neural networks):

- **Generator**: This is the generative model itself. It takes a probability distribution (random noise) as input and tries to generate a realistic output image. Its purpose is similar to the decoder part of the VAE.
- **Discriminator**: This takes two alternating inputs: real images of the training dataset or generated fake samples from the generator. It tries to determine whether the input image comes from the real images or the generated ones.

The two networks are trained together as a system. On the one hand, the discriminator tries to get better at distinguishing between real and fake images. On the other hand, the generator tries to output more realistic images so that it can *deceive* the discriminator into thinking that the generated images are real. To use the analogy in the original paper, you can think of the generator as a team of counterfeiters, trying to produce fake currency. Conversely, the discriminator acts as a police officer, trying to capture the fake money, and the two are constantly trying to deceive each other (hence the name adversarial). The ultimate goal of the system is to make the generator so good that the discriminator can't distinguish between real and fake images. Even though the discriminator performs classification, a GAN is still unsupervised, since we don't need labels for the images. In the next section, we'll discuss the process of training in the context of the GAN framework.

Training GANs

Our main goal is for the generator to produce realistic images, and the GAN framework is a vehicle for that goal. We'll train the generator and the discriminator separately and sequentially (one after the other) and alternate between the two phases multiple times.

Before going into more detail, let's use the following diagram to introduce some notations:

- We'll denote the generator with $G(\mathbf{z}, \theta_g)$, where θ_g is the network weights and $\mathbf{z}$ is the latent vector, which serves as an input to the generator. Think of it as a random seed value to kickstart the image-generation process. It is similar to the latent vector in VAEs. $\mathbf{z}$ has a probability distribution, $p_z(\mathbf{z})$, which is usually random normal or random uniform. The generator outputs fake samples, $\mathbf{x}$, with a probability distribution of $p_g(\mathbf{x})$. You can think of $p_g(\mathbf{x})$ as the probability distribution of the real data according to the generator.

- We'll denote the discriminator with $D(\mathbf{x}, \theta_d)$, where θ_d is the network weights. It takes either real data with the $\mathbf{x} \sim p_{data}(\mathbf{x})$ distribution or generated samples, $\mathbf{x} \sim p_g(\mathbf{x})$, as input. The discriminator is a binary classifier that outputs whether the input image is part of the real (network output 1) or the generated data (network output 0).
- During training, we'll denote the discriminator and generator loss functions with $J^{(D)}$ and $J^{(G)}$, respectively.

The following is a more detailed diagram of a GAN framework:

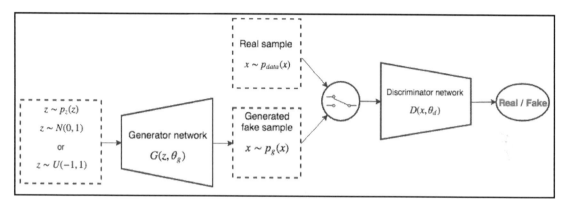

A detailed example of a GAN

GAN training is different compared to training a regular DNN because we have two networks. We can think of it as a sequential minimax zero-sum game of two players (generator and discriminator):

- **Sequential**: This means that the players take turns after one another, similar to chess or tic-tac-toe (as opposed to simultaneously). First, the discriminator tries to minimize $J^{(D)}$, but it can only do so by adjusting the weights, θ_d. Next, the generator tries to minimize $J^{(G)}$, but it can only adjust the weights, θ_g. We repeat this process multiple times.
- **Zero-sum**: This means that the gains or losses of one player are balanced by the gains or losses of the opposite player. That is, the sum of the generator's loss and the discriminator's loss is always 0:

$$J^{(G)} = -J^{(D)}$$

- **Minimax**: This means that the strategy of the first player (generator) is to **minimize** the opponent's (discriminator) **maximum** score (hence the name). When we train the discriminator, it becomes better at distinguishing between real and fake samples (minimizing $J^{(D)}$). Next, when we train the generator, it tries to step up to the level of the new and improved discriminator (we minimize $J^{(G)}$, which is equivalent to maximizing $J^{(D)}$). The two networks are in constant competition. We'll denote the minimax game with the following formula, where V is the loss function:

$$\min_{G} \max_{D} V(G, D)$$

Let's assume that, after a number of training steps, both $J^{(G)}$ and $J^{(D)}$ will be at some local minimum. Here, the solution to the minimax game is called the Nash equilibrium. A Nash equilibrium happens when one of the actors doesn't change its action, regardless of what the other actor may do. A Nash equilibrium in a GAN framework happens when the generator becomes so good that the discriminator is no longer able to distinguish between generated and real samples. That is, the discriminator output will always be half, regardless of the presented input.

Now that we have had an overview of GANs, let's discuss how to train them. We'll start with the discriminator and then we'll continue with the generator.

Training the discriminator

The discriminator is a classification neural network and we can train it in the usual way, that is, using gradient descent and backpropagation. However, the training set is composed of real and generated samples. Let's learn how to incorporate that in the training process:

1. Depending on the input sample (real or fake), we have two paths:
   - Select the sample from the real data, $x \sim p_{data}(x)$, and use it to produce $D(x)$.
   - Generate a fake sample, $x \sim p_g(x)$. Here, the generator and discriminator work as a single network. We start with a random vector, z, which we use to produce the generated sample, $G(z)$. Then, we use it as input to the discriminator to produce the final output, $D(G(z))$.

2. Next, we compute the loss function, which reflects the duality of the training data (more on that later).

3. Finally, we backpropagate the error gradient and update the weights. Although the two networks work together, the generator weights, θ_g, will be locked and we'll only update the discriminator weights, θ_d. This ensures that we'll improve the discriminatory performance by making it better, as opposed to making the generator worse.

To understand discriminator loss, let's recall the formula for cross-entropy loss:

$$H(p,q) = -\sum_{i=1}^{n} p_i(\mathbf{x})\log(q_i(\mathbf{x}))$$

Here, $q_i(\mathbf{x})$ is the estimated probability of the output belonging to the *i*-th class (out of *n* total classes) and $p_i(\mathbf{x})$ is the actual probability. For the sake of simplicity, we'll assume that we apply the formula over a single training sample. In the case of binary classification, this formula can be simplified, as follows:

$$H(p,q) = -(p(\mathbf{x})\log q(\mathbf{x}) + (1 - p(\mathbf{x}))\log(1 - q(\mathbf{x})))$$

When the target probabilities are $p(\mathbf{x}) \rightarrow \{0,1\}$ (one-hot-encoding), one of the loss terms is always 0.

We can expand the formula for a mini-batch of *m* samples:

$$H(p,q) = -\frac{1}{m}\sum_{j=1}^{m}(p(\mathbf{x}_j)\log(q(\mathbf{x}_j)) + (1 - p(\mathbf{x}_j))\log(1 - q(\mathbf{x}_j)))$$

Knowing all this, let's define the discriminator loss:

$$J^{(D)} = -\frac{1}{2}\mathbb{E}_{\mathbf{x}\sim p_{data}(\mathbf{x})}\log(D(\mathbf{x})) - \frac{1}{2}\mathbb{E}_{\mathbf{z}\sim p_z(\mathbf{z})}\log(1 - D(G(\mathbf{z})))$$

Although it seems complex, this is just cross-entropy loss for a binary classifier with some GAN-specific bells and whistles. Let's discuss them:

- The two components of the loss reflect the two possible classes (real or fake), which are equal in number in the training set.
- $\frac{1}{2}\mathbb{E}_{\mathbf{x} \sim p_{data}(\mathbf{x})} \log D(\mathbf{x})$ is the loss when the input is sampled from real data. Ideally, in such cases, we'll have $D(x) = 1$.
- In this context, the expectation term, $\mathbb{E}_{\mathbf{x} \sim p_{data}(\mathbf{x})}$, implies that $\mathbf{x}$ is sampled from $p_{data}(\mathbf{x})$. In essence, this part of the loss means that, when we sample $\mathbf{x}$ from $p_{data}(\mathbf{x})$, we expect the discriminator output, $D(\mathbf{x}) = 1$. Finally, 0.5 is the cumulative class probability of the real data, $p_{data}(\mathbf{x})$, since it comprises exactly half of the whole set.

- $\frac{1}{2}\mathbb{E}_{\mathbf{z} \sim p_z(\mathbf{z})} \log(1 - D(G(\mathbf{z})))$ is the loss when the input is sampled from generated data. Here, we can make the same observations that we made with the real data component. However, this term is maximized when $D(G(\mathbf{z})) = 0$.

To summarize, the discriminator loss will be zero when $D(\mathbf{x}) = 1$ for all $\mathbf{x} \sim p_{data}(\mathbf{x})$ and $D(\mathbf{x}) = 0$ for all generated $\mathbf{x} \sim p_g(\mathbf{x})$ (or $\mathbf{x} = G(\mathbf{z})$).

Training the generator

We'll train the generator by making it better at deceiving the discriminator. To do this, we'll need both networks, similar to the way we trained the discriminator with fake samples:

1. We start with a random latent vector, $\mathbf{z}$, and feed it through both the generator and discriminator to produce the output, $D(G(\mathbf{z}))$.
2. The loss function is the same as the discriminator loss. However, our goal here is to maximize rather than minimize it, since we want to deceive the discriminator.
3. In the backward pass, the discriminator weights, θ_d, are locked and we can only adjust θ_g. This forces us to maximize the discriminator loss by making the generator better, instead of making the discriminator worse.

You may have noticed that, in this phase, we only use generated data. Since the discriminator weights are locked, we can ignore the part of the loss function that deals with real data. Therefore, we can simplify it to the following:

$$J^{(G)} = \mathbb{E}_{\mathbf{z} \sim p_z(\mathbf{z})} \log(1 - D(G(\mathbf{z})))$$

The derivative (gradient) of this formula is $-\frac{1}{1-D(G(\mathbf{z}))}$, which can be seen in the following diagram as an uninterrupted line. This imposes a limitation on the training. Early on, when the discriminator can easily distinguish between real and fake samples ($D(G(\mathbf{z})) \approx 0$), the gradient will be close to zero. This will result in little learning of the weights, θ_g (another manifestation of the vanishing gradient problem):

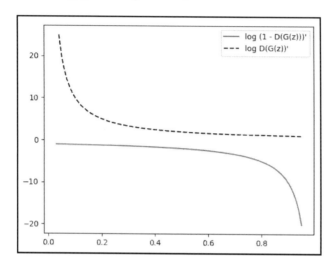

Gradients of the two generator loss functions

We can solve this issue by using a different loss function:

$$J^{(G)} = -\mathbb{E}_{\mathbf{z} \sim p_z(\mathbf{z})} \log(D(G(\mathbf{z})))$$

The derivative of this function is displayed in the preceding diagram with a dashed line. This loss is still minimized when $D(G(\mathbf{z})) \approx 1$ and when the gradient is large; that is, when the generator underperforms. With this loss, the game is no longer zero-sum, but this won't have a practical effect on the GAN framework. Now, we have all the ingredients we need to define the GAN training algorithm. We'll do this in the next section.

Putting it all together

With our newfound knowledge, we can define the minimax objective in full:

$$\min_{G} \max_{D} V(G, D) = \frac{1}{2} \mathbb{E}_{\mathbf{x} \sim p_{data}(\mathbf{x})} \log(D(\mathbf{x})) + \frac{1}{2} \mathbb{E}_{\mathbf{z} \sim p_z(\mathbf{z})} \log(1 - D(G(\mathbf{z})))$$

In short, the generator tries to minimize the objective, while the discriminator tries to maximize it. Note that, while the discriminator should minimize its loss, the minimax objective is a negative of the discriminator loss, and therefore the discriminator has to maximize it.

The following step-by-step training algorithm was introduced by the authors of the GAN framework.

Repeat this for a number of iterations:

1. Repeat for k steps, where k is a hyperparameter:
    - Sample a mini-batch of m random samples from the latent space, $\{z^{(1)}, z^{(2)}, \ldots z^{(m)}\} \sim p_g(z)$
    - Sample a mini-batch of m samples from the real data, $\{x^{(1)}, x^{(2)}, \ldots x^{(m)}\} \sim p_{data}(x)$
    - Update the discriminator weights, θ_d, by ascending the stochastic gradient of its cost:

    $$\nabla_{\theta_d} \frac{1}{m} \sum_{i=1}^{m} [\log(D(x^{(i)})) + \log(1 - D(G(z^{(i)})))]$$

2. Sample a mini-batch of m random samples from the latent space, $\{z^{(1)}, z^{(2)}, \ldots z^{(m)}\} \sim p_g(z)$.

3. Update the generator by descending the stochastic gradient of its cost:

    $$\nabla_{\theta_g} \frac{1}{m} \sum_{i=1}^{m} \log(1 - D(G(z^{(i)})))$$

    Alternatively, we can use the updated cost function we introduced in the *Training the generator* section:

    $$-\nabla_{\theta_g} \frac{1}{m} \sum_{i=1}^{m} \log(D(G(z^{(i)})))$$

Now that we know how to train GANs, let's discuss some of the problems we may face while training them.

Problems with training GANs

Training GAN models has some major pitfalls:

- The gradient descent algorithm is designed to find the minimum of the loss function, rather than the Nash equilibrium, which is not the same thing. As a result, sometimes the training may fail to converge and could oscillate instead.

- Recall that the discriminator output is a sigmoid function that represents the probability of the example being real or fake. If the discriminator becomes too good at this task, the probability output will converge to either 0 or 1 at every training sample. This would mean that the error gradient will always be 0, which will prevent the generator from learning anything. On the other hand, if the discriminator is bad at recognizing fakes from real images, it will backpropagate the wrong information to the generator. Therefore, the discriminator shouldn't be either too good or too bad for the training to succeed. In practice, this means that we cannot train it until convergence.

- **Mode collapse** is a problem where the generator can generate a limited number of images (or even just one), regardless of the latent input vector value. To understand why this happens, let's focus on a single generator training episode that tries to minimize $\mathbb{E}_{\mathbf{z} \sim p_z(\mathbf{z})} \log(1 - D(G(\mathbf{z})))$ while the weights of the discriminator are fixed. In other words, the generator tries to generate a fake image, $\mathbf{x}^*$, so that $\mathbf{x}^* = \arg\max_{x} D(\mathbf{x})$. However, the loss function does not force the generator to create a unique image, $\mathbf{x}^*$, for different values of the input latent vector. That is, the training can modify the generator in a way where it completely decouples the generated image, $\mathbf{x}^*$, from the latent vector value and, at the same time, still minimize the loss function. For example, a GAN for generating new MNIST images could only generate the number 4, regardless of the input. Once we update the discriminator, the previous value, $\mathbf{x}^*$, may not be optimal anymore, which would force the generator to generate new and different images. Nevertheless, mode collapse may recur in different stages of the training process.

Now that we are familiar with the GAN framework, we'll discuss several different types of GAN.

Types of GAN

Since the GAN framework was first introduced, a lot of new variations have emerged. In fact, there are so many new GANs now that, in order to stand out, the authors have come up with creative GAN names, such as BicycleGAN, DiscoGAN, GANs for LIFE, and ELEGANT. In the next few sections, we'll discuss some of them. All of the examples have been implemented with TensorFlow 2.0 and Keras.

The code for DCGAN, CGAN, WGAN, and CycleGAN is partially inspired by `https://github.com/eriklindernoren/Keras-GAN`. You can find the full implementations of all the examples in this chapter at `https://github.com/PacktPublishing/Advanced-Deep-Learning-with-Python/tree/master/Chapter05`.

Deep Convolutional GAN

In this section, we'll implement the **Deep Convolutional GAN (DCGAN**, *Unsupervised Representation Learning with Deep Convolutional Generative Adversarial Networks*, `https://arxiv.rg/abs/1511.06434`). In the original GAN framework proposal, the authors only used fully-connected networks. In contrast, in DCGANs both the generator and the discriminator are CNNs. They have some constraints that help stabilize the training process. You can think of these as general guidelines for GAN training and not just for DCGANs:

- The discriminator uses strided convolutions instead of pooling layers.
- The generator uses transpose convolutions to upsample the latent vector, z, to the size of the generated image.
- Both networks use batch normalization.
- No fully-connected layers, with the exception of the last layer of the discriminator.
- LeakyReLU activations for all the layers of the generator and discriminator, except their outputs. The generator output layer uses Tanh activation (which has a range of (-1, 1)) to mimic the properties of real-world data. The discriminator has a single sigmoid output (recall that it's in the range of (0, 1)) because it measures the probability of the sample being real or fake.

In the following diagram, we can see a sample generator network in the DCGAN framework:

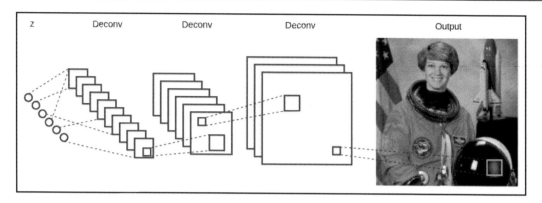

Generator network with transpose convolutions

Implementing DCGAN

In this section, we'll implement DCGAN, which generates new MNIST images. This example will serve as a blueprint for all GAN implementations in upcoming sections. Let's get started:

1. Let's start by importing the necessary modules and classes:

```
import matplotlib.pyplot as plt
import numpy as np
from tensorflow.keras.datasets import mnist
from tensorflow.keras.layers import \
    Conv2D, Conv2DTranspose, BatchNormalization, Dropout, Input, \
    Dense, Reshape, Flatten
from tensorflow.keras.layers import LeakyReLU
from tensorflow.keras.models import Sequential, Model
from tensorflow.keras.optimizers import Adam
```

2. Implement the `build_generator` function. We'll follow the guidelines that were outlined at the beginning of this section—upsampling with transpose convolutions, batch normalization, and LeakyReLU activations. The model starts with a fully-connected layer to upsample the 1D latent vector. Then, the vector is upsampled with a series of `Conv2DTranspose`. The final `Conv2DTranspose` has a `tanh` activation and the generated image has only 1 channel:

```
def build_generator(latent_input: Input):
    model = Sequential([
        Dense(7 * 7 * 256, use_bias=False,
        input_shape=latent_input.shape[1:]),
        BatchNormalization(), LeakyReLU(),
```

```
            Reshape((7, 7, 256)),

            # expand the input with transposed convolutions
            Conv2DTranspose(filters=128, kernel_size=(5, 5),
                            strides=(1, 1),
                            padding='same', use_bias=False),
            BatchNormalization(), LeakyReLU(),

            # gradually reduce the volume depth
            Conv2DTranspose(filters=64, kernel_size=(5, 5),
                            strides=(2, 2),
                            padding='same', use_bias=False),
            BatchNormalization(), LeakyReLU(),

            Conv2DTranspose(filters=1, kernel_size=(5, 5),
                            strides=(2, 2), padding='same',
                            use_bias=False, activation='tanh'),
    ])

    # this is forward phase
    generated = model(latent_input)

    return Model(z, generated)
```

3. Build the discriminator. Again, it's a simple CNN with stride convolutions:

```
def build_discriminator():
    model = Sequential([
        Conv2D(filters=64, kernel_size=(5, 5), strides=(2, 2),
               padding='same', input_shape=(28, 28, 1)),
        LeakyReLU(), Dropout(0.3),
        Conv2D(filters=128, kernel_size=(5, 5), strides=(2, 2),
               padding='same'),
        LeakyReLU(), Dropout(0.3),
        Flatten(),
        Dense(1, activation='sigmoid'),
    ])

    image = Input(shape=(28, 28, 1))
    output = model(image)

    return Model(image, output)
```

4. Implement the `train` function with the actual GAN training. This function implements the procedure that was outlined in the *Putting it all together* subsection in the *Training GANs* section. We'll start with the function declaration and the initialization of the variables:

```
def train(generator, discriminator, combined, steps, batch_size):
    # Load the dataset
    (x_train, _), _ = mnist.load_data()

    # Rescale in [-1, 1] interval
    x_train = (x_train.astype(np.float32) - 127.5) / 127.5
    x_train = np.expand_dims(x_train, axis=-1)

    # Discriminator ground truths
    real = np.ones((batch_size, 1))
    fake = np.zeros((batch_size, 1))

    latent_dim = generator.input_shape[1]
```

We'll continue with the training loop, where we alternate one discriminator training episode with one generator training episode. First, we train the `discriminator` on 1 batch of `real_images` and one batch of `generated_images`. Then, we train the generator (which includes the `discriminator` as well) on the same batch of `generated_images`. Note that we label these images as real because we want to maximize the `discriminator` loss. The following is the implementation (please note the indentation; this is still part of the `train` function):

```
for step in range(steps):
    # Train the discriminator

    # Select a random batch of images
    real_images = x_train[np.random.randint(0, x_train.shape[0],
    batch_size)]

    # Random batch of noise
    noise = np.random.normal(0, 1, (batch_size, latent_dim))

    # Generate a batch of new images
    generated_images = generator.predict(noise)

    # Train the discriminator
    discriminator_real_loss = discriminator.train_on_batch
    (real_images, real)
    discriminator_fake_loss = discriminator.train_on_batch
    (generated_images, fake)
```

```
        discriminator_loss = 0.5 * np.add(discriminator_real_loss,
        discriminator_fake_loss)

        # Train the generator
        # random latent vector z
        noise = np.random.normal(0, 1, (batch_size, latent_dim))

        # Train the generator
        # Note that we use the "valid" labels for the generated images
        # That's because we try to maximize the discriminator loss
        generator_loss = combined.train_on_batch(noise, real)

        # Display progress
        print("%d [Discriminator loss: %.4f%%, acc.: %.2f%%] [Generator
        loss: %.4f%%]" % (step, discriminator_loss[0], 100 *
        discriminator_loss[1], generator_loss))
```

5. Implement a boilerplate function, `plot_generated_images`, to display some generated images after the training is finished:

   1. Create an nxn grid (the `figure` variable).

   2. Create nxn random latent vectors (the `noise` variable)—one for each generated image.

   3. Generate the images and place them in the grid cells.

   4. Display the result.

The following is the implementation:

```
def plot_generated_images(generator):
    n = 10
    digit_size = 28

    # big array containing all images
    figure = np.zeros((digit_size * n, digit_size * n))

    latent_dim = generator.input_shape[1]

    # n*n random latent distributions
    noise = np.random.normal(0, 1, (n * n, latent_dim))

    # generate the images
    generated_images = generator.predict(noise)

    # fill the big array with images
    for i in range(n):
        for j in range(n):
            slice_i = slice(i * digit_size, (i + 1) * digit_size)
```

```
            slice_j = slice(j * digit_size, (j + 1) * digit_size)
            figure[slice_i, slice_j] = np.reshape
                            (generated_images[i * n + j], (28, 28))
```

```
    # plot the results
    plt.figure(figsize=(6, 5))
    plt.axis('off')
    plt.imshow(figure, cmap='Greys_r')
    plt.show()
```

6. Build the full GAN model by including the `generator`, `discriminator`, and the `combined` network. We'll use the latent vector that's 64 in size (the `latent_dim` variable) and we'll run the training for 50,000 batches using the Adam optimizer (this may take a while). Then, we'll plot the results:

```
latent_dim = 64

# Build the generator
# Generator input z
z = Input(shape=(latent_dim,))

generator = build_generator(z)

generated_image = generator(z)

# we'll use Adam optimizer
optimizer = Adam(0.0002, 0.5)

# Build and compile the discriminator
discriminator = build_discriminator()
discriminator.compile(loss='binary_crossentropy',
                    optimizer=optimizer,
                    metrics=['accuracy'])

# Only train the generator for the combined model
discriminator.trainable = False

# The discriminator takes generated image as input and determines
validity
real_or_fake = discriminator(generated_image)

# Stack the generator and discriminator in a combined model
# Trains the generator to deceive the discriminator
combined = Model(z, real_or_fake)
combined.compile(loss='binary_crossentropy', optimizer=optimizer)

train(generator, discriminator, combined, steps=50000,
```

```
batch_size=100)

plot_generated_images(generator)
```

If everything goes as planned, we should see something similar to the following:

Newly generated MNIST images

This concludes our discussion of DCGANs. In the next section, we'll discuss another type of GAN model called the Conditional GAN.

Conditional GAN

The conditional GAN (CGAN, *Conditional Generative Adversarial Nets,* https://arxiv.org/abs/1411.1784) is an extension of the GAN model where both the generator and discriminator receive some additional conditioning input information. This could be the class of the current image or some other property:

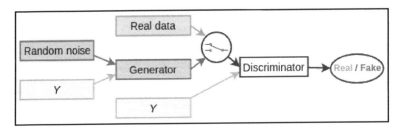

Conditional GAN. *Y* represents the conditional input for the generator and discriminator

For example, if we train a GAN to generate new MNIST images, we could add an additional input layer with values of one-hot encoded image labels. CGANs have the disadvantage that they are not strictly unsupervised and we need some kind of label for them to work. However, they have some other advantages:

- By using more well-structured information for training, the model can learn better data representations and generate better samples.
- In regular GANs, all the image information is stored in the latent vector, $\mathbf{z}$. This poses a problem: since z can be complex, we don't have much control over the properties of the generated image. For example, suppose that we want our MNIST GAN to generate a certain digit; say, 7. We would have to experiment with different latent vectors until we reach the desired output. But with CGAN, we could simply combine the one-hot vector of 7 with some random $\mathbf{z}$ and the network will generate the correct digit. We could still try different values for $\mathbf{z}$ and the model would generate different versions of the digit, that is, 7. In short, CGAN provides a way for us to control (condition) the generator output.

Because of the conditional input, we'll modify the minimax objective to include the condition, y, as well:

$$\min_G \max_D V(G, D) = \frac{1}{2}\mathbb{E}_{\mathbf{x}\sim p_{data}(\mathbf{x})}[log(D(\mathbf{x}|y))] + \frac{1}{2}\mathbb{E}_{\mathbf{z}\sim p_z(\mathbf{z})}[log(1 - D(G(\mathbf{z}|y)))]$$

Implementing CGAN

The blueprint for the CGAN implementation is very similar to the DCGAN example in the *Implementing DCGAN* section. That is, we'll implement CGAN in order to generate new images of the MNIST dataset. For the sake of simplicity (and diversity), we'll use fully connected generators and discriminators. To avoid repetition, we'll only show modified sections of the code compared to DCGAN. You can find the full example in this book's GitHub repository.

The first significant difference is the definition of the generator:

```
def build_generator(z_input: Input, label_input: Input):
    model = Sequential([
        Dense(128, input_dim=latent_dim),
        LeakyReLU(alpha=0.2), BatchNormalization(momentum=0.8),
        Dense(256),
        LeakyReLU(alpha=0.2), BatchNormalization(momentum=0.8),
        Dense(512),
        LeakyReLU(alpha=0.2), BatchNormalization(momentum=0.8),
        Dense(np.prod((28, 28, 1)), activation='tanh'),
```

```
        # reshape to MNIST image size
        Reshape((28, 28, 1))
    ])
    model.summary()

    # the latent input vector z
    label_embedding = Embedding(input_dim=10,
    output_dim=latent_dim)(label_input)
    flat_embedding = Flatten()(label_embedding)

    # combine the noise and label by element-wise multiplication
    model_input = multiply([z_input, flat_embedding])
    image = model(model_input)

    return Model([z_input, label_input], image)
```

Although it's a fully-connected network, we still follow the GAN network design guidelines that were defined in the *Deep Convolutional GANs* section. Let's discuss the way we combine the latent vector, z_input, with the conditional label, label_input (an integer with values from 0 to 9). We can see that label_input is transformed with an Embedding layer. This layer does two things:

- Converts the integer value, label_input, into a one-hot representation with a length of input_dim
- Uses the one-hot representation as an input for a fully-connected layer with the size of output_dim

The embedding layer allows us to obtain unique vector representations for each possible input value. In this case, the output of label_embedding has the same dimensions as the size of the latent vector and z_input. label_embedding is combined with the latent vector, z_input, with the help of element-wise multiplication in the model_input variable, which serves as an input for the rest of the network.

Next, we'll focus on the discriminator, which is also a fully-connected network and uses the same embedding mechanism as the generator. This time, the embedding output size is np.prod((28, 28, 1)), which is equal to 784 (the size of the MNIST images):

```
def build_discriminator():
    model = Sequential([
        Flatten(input_shape=(28, 28, 1)),
        Dense(256),
        LeakyReLU(alpha=0.2),
        Dense(128),
        LeakyReLU(alpha=0.2),
        Dense(1, activation='sigmoid'),
```

```
], name='discriminator')
model.summary()

image = Input(shape=(28, 28, 1))
flat_img = Flatten()(image)

label_input = Input(shape=(1,), dtype='int32')
label_embedding = Embedding(input_dim=10, output_dim=np.prod(
(28, 28, 1)))(label_input)
flat_embedding = Flatten()(label_embedding)

# combine the noise and label by element-wise multiplication
model_input = multiply([flat_img, flat_embedding])

validity = model(model_input)

return Model([image, label_input], validity)
```

The rest of the example code is very similar to the DCGAN example. The only other differences are trivial—they account for the multiple inputs (latent vector and embedding) for the networks. The `plot_generated_images` function has an additional parameter, which allows it to generate images for random latent vectors and a specific conditional label (in this case, a digit). In the following, we can see the newly generated images for conditional labels 3, 8, and 9:

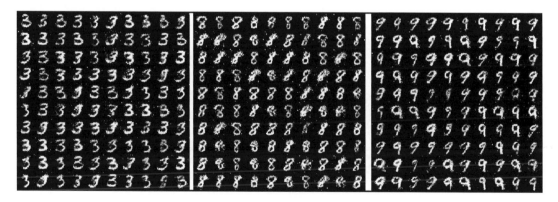

CGAN for conditional labels 3, 8, and 9

This concludes our discussion of CGANs. In the next section, we'll discuss another type of GAN model called the Wasserstein GAN.

Wasserstein GAN

To understand the Wasserstein GAN (WGAN, https://arxiv.org/abs/1701.07875), let's recall that, in the *Training GANs* section, we denoted the probability distribution of the generator with p_g and the probability distribution of the real data with p_{data}. In the process of training the GAN model, we update the generator weights and so we change p_g. The goal of the GAN framework is to converge p_g to p_{data} (this is also valid for other types of generative model, such as VAE), that is, the probability distribution of the generated images should be the same as the real ones, which would result in realistic images. WGAN uses a new way to measure the distance between the two distributions called the Wasserstein distance (or the **Earth mover's distance (EMD)**). To understand it, let's start with the following diagram:

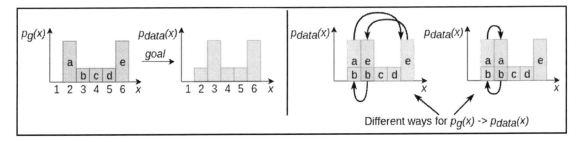

An example of EMD. Left: Initial and target distributions: Right: Two different ways to transform p_g into p_{data}

For the sake of simplicity, we'll assume that the p_g and p_{data} are distributions discrete (the same rule applies for continuous distributions). We can transform p_g into p_{data} by moving the columns (a, b, c, d, e) left or right along the x axis. Each transfer of 1 position has a cost of 1. For example, the cost to move column *a* from its initial position, 2, to position 6 is 4. The right-hand side of the preceding diagram shows two ways of doing this. In the first case, we have *total cost = cost(a:2->6) + cost(e:6->3) + cost(b:3->2) = 4 +3 + 1 = 8*. In the second case, we have *total cost = cost(a:2->3) + cost(b:2->1) = 1 + 1 = 2*. EMD is the minimal total cost it takes to transform one distribution into the other. Therefore, in this example, we have EMD = 2.

We now have a basic idea of what EMD is, but we still don't know why it's necessary to use this metric in the GAN model. The WGAN paper provides an elaborate but somewhat complex answer to this question. In this section, we'll try to explain it. To start, let's note that the generator starts with a low-dimensional latent vector, z, and then transforms it into a high-dimensional generated image (for example, 784, in the case of MNIST). The output size of the image also implies a high-dimensional distribution of the generated data, p_g. However, its intrinsic dimensions (the latent vector, z) are much lower. Because of this p_g will be excluded from big sections of the high-dimensional feature space. On the other hand, p_{data} is truly high dimensional because it doesn't start from a latent vector; instead, it represents the real data with its full richness. Therefore, it's very likely that p_g and p_{data} don't intersect anywhere in the feature space.

To understand why this matters, let's note that we can transform the generator and discriminator cost functions (see the *Training GANs* section) into functions of the KL and the **Jensen–Shannon (JS,** https://en.wikipedia.org/wiki/Jensen%E2%80%93Shannon_divergence) divergence. The problem with these metrics is that they provide a zero gradient when the two distributions don't intersect. That is, no matter what the distance between the two distributions is (small or large), if they don't intersect, the metrics won't provide any information about the actual difference between them. However, as we just explained, it's very likely that the distributions won't intersect. Contrary to this, the Wasserstein distance works regardless of whether the distributions intersect or not, which makes it a better candidate for the GAN model. We can illustrate this issue visually with the following diagram:

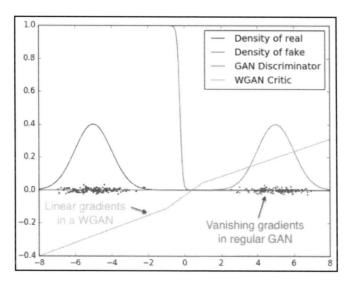

The advantage of the Wasserstein distance over the regular GAN discriminator. Source: https://arxiv.org/abs/1701.07875

Here, we can see two non-intersecting Gaussian distributions, P_g and P_{data} (to the left and to the right, respectively). The regular GAN discriminator output is the sigmoid function (with a range of $(0, 1)$), which tells us the probability of the input being fake or not. In this case, the sigmoid output is meaningful in a very narrow range (centered around 0) and converges toward 0 or 1 in all other areas. This is a manifestation of the same problem we outlined in the *Problems with training GANs* section. It leads to vanishing gradients, which prevents error backpropagation to the generator. In contrast, the WGAN doesn't give us binary feedback on whether an image is real or fake and instead provides an actual distance measurement between the two distributions (also displayed in the preceding diagram). This distance is more useful than binary classification because it will provide a better indication of how to update the generator. To reflect this, the authors of the paper have renamed the discriminator and called it **critic**.

The following screenshot shows the WGAN algorithm as it's described in the paper:

Algorithm 1 WGAN, our proposed algorithm. All experiments in the paper used the default values $\alpha = 0.00005$, $c = 0.01$, $m = 64$, $n_{critic} = 5$.

Require: : α, the learning rate. c, the clipping parameter. m, the batch size. n_{critic}, the number of iterations of the critic per generator iteration.
Require: : w_0, initial critic parameters. θ_0, initial generator's parameters.

1: **while** θ has not converged **do**
2:      **for** $t = 0, ..., n_{critic}$ **do**
3:          Sample $\{x^{(i)}\}_{i=1}^m \sim \mathbb{P}_r$ a batch from the real data.
4:          Sample $\{z^{(i)}\}_{i=1}^m \sim p(z)$ a batch of prior samples.
5:          $g_w \leftarrow \nabla_w \left[\frac{1}{m} \sum_{i=1}^m f_w(x^{(i)}) - \frac{1}{m} \sum_{i=1}^m f_w(g_\theta(z^{(i)})) \right]$
6:          $w \leftarrow w + \alpha \cdot \text{RMSProp}(w, g_w)$
7:          $w \leftarrow \text{clip}(w, -c, c)$
8:      **end for**
9:      Sample $\{z^{(i)}\}_{i=1}^m \sim p(z)$ a batch of prior samples.
10:     $g_\theta \leftarrow -\nabla_\theta \frac{1}{m} \sum_{i=1}^m f_w(g_\theta(z^{(i)}))$
11:     $\theta \leftarrow \theta - \alpha \cdot \text{RMSProp}(\theta, g_\theta)$
12: **end while**

Here, f_w denotes the critic, g_w is the critic weight update, and g_θ is the generator weight update. Although the theory behind WGAN is sophisticated, in practice we can implement it by making relatively few changes to the regular GAN model:

- Remove the output sigmoid activation of the discriminator.
- Replace the log generator/discriminator loss functions with an EMD-derived loss.

- Clip the critic weights after each mini-batch so that their absolute values are smaller than a constant, *c*. This requirement enforces the so-called Lipschitz constraint on the critic, which makes it possible to use the Wasserstein distance (more on this in the paper itself). Without getting into the details, we'll just mention that weight clipping can lead to undesired behavior. One successful solution to these issues has been the gradient penalty (WGAN-GP, *Improved Training of Wasserstein GANs*, https://arxiv.org/abs/1704.00028), which does not suffer from the same problems.
- The authors of the paper reported that optimization methods without momentum (SGD, RMSProp) work better than those with momentum.

Implementing WGAN

Now that we have a basic idea of how the Wasserstein GAN works, let's implement it. Once again, we'll use the DCGAN blueprint and omit the repetitive code snippets so that we can focus on the differences. The build_generator and build_critic functions instantiate the generator and the critic, respectively. For the sake of simplicity, the two networks contain only fully connected layers. All the hidden layers have LeakyReLU activations. Following the paper's guidelines, the generator has Tanh output activation and the critic has a single scalar output (no sigmoid activation, though). Next, let's implement the train method since it contains some WGAN specifics. We'll start with the method's declaration and the initialization of the training process:

```
def train(generator, critic, combined, steps, batch_size, n_critic,
clip_value):
    # Load the dataset
    (x_train, _), _ = mnist.load_data()

    # Rescale in [-1, 1] interval
    x_train = (x_train.astype(np.float32) - 127.5) / 127.5

    # We use FC networks, so we flatten the array
    x_train = x_train.reshape(x_train.shape[0], 28 * 28)

    # Discriminator ground truths
    real = np.ones((batch_size, 1))
    fake = -np.ones((batch_size, 1))

    latent_dim = generator.input_shape[1]
```

Then, we'll continue with the training loop, which follows the steps of the WGAN algorithm we described earlier in this section. The inner loop trains the `critic n_critic` steps for each training step of the `generator`. In fact, this is the main difference between training the `critic` and training the `discriminator` in the train function of the *Implementing DCGAN* section, where the discriminator and the generator alternate at each step. Additionally, the `weights` critic is clipped after each mini-batch. The following is the implementation (please note the indentation; this code is part of the `train` function):

```
for step in range(steps):
    # Train the critic first for n_critic steps
    for _ in range(n_critic):
        # Select a random batch of images
        real_images = x_train[np.random.randint(0, x_train.shape[0],
        batch_size)]

        # Sample noise as generator input
        noise = np.random.normal(0, 1, (batch_size, latent_dim))

        # Generate a batch of new images
        generated_images = generator.predict(noise)

        # Train the critic
        critic_real_loss = critic.train_on_batch(real_images, real)
        critic_fake_loss = critic.train_on_batch(generated_images,
        fake)
        critic_loss = 0.5 * np.add(critic_real_loss, critic_fake_loss)

        # Clip critic weights
        for l in critic.layers:
            weights = l.get_weights()
            weights = [np.clip(w, -clip_value, clip_value) for w in
            weights]
            l.set_weights(weights)

    # Train the generator
    # Note that we use the "valid" labels for the generated images
    # That's because we try to maximize the discriminator loss
    generator_loss = combined.train_on_batch(noise, real)

    # Display progress
    print("%d [Critic loss: %.4f%%] [Generator loss: %.4f%%]" %
        (step, critic_loss[0], generator_loss))
```

Next, we'll implement the derivative of the Wasserstein loss itself. It is a TF operation that represents the mean value of the product of the network output and the labels (real or fake):

```
def wasserstein_loss(y_true, y_pred):
    """The Wasserstein loss implementation"""
    return tensorflow.keras.backend.mean(y_true * y_pred)
```

Now, we can build the full GAN model. This step is similar to the other GAN models:

```
latent_dim = 100

# Build the generator
# Generator input z
z = Input(shape=(latent_dim,))

generator = build_generator(z)

generated_image = generator(z)

# we'll use RMSprop optimizer
optimizer = RMSprop(lr=0.00005)

# Build and compile the discriminator
critic = build_critic()
critic.compile(optimizer, wasserstein_loss,
                metrics=['accuracy'])

# The discriminator takes generated image as input and determines validity
real_or_fake = critic(generated_image)

# Only train the generator for the combined model
critic.trainable = False

# Stack the generator and discriminator in a combined model
# Trains the generator to deceive the discriminator
combined = Model(z, real_or_fake)
combined.compile(loss=wasserstein_loss, optimizer=optimizer)
```

Finally, let's initiate training and evaluation:

```
# train the GAN system
train(generator, critic, combined,
      steps=40000, batch_size=100, n_critic=5, clip_value=0.01)

# display some random generated images
plot_generated_images(generator)
```

Once we run this example, WGAN will produce the following images after training 40,000 mini-batches (this may take a while):

WGAN MNIST generator results

This concludes our discussion of WGANs. In the next section, we'll discuss how to implement image-to-image translation with CycleGAN.

Image-to-image translation with CycleGAN

In this section, we'll discuss **Cycle-Consistent Adversarial Networks** (**CycleGAN**, *Unpaired Image-to-Image Translation using Cycle-Consistent Adversarial Networks*, https://arxiv.org/abs/1703.10593) and their application for image-to-image translation. To quote the paper itself, image-to-image translation is a class of vision and graphics problems where the goal is to learn the mapping between an input image and an output image using a training set of aligned image pairs. For example, if we have grayscale and RGB versions of the same image, we can train an ML algorithm to colorize grayscale images or vice versa.

Another example is image segmentation (Chapter 3, *Object Detection and Image Segmentation*), where the input image is translated into a segmentation map of the same image. In the latter case, we train the model (U-Net, Mask R-CNN) with image/segmentation map pairs. However, paired training data may not be available for many tasks. CycleGAN presents a way for us to transform an image from the source domain, X, into the target domain, Y, in the absence of paired samples. The following image shows some examples of paired and unpaired images:

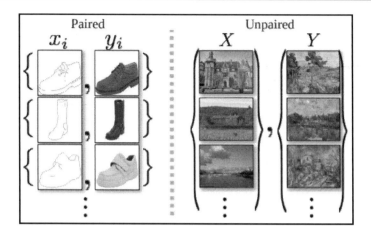

Left: Paired training samples with the corresponding source and target images: Right: Unpaired training samples. where the source and target images don't correspond.
Source: https://arxiv.org/abs/1703.10593

 The *Image-to-Image Translation with Conditional Adversarial Networks* (known as Pix2Pix, https://arxiv.org/abs/1611.07004) paper from the same team also does image-to-image translation for paired training data.

But how does CycleGAN do this? First, the algorithm assumes that, although there are no direct pairs in the two sets, there is still some relationship between the two domains. For example, these could be photographs of the same scene but from different angles. CycleGAN aims to learn this set-level relationship, rather than the relationships between distinct pairs. In theory, the GAN model lends itself to this task well. We can train a generator that maps $G : X \rightarrow Y$, which produces an image, $\hat{y} = G(\mathbf{x}), \mathbf{x} \in X$, that a discriminator cannot distinguish from the target images, $\mathbf{y} \in Y$. More specifically, the optimal G should translate the domain, X, into a domain, $\hat{Y}$, with an identical distribution to domain Y. In practice, the authors of the paper discovered that such a translation does not guarantee that an individual input, x, and output, y, are paired up in a meaningful way—there are infinitely many mappings, G, that will create the same distribution over $\hat{y}$. They also found that this GAN model suffers from the familiar mode collapse problem.

CycleGAN tries to solve these issues with the so-called **cycle consistency**. To understand what this is, let's say that we translate a sentence from English into German. The translation will be cycle-consistent if we translate the sentence back from German into English and we arrive at the original sentence we started with. In a mathematical context, if we have a translator, $G : X \rightarrow Y$, and another translator, $F : Y \rightarrow X$, the two should be inverses of each other.

To explain how CycleGAN implements cycle consistency, let's start with the following diagram:

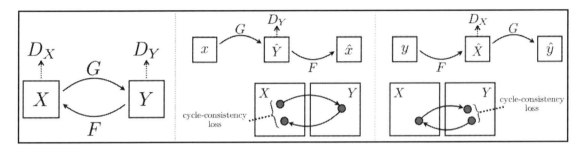

Left: Overall CycleGAN schema: Middle: Forward cycle-consistency loss: Right: Backward cycle-consistency loss. Source: https://arxiv.org/abs/1703.10593

The model has two generators, $G : X \to Y$ and $F : Y \to X$, and two associated discriminators, D_x and D_y, respectively (left in the preceding diagram). Let's take a look at G first. It takes an input image, $\mathbf{x} \in X$, and generates $\hat{\mathbf{y}} = G(\mathbf{x})$, which look similar to the images from domain Y. D_y aims to discriminate between real images, $\mathbf{y} \in Y$, and the generated $\hat{\mathbf{y}} \in \hat{Y}$. This part of the model functions like a regular GAN and uses the regular minimax GAN adversarial loss:

$$ J(G, D_Y, X, Y) = \mathbb{E}_{\mathbf{y} \sim p_{data}(\mathbf{y})}\left[\log D_Y(\mathbf{y})\right] + \mathbb{E}_{\mathbf{x} \sim p_{data}(\mathbf{x})}\left[\log(1 - D_Y(G(\mathbf{x})))\right] $$

The first term represents the original images, y, and the second represents the images that were generated by G. The same formula is valid for the generator, F. As we mentioned previously, this loss only ensures that $\hat{\mathbf{y}}$ will have the same distribution as the images from Y, but doesn't create a meaningful pair of $\mathbf{x}$ and $\mathbf{y}$. To quote the paper: with a large enough capacity, a network can map the same set of input images to any random permutation of images in the target domain, where any of the learned mappings can induce an output distribution that matches the target distribution. Thus, adversarial losses alone cannot guarantee that the learned function can map an individual input, $\mathbf{x}_i$, to the desired output, $\mathbf{y}_i$.

The authors of the paper argue that the learned mapping functions should be cycle-consistent (preceding diagram, middle). For each image, $\mathbf{x} \in X$, the image translation cycle should be able to bring $\mathbf{x}$ back to the original image (this is called forward cycle consistency). G generates a new image, $\hat{\mathbf{y}}$, which serves as an input to F, which in turn generates a new image, $\hat{\mathbf{x}}$, where $\mathbf{x} \approx \hat{\mathbf{x}}$: $\mathbf{x} \to G(\mathbf{x}) \to F(G(\mathbf{x})) \approx \mathbf{x}$. G and F should also satisfy backward cycle consistency (preceding diagram, right): $\mathbf{y} \to F(\mathbf{y}) \to G(F(\mathbf{y})) \approx \mathbf{y}$.

This new path creates an additional cycle-consistency loss term:

$$J_{cyc}(G,F) = \mathbb{E}_{\mathbf{x} \sim p_{data}(\mathbf{x})} \left[\|F(G(\mathbf{x})) - \mathbf{x}|_1 \right] + \mathbb{E}_{\mathbf{y} \sim p_{data}(\mathbf{y})} \left[\|G(F(\mathbf{y})) - \mathbf{y}|_1 \right]$$

This measures the absolute difference between the original images, that is, x and y, and their generated counterparts, $\hat{x}$ and $\hat{y}$. Note that these paths can be viewed as jointly training two autoencoders, $F \circ G : X \rightarrow X$ and $G \circ F : Y \rightarrow Y$. Each autoencoder has a special internal structure: it maps an image to itself with the help of an intermediate representation – the translation of the image into another domain.

The full CycleGAN objective is a combination of the cycle consistency loss and the adversarial losses of F and G:

$$\begin{aligned} J(G,F,D_X,D_Y) &= J_{GAN}(G,D_Y,X,Y) \\ &+ J_{GAN}(F,D_X,Y,X) \\ &+ \lambda J_{cyc}(G,F) \end{aligned}$$

Here, the coefficient, λ, controls the relative importance between the two losses. CycleGAN aims to solve the following minimax objective:

$$G^*, F^* = \arg \min_{G,F} \max_{D_X,D_Y} \mathcal{L}(G,F,D_X,D_Y)$$

Implementing CycleGAN

This example contains several source files located at `https://github.com/ PacktPublishing/Advanced-Deep-Learning-with-Python/tree/master/Chapter05/ cyclegan`. Besides TF, the code also depends on `tensorflow_addons` and `imageio` packages. You can install them with the `pip` package installer. We'll implement CycleGAN for multiple training datasets, all of which were provided by the authors of the paper. Before you run the example, you have to download the relevant dataset with the help of the `download_dataset.sh` executable script, which uses the dataset name as an argument. The list of available datasets is included in the file. Once you've downloaded this, you can access the images with the help of the `DataLoader` class, which is located in the `data_loader.py` module (we won't include its source code here). Suffice to say that the class can load mini-batches and whole datasets of normalized images as `numpy` arrays. We'll also omit the usual imports.

Building the generator and discriminator

First, we'll implement the `build_generator` function. The GAN models we've looked at so far started with some sort of latent vector. But here, the generator input is an image from one of the domains and the output is an image from the opposite domain. Following the paper's guidelines, the generator is a U-Net style network. It has a downsampling encoder, an upsampling decoder, and shortcut connections between the corresponding encoder/decoder blocks. We'll start with the `build_generator` definition:

```
def build_generator(img: Input) -> Model:
```

The U-Net downsampling encoder consists of a number of convolutional layers with `LeakyReLU` activations, followed by `InstanceNormalization`. The difference between batch and instance normalization is that batch normalization computes its parameters across the whole mini-batch, while instance normalization computes them separately for each image of the mini-batch. For clarity, we'll implement a separate subroutine called `downsampling2d`, which defines one such layer. We'll use this function to build the necessary number of layers when we build the network encoder (please note the indentation here; `downsampling2d` is a subroutine defined within `build_generator`):

```
def downsampling2d(layer_input, filters: int):
    """Layers used in the encoder"""
    d = Conv2D(filters=filters,
            kernel_size=4,
            strides=2,
            padding='same')(layer_input)
    d = LeakyReLU(alpha=0.2)(d)
    d = InstanceNormalization()(d)
    return d
```

Next, let's focus on the decoder, which isn't implemented with transpose convolutions. Instead, the input data is upsampled with the `UpSampling2D` operation, which simply duplicates each input pixel as a 2×2 patch. This is followed by a regular convolution to smooth out the patches. This smoothed output is concatenated with the shortcut (or `skip_input`) connection from the corresponding encoder block. The decoder consists of a number of such upsampling blocks. For clarity, we'll implement a separate subroutine called `upsampling2d`, which defines one such block. We'll use it to build the necessary number of blocks for the network decoder (please note the indentation here; `upsampling2d` is a subroutine defined within `build_generator`):

```
def upsampling2d(layer_input, skip_input, filters: int):
    """
    Layers used in the decoder
    :param layer_input: input layer
    :param skip_input: another input from the corresponding encoder
```

```
block
        :param filters: number of filters
        """
        u = UpSampling2D(size=2)(layer_input)
        u = Conv2D(filters=filters,
                kernel_size=4,
                strides=1,
                padding='same',
                activation='relu')(u)
        u = InstanceNormalization()(u)
        u = Concatenate()([u, skip_input])
        return u
```

Next, we'll implement the full definition of the U-Net using the subroutines we just defined (please note the indentation here; the code is part of `build_generator`):

```
# Encoder
gf = 32
d1 = downsampling2d(img, gf)
d2 = downsampling2d(d1, gf * 2)
d3 = downsampling2d(d2, gf * 4)
d4 = downsampling2d(d3, gf * 8)

# Decoder
# Note that we concatenate each upsampling2d block with
# its corresponding downsampling2d block, as per U-Net
u1 = upsampling2d(d4, d3, gf * 4)
u2 = upsampling2d(u1, d2, gf * 2)
u3 = upsampling2d(u2, d1, gf)

u4 = UpSampling2D(size=2)(u3)
output_img = Conv2D(3, kernel_size=4, strides=1, padding='same',
activation='tanh')(u4)

model = Model(img, output_img)

model.summary()

return model
```

Then, we should implement the `build_discriminator` function. We'll omit the implementation here because it is a fairly straightforward CNN, similar to those shown in the previous examples (you can find this in the book's GitHub repository). The only difference is that, instead of using batch normalization, it uses instance normalization.

Putting it all together

At this point, we usually implement the `train` method, but because CycleGAN has more components, we'll show you how to build the entire model. First, we instantiate the `data_loader` object, where you can specify the name of the training set (feel free to experiment with the different datasets). All the images will be resized to `img_res=(IMG_SIZE, IMG_SIZE)` for the network input, where `IMG_SIZE = 256` (you can also try `128` to speed up the training process):

```
# Input shape
img_shape = (IMG_SIZE, IMG_SIZE, 3)

# Configure data loader
data_loader = DataLoader(dataset_name='facades',
                         img_res=(IMG_SIZE, IMG_SIZE))
```

Then, we'll define the optimizer and the loss weights:

```
lambda_cycle = 10.0  # Cycle-consistency loss
lambda_id = 0.1 * lambda_cycle  # Identity loss

optimizer = Adam(0.0002, 0.5)
```

Next, we'll create the two generators, `g_XY` and `g_YX`, and their corresponding discriminators, `d_Y` and `d_X`. We'll also create the `combined` model to train both generators simultaneously. Then, we'll create the composite loss function, which contains an additional identity mapping term. You can read more about it in the respective paper, but in short, it helps preserve color composition between the input and the output when translating images from the painting domain to the photo domain:

```
# Build and compile the discriminators
d_X = build_discriminator(Input(shape=img_shape))
d_Y = build_discriminator(Input(shape=img_shape))
d_X.compile(loss='mse', optimizer=optimizer, metrics=['accuracy'])
d_Y.compile(loss='mse', optimizer=optimizer, metrics=['accuracy'])

# Build the generators
img_X = Input(shape=img_shape)
g_XY = build_generator(img_X)

img_Y = Input(shape=img_shape)
g_YX = build_generator(img_Y)

# Translate images to the other domain
fake_Y = g_XY(img_X)
fake_X = g_YX(img_Y)
```

```
# Translate images back to original domain
reconstr_X = g_YX(fake_Y)
reconstr_Y = g_XY(fake_X)

# Identity mapping of images
img_X_id = g_YX(img_X)
img_Y_id = g_XY(img_Y)

# For the combined model we will only train the generators
d_X.trainable = False
d_Y.trainable = False

# Discriminators determines validity of translated images
valid_X = d_X(fake_X)
valid_Y = d_Y(fake_Y)

# Combined model trains both generators to fool the two discriminators
combined = Model(inputs=[img_X, img_Y],
                 outputs=[valid_X, valid_Y,
                          reconstr_X, reconstr_Y,
                          img_X_id, img_Y_id])
```

Next, let's configure the `combined` model for training:

```
combined.compile(loss=['mse', 'mse',
                       'mae', 'mae',
                       'mae', 'mae'],
                 loss_weights=[1, 1,
                               lambda_cycle, lambda_cycle,
                               lambda_id, lambda_id],
                 optimizer=optimizer)
```

Once the model is ready, we initiate the training process with the `train` function. In line with the paper's guidelines, we will use a mini-batch of size 1:

```
train(epochs=200, batch_size=1, data_loader=data_loader,
      g_XY=g_XY,
      g_YX=g_YX,
      d_X=d_X,
      d_Y=d_Y,
      combined=combined,
      sample_interval=200)
```

Finally, we'll implement the `train` function. It is somewhat similar to the previous GAN models, but it also takes the two pairs of generators and discriminators into account:

```python
def train(epochs: int, data_loader: DataLoader,
          g_XY: Model, g_YX: Model, d_X: Model, d_Y: Model,
          combined:Model, batch_size=1, sample_interval=50):
    start_time = datetime.datetime.now()

    # Calculate output shape of D (PatchGAN)
    patch = int(IMG_SIZE / 2 ** 4)
    disc_patch = (patch, patch, 1)

    # GAN loss ground truths
    valid = np.ones((batch_size,) + disc_patch)
    fake = np.zeros((batch_size,) + disc_patch)

    for epoch in range(epochs):
        for batch_i, (imgs_X, imgs_Y) in
        enumerate(data_loader.load_batch(batch_size)):
            # Train the discriminators

            # Translate images to opposite domain
            fake_Y = g_XY.predict(imgs_X)
            fake_X = g_YX.predict(imgs_Y)

            # Train the discriminators (original images = real /
            translated = Fake)
            dX_loss_real = d_X.train_on_batch(imgs_X, valid)
            dX_loss_fake = d_X.train_on_batch(fake_X, fake)
            dX_loss = 0.5 * np.add(dX_loss_real, dX_loss_fake)

            dY_loss_real = d_Y.train_on_batch(imgs_Y, valid)
            dY_loss_fake = d_Y.train_on_batch(fake_Y, fake)
            dY_loss = 0.5 * np.add(dY_loss_real, dY_loss_fake)

            # Total discriminator loss
            d_loss = 0.5 * np.add(dX_loss, dY_loss)

            # Train the generators
            g_loss = combined.train_on_batch([imgs_X, imgs_Y],
                                             [valid, valid,
                                              imgs_X, imgs_Y,
                                              imgs_X, imgs_Y])

            elapsed_time = datetime.datetime.now() - start_time

            # Plot the progress
            print("[Epoch %d/%d] [Batch %d/%d] [D loss: %f, acc: %3d%%]
```

```
[G loss: %05f, adv: %05f, recon: %05f, id: %05f] time: %s " \
% (epoch, epochs, batch_i, data_loader.n_batches, d_loss[0],
100 * d_loss[1], g_loss[0], np.mean(g_loss[1:3]),
np.mean(g_loss[3:5]), np.mean(g_loss[5:6]), elapsed_time))

# If at save interval => save generated image samples
if batch_i % sample_interval == 0:
    sample_images(epoch, batch_i, g_XY, g_YX, data_loader)
```

The training may take a while to finish, but the process will generate images after each `sample_interval` batch. The following shows some examples of the images that were generated by the Center for Machine Perception facade database (`http://cmp.felk.cvut.cz/~tylecr1/facade/`). It contains building facades, where each pixel is labeled as one of multiple facade-related categories, such as windows, doors, balconies, and so on:

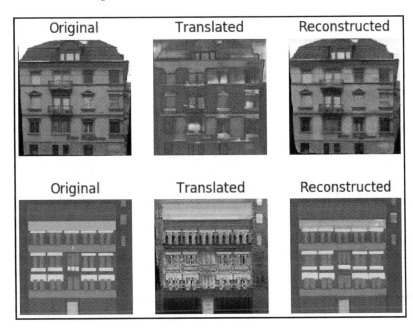

An example of CycleGAN image-to-image translation

This concludes our discussion of GANs. Next, we'll focus on a different type of generative model called artistic style transfer.

Introducing artistic style transfer

In this final section, we'll discuss artistic style transfer. Similar to one of the applications of CycleGAN, it allows us to use the style (or texture) of one image to reproduce the semantic content of another. Although it can be implemented with different algorithms, the most popular way was introduced in 2015 in the *A Neural Algorithm of Artistic Style* paper (https://arxiv.org/abs/1508.06576). It's also known as neural style transfer and it uses (you guessed it!) CNNs. The basic algorithm has been improved and tweaked over the past few years, but in this section we'll explore its original form as this will give us a good foundation for understanding the latest versions.

The algorithm takes two images as input:

- The content image (C) we would like to redraw
- The style image (I) whose style (texture) we'll use to redraw C

The result of the algorithm is a new image: $G = C + S$. The following is an example of neural style transfer:

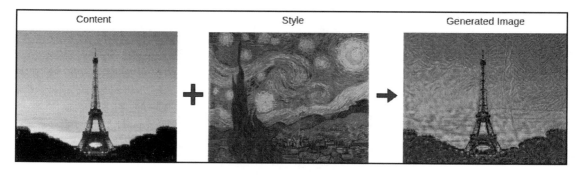

An example of neural style transfer

To understand how neural style transfer works, let's recall that CNNs learn a hierarchical representation of their features. We know that initial convolutional layers learn basic features, such as edges and lines. Conversely, deeper layers learn more complex features, such as faces, cars, and trees. Knowing this, let's look at the algorithm itself:

1. Like many other tasks (for example, Chapter 3, *Object Detection and Image Segmentation*), this algorithm starts with a pretrained VGG network.

2. Feed the network with the content image, C. Extract and store the output activations (or feature maps or slices) of one or more of the hidden convolutional layers in the middle of the network. Let's denote these activations with A_c^l, where l is the index of the layer. We're interested in the middle layers because the level of feature abstraction encoded in them is best suited for this task.

3. Do the same with the style image, S. This time, denote the style activations of the l layer with A_s^l. The layers we choose for the content and style are not necessarily the same.

4. Generate a single random image (white noise), G. This random image will gradually turn into the end result of the algorithm. We'll repeat this for a number of iterations:

    1. Propagate G through the network. This is the only image we'll use throughout the whole process. Like we did previously, we'll store the activations for all the l layers (here, l is a combination of all layers we used for the content and style images). Let's denote these activations with A_g^l.

    2. Compute the difference between the random noise activations, A_g^l, on one hand and A_c^l and A_s^l on the other. These will be the two components of our loss function:

        - $J_c(C, G) = \frac{1}{2} \sum_l (A_c^l - A_g^l)^2$, known as the **content loss**: This is just the MSE over the element-wise difference between the two activations of all l layers.

        - $J_s(S, G)$, known as the **style loss**: This is similar to the content loss, but instead of raw activations we'll compare their **gram matrices** (we won't go into this in any detail).

    3. Use the content and style losses to compute the total loss, $J(G) = \alpha J_C(C, G) + \beta J_s(S, G)$, which is just a weighted sum of the two. The α and β coefficients determine which of the components will carry more weight.

    4. Backpropagate the gradients to the start of the network and update the generated image, $G \leftarrow G - \frac{d}{dG} J(G)$. In this way, we make G more similar to both the content and style images since the loss function is a combination of both.

This algorithm makes it possible for us to harness the powerful representational power of CNNs for artistic style transfer. It does this with a novel loss function and the smart use of backpropagation.

If you are interested in implementing neural style transfer, check out the official PyTorch tutorial at `https://pytorch.org/tutorials/advanced/neural_style_tutorial.html`. Alternatively, go to `https://www.tensorflow.org/beta/tutorials/generative/style_transfer` for the TF 2.0 implementation.

One shortcoming of this algorithm is that it's relatively slow. Typically, we have to repeat this pseudo-training procedure for a couple of hundred iterations to produce a visually appealing result. Fortunately, the paper *Perceptual Losses for Real-Time Style Transfer and Super-Resolution* (`https://arxiv.org/abs/1603.08155`) builds on top of the original algorithm to provide a solution, which is three orders of magnitude faster.

Summary

In this chapter, we discussed how to create new images with generative models, which is one of the most exciting deep learning areas at the moment. We learned about the theoretical foundations of VAEs and then we implemented a simple VAE to generate new MNIST digits. Then, we described the GAN framework and we discussed and implemented multiple types of GAN, including DCGAN, CGAN, WGAN, and CycleGAN. Finally, we mentioned the neural style transfer algorithm. This chapter concludes a series of four chapters dedicated to computer vision and I really hope you've enjoyed them.

In the next few chapters, we'll talk about Natural Language Processing and recurrent networks.

Section 3: Natural Language and Sequence Processing

3

In this section, we'll discuss recurrent networks, natural language, and sequence processing. We'll talk about the state-of-the art techniques in natural language processing, such as sequence and attention models, as well as Google's BERT.

This section contains the following chapters:

- Chapter 6, *Language Modeling*
- Chapter 7, *Understanding Recurrent Networks*
- Chapter 8, *Sequence-to-Sequence Models and Attention*

6
Language Modeling

This chapter is the first of several in which we'll discuss different neural network algorithms in the context of **natural language processing (NLP)**. NLP teaches computers to process and analyze natural language data in order to perform tasks such as machine translation, sentiment analysis, natural language generation, and so on. But to successfully solve such complex problems, we have to represent the natural language in a way that the computer can understand, and this is not a trivial task.

To understand why, let's go back to image recognition. The neural network input is fairly intuitive—a 2D tensor with preprocessed pixel intensities, which preserves the spatial features of the image. Let's take a 28 x 28 MNIST image, which contains 784 pixels. All the information about the digit in the image is contained within these pixels only and we don't need any external information to classify the image. We can also safely assume that each pixel (perhaps excluding the ones near the image borders) carries the same information weight. Therefore, we feed them all to the network to do its magic and we let the results speak for themselves.

Now, let's focus on text data. Unlike an image, we have 1D (as opposed to 2D) data—a single long sequence of words. A general rule of thumb is that a single-spaced A4 page contains 500 words. To feed a network (or any ML algorithm) the informational equivalent of a single MNIST image, we need 1.5 pages of text. The text structure has several hierarchical levels; starting from characters, then words, sentences, and paragraphs, all of which can fit within 1.5 pages of text. All the pixels of the image relate to one digit; however, we don't know whether all the words relate to the same subject. To avoid this complexity, NLP algorithms usually work with shorter sequences. Even though some algorithms use **recurrent neural networks (RNNs)**, which take into account all previous inputs, in practice, they are still limited to a relatively short window of the immediately preceding words. Therefore, an NLP algorithm has to do more (perform well) with less (a smaller amount of input information).

To help us with this, we'll use a special type of vector word representation (language model). The language models we'll discuss use the context of a word (its surrounding words) to create a unique embedding vector associated with that word. These vectors carry more information about the word, compared to, say, one-hot encoding. They serve as a base for various NLP tasks.

In this chapter, we will cover the following topics:

- Understanding *n*-grams
- Introducing neural language models:
    - Neural probabilistic language model
    - Word2Vec and fastText
    - Global Vectors for Word Representation

- Implementing language models

Understanding n-grams

A word-based language model defines a probability distribution over sequences of words. Given a sequence of words of length *m* (for example, a sentence), it assigns a probability *P(w1, ... , w_m)* to the full sequence of words. We can use these probabilities as follows:

- To estimate the likelihood of different phrases in NLP applications.
- As a generative model to create new text. A word-based language model can compute the likelihood of a given word following a sequence of words.

The inference of the probability of a long sequence, say w_1, ..., w_m, is typically infeasible. We can calculate the joint probability of *P(w_1, ... , w_m)* with the chain rule of joint probability (Chapter 1, *The Nuts and Bolts of Neural Networks*):

$$P(w_1, \ldots, w_m) = P(w_m | w_1, \ldots, w_{m-1}) \ldots P(w_3 | w_1, w_2) P(w_2 | w_1) P(w_1)$$

The probability of the later words given the earlier words would be especially difficult to estimate from the data. That's why this joint probability is typically approximated by an independence assumption that the *i*-th word is only dependent on the *n-1* previous words. We'll only model the joint probabilities of combinations of *n* sequential words, called *n*-grams. For example, in the phrase *the quick brown fox*, we have the following *n*-grams:

- **1-gram**: *The*, *quick*, *brown*, and *fox* (also known as a unigram).
- **2-grams**: *The quick*, *quick brown*, and *brown fox* (also known as a bigram).

- **3-grams**: *The quick brown* and *quick brown fox* (also known as a trigram).
- **4-grams**: *The quick brown fox*.

The inference of the joint distribution is approximated with the help of *n*-gram models that split the joint distribution into multiple independent parts.

 The term *n*-grams can refer to other types of sequences of length *n*, such as *n* characters.

If we have a large corpus of text, we can find all the *n*-grams up until a certain *n* (typically 2 to 4) and count the occurrence of each *n*-gram in that corpus. From these counts, we can estimate the probabilities of the last word of each *n*-gram, given the previous *n-1* words:

- **1-gram**:
$$P(word) = \frac{count(word)}{\text{total number of words in corpus}}$$

- **2-gram**:
$$P(w_i|w_{i-1}) = \frac{count(w_{i-1},w_i)}{count(w_{i-1})}$$

- **N-gram**:
$$P(w_{n+i}|w_n,\dots,w_{n+i-1}) = \frac{count(w_n,\dots,w_{n+i-1},w_{n+i})}{count(w_n,\dots,w_{n+i-1})}$$

The independent assumption that the *i*-th word is only dependent on the previous *n-1* words can now be used to approximate the joint distribution.

For example, for a unigram, we can approximate the joint distribution by using the following formula:

$$P(w_1,\dots,w_m) = P(w_1)P(w_2)P(w_3)\dots P(w_m)$$

For a trigram, we can approximate the joint distribution by using the following formula:

$$P(w_1,\dots,w_m) = P(w_1)P(w_2|w_1)P(w_3|w_1,w_2)\dots P(w_m|w_{m-2},w_{m-1})$$

We can see that, based on the vocabulary size, the number of *n*-grams grows exponentially with *n*. For example, if a small vocabulary contains 100 words, then the number of possible 5-grams would be *100^5 = 10,000,000,000* different 5-grams. In comparison, the entire works of Shakespeare contain around 30,000 different words, illustrating the infeasibility of using *n*-grams with a large *n*. Not only is there the issue of storing all the probabilities, but we would also need a very large text corpus to create decent *n*-gram probability estimations for larger values of *n*.

This problem is known as the curse of dimensionality. When the number of possible input variables (words) increases, the number of different combinations of these input values increases exponentially. The curse of dimensionality arises when the learning algorithm needs at least one example per relevant combination of values, which is the case in *n*-gram modeling. The larger our *n*, the better we can approximate the original distribution and the more data we would need to make good estimations of the *n*-gram probabilities.

Now that we are familiar with the *n*-gram model and the curse of dimensionality, let's discuss how to solve it with the help of neural language models.

Introducing neural language models

One way to overcome the curse of dimensionality is by learning a lower-dimensional, distributed representation of the words (*A Neural Probabilistic Language Model*, http://www. jmlr.org/papers/volume3/bengio03a/bengio03a.pdf). This distributed representation is created by learning an embedding function that transforms the space of words into a lower-dimensional space of word embeddings as follows:

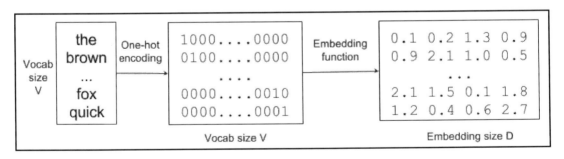

Words -> one-hot encoding -> word embedding vectors

Words from the vocabulary with size V are transformed into one-hot encoding vectors of size V (each word is encoded uniquely). Then, the embedding function transforms this V-dimensional space into a distributed representation of size D (here, $D=4$).

The idea is that the embedding function learns semantic information about the words. It associates each word in the vocabulary with a continuous-valued vector representation, that is, the word embedding. Each word corresponds to a point in this embedding space, and different dimensions correspond to the grammatical or semantic properties of these words.

The goal is to ensure that the words close to each other in the embedding space have similar meanings. In this way, the information that some words are semantically similar can be exploited by the language model. For example, it might learn that *fox* and *cat* are semantically related and that both *the quick brown fox* and *the quick brown cat* are valid phrases. A sequence of words can then be replaced with a sequence of embedding vectors that capture the characteristics of these words. We can use this sequence as a base for various NLP tasks. For example, a classifier trying to classify the sentiment of an article might be trained on using previously learned word embeddings, instead of one-hot encoding vectors. In this way, the semantic information of the words becomes readily available for the sentiment classifier.

Word embeddings are one of the central paradigms when solving NLP tasks. We can use them to improve the performance of other tasks where there might not be a lot of labeled data available. Next, we'll discuss the first neural language model that was introduced in 2001 (which serves as an example that many of the concepts in deep learning are not new).

 We usually denote vectors with bold non-italic lowercase letters, such as **w**. But the convention in neural language models is to use italic lowercase, such as w. In this chapter, we'll use this convention.

In the next section, we will take a look at the **neural probabilistic language model** (NPLM).

Neural probabilistic language model

It is possible to learn the language model and, implicitly, the embedding function via a feedforward fully connected network. Given a sequence of *n-1* words (w_{t-n+1}, ..., w_{t-1}), it tries to output the probability distribution of the next word, w_t (the following diagram is based on `http://www.jmlr.org/papers/volume3/bengio03a/bengio03a.pdf`):

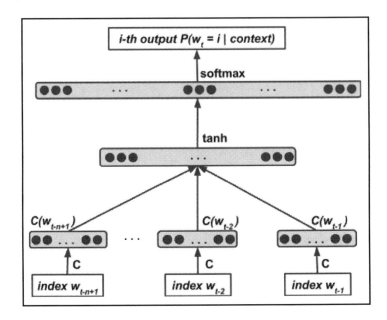

A neural network language model that outputs the probability distribution of the word w_t, given the words w_{t-n+1} ... w_{t-1}. C is the embedding matrix

The network layers play different roles, such as the following:

1. The embedding layer takes the one-hot representation of the word w_i and transforms it into the word's embedding vector by multiplying it with the embedding matrix, **C**. This computation can be efficiently implemented with table lookup. The embedding matrix, **C**, is shared between the words, so all words use the same embedding function. **C** is a $V * D$ matrix, where V is the size of the vocabulary and D is the size of the embedding. In other words, the matrix, **C**, represents the network weights of the hidden *tanh* layer.

2. The resulting embeddings are concatenated and serve as an input to the hidden layer, which uses *tanh* activation. The output of the hidden layer is thus represented by the $\mathbf{z} = \tanh(\mathbf{H} \cdot (\text{concat}(\mathbf{C}(w_{t-n+1}), \ldots, \mathbf{C}(w_{t-1})) + d))$ function, where $\mathbf{H}$ represents the embedding to hidden layer weights and d represents the hidden biases.

3. Finally, we have the output layer with weights, $\mathbf{U}$, bias, b, and softmax activation, which map the hidden layer to the word space probability distribution: $y = \text{softmax}(\mathbf{U}\mathbf{z} + b)$.

This model simultaneously learns an embedding of all the words in the vocabulary (embedding layer) and a model of the probability function for sequences of words (network output). It is able to generalize this probability function to sequences of words that were not seen during training. A specific combination of words in the test set might not be seen in the training set, but a sequence with similar embedding features is much more likely to be seen during training. Since we can construct the training data and labels based on the positions of the words (which already exist in the text), training this model is an unsupervised learning task. Next, we'll discuss the word2vec language model, which was introduced in 2013 and sparked an interest in the field of NLP in the context of neural networks.

Word2Vec

A lot of research has gone into creating better word embedding models, in particular by omitting learning the probability function over sequences of words. One of the most popular ways to do this is with word2vec (http://papers.nips.cc/paper/5021-distributed-representations-of-words-and-phrases-and-their-compositionality.pdf and https://arxiv.org/abs/1301.3781, https://arxiv.org/abs/1310.4546). Similar to NPLM, word2vec creates embedding vectors based on the context (surrounding words) of the word in focus. It comes in two flavors: **continuous bag of words** (CBOW) and **Skip-gram**. We'll start with CBOW and then we'll discuss Skip-gram.

CBOW

CBOW predicts the most likely word given its context (surrounding words). For example, given the sequence *The quick _____ fox jumps*, the model will predict *brown*. The context is the n preceding and the n following words of the word in focus (unlike NPLM, where only the preceding words participate). The following screenshot shows the context window as it slides across the text:

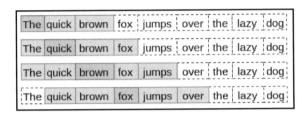

A word2vec sliding context window with $n = 2$. The same type of context window applies to both CBOW and Skip-gram

CBOW takes all words within the context with equal weights and doesn't consider their order (hence the *bag* in the name). It is somewhat similar to NPLM, but because it learns only the embedding vectors, we'll train the model with the help of the following simple neural network:

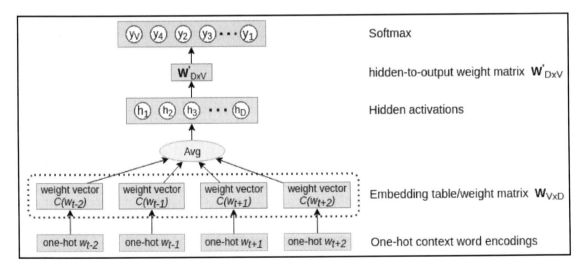

A CBOW model network

Here's how it works:

- The network has input, hidden, and output layers.
- The input is the one-hot encoded word representations. The one-hot encoded vector size of each word is equal to the size of the vocabulary, V.
- The embedding vectors are represented by the input-to-hidden weights, $\mathbf{W}_{V \times D}$, of the network. They are $V \times D$-shaped matrix, where D is the length of the embedding vector (which is the same as the number of units in the hidden layer). As in NPLM, we can think of the weights as a lookup table, where each row represents one word embedding vector. Because each input word is one-hot encoded, it will always activate a single row of the weights. That is, for each input sample (word), only the word's own embedding vector will participate.
- The embedding vectors of all context words are averaged to produce the output of the hidden network layer (there is no activation function).
- The hidden activations serve as input to the output softmax layer of size V (with the weight vector $\mathbf{W'}_{D \times V}$), which predicts the most likely word to be found in the context (proximity) of the input words. The index with the highest activation represents the one-hot encoded related word.

We'll train the network with gradient descent and backpropagation. The training set consists of (context and label) one-hot encoded pairs of words, appearing in close proximity to each other in the text. For example, if part of the text is the sequence [the, quick, brown, fox, jumps] and $n = 2$, the training tuples will include ([quick, brown], the), ([the, brown, fox], quick), ([the, quick, fox jumps], brown), and so on. Since we are only interested in the embeddings, $\mathbf{W}_{V \times D}$, we'll discard the rest of the network weights, $\mathbf{W'}_{V \times D}$, when the training is finished.

CBOW will tell us which word is most likely to appear in a given context. This could be a problem for rare words. For example, given the context *The weather today is really* ____, the model will predict the word *beautiful* rather than *fabulous* (hey, it's just an example). CBOW is several times faster to train than the Skip-gram and achieves slightly better accuracy for frequent words.

Skip-gram

Given an input word, the Skip-gram model can predict its context (the opposite of CBOW). For example, the word *brown* will predict the words *The quick fox jumps*. Unlike CBOW, the input is a single one-hot word. But how do we represent the context words in the output? Instead of trying to predict the whole context (all surrounding words) simultaneously, Skip-gram transforms the context into multiple training pairs such as (fox, the), (fox, quick), (fox, brown), and (fox, jumps). Once again, we can train the model with a simple one-layer network:

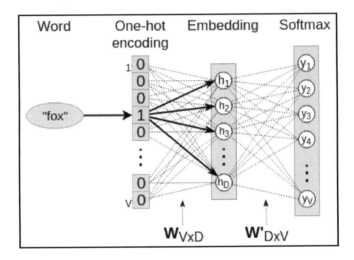

A Skip-gram model network

As with CBOW, the output is a softmax, which represents the one-hot encoded most probable context word. The input-to-hidden weights, $\mathbf{W}_{VxD}$, represent the word embeddings lookup table and the hidden-to-output weights, $\mathbf{W}'_{DxV}$, are only relevant during training. The hidden layer doesn't have an activation function (that is, it uses linear activation).

We'll train the model with backpropagation (no surprises here). Given a sequence of words, $w_1, ..., w_M$, the objective of the Skip-gram model is to maximize the average log probability where n is the window size:

$$\frac{1}{M} \sum_{m=1}^{M} \sum_{-n \leq i \leq n, \ i \neq 0} \log p(w_{m+i} | w_m)$$

The model defines the probability, $P(w_{m+i}|w_m)$, as the following:

$$P(w_O|w_I) = \frac{\exp({\mathbf{v}'_{w_O}}^\mathsf{T} \mathbf{v}_{w_I})}{\sum_{w=1}^{V} \exp({\mathbf{v}'_w}^\mathsf{T} \mathbf{v}_{w_I})}$$

In this example, w_I and w_O are the input and output words and $\mathbf{v}_w$ and $\mathbf{v}'_w$ are the corresponding word vectors in the input and output weights $\mathbf{W}_{V \times D}$ and $\mathbf{W}'_{D \times V}$, respectively (we keep the original notation of the paper). Since the net doesn't have a hidden activation function, its output value for one input/output word pair is simply the multiplication of the input word vector, $\mathbf{v}_{w_I}$, and the output word vector, $\mathbf{v}'_{w_O}$ (hence the transpose operation).

The authors of the word2vec paper note that word representations cannot represent idiomatic phrases that are not compositions of the individual words. For example, *New York Times* is a newspaper, and not just a natural combination of the meanings of *New, York,* and *Times*. To overcome this, the model can be extended to include whole phrases. However, this significantly increases the vocabulary size. And, as we can see from the preceding formula, the softmax denominator needs to compute the output vectors for all words of the vocabulary. Additionally, every weight of the $\mathbf{W}'_{D \times V}$ matrix is updated on every training step, which slows the training.

To solve this, we can replace the softmax with the so-called **negative sampling (NEG)**. For each training sample, we'll take the positive training pair (for example, (fox, brown)), as well as k additional negative pairs (for example, (fox, puzzle)), where k is usually in the range of [5,20]. Instead of predicting the word that best matches the input word (softmax), we'll simply predict whether the current pair of words is true or not. In effect, we convert the multinomial classification problem (classify as one of many classes) to a binary logistic regression (or binary classification) problem. By learning the distinction between positive and negative pairs, the classifier will eventually learn the word vectors in the same way, as with multinomial classification. In word2vec, the words for the negative pairs are drawn from a special distribution, which draws less frequent words more often, compared to more frequent ones.

Some of the most frequent words to occur carry less information value compared to the rare words. Examples of such words are the definite and indefinite articles *a*, *an*, and *the*. The model will benefit more from observing the pairs *London* and *city* compared to *the* and *city* because almost all words co-occur frequently with *the*. The opposite is also true—the vector representations of frequent words do not change significantly after training on a large number of examples. To counter the imbalance between the rare and frequent words, the authors of the paper propose a subsampling approach, where each word, w_i, of the training set is discarded with some probability, computed by the heuristic formula where $f(w_i)$ is the frequency of word w_i and t is a threshold (usually around 10^{-5}):

$$P(w_i) = 1 - \sqrt{\frac{t}{f(w_i)}}$$

It aggressively subsamples words with a frequency of greater than t, but also preserves the ranking of the frequencies.

In conclusion, we can say that, in general, Skip-gram performs better on rare words compared to CBOW, but it takes longer to train.

fastText

fastText (https://fasttext.cc/) is a library for learning word embeddings and text classification created by the **Facebook AI Research (FAIR)** group. Word2Vec treats each word in the corpus as an atomic entity and generates a vector for each word, but this approach ignores the internal structure of the words. In contrast, fastText decomposes each word, w, to a bag of character n-grams. For example, if $n = 3$, we can decompose the word *there* to the character 3-grams and the special sequence *<there>* for the whole word:

<th, the, her, ere, re>

Note the use of the special characters < and > to indicate the start and the end of the word. This is necessary to avoid mismatching between n-grams from different words. For example, the word *her* will be represented as *<her>* and it will not be mistaken for the n-gram *her* from the word *there*. The authors of fastText suggest $3 \le n \le 6$.

Recall the softmax formula we introduced in the *Skip-gram* section. Let's generalize it by replacing the vector multiplication operation of the word2vec network with a generic scoring function, *s*, where w_t is the input word and w_c is the context word:

$$P(w_c|w_t) = \frac{\exp(s(w_t, w_c))}{\sum_{w=1}^{V} \exp(s(w_t, w_j))}$$

In the case of fastText, we'll represent a word with the sum of the vector representations of its *n*-grams. Let's denote the set of *n*-grams that appear in word *w* with $G_w = \{1 \ldots G\}$, the vector representation of an *n*-gram, *g*, with $\mathbf{v}_g$, and the potential vector of the context word, *c*, with $\mathbf{v}'_c$. Then, the scoring function defined by fastText becomes the following:

$$s(w, c) = \sum_{g \in G_{w_t}} \mathbf{v}_g^{\mathsf{T}} \mathbf{v}'_c$$

In effect, we train the fastText model with Skip-gram type word pairs, but the input word is represented as a bag of *n*-grams.

Using character *n*-grams has several advantages over the traditional word2vec model:

- It can classify unknown or misspelled words if they share *n*-grams with other words familiar to the model.
- It can generate better word embeddings for rare words. Even if a word is rare, its character *n*-grams are still shared with other words, so the embeddings can still be good.

Now that we are familiar with word2vec, we'll introduce the Global Vectors for Word Representation language model, which improves some word2vec deficiencies.

Global Vectors for Word Representation model

One disadvantage of word2vec is that it only uses the local context of words and doesn't consider their global co-occurrences. In this way, the model loses a readily available, valuable source of information. As the name suggests, the **Global Vectors for Word Representation (GloVe)** model tries to solve this (`https://nlp.stanford.edu/pubs/glove.pdf`).

The algorithm starts with the global word-word co-occurrence matrix, **X**. A cell, X_{ij}, indicates how often the word j appears in the context of word i. The following table shows the co-occurrence matrix for a window with size $n = 2$ of the sequence *I like DL. I like NLP. I enjoy cycling*:

$n = 2$	I	like	DL	NLP	enjoy	cycling	.
I	0	2	2	2	1	1	2
like	2	0	1	1	0	0	2
DL	2	1	0	0	0	0	1
NLP	2	1	0	0	0	0	1
enjoy	1	0	0	0	0	1	2
cycling	1	0	0	0	1	0	1
.	2	2	1	1	2	1	0

A co-occurrence matrix of the sequence I like DL. I like NLP. I enjoy cycling

Let's denote the number of times any word appears in the context of word i with $X_i = \sum_k X_{ik}$ and the probability that word j appears in the context of word i with $P_{ij} = P(j|i) = X_{ij}/X_i$. To better understand how this can help us, we'll use an example that shows the co-occurrence probabilities for the target words *ice* and *steam* with selected context words from a 6 billion token corpus:

Probability and Ratio	$k = solid$	$k = gas$	$k = water$	$k = fashion$
$P(k|ice)$	1.9×10^{-4}	6.6×10^{-5}	3.0×10^{-3}	1.7×10^{-5}
$P(k|steam)$	2.2×10^{-5}	7.8×10^{-4}	2.2×10^{-3}	1.8×10^{-5}
$P(k|ice)/P(k|steam)$	8.9	8.5×10^{-2}	1.36	0.96

Co-occurrence probabilities for the target words ice and steam with selected context words from a 6 billion token corpus: source: https://nlp.stanford.edu/pubs/glove.pdf

The bottom row shows the ratio of the probabilities. The word **solid** (the first column) is related to **ice**, but less related to **steam**, so the ratio between their probabilities is large. Conversely, **gas** is more related to **steam** than to **ice** and the ratio between their probabilities is very small. The words **water** and **fashion** are equally related to both target words, hence the ratio of the probabilities is close to one. The ratio is better in distinguishing relevant words (**solid** and **gas**) from irrelevant words (**water** and **fashion**), compared to the raw probabilities. Additionally, it is better at discriminating between the two relevant words.

With the previous argument, the authors of GloVe propose starting the word vector learning with the ratios of co-occurrence probabilities, rather than the probabilities themselves. With that starting point, and keeping in mind that the ratio P_{ik}/P_{jk} depends on three words—i, j, and k—we can define the most general form of the GloVe model as follows, where $w \in \mathbb{R}^D$ are the word vectors and $\tilde{w} \in \mathbb{R}^D$ is a special context vector, which we'll discuss later ($\mathbb{R}^D$ is the D-dimensional vector space of real numbers):

$$F(w_i, w_j, \tilde{w}_k) = \frac{P_{ik}}{P_{jk}}$$

In other words, F is such a function that, when computed with these three specific vectors (we assume that we already know them), will output the ratio of probabilities. Furthermore, F should encode the information of the probabilities ratio because we've already identified its importance. Since vector spaces are inherently linear, one way to encode this information is with the vector difference of the two target words. Therefore, the function becomes the following:

$$F(w_i - w_j, \tilde{w}_k) = \frac{P_{ik}}{P_{jk}}$$

Next, let's note that the function arguments are vectors, but the ratio of probabilities is scalar. To solve this issue, we can take the dot product of the arguments:

$$F((w_i - w_j)^\mathsf{T} \tilde{w}_k) = \frac{P_{ik}}{P_{jk}}$$

Then, let's observe that the distinction between a word and its context word is arbitrary and we can freely exchange the two roles. Therefore, we should have $F(w_i, w_j, \tilde{w}_k) = F(w_j, w_i, \tilde{w}_k)$, but the preceding equation doesn't satisfy this condition. Long story short (there is a more detailed explanation in the paper), to satisfy this condition, we need to introduce another restriction in the form of the following equation where, b_i and $\tilde{b}_k$ are bias scalar values:

$$w_i^\mathsf{T} \tilde{w}_k + b_i + \tilde{b}_k = \log(X_{ik})$$

One issue with this formula is that *log(0)* is undefined, but the majority of the X_{ik} entries will be *0*. Additionally, it takes all co-occurrences with the same weight, but rare co-occurrences are noisy and carry less information than the more frequent ones. To solve all these issues, the authors propose a least squares regression model with a weighting function, $f(X_{ij})$, for each co-occurrence. The model has the following cost function:

$$J = \sum_{i,j=1}^{V} f(X_{ij})(w_i^T \tilde{w}_j + b_i + \tilde{b}_j - \log(X_{ij}))^2$$

Finally, the weighting function, *f*, should satisfy several properties. First, *f(0) = 0*. Then, *f(x)* should be non-decreasing so that rare co-occurrences are not overweighted. And finally, *f(x)* should be relatively small for large values of *x*, so that frequent co-occurrences are not overweighted. Based on these properties and their experiments, the authors propose the following function:

$$f(x) = \begin{cases} (x/x_{max})^\alpha & \text{if } x < x_{max} \\ 1 & \text{otherwise} \end{cases}$$

The following graph shows *f(x)*:

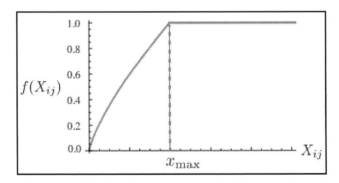

Weighting function $f(X_{ij})$ with a cut-off value of $x_{max}= 100$ and $\alpha = 3/4$. The authors' experiments show that these parameters work best: source: https://nlp.stanford.edu/pubs/glove.pdf

The model generates two sets of word vectors: W and $\tilde{W}$. When X is symmetric, W and $\tilde{W}$ are equivalent and differ only as a result of their random initializations. But the authors note that training an ensemble of networks and averaging their results usually helps to prevent overfitting. To mimic this behavior, they choose to use the sum $W + \tilde{W}$ as the final word vectors, observing a small increase in the performance.

This concludes our discussion about neural language models. In the next section, we'll see how to train and visualize a word2vec model.

Implementing language models

In this section, we'll implement a short pipeline for preprocessing text sequences and training a word2vec model with the processed data. We'll also implement another example to visualize embedding vectors and check some of their interesting properties.

The code in this section requires the following Python packages:

- **Gensim** (version 3.80, `https://radimrehurek.com/gensim/`) is an open source Python library for unsupervised topic modeling and NLP. It supports all three models that we have discussed so far (word2vec, GloVe, and fastText).
- The **Natural Language Toolkit** (**NLTK**, `https://www.nltk.org/`, ver 3.4.4) is a Python suite of libraries and programs for symbolic and statistical NLP.
- Scikit-learn (ver 0.19.1, `https://scikit-learn.org/`) is an open source Python ML library with various classification, regression, and clustering algorithms. More specifically, we'll use **t-Distributed Stochastic Neighbor Embedding** (**t-SNE**, `https://lvdmaaten.github.io/tsne/`) to visualize high-dimensional embedding vectors (more on that later).

With this introduction, let's continue with training the language model.

Training the embedding model

In the first example, we'll train a word2vec model on the classic novel *War and Peace* by Leo Tolstoy. The novel is stored as a regular text file in the code repository. Let's start:

1. As the tradition goes, we'll do the imports:

```
import logging
import pprint  # beautify prints

import gensim
import nltk
```

2. Then, we'll set the logging level to `INFO` so we can track the training progress:

```
logging.basicConfig(level=logging.INFO)
```

3. Next, we'll implement the text tokenization pipeline. Tokenization refers to the breaking up of a text sequence into pieces (or **tokens**) such as words, keywords, phrases, symbols, and other elements. Tokens can be individual words, phrases, or even whole sentences. We'll implement two-level tokenization; first, we'll split the text into sentences and then we'll split each sentence into individual words:

```
class TokenizedSentences:
    """Split text to sentences and tokenize them"""

    def __init__(self, filename: str):
        self.filename = filename

    def __iter__(self):
        with open(self.filename) as f:
            corpus = f.read()

        raw_sentences = nltk.tokenize.sent_tokenize(corpus)
        for sentence in raw_sentences:
            if len(sentence) > 0:
                yield gensim.utils.simple_preprocess(sentence,
min_len=2, max_len=15)
```

The `TokenizedSentences` iterator takes as an argument the text filename, where the novel is located. Here's how the rest of it works:

1. The iteration starts by reading the full contents of the file in the `corpus` variable.
2. The raw text is split into a list of sentences (the `raw_sentences` variable) with the help of NLTK's `nltk.tokenize.sent_tokenize(corpus)` function. For example, it will return a `['I like DL.', 'I like NLP.', 'I enjoy cycling.']` for input list `'I like DL. I like NLP. I enjoy cycling.'`.
3. Next, each `sentence` is preprocessed with the `gensim.utils.simple_preprocess(sentence, min_len=2, max_len=15)` function. It converts a document into a list of lowercase tokens, ignoring tokens that are too short or too long. For example, the `'I like DL'` sentence will be tokenized to the `['like', 'dl']` list. The punctuation characters are also removed. The tokenized sentence is yielded as the final result.

4. Then, we'll instantiate `TokenizedSentences`:

```
sentences = TokenizedSentences('war_and_peace.txt')
```

5. Next, we'll instantiate Gensim's word2vec training model:

```
model = gensim.models.word2vec. \
    Word2Vec(sentences=sentences,
             sg=1,  # 0 for CBOW and 1 for Skip-gram
             window=5,  # the size of the context window
             negative=5,  # negative sampling word count
             min_count=5,  # minimal word occurrences to include
             iter=5,  # number of epochs
             )
```

The model takes `sentences` as a training dataset. `Word2Vec` supports all parameters and variants of the model that we've discussed in this chapter. For example, you can switch between CBOW or Skip-gram with the `sg` parameter. You can also set the context window size, negative sampling count, number of epochs, and other things. You can explore all parameters in the code itself.

Alternatively, you can use the fastText model by replacing `gensim.models.word2vec.Word2Vec` with `gensim.models.fasttext.FastText` (it works with the same input parameters).

6. The `Word2Vec` constructor also initiates the training. After a short time (you don't need the GPU, as the training dataset is small), the generated embedding vectors are stored in the `model.wv` object. On one hand, it acts like a dictionary and you can access the vector for each word with `model.wv['WORD_GOES_HERE']`, however, it also supports some other interesting functionality. You can measure the similarity between different words based on the difference of their word vectors with the `model.wv.most_similar` method. First, it converts each word vector to a unit vector (a vector with a length of one). Then, it computes the dot product between the unit vector of the target word and the unit vectors of all other words. The higher the dot product between two vectors, the more similar they are. For example, `pprint.pprint(model.wv.most_similar(positive='mother', topn=5))` will output the five most similar words to the word `'mother'` and their dot products:

```
[('sister', 0.9024157524108887),
 ('daughter', 0.8976515531539917),
 ('brother', 0.8965438008308411),
 ('father', 0.8935455679893494),
 ('husband', 0.8779271245002747)]
```

The result serves as a kind of proof that the word vectors correctly encode the meaning of the words. The word `'mother'` is indeed related by meaning to `'sister'`, `'daughter'`, and so on.

We can also find the most similar words to a combination of target words. For example, `model.wv.most_similar(positive=['woman', 'king'], topn=5)` will take the mean of the word vectors of `'woman'` and `'king'` and then it will find the words with the most similar vectors to the new mean value:

```
[('heiress', 0.9176832437515259), ('admirable',
0.9104862213134766), ('honorable', 0.9047746658325195),
('creature', 0.9040032625198364), ('depraved', 0.9013445973396301)]
```

We can see that some of the words are relevant (`'heiress'`), but most aren't (`'creature'`, `'admirable'`). Perhaps our training dataset is too small to capture more complex relations like these.

Visualizing embedding vectors

To obtain better word vectors, compared to the ones in the *Training embedding model* section, we'll train another word2vec model. However, this time, we will use a larger corpus—the `text8` dataset, which consists of the first 100,000,000 bytes of plain text from Wikipedia. The dataset is included in Gensim and it's tokenized as a single long list of words. With that, let's start:

1. As usual, the imports are first. We'll also set the logging to `INFO` for good measure:

```
import logging
import pprint  # beautify prints

import gensim.downloader as gensim_downloader
import matplotlib.pyplot as plt
import numpy as np
from gensim.models.word2vec import Word2Vec
from sklearn.manifold import TSNE

logging.basicConfig(level=logging.INFO)
```

2. Next, we'll train the `Word2vec` model. This time, we'll use CBOW for faster training. We'll load the dataset with `gensim_downloader.load('text8')`:

```
model = Word2Vec(
    sentences=gensim_downloader.load('text8'),  # download and load
the text8 dataset
    sg=0, size=100, window=5, negative=5, min_count=5, iter=5)
```

3. To see if this model is better, we can try to find the words most similar to `'woman'` and `'king'`, but most dissimilar to `'man'`. Ideally, one of the words would be `'queen'`. We can do this with the expression `pprint.pprint(model.wv.most_similar(positive=['woman', 'king'], negative=['man']))`. The output is as follows:

```
[('queen', 0.6532326936721802), ('prince', 0.6139929294586182),
('empress', 0.6126195192337036), ('princess', 0.6075714230537415),
('elizabeth', 0.588543176651001), ('throne', 0.5846244692802429),
('daughter', 0.5667101144790649), ('son', 0.5659586191177368),
('isabella', 0.5611927509307861), ('scots', 0.5606790781021118)]
```

Indeed, the most similar word is `'queen'`, but the rest of the words are relevant as well.

4. Next, we'll display the words in a 2D plot with the help of a t-SNE visualization model on the collected word vectors. The t-SNE models each high-dimensional embedding vector on a two- or three-dimensional point in a way where similar objects are modeled on nearby points and dissimilar objects are modeled on distant points with a high probability. We'll start with several `target_words` and then we'll collect clusters of the *n* most similar words (and their vectors) to each target word. The following is the code that does this:

```
target_words = ['mother', 'car', 'tree', 'science', 'building',
'elephant', 'green']
word_groups, embedding_groups = list(), list()

for word in target_words:
    words = [w for w, _ in model.most_similar(word, topn=5)]
    word_groups.append(words)

    embedding_groups.append([model.wv[w] for w in words])
```

5. Then, we'll train a t-SNE visualization model on the collected clusters with the following parameters:

- `perplexity` is loosely related to the number of nearest neighbors considered when matching the original and the reduced vectors for each point. In other words, it determines whether the algorithm will focus on the local or the global properties of the data.
- `n_components=2` specifies the number of output vector dimensions.
- `n_iter=5000` is the number of training iterations.
- `init='pca'` to use **principal component analysis (PCA)**-based initialization.

The model takes the `embedding_groups` clusters as input and outputs the `embeddings_2d` array with 2D embedding vectors. The following is the implementation:

```
# Train the t-SNE algorithm
embedding_groups = np.array(embedding_groups)
m, n, vector_size = embedding_groups.shape
tsne_model = TSNE(perplexity=8, n_components=2, init='pca',
n_iter=5000)

# generate 2d embeddings from the original 100d ones
embeddings_2d = tsne_model.fit_transform(embedding_groups.reshape(m
* n, vector_size))
embeddings_2d = np.array(embeddings_2d).reshape(m, n, 2)
```

6. Next, we'll display the new 2D embeddings. To do this, we'll initialize the plot and some of its properties for better visibility:

```
# Plot the results
plt.figure(figsize=(16, 9))
# Different color and marker for each group of similar words
color_map = plt.get_cmap('Dark2')(np.linspace(0, 1,
len(target_words)))
markers = ['o', 'v', 's', 'x', 'D', '*', '+']
```

7. Then, we'll iterate over each `similar_words` cluster and we'll display its words on a scatter plot as points. We'll use a unique marker for each cluster. The points will be annotated with their corresponding words:

```
# Iterate over all groups
for label, similar_words, emb, color, marker in \
        zip(target_words, word_groups, embeddings_2d, color_map,
markers):
    x, y = emb[:, 0], emb[:, 1]
```

```
# Plot the points of each word group
plt.scatter(x=x, y=y, c=color, label=label, marker=marker)

# Annotate each point with its corresponding caption
for word, w_x, w_y in zip(similar_words, x, y):
    plt.annotate(word, xy=(w_x, w_y), xytext=(0, 15),
                 textcoords='offset points', ha='center',
va='top', size=10)
```

8. Finally, we'll display the plot:

```
plt.legend()
plt.grid(True)
plt.show()
```

We can see how each cluster of related words is grouped in a close region of the 2D plot:

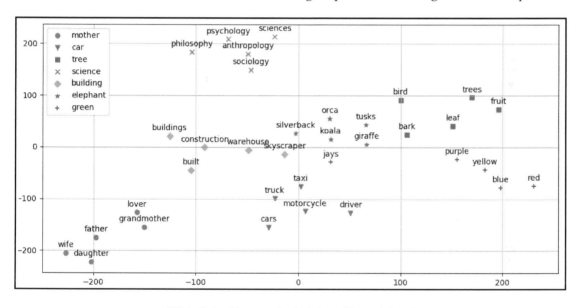

t-SNE visualization of the target words and their clusters of the most similar words

The graph, once again, proves that the obtained word vectors contain relevant information for the words. With the end of this example, we conclude the chapter as well.

Summary

This was the first chapter devoted to NLP. Appropriately, we started with the basic building blocks of most NLP algorithms today—the words and their context-based vector representations. We started with *n*-grams and the need to represent words as vectors. Then, we discussed the word2vec, fastText, and GloVe models. Finally, we implemented a simple pipeline to train an embedding model and we visualized word vectors with t-SNE.

In the next chapter, we'll discuss RNNs—a neural network architecture that naturally lends itself to NLP tasks.

7
Understanding Recurrent Networks

In Chapter 1, *The Nuts and Bolts of Neural Networks*, and Chapter 2, *Understanding Convolutional Networks*, we took an in-depth look at the properties of general feedforward networks and their specialized incarnation, **Convolutional Neural Networks (CNNs)**. In this chapter, we'll close this story arc with **Recurrent Neural Networks (RNNs)**. The NN architectures we discussed in the previous chapters take in a fixed-sized input and provide a fixed-sized output. RNNs lift this constraint with their ability to process input sequences of a variable length by defining a recurrent relationship over these sequences (hence the name). If you are familiar with some of the topics that will be discussed in this chapter, you can skip them.

In this chapter, we will cover the following topics:

- Introduction to RNNs
- Introducing long short-term memory
- Introducing gated recurrent units
- Implementing text classification

Introduction to RNNs

RNNs are neural networks that can process sequential data with a variable length. Examples of such data include the words of a sentence or the price of stock at various moments in time. By using the word sequential, we imply that the elements of the sequence are related to each other and that their order matters. For example, if we take a book and randomly shuffle all of the words in it, the text will lose its meaning, even though we'll still know the individual words. Naturally, we can use RNNs to solve tasks that relate to sequential data. Examples of such tasks are language translation, speech recognition, predicting the next element of a time series, and so on.

RNNs get their name because they apply the same function over a sequence recurrently. We can define an RNN as a recurrence relation:

$$\mathbf{s}_t = f(\mathbf{s}_{t-1}, \mathbf{x}_t)$$

Here, f is a differentiable function, $\mathbf{s}_t$ is a vector of values called the internal network state (at step t), and $\mathbf{x}_t$ is the network input at step t. Unlike regular networks, where the state only depends on the current input (and network weights), here, $\mathbf{s}_t$ is a function of both the current input as well as the previous state, $\mathbf{s}_{t-1}$. You can think of $\mathbf{s}_{t-1}$ as the network's summary of all of the previous inputs. This is unlike the regular feedforward networks (including CNNs), which take only the current input sample as input. The recurrence relationship defines how the state evolves step by step over the sequence via a feedback loop over previous states, as illustrated in the following diagram:

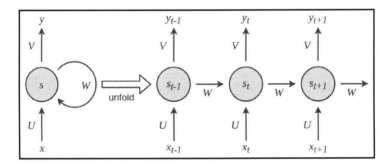

Left: Visual illustration of the RNN recurrence relation: $s_t = Ws_{t-1} + Ux_t$. The final output will be $y_t = Vs_t$. Right: The RNN states are recurrently unfolded over the sequence $t-1$, t, $t+1$. Note that the parameters U, V, and W are shared between all steps

The RNN has three sets of parameters (or weights):

- **U** transforms the input, $\mathbf{x}_t$, into the state, $\mathbf{s}_t$.
- **W** transforms the previous state, $\mathbf{s}_{t-1}$, into the current state, $\mathbf{s}_t$.
- **V** maps the newly computed internal state, $\mathbf{s}_t$, to the output, $\mathbf{y}_t$.

U, **V**, and **W** apply linear transformation over their respective inputs. The most basic case of such a transformation is the familiar weighted sum we know and love. We can now define the internal state and the network output as follows:

$$\mathbf{s}_t = f(\mathbf{W}\mathbf{s}_{t-1} + \mathbf{U}\mathbf{x}_t)$$

$$\mathbf{y}_t = \mathbf{V}\mathbf{s}_t$$

Here, f is the non-linear activation function (such as tanh, sigmoid, or ReLU).

For example, in a word-level language model, the input, *x*, will be a sequence of words encoded in input vectors *(*$\mathbf{x}_1$ ... $\mathbf{x}_t$ ...*)*. The state, *s*, will be a sequence of state vectors *(*$\mathbf{s}_1$ ... $\mathbf{s}_t$ ...*)*. Finally, the output, *y*, will be a sequence of probability vectors *(*$\mathbf{y}_1$ ... $\mathbf{y}_t$ ... *)* of the next words in the sequence.

Note that, in an RNN, each state is dependent on all of the previous computations through this recurrence relation. An important implication of this is that RNNs have memory over time because the states, *s*, contain information based on the previous steps. In theory, RNNs can remember information for an arbitrarily long period of time, but in practice, they are limited to looking back only a few steps. We will address this issue in more detail in the *Vanishing and exploding gradients* section.

The RNN we described here is somewhat equivalent to a single layer regular neural network (with an additional recurrence relationship). As we now know from `Chapter 1`, *The Nuts and Bolts of Neural Networks*, a network with a single layer has some serious limitations. Fear not! As with regular networks, we can stack multiple RNNs to form a **stacked RNN**. The cell state, $\mathbf{s}^l_t$, of an RNN cell at level *l* at time *t* will take the output, $\mathbf{y}^{l-1}_t$, of the RNN cell from level *l-1* and the previous cell state, $\mathbf{s}^l_{t-1}$, of the cell at the same level, *l*, as the input:

$$\mathbf{s}^l_t = f(\mathbf{s}^l_{t-1}, \mathbf{y}^{l-1}_t)$$

In the following diagram, we can see an unfolded, stacked RNN:

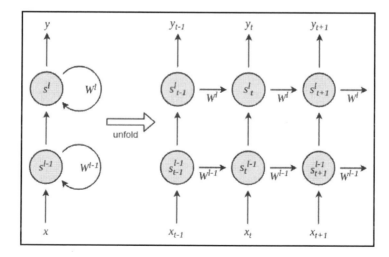

Stacked RNN

The RNN we've discussed so far takes the preceding elements of the sequence to produce an output. This makes sense for tasks such as time series prediction, where we want to predict the next element of the series based on the previous elements. But it also imposes unnecessary limitations on other tasks, such as the ones from the NLP domain. As we saw in Chapter 6, *Language Modeling*, we can obtain a lot of information about a word by its context and it makes sense to extract that context from both the preceding and succeeding words.

We can extend the regular RNN to the so-called **bidirectional RNN** to cover this scenario, as shown in the following diagram:

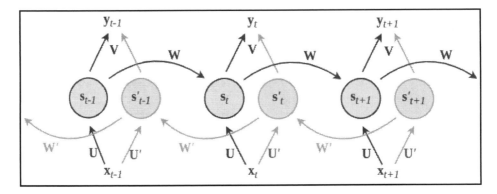

Bidirectional RNN

This network has two propagation loops working in both directions, that is, left to right from steps *t* to *t+1* and right to left from steps *t+1* to *t*. We'll denote the right to left propagation related notations with the prim symbol (not to be confused with derivatives). At each time step, *t*, the network maintains two internal state vectors: s_t for the left to right propagation and s'_t for the right to left propagation. The right to left phase has its own set of input weights, U' and W', mirroring the weights, U and W, for the left to right phase. The formula for the right to left hidden state vector is as follows:

$$s'_t = f(W's'_{t+1} + U'x_t)$$

The output of the network, y_t, is a combination of the internal states, s_t and s_{t+1}. One way to combine them is with concatenation. In this case, we'll denote the weight matrix of the concatenated states to the output with **V**. Here, the formula for the output is as follows:

$$y_t = V[s_t; s'_t]$$

Alternatively, we can simply sum the two state vectors:

$$\mathbf{y}_t = \mathbf{V}(\mathbf{s}_t + \mathbf{s}'_t)$$

Because RNNs are not limited to processing fixed-size inputs, they really expand the possibilities of what we can compute with neural networks, such as sequences of different lengths or images of varied sizes.

Let's go over some different combinations:

- **One-to-one**: This is non-sequential processing, such as feedforward neural networks and CNNs. Note that, there isn't much difference between a feedforward network and applying an RNN to a single time step. An example of one-to-one processing is image classification, which we looked at in Chapter 2, *Understanding Convolutional Networks*, and Chapter 3, *Advanced Convolutional Networks*.

- **One-to-many**: This processing generates a sequence based on a single input, for example, caption generation from an image (*Show and Tell: A Neural Image Caption Generator*, https://arxiv.org/abs/1411.4555).

- **Many-to-one**: This processing outputs a single result based on a sequence, for example, sentiment classification of text.

- **Many-to-many indirect**: A sequence is encoded into a state vector, after which this state vector is decoded into a new sequence, for example, language translation (*Learning Phrase Representations using RNN Encoder-Decoder for Statistical Machine Translation*, https://arxiv.org/abs/1406.1078 and *Sequence to Sequence Learning with Neural Networks*, http://papers.nips.cc/paper/5346-sequence-to-sequence-learning-with-neural-networks.pdf).

- **Many-to-many direct:** This outputs a result for each input step, for example, frame phoneme labeling in speech recognition.

 The many-to-many models are often referred to as **sequence-to-sequence (seq2seq)** models.

The following is a graphical representation of the preceding input-output combinations:

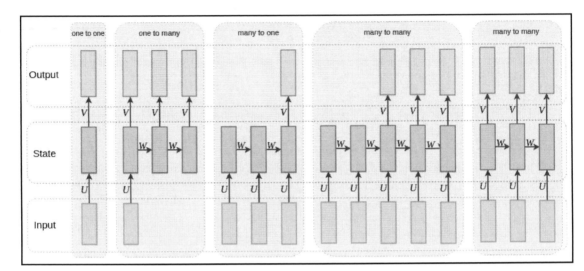

RNN input-output combinations: Inspired by http://karpathy.github.io/2015/05/21/rnn-effectiveness/.

Now that we've introduced RNNs, in the next section, we'll implement a simple RNN example from scratch to improve our knowledge.

RNN implementation and training

In the preceding section, we briefly discussed what RNNs are and what problems they can solve. Let's dive into the details of an RNN and how to train it with a very simple toy example: counting ones in a sequence.

In this problem, we will teach a basic RNN how to count the number of ones in the input and then output the result at the end of the sequence. This is an example of a many-to-one relationship, which we defined in the previous section.

We'll implement this example with Python (no DL libraries) and NumPy. An example of the input and output is as follows:

```
In: (0, 0, 0, 0, 1, 0, 1, 0, 1, 0)
Out: 3
```

The RNN we'll use is illustrated in the following diagram:

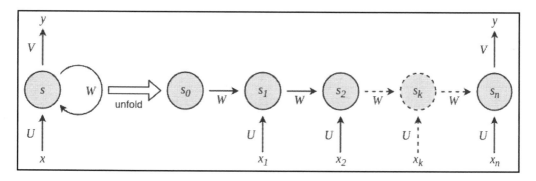

Basic RNN for counting ones in the input

The network will have only two parameters: an input weight, **U**, and a recurrence weight, **W**. The output weight, **V**, is set to 1 so that we just read out the last state as the output, **y**.

 Since s_t, x_t, U, and W are scalar values, we won't use the matrix notation (bold capital letters) in the *RNN implementation and training* section and its subsections. However, note that the generic versions of these formulas use matrix and vector parameters.

Before we continue, let's add some code so that our example can be executed. We'll import numpy and define our training and data, x, and labels, y. x is two-dimensional since the first dimension represents the sample in the mini-batch. For the sake of simplicity, we'll use a mini-batch with a single sample:

```
import numpy as np

# The first dimension represents the mini-batch
x = np.array([[0, 0, 0, 0, 1, 0, 1, 0, 1, 0]])

y = np.array([3])
```

The recurrence relation defined by this network is $s_t = f(W s_{t-1} + U x_t)$. Note that this is a linear model since we don't apply a non-linear function in this formula. We can implement a recurrence relationship as follows:

```
def step(s, x, U, W):
    return x * U + s * W
```

The states, s_t, and the weights, W and U, are single scalar values. A good solution to this is to just get the sum of the inputs across the sequence. If we set $U=1$, then whenever input is received, we will get its full value. If we set $W=1$, then the value we would accumulate would never decay. So, for this example, we would get the desired output: 3.

Nevertheless, let's use this simple example to network the training and implementation of this neural network. This will be interesting, as we will see in the rest of this section. First, let's look at how we can get this result through backpropagation.

Backpropagation through time

Backpropagation through time is the typical algorithm we use to train recurrent networks (*Backpropagation Through Time: What It Does and How to Do It*, http://axon.cs.byu.edu/~martinez/classes/678/Papers/Werbos_BPTT.pdf). As the name suggests, it's based on the backpropagation algorithm we discussed in Chapter 1, *The Nuts and Bolts of Neural Networks*.

The main difference between regular backpropagation and backpropagation through time is that the recurrent network is unfolded through time for a certain number of time steps (as illustrated in the preceding diagram). Once the unfolding is complete, we end up with a model that is quite similar to a regular multi-layer feedforward network, that is, one hidden layer of that network represents one step through time. The only differences are that each layer has multiple inputs: the previous state, s_{t-1}, and the current input, x_t. The parameters U and W are shared between all of the hidden layers.

The forward pass unwraps the RNN along the sequence and builds a stack of states for each step. In the following code block, we can see an implementation of the forward pass, which returns the activation, s, for each recurrent step and each sample in the batch:

```
def forward(x, U, W):
    # Number of samples in the mini-batch
    number_of_samples = len(x)

    # Length of each sample
    sequence_length = len(x[0])

    # Initialize the state activation for each sample along the sequence
    s = np.zeros((number_of_samples, sequence_length + 1))

    # Update the states over the sequence
    for t in range(0, sequence_length):
        s[:, t + 1] = step(s[:, t], x[:, t], U, W)   # step function

    return s
```

Now that we have our forward step and loss function, we can define how the gradient is propagated backward. Since the unfolded RNN is equivalent to a regular feedforward network, we can use the backpropagation chain rule we introduced in Chapter 1, *The Nuts and Bolts of Neural Networks*.

Because the weights, W and U, are shared across the layers, we'll accumulate the error derivatives for each recurrent step, and in the end, we'll update the weights with the accumulated value.

First, we need to get the gradient of the output, s_t, with respect to the loss function ($\partial J / \partial s$). Once we have it, we'll propagate it backward through the stack of activities we built during the forward step. This backward pass pops activities off of the stack to accumulate their error derivatives at each time step. The recurrence relation to propagate this gradient through the network can be written as follows (chain rule):

$$\frac{\partial J}{\partial s_{t-1}} = \frac{\partial J}{\partial s_t} \frac{\partial s_t}{\partial s_{t-1}} = \frac{\partial J}{\partial s_t} W$$

Here, J is the loss function.

The gradients of the weights, U and W, are accumulated as follows:

$$\frac{\partial J}{\partial U} = \sum_{t=0}^{n} \frac{\partial J}{\partial s_t} x_t$$

$$\frac{\partial J}{\partial W} = \sum_{t=0}^{n} \frac{\partial J}{\partial s_t} s_{t-1}$$

The following is an implementation of the backward pass:

1. The gradients for U and W are accumulated in gU and gW, respectively:

```
def backward(x, s, y, W):
    sequence_length = len(x[0])

    # The network output is just the last activation of sequence
    s_t = s[:, -1]

    # Compute the gradient of the output w.r.t. MSE loss function
      at final state
    gS = 2 * (s_t - y)

    # Set the gradient accumulations to 0
```

```
    gU, gW = 0, 0

    # Accumulate gradients backwards
    for k in range(sequence_length, 0, -1):
        # Compute the parameter gradients and accumulate the
          results
        gU += np.sum(gS * x[:, k - 1])
        gW += np.sum(gS * s[:, k - 1])

        # Compute the gradient at the output of the previous layer
        gS = gS * W

    return gU, gW
```

2. We can now try to use gradient descent to optimize our network. We compute `gradients` (using mean square error) with the help of the `backward` function and we use them to update the `weights` value:

```
def train(x, y, epochs, learning_rate=0.0005):
    """Train the network"""

    # Set initial parameters
    weights = (-2, 0) # (U, W)

    # Accumulate the losses and their respective weights
    losses = list()
    gradients_u = list()
    gradients_w = list()

    # Perform iterative gradient descent
    for i in range(epochs):
        # Perform forward and backward pass to get the gradients
        s = forward(x, weights[0], weights[1])

        # Compute the loss
        loss = (y[0] - s[-1, -1]) ** 2

        # Store the loss and weights values for later display
        losses.append(loss)

        gradients = backward(x, s, y, weights[1])
        gradients_u.append(gradients[0])
        gradients_w.append(gradients[1])

        # Update each parameter `p` by p = p - (gradient *
          learning_rate).
        # `gp` is the gradient of parameter `p`
        weights = tuple((p - gp * learning_rate) for p, gp in
```

```
        zip(weights, gradients))

    print(weights)

    return np.array(losses), np.array(gradients_u),
    np.array(gradients_w)
```

3. Next, we'll implement the related `plot_training` function, which displays the `loss` function and the gradients for each weight over the epochs:

```
def plot_training(losses, gradients_u, gradients_w):
    import matplotlib.pyplot as plt

    # remove nan and inf values
    losses = losses[~np.isnan(losses)][:-1]
    gradients_u = gradients_u[~np.isnan(gradients_u)][:-1]
    gradients_w = gradients_w[~np.isnan(gradients_w)][:-1]

    # plot the weights U and W
    fig, ax1 = plt.subplots(figsize=(5, 3.4))

    ax1.set_ylim(-3, 20)
    ax1.set_xlabel('epochs')
    ax1.plot(gradients_u, label='grad U', color='blue',
    linestyle=':')
    ax1.plot(gradients_w, label='grad W', color='red', linestyle='-
    ')
    ax1.legend(loc='upper left')

    # instantiate a second axis that shares the same x-axis
    # plot the loss on the second axis
    ax2 = ax1.twinx()

    # uncomment to plot exploding gradients
    ax2.set_ylim(-3, 10)
    ax2.plot(losses, label='Loss', color='green')
    ax2.tick_params(axis='y', labelcolor='green')
    ax2.legend(loc='upper right')

    fig.tight_layout()

    plt.show()
```

4. Finally, we can run this code:

```
losses, gradients_u, gradients_w = train(x, y, epochs=150)
plot_training(losses, gradients_u, gradients_w)
```

The preceding code produces the following diagram:

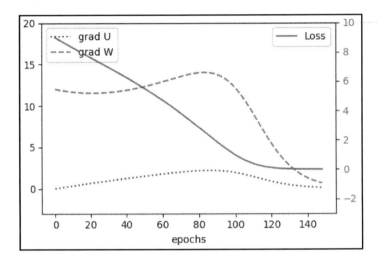

The RNN loss: the uninterrupted line represents the loss. where the dashed lines represent the weight gradients during training

Now that we've learned about backpropagation through time, let's discuss how the familiar vanishing and exploding gradient problems affect it.

Vanishing and exploding gradients

The preceding example has an issue, though. Let's run the training process with a longer sequence:

```
x = np.array([[0, 0, 0, 0, 1, 0, 1, 0, 1, 0, 0, 0, 0, 0, 1, 0, 1, 0, 1, 0,
0, 0, 0, 0, 1, 0, 1, 0, 1, 0, 0, 0, 0, 0, 1, 0, 1, 0, 1, 0]])

y = np.array([12])

losses, gradients_u, gradients_w = train(x, y, epochs=150)
plot_training(losses, gradients_u, gradients_w)
```

The output is as follows:

```
Sum of ones RNN from scratch
chapter07-rnn/simple_rnn.py:5: RuntimeWarning: overflow encountered in
multiply
   return x * U + s * W
chapter07-rnn/simple_rnn.py:40: RuntimeWarning: invalid value encountered
in multiply
   gU += np.sum(gS * x[:, k - 1])
```

```
chapter07-rnn/simple_rnn.py:41: RuntimeWarning: invalid value encountered
in multiply
  gW += np.sum(gS * s[:, k - 1])
(nan, nan)
```

The reason for these warnings is that the final parameters, U and W, end up as **Not a Number (NaN)**. To display the gradients properly, we'll need to change the scale of the gradient axis in the `plot_training` function from `ax1.set_ylim(-3, 20)` to `ax1.set_ylim(-3, 600)`, as well as the scale of the loss axis from `ax2.set_ylim(-3, 10)` to `ax2.set_ylim(-3, 200)`.

Now, the program will produce the following diagram of the new loss and gradients:

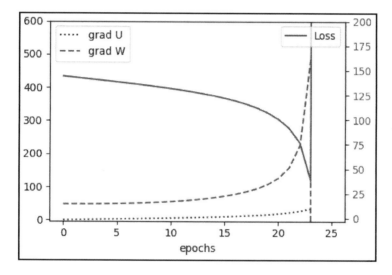

Parameters and loss function during exploding gradients scenario

In the initial epochs, the gradients slowly increase, similar to the way they increased for the shorter sequence. However, when they get to epoch 23 (the exact epoch is unimportant, though), the gradient becomes so large that it goes out of the range of the `float` variable and becomes NaN (as illustrated by the jump in the plot). This problem is known as exploding gradients. We can stumble upon exploding gradients in a regular feedforward NN, but it is especially pronounced in RNNs. To understand why, let's recall the recurrent gradient propagation chain rule for the two consecutive sequence steps we defined in the *Backpropagation through time* section:

$$\frac{\partial J}{\partial s_{t-1}} = \frac{\partial J}{\partial s_t}\frac{\partial s_t}{\partial s_{t-1}} = \frac{\partial J}{\partial s_t}W$$

Depending on the sequence's length, an unfolded RNN can be much deeper compared to a regular network. At the same time, the weights, *W*, of an RNN are shared across all of the steps. Therefore, we can generalize this formula to compute the gradient between two non-consecutive steps of the sequence. Because *W* is shared, the equation forms a geometric progression:

$$\frac{\partial s_t}{\partial s_{t-k}} = \frac{\partial s_t}{\partial s_{t-1}} \frac{\partial s_{t-1}}{\partial s_{t-2}} \cdots \cdots \frac{\partial s_{t-k+1}}{\partial s_{t-k}} = \prod_{j=1}^{k} \frac{\partial s_{t-j+1}}{\partial s_{t-j}} = W^k$$

In our simple linear RNN, the gradient grows exponentially if $|W| > 1$ (exploding gradient), where *W* is a single scalar weight, for example, 50 time steps over W=1.5 is $W^{50} \approx 637621500$. The gradient shrinks exponentially if $|W| < 1$ (vanishing gradient), for example, 10 time steps over W=0.6 is $W^{20} = 0.00097$. If the weight parameter, **W**, is a matrix instead of a scalar, this exploding or vanishing gradient is related to the largest eigenvalue (ϱ) of **W** (also known as a spectral radius). It is sufficient for $\varrho < 1$ for the gradients to vanish, and it is necessary for $\varrho > 1$ for them to explode.

The vanishing gradients problem, which we first mentioned in `Chapter 1`, *The Nuts and Bolts of Neural Networks*, has another more subtle effect in RNNs. The gradient decays exponentially over the number of steps to a point where it becomes extremely small in the earlier states. In effect, they are overshadowed by the larger gradients from more recent time steps, and the network's ability to retain the history of these earlier states vanishes. This problem is harder to detect because the training will still work and the network will produce valid outputs (unlike with exploding gradients). It just won't be able to learn long-term dependencies.

Now, we are familiar with some of the problems of RNNs. This knowledge will serve us well because, in the next section, we'll discuss how to solve these problems with the help of a special type of RNN.

Introducing long short-term memory

Hochreiter and Schmidhuber studied the problems of vanishing and exploding gradients extensively and came up with a solution called **Long Short-Term Memory** (**LSTM**, `https://www.bioinf.jku.at/publications/older/2604.pdf`). LSTMs can handle long-term dependencies due to a specially crafted memory cell. In fact, they work so well that most of the current accomplishments in training RNNs on a variety of problems are due to the use of LSTMs. In this section, we'll explore how this memory cell works and how it solves the vanishing gradients issue.

The key idea of LSTM is the cell state, c_t (in addition to the hidden RNN state, h_t), where the information can only be explicitly written in or removed so that the state stays constant if there is no outside interference. The cell state can only be modified by specific gates, which are a way to let information pass through. These gates are composed of a sigmoid function and element-wise multiplication. Because the sigmoid only outputs values between 0 and 1, the multiplication can only reduce the value running through the gate. A typical LSTM is composed of three gates: a forget gate, an input gate, and an output gate. The cell state, input, and output are all vectors so that the LSTM can hold a combination of different information blocks at each time step.

The following is a diagram of an LSTM cell:

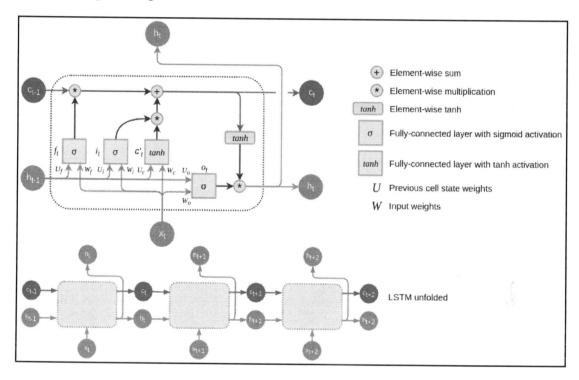

Top: LSTM cell; bottom: Unfolded LSTM cell: Inspired by http://colah.github.io/posts/2015-08-Understanding-LSTMs/.

Before we continue, let's introduce some notations. x_t, c_t, and h_t are the LSTM's input, cell memory state, and output (or hidden state) vectors in moment t. c'_t is the candidate cell state vector (more on that later). The input, x_t, and the previous cell output, h_{t-1}, are connected to each gate and the candidate cell vector with sets of fully connected weights, $\mathbf{W}$ and $\mathbf{U}$, respectively. f_t, i_t, and o_t are the forget, input, and output gates of the LSTM cell. These gates are fully connected layers with sigmoid activations.

Let's start with the forget gate, $\mathbf{f}_t$. As the name suggests, it decides whether we want to erase parts of the existing cell state or not. It bases its decision on the weighted vector sum of the output of the previous cell, $\mathbf{h}_{t-1}$, and the current input, $\mathbf{x}_t$:

$$f_t = \sigma(\mathbf{W}_f \mathbf{x}_t + \mathbf{U}_f \mathbf{h}_{t-1})$$

From the preceding diagram, we can see that the forget gate applies element-wise sigmoid activations on each element of the previous state vector, $\mathbf{c}_{t-1}$: $\mathbf{f}_t * \mathbf{c}_{t-1}$. Again, note that because the operation is element-wise, the values of this vector are squashed in the [0, 1] range. An output of 0 erases a specific $\mathbf{c}_{t-1}$ cell block completely and an output of 1 allows the information in that cell block to pass through. This means that the LSTM can get rid of irrelevant information in its cell state vector.

 The forget gate was not in the original LSTM that was proposed by Hochreiter. Instead, it was proposed in *Learning to Forget: Continual Prediction with LSTM* (http://citeseerx.ist.psu.edu/viewdoc/download?doi=10.1.1.55.5709&rep=rep1&type=pdf).

The input gate, $\mathbf{i}_t$, decides what new information is going to be added to the memory cell in a multi-step process. The first step determines whether any information is going to be added. As in the forget gate, it bases its decision on $\mathbf{h}_{t-1}$ and $\mathbf{x}_t$: it outputs 0 or 1 through the sigmoid function for each cell of the candidate state vector. An output of 0 means that no information is added to that cell block's memory. As a result, the LSTM can store specific pieces of information in its cell state vector:

$$i_t = \sigma(\mathbf{W}_i \mathbf{x}_t + \mathbf{U}_i \mathbf{h}_{t-1})$$

In the next step, we compute the new candidate cell state, $\mathbf{c}'_t$. It is based on the previous output, $\mathbf{h}_{t-1}$, and the current input, $\mathbf{x}_t$, and is transformed via a tanh function:

$$c'_t = \tanh(\mathbf{W}_c \mathbf{x}_t + \mathbf{U}_c \mathbf{h}_{t-1})$$

Next, c'_t is combined with the sigmoid outputs of the input gate via element-wise multiplication, $\mathbf{i}_t * \mathbf{c}'_t$.

To recap, the forget and input gates decide what information to forget and include from the previous and candidate cell states, respectively. The final version of the new cell state, c_t, is just an element-wise sum between these two components:

$$c_t = \mathbf{f}_t * \mathbf{c}_{t-1} \oplus \mathbf{i}_t * \mathbf{c}'_t$$

Next, let's focus on the output gate, which decides what the total cell output is going to be. It takes $\mathbf{h}_{t-1}$ and $\mathbf{x}_t$ as inputs and outputs, that is, 0 or 1 (via the sigmoid function), for each block of the cell's memory. Like before, 0 means that the block doesn't output any information and 1 means that the block can pass through as a cell's output. Therefore, the LSTM can output specific blocks of information from its cell state vector:

$$\mathbf{o}_t = \sigma(\mathbf{W}_o\mathbf{x}_t + \mathbf{U}_o\mathbf{h}_{t-1})$$

Finally, the LSTM cell output is transferred by a tanh function:

$$\mathbf{h}_t = \mathbf{o}_t * \tanh(\mathbf{c}_t)$$

Because all of these formulas are derivable, we can chain LSTM cells together, just like when we chain simple RNN states together and train the network via backpropagation through time.

But how does the LSTM protect us from vanishing gradients? Let's start with the forward phase. Notice that the cell state is copied identically from step to step if the forget gate is 1 and the input gate is 0: $\mathbf{c}_t = \mathbf{f}_t * \mathbf{c}_{t-1} \oplus \mathbf{i}_t * \mathbf{c}'_t = 1 * \mathbf{c}_{t-1} \oplus 0 * \mathbf{c}'_t = \mathbf{c}_{t-1}$. Only the forget gate can completely erase the cell's memory. As a result, the memory can remain unchanged over a long period of time. Also, note that the input is a tanh activation that's been added to the current cell's memory. This means that the cell's memory doesn't blow up and is quite stable.

Let's use an example to demonstrate how a LSTM cell is unfolded. For the sake of simplicity, we'll assume that it has one-dimensional (single scalar value) input, state, and output vectors. Because the values are scalar, we won't use vector notation for the rest of this example:

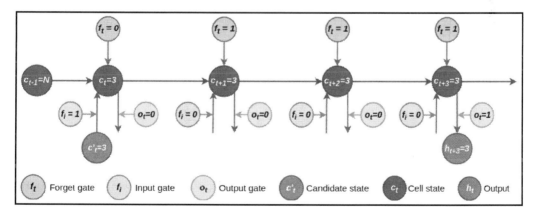

Unrolling an LSTM through time: Inspired by http://nikhilbuduma.com/2015/01/11/a-deep-dive-into-recurrent-neural-networks/.

The process is as follows:

1. First, we have a value of 3 as a candidate state. The input gate is set to $f_i = 1$ and the forget gate is set to $f_t = 0$. This means that the previous state, $c_{t-1} = N$, is erased and is replaced with the new state, $c_t = 0 * N \oplus 1 * 3 = 3$.

2. For the next two time steps, the forget gate is set to 1, while the input gate is set to 0. By doing this, all of the information is kept throughout these steps and no new information is added because the input gate is set to 0:
$c_{t+1} = 1 * 3 \oplus 0 * c'_{t+1} = 3$.

3. Finally, the output gate is set to $o_t = 1$ and 3 is output and remains unchanged. We have successfully demonstrated how the internal state is stored across multiple steps.

Next, let's focus on the backward phase. The cell state, c_t, can mitigate the vanishing/exploding gradients as well with the help of the forget gate, f_t. Like the regular RNN, we can use the chain rule to compute the partial derivative, $\partial c_t / \partial c_{t-1}$, for two consecutive steps. Following the formula $c_t = f_t * c_{t-1} \oplus i_t * c'_t$ and without going into details, its partial derivative is as follows:

$$\frac{\partial c_t}{\partial c_{t-1}} \approx f_t$$

We can generalize this to non-consecutive steps as well:

$$\frac{\partial c_t}{\partial c_{t-k}} = \frac{\partial c_t}{\partial c_{t-1}} \frac{\partial c_{t-1}}{\partial c_{t-2}} \cdots \frac{\partial c_{t-k+1}}{\partial c_{t-k}} \approx \prod_{j=1}^{k} f_{t-j+1}$$

If the forget gate values are close to 1, gradient information can pass back through the network states almost unchanged. This is because f_t uses sigmoid activation and information flow is still subject to the vanishing gradient that's specific to sigmoid activations (Chapter 1, *The Nuts and Bolts of Neural Networks*). But unlike the gradients in the regular RNN, f_t has a different value at each time step. Therefore, this is not a geometric progression and the vanishing gradient effect is less pronounced.

We can stack LSTM cells in the same way as we stack regular RNNs, with the exception that a cell state of step *t* at one level serves as an input to the cell state of the same level at step *t+1*. The following diagram shows an unfolded stacked LSTM:

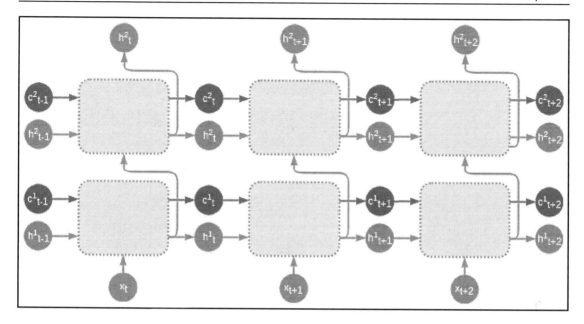

Stacked LSTM

Now that we've introduced LSTM, let's solidify our knowledge by implementing it in the next section.

Implementing LSTM

In this section, we'll implement an LSTM cell with PyTorch 1.3.1. First, let's note that PyTorch already has an LSTM implementation, which is available at `torch.nn.LSTM`. However, our goal is to understand how the LSTM cell works, so we'll implement our own version from scratch instead. The cell will be a subclass of `torch.nn.Module` and we'll use it as a building block for larger models. The source code for this example is available at `https://github.com/PacktPublishing/Advanced-Deep-Learning-with-Python/tree/master/Chapter07/lstm_cell.py`. Let's get started:

1. First, we'll do the imports:

```
import math
import typing

import torch
```

2. Next, we'll implement the class and the __init__ method:

```
class LSTMCell(torch.nn.Module):

    def __init__(self, input_size: int, hidden_size: int):
        """
        :param input_size: input vector size
        :param hidden_size: cell state vector size
        """

        super(LSTMCell, self).__init__()
        self.input_size = input_size
        self.hidden_size = hidden_size

        # combine all gates in a single matrix multiplication
        self.x_fc = torch.nn.Linear(input_size, 4 * hidden_size)
        self.h_fc = torch.nn.Linear(hidden_size, 4 * hidden_size)

        self.reset_parameters()
```

To understand the role of the fully connected layers, self.x_fc and self.h_fc, let's recall that the candidate cell state and the input, forget, and output gates all depend on the weighted vector sum of the input, $\mathbf{x}_t$, and the previous cell output, $\mathbf{h}_{t-1}$. Therefore, instead of having eight separate $W_{i,f,c,o}\mathbf{x}_t$ and $U_{i,f,c,o}\mathbf{h}_{t-1}$ operations for each cell, we can combine these and make two large fully connected layers, self.x_fc and self.h_fc, each with an output size of 4 * hidden_size. Once we need the output for a specific gate, we can extract the necessary slice from either of the two tensor outputs of the fully connected layers (we'll see how to do that in the implementation of the forward method).

3. Let's continue with the reset_parameters method, which initializes all of the weights of the network with the LSTM-specific Xavier initializer (if you copy and paste this code directly, you may have to check the indentation):

```
def reset_parameters(self):
    """Xavier initialization """
    size = math.sqrt(3.0 / self.hidden_size)
    for weight in self.parameters():
        weight.data.uniform_(-size, size)
```

4. Next, we'll start implementing the `forward` method, which contains all of the LSTM execution logic we described in the *Introducing long short-term memory* section. It takes the current mini-batch at step *t*, as well as a tuple that contains the cell output and cell state at step *t-1*, as input:

```
def forward(self,
               x_t: torch.Tensor,
               hidden: typing.Tuple[torch.Tensor, torch.Tensor] =
    (None, None)) \
          -> typing.Tuple[torch.Tensor, torch.Tensor]:
      h_t_1, c_t_1 = hidden # t_1 is equivalent to t-1

      # in case of more than 2-dimensional input
      # flatten the tensor (similar to numpy.reshape)
      x_t = x_t.view(-1, x_t.size(1))
      h_t_1 = h_t_1.view(-1, h_t_1.size(1))
      c_t_1 = c_t_1.view(-1, c_t_1.size(1))
```

5. We'll continue by computing activations for all three gates and the candidate state simultaneously. It's as simple as doing the following:

```
gates = self.x_fc(x_t) + self.h_fc(h_t_1)
```

6. Next, we'll split the output for each gate:

```
i_t, f_t, candidate_c_t, o_t = gates.chunk(4, 1)
```

7. Then, we'll apply the `activation` functions over them:

```
i_t, f_t, candidate_c_t, o_t = \
    i_t.sigmoid(), f_t.sigmoid(), candidate_c_t.tanh(),
o_t.sigmoid()
```

8. Next, we'll compute the new cell state, c_i:

```
c_t = torch.mul(f_t, c_t_1) + torch.mul(i_t, candidate_c_t)
```

9. Finally, we'll compute the cell output, `ht`, and we'll return it along with the new cell state, c_i:

```
h_t = torch.mul(o_t, torch.tanh(c_t))
return h_t, c_t
```

Once we have the LSTM cell, we can apply it to the same task of counting the ones in a sequence, like we did with the regular RNN. We'll only include the most relevant parts of the source code, but the full example is available at `https://github.com/PacktPublishing/Advanced-Deep-Learning-with-Python/tree/master/Chapter07/lstm_gru_count_1s.py`. This time, we'll use a full training set of 10,000 binary sequences that have a length of 20 (these are arbitrary numbers). The premise of the implementation is similar to the RNN example: we feed the binary sequence to the LSTM in a recurrent manner and the cell outputs the predicted count of the ones as a single scalar value (regression task). However, our `LSTMCell` implementation has two limitations:

- It only covers a single step of the sequence.
- It outputs the cell state and the network output vector. This is a regression task and we have a single output value, but the cell state and network output have more dimensions.

To solve these problems, we'll implement a custom `LSTMModel` class, which extends `LSTMCell`. It feeds the `LSTMCell` instance with all of the elements of the sequence and handles the transition of the cell state and network output from one element of the sequence to the next.

Once the final output has been produced, it is fed to a fully connected layer, which transforms it into a single scalar value that represents the network's prediction of the number of ones. The following is the implementation of this:

```python
class LSTMModel(torch.nn.Module):
    def __init__(self, input_dim, hidden_size, output_dim):
        super(LSTMModel, self).__init__()
        self.hidden_size = hidden_size

        # Our own LSTM implementation
        self.lstm = LSTMCell(input_dim, hidden_size)

        # Fully connected output layer
        self.fc = torch.nn.Linear(hidden_size, output_dim)

    def forward(self, x):
        # Start with empty network output and cell state to initialize the
sequence
        c_t = torch.zeros((x.size(0), self.hidden_size)).to(x.device)
        h_t = torch.zeros((x.size(0), self.hidden_size)).to(x.device)

        # Iterate over all sequence elements across all sequences of the
mini-batch
        for seq in range(x.size(1)):
            h_t, c_t = self.lstm(x[:, seq, :], (h_t, c_t))
```

```
# Final output layer
return self.fc(h_t)
```

Now, we'll jump straight to the train/test setup stage (recall that this is just a snippet of the full source code):

1. First, we'll generate the training and testing datasets. The `generate_dataset` function returns an instance of `torch.utils.data.TensorDataset`. It contains `TRAINING_SAMPLES = 10000` two-dimensional tensors of binary sequences with a length of `SEQUENCE_LENGTH = 20` and scalar value labels for the number of ones in each sequence:

   ```
   train = generate_dataset(SEQUENCE_LENGTH, TRAINING_SAMPLES)
   train_loader = torch.utils.data.DataLoader(train,
   batch_size=BATCH_SIZE, shuffle=True)

   test = generate_dataset(SEQUENCE_LENGTH, TEST_SAMPLES)
   test_loader = torch.utils.data.DataLoader(test,
   batch_size=BATCH_SIZE, shuffle=True)
   ```

2. We'll instantiate the model with `HIDDEN_UNITS = 20`. The model takes a single input (each sequence element) and outputs a single value (number of ones):

   ```
   model = LSTMModel(input_size=1, hidden_size=HIDDEN_UNITS,
   output_size=1)
   ```

3. Next, we'll instantiate the `MSELoss` function (because of the regression) and the Adam optimizer:

   ```
   loss_function = torch.nn.MSELoss()
   optimizer = torch.optim.Adam(model.parameters())
   ```

4. Finally, we can run the training/testing cycle for `EPOCHS = 10`. The `train_model` and `test_model` functions are the same as the ones we implemented in the *Implementing transfer learning with PyTorch* section of Chapter 2, *Understanding Convolutional Networks*:

   ```
   for epoch in range(EPOCHS):
       print('Epoch {}/{}'.format(epoch + 1, EPOCHS))

       train_model(model, loss_function, optimizer, train_loader)
       test_model(model, loss_function, test_loader)
   ```

If we run this example, the network will achieve 100% test accuracy in 5-6 epochs.

Now that we've learned about LSTMs, let's shift our attention to gated recurrent units. This is another type of recurrent block that tries to replicate the properties of LSTM, but with a simplified structure.

Introducing gated recurrent units

A **Gated Recurrent Unit (GRU)** is a type of recurrent block that was introduced in 2014 (*Learning Phrase Representations using RNN Encoder-Decoder for Statistical Machine Translation*, `https://arxiv.org/abs/1406.1078` and *Empirical Evaluation of Gated Recurrent Neural Networks on Sequence Modeling*, `https://arxiv.org/abs/1412.3555`) as an improvement over LSTM. A GRU unit usually has similar or better performance than an LSTM, but it does so with fewer parameters and operations:

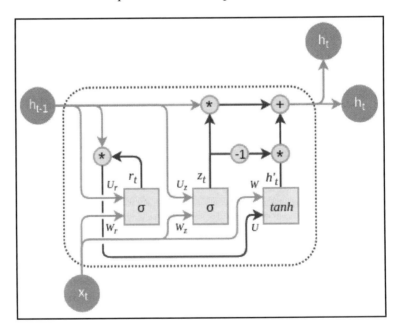

A GRU cell

Similar to the *classic* RNN, a GRU cell has a single hidden state, $\mathbf{h}_t$. You can think of it as a combination of the hidden and cell states of an LSTM. The GRU cell has two gates:

- An update gate, $\mathbf{z}_t$, which combines the input and forget LSTM gates. It decides what information to discard and what new information to include in its place, based on the network input, $\mathbf{x}_t$, and the previous cell hidden state, $\mathbf{h}_{t-1}$. By combining the two gates, we can ensure that the cell will forget information, but only when we are going to include new information in its place:

$$\mathbf{z}_t = \sigma(\mathbf{W}_z\mathbf{x}_t + \mathbf{U}_z\mathbf{h}_{t-1})$$

- A reset gate, $\mathbf{r}_t$, which uses the previous cell state, $\mathbf{h}_{t-1}$, and the network input, $\mathbf{x}_t$, to decide how much of the previous state to pass through:

$$\mathbf{r}_t = \sigma(\mathbf{W}_r\mathbf{x}_t + \mathbf{U}_r\mathbf{h}_{t-1})$$

Next, we have the candidate state, $\mathbf{h}'_t$:

$$\mathbf{h}'_t = \tanh(\mathbf{W}\mathbf{x}_t + \mathbf{U}(\mathbf{r}_t * \mathbf{h}_{t-1}))$$

Finally, the GRU output, $\mathbf{h}_t$, at time t is an element-wise sum between the previous output, $\mathbf{h}_{t-1}$, and the candidate output, $\mathbf{h}'_t$:

$$\mathbf{h}_t = \mathbf{z}_t * \mathbf{h}_{t-1} \oplus (1 - \mathbf{z}_t) * \mathbf{h}'_t$$

Since the update gate allows us to both forget and store data, it is directly applied over the previous output, $\mathbf{h}_{t-1}$, and applied over the candidate output, $\mathbf{h}'_t$.

Implementing GRUs

In this section, we'll implement a GRU cell with PyTorch 1.3.1 by following the blueprint from the *Implementing LSTM* section. Let's get started:

1. First, we'll do the imports:

```
import math
import torch
```

2. Next, we'll write the class definition and the `init` method. In LSTM, we were able to create a shared fully connected layer for all gates, because each gate required the same input combination of x_t and h_{t-1}. The GRU gates use different inputs, so we'll create separate fully connected operations for each GRU gate:

```python
class GRUCell(torch.nn.Module):

    def __init__(self, input_size: int, hidden_size: int):
        """
        :param input_size: input vector size
        :param hidden_size: cell state vector size
        """

        super(GRUCell, self).__init__()
        self.input_size = input_size
        self.hidden_size = hidden_size

        # x to reset gate r
        self.x_r_fc = torch.nn.Linear(input_size, hidden_size)

        # x to update gate z
        self.x_z_fc = torch.nn.Linear(input_size, hidden_size)

        # x to candidate state h'(t)
        self.x_h_fc = torch.nn.Linear(input_size, hidden_size)

        # network output/state h(t-1) to reset gate r
        self.h_r_fc = torch.nn.Linear(hidden_size, hidden_size)

        # network output/state h(t-1) to update gate z
        self.h_z_fc = torch.nn.Linear(hidden_size, hidden_size)

        # network state h(t-1) passed through the reset gate r
        # towards candidate state h(t)
        self.hr_h_fc = torch.nn.Linear(hidden_size, hidden_size)
```

We'll omit the definition of `reset_parameters` because it's the same as it is in `LSTMCell`.

3. Then, we'll implement the `forward` method with the cell by following the steps we described in the *Gated recurrent units* section. The method takes the current input vector, x_t, and the previous cell state/output, h_{t-1}, as input. First, we'll compute the forget and update gates, similar to how we computed the gates in the LSTM cell:

```python
def forward(self,
            x_t: torch.Tensor,
            h_t_1: torch.Tensor = None) \
        -> torch.Tensor:

    # compute update gate vector
    z_t = torch.sigmoid(self.x_z_fc(x_t) + self.h_z_fc(h_t_1))

    # compute reset gate vector
    r_t = torch.sigmoid(self.x_r_fc(x_t) + self.h_r_fc(h_t_1))
```

4. Next, we'll compute the new candidate state/output, which uses the reset gate:

```python
candidate_h_t = torch.tanh(self.x_h_fc(x_t) +
    self.hr_h_fc(torch.mul(r_t, h_t_1)))
```

5. Finally, we'll compute the new output based on the candidate state and the update gate:

```python
h_t = torch.mul(z_t, h_t_1) + torch.mul(1 - z_t, candidate_h_t)
```

We can implement the counting of ones task with a GRU cell in the same way that we did with LSTM. To avoid repetition, we won't include the implementation here, but it is available at `https://github.com/PacktPublishing/Advanced-Deep-Learning-with-Python/tree/master/Chapter07/lstm_gru_count_1s.py`.

This concludes our discussion about various types of RNNs. Next, we'll channel this knowledge by implementing a text sentiment analysis example.

Implementing text classification

Let's recap on this chapter so far. We started by implementing an RNN using only `numpy`. Then, we continued with an LSTM implementation using primitive PyTorch operations. We'll conclude this arc by training the default PyTorch 1.3.1 LSTM implementation for a text classification problem. This example also requires the `torchtext` 0.4.0 package. Text classification (or categorization) refers to the task of assigning categories (or labels) depending on its contents. Text classification tasks include spam detection, topic labeling, and sentiment analysis. This type of problem is an example of a *many-to-one* relationship, which we defined in the *Introduction to RNNs* section.

In this section, we'll implement a sentiment analysis example over the Large Movie Review Dataset (`http://ai.stanford.edu/~amaas/data/sentiment/`), which consists of 25,000 training and 25,000 testing reviews of popular movies. Each review has a binary label that indicates whether it is positive or negative. Besides PyTorch, we'll use the `torchtext` package (`https://torchtext.readthedocs.io/`). It consists of data processing utilities and popular datasets for natural language. You'll also need to install the `spacy` open source software library (`https://spacy.io`) for advanced NLP, which we'll use to tokenize the dataset.

The sentiment analysis algorithm is displayed in the following diagram:

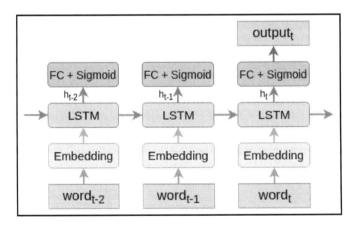

Sentiment analysis with word embeddings and LSTM

Let's describe the algorithm steps (these are valid for any text classification algorithm):

1. Each word of the sequence is replaced with its embedding vector (Chapter 6, *Language Modeling*). These embeddings can be produced with word2vec, fastText, GloVe, and so on.

2. The word embedding is fed as input to the LSTM cell.

3. The cell output, $\mathbf{h}_t$, serves as input to a fully connected layer with a single output unit. The unit uses sigmoid activation, which represents the probability of the review to be positive (1) or negative (0). If the problem is multinomial (and not binary), we can replace the sigmoid with softmax.

4. The network output for the final element of the sequence is taken as a result for the whole sequence.

Now that we have provided an overview of the algorithm, let's implement it. We'll only include the interesting portions of the code, but the full implementation is available at `https://github.com/PacktPublishing/Advanced-Deep-Learning-with-Python/tree/master/Chapter07/sentiment_analysis.py`.

This example is partially based on `https://github.com/bentrevett/pytorch-sentiment-analysis`.

Let's get started:

1. First, we'll add the imports:

```
import torch
import torchtext
```

2. Next, we'll instantiate a `torchtext.data.Field` object:

```
TEXT = torchtext.data.Field(
    tokenize='spacy',  # use SpaCy tokenizer
    lower=True,  # convert all letters to lower case
    include_lengths=True,  # include the length of the movie review
)
```

This object declares a text processing pipeline, which starts with the raw text and outputs a tensor representation of the text. More specifically, it uses the `spacy` tokenizer, converts all of the letters into lowercase, and includes the length (in words) of each movie review.

3. Then, we'll do the same for the labels (positive or negative):

```
LABEL = torchtext.data.LabelField(dtype=torch.float)
```

4. Next, we'll instantiate the training and testing dataset splits:

```
train, test = torchtext.datasets.IMDB.splits(TEXT, LABEL)
```

The movie review dataset is included in `torchtext` and we don't need to do any additional work. The `splits` method takes the `TEXT` and `LABEL` fields as parameters. By doing this, the specified pipelines are applied over the selected dataset.

5. Then, we'll instantiate the vocabulary:

```
TEXT.build_vocab(train, vectors=torchtext.vocab.GloVe(name='6B',
dim=100))
LABEL.build_vocab(train)
```

The vocabulary presents a mechanism for the numerical representation of the words. In this case, the numerical representation of the `TEXT` field is a pretrained 100d GloVe vector. On the other hand, the labels in the dataset have a string value of either `pos` or `neg`. The role of the vocabulary here is to assign numbers (0 and 1) to these two labels.

6. Next, we'll define iterators for the training and testing datasets, where `device` represents either GPU or CPU. The iterators will return one mini-batch at each call:

```
train_iter, test_iter = torchtext.data.BucketIterator.splits(
    (train, test), sort_within_batch=True, batch_size=64,
device=device)
```

7. We'll proceed by implementing and instantiating the `LSTMModel` class. This is at the core of the program, which implements the algorithm steps we defined in the diagram at the beginning of this section:

```
class LSTMModel(torch.nn.Module):
    def __init__(self, vocab_size, embedding_size, hidden_size,
output_size, pad_idx):
        super().__init__()

        # Embedding field
self.embedding=torch.nn.Embedding(num_embeddings=vocab_size,
        embedding_dim=embedding_size,padding_idx=pad_idx)
```

```
# LSTM cell
self.rnn = torch.nn.LSTM(input_size=embedding_size,
hidden_size=hidden_size)

# Fully connected output
self.fc = torch.nn.Linear(hidden_size, output_size)

def forward(self, text_sequence, text_lengths):
# Extract embedding vectors
embeddings = self.embedding(text_sequence)

# Pad the sequences to equal length
packed_sequence =torch.nn.utils.rnn.pack_padded_sequence
(embeddings, text_lengths)

packed_output, (hidden, cell) = self.rnn(packed_sequence)

return self.fc(hidden)


model = LSTMModel(vocab_size=len(TEXT.vocab),
                embedding_size=EMBEDDING_SIZE,
                hidden_size=HIDDEN_SIZE,
                output_size=1,
                pad_idx=TEXT.vocab.stoi[TEXT.pad_token])
```

LSTMModel processes a mini-batch of sequences (in this case, movie reviews) with varying lengths. However, the mini-batch is a tensor, which assigns slices with equal length for each sequence. Because of this, all of the sequences are padded in advance with a special symbol to reach the length of the longest sequence in the batch. The padding_idx parameter in the constructor of torch.nn.Embedding represents the index of the padding symbol in the vocabulary. But using sequences with padding will lead to unnecessary calculations for the padded portions. Because of this, the forward propagation of the model takes both the text mini-batch and text_lengths of each sequence as parameters. They are fed to the pack_padded_sequence function, which transforms them into a packed_sequence object. We do all of this because the self.rnn object (the instance of torch.nn.LSTM) has a special routine for processing packed sequences, which optimizes the computation with respect to the padding.

8. Next, we'll copy the GloVe word embedding vectors to the embedding layer of the model:

```
model.embedding.weight.data.copy_(TEXT.vocab.vectors)
```

9. Then, we'll set the embedding entries for the padding and unknown tokens to zeros so that they don't influence the propagation:

```
model.embedding.weight.data[TEXT.vocab.stoi[TEXT.unk_token]] =
torch.zeros(EMBEDDING_SIZE)
model.embedding.weight.data[TEXT.vocab.stoi[TEXT.pad_token]] =
torch.zeros(EMBEDDING_SIZE)
```

10. Finally, we can run the whole thing with the following code (the `train_model` and `test_model` functions are the same as they were previously):

```
optimizer = torch.optim.Adam(model.parameters())
loss_function = torch.nn.BCEWithLogitsLoss().to(device)

model = model.to(device)

for epoch in range(5):
    print(f"Epoch {epoch + 1}/5")
    train_model(model, loss_function, optimizer, train_iter)
    test_model(model, loss_function, test_iter)
```

If everything works as intended, the model will achieve a test accuracy of around 88%.

Summary

In this chapter, we discussed RNNs. First, we started with the RNN and backpropagation through time theory. Then, we implemented an RNN from scratch to solidify our knowledge on the subject. Next, we moved on to more complex LSTM and GRU cells using the same pattern: a theoretical explanation, followed by a practical PyTorch implementation. Finally, we combined our knowledge from Chapter 6, *Language Modeling*, with the new material from this chapter for a full-featured sentiment analysis task implementation.

In the next chapter, we'll discuss seq2seq models and their variations—an exciting new development in sequence processing.

8
Sequence-to-Sequence Models and Attention

In Chapter 7, *Understanding Recurrent Networks,* we outlined several types of recurrent models, depending on the input-output combinations. One of them is **indirect many-to-many** or **sequence-to-sequence (seq2seq)**, where an input sequence is transformed into another, different output sequence, not necessarily with the same length as the input. Machine translation is the most popular type of seq2seq task. The input sequences are the words of a sentence in one language and the output sequences are the words of the same sentence translated into another language. For example, we can translate the English sequence **tourist attraction** to the German **touristenattraktion**. Not only is the output sentence a different length, but there is no direct correspondence between the elements of the input and output sequences. In particular, one output element corresponds to a combination of two input elements.

Machine translation that's implemented with a single neural network is called **neural machine translation** (**NMT**). Other types of indirect many-to-many tasks include speech recognition, where we take different time frames of an audio input and convert them into a text transcript, question-answering chatbots, where the input sequences are the words of a textual question and the output sequence is the answer to that question, and text summarization, where the input is a text document and the output is a short summary of the text's contents.

In this chapter, we'll introduce the attention mechanism—a new type of algorithm for seq2seq tasks. It allows direct access to any element of the input sequence. This is unlike a **recurrent neural network (RNN)**, which summarizes the whole sequence in a single hidden state vector and prioritizes recent sequence elements over older ones.

This chapter will cover the following topics:

- Introducing seq2seq models
- Seq2seq with attention
- Understanding transformers
- Transformer language models:
    - Bidirectional encoder representations from transformers
    - Transformer-XL
    - XLNet

Introducing seq2seq models

Seq2seq, or encoder-decoder (see *Sequence to Sequence Learning with Neural Networks* at `https://arxiv.org/abs/1409.3215`), models use RNNs in a way that's especially suited for solving tasks with indirect many-to-many relationships between the input and the output. A similar model was also proposed in another pioneering paper, *Learning Phrase Representations using RNN Encoder-Decoder for Statistical Machine Translation* (go to `https://arxiv.org/abs/1406.1078` for more information). The following is a diagram of the seq2seq model. The input sequence [**A, B, C, <EOS>**] is decoded into the output sequence [**W, X, Y, Z, <EOS>**]:

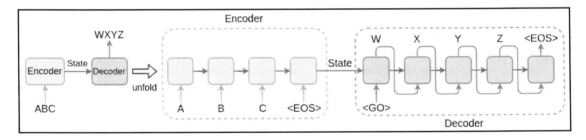

A seq2seq model case by https://arxiv.org/abs/1409.3215

The model consists of two parts: an encoder and a decoder. Here's how the inference part works:

- The encoder is an RNN. The original paper uses LSTM, but GRU or other types would also work. Taken by itself, the encoder works in the usual way—it reads the input sequence, one step at a time, and updates its internal state after each step. The encoder will stop reading the input sequence once a special **<EOS>**—end of sequence—symbol is reached. If we assume that we use a textual sequence, we'll use word-embedding vectors as the encoder input at each step, and the **<EOS>** symbol signals the end of a sentence. The encoder output is discarded and has no role in the seq2seq model, as we're only interested in the hidden encoder state.

- Once the encoder is finished, we'll signal the decoder so that it can start generating the output sequence with a special **<GO>** input signal. The encoder is also an RNN (LSTM or GRU). The link between the encoder and the decoder is the most recent encoder internal state vector $\mathbf{h}_t$ (also known as the **thought vector**), which is fed as the recurrence relation at the first decoder step. The decoder output y_{t+1} at step *t+1* is one element of the output sequence. We'll use it as an input at step *t+2*, then we'll generate new output, and so on (this type of model is called **autoregressive**). In the case of textual sequences, the decoder output is a softmax over all the words in the vocabulary. At each step, we take the word with the highest probability and we feed it as input to the next step. Once **<EOS>** becomes the most probable symbol, the decoding is finished.

The training of the model is supervised, and the model needs to know both the input sequence and its corresponding target output sequence (for example, the same text in multiple languages). We feed the input sequence to the decoder, generate the thought vector h_t, and use it to initiate the output sequence generation from the decoder. However, the decoder uses a process called **teacher forcing**—the decoder input at step *t* is not the decoder output of step *t-1*. Instead, the input at step *t* is always the correct character from the target sequence at step *t-1*. For example, let's say that the correct target sequence until step *t* is [**W**, **X**, **Y**], but the current decoder-generated output sequence is [**W**, **X**, **Z**]. With teacher forcing, the decoder input at step *t+1* will be **Y** instead of **Z**. In other words, the decoder learns to generate target values [t+1, ...] given target values [..., t]. We can think of this in the following way: the decoder input is the target sequence, while its output (target values) is the same sequence, but shifted one position to the right.

To summarize, the seq2seq model solves the problem of varying input/output sequence lengths by encoding the input sequence in a fixed-length state vector and then using this vector as a base to generate the output sequence. We can formalize this by saying that it tries to maximize the following probability:

$$P(y_1, \ldots, y_{T'} | x_1, \ldots, x_T) = \prod_{t=1}^{T'} P(y_t | \mathbf{v}, y_1, \ldots, y_{t-1})$$

This is equivalent to the following:

$$P(y_1, \ldots, y_{T'} | x_1, \ldots, x_T) = P(y_1 | \mathbf{v}) \, P(y_2 | \mathbf{v}, y_1) \ldots P(y_{T'} | \mathbf{v}, y_1, \ldots, y_{T'-1})$$

Let's look at the elements of this formula in more detail:

- $P(y_1, \ldots, y_{T'} | x_1, \ldots, x_T)$ is the conditional probability where $(x_1, \ldots, x_T)$ is the input sequence with length T and $(y_1, \ldots, y_{T'})$ is the output sequence with length T'.
- The element v is the fixed-length encoding of the input sequence (the thought vector).
- $P(y_{T'} | \mathbf{v}, y_1, \ldots, y_{T'-1})$ is the probability of an output word $y_{T'}$ given prior words y, as well as the vector v.

The original seq2seq paper introduces a few tricks to enhance the training and performance of the model:

- The encoder and decoder are two separate LSTMs. In the case of NMTs, this makes it possible to train different decoders with the same encoder.
- The experiments of the authors of the paper demonstrated that stacked LSTMs perform better than the ones with a single layer.
- The input sequence is fed to the decoder in reverse. For example, **ABC -> WXYZ** would become **CBA -> WXYZ**. There is no clear explanation of why this works, but the authors have shared their intuition: since this is a step-by-step model, if the sequences were in normal order, each source word in the source sentence would be far from its corresponding word in the output sentence. If we reverse the input sequence, the average distance between input/output words won't change, but the first input words will be very close to the first output words. This will help the model to establish better *communication* between the input and output sequences.

- Besides <EOS> and <GO>, the model also uses the following two special symbols (we've already encountered them in the *Implementing text classification* section of `Chapter 7`, *Understanding Recurrent Networks*):
  - <UNK>—**unknown**: This is used to replace rare words so that the vocabulary size doesn't grow too large.
  - <PAD>: For performance reasons, we have to train the model with sequences of a fixed length. However, this contradicts the real-world training data, where the sequences can have arbitrary lengths. To solve this, shorter sequences are filled with the special <PAD> symbol.

Now that we've introduced the base seq2seq model architecture, we'll learn how to extend it with the attention mechanism.

Seq2seq with attention

The decoder has to generate the entire output sequence based solely on the thought vector. For this to work, the thought vector has to encode all of the information of the input sequence; however, the encoder is an RNN, and we can expect that its hidden state will carry more information about the latest sequence elements than the earliest. Using LSTM cells and reversing the input helps, but cannot prevent it entirely. Because of this, the thought vector becomes something of a bottleneck. As a result, the seq2seq model works well for short sentences, but the performance deteriorates for longer ones.

Bahdanau attention

We can solve this problem with the help of the **attention mechanism** (see *Neural Machine Translation by Jointly Learning to Align and Translate* at `https://arxiv.org/abs/1409.0473`), an extension of the seq2seq model, that provides a way for the decoder to work with all encoder hidden states, not just the last one.

> The type of attention mechanism in this section is called Bahdanau attention, after the author of the original paper.

Besides solving the bottleneck problem, the attention mechanism has some other advantages. For one, the immediate access to all previous states helps to prevent the vanishing gradients problem. It also allows for some interpretability of the results because we can see what parts of the input the decoder was focusing on.

The following diagram shows how attention works:

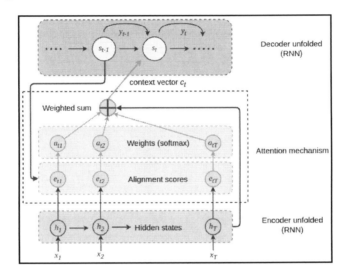

Attention mechanism

Don't worry—it looks scarier than it actually is. We'll go through this diagram from top to bottom: the attention mechanism works by plugging an additional **context vector** c_t between the encoder and the decoder. The hidden decoder state s_t at time t is now a function not only of the hidden state and decoder output at step $t-1$, but also of the context vector c_t:

$$s_t = f(s_{t-1}, y_{t-1}, c_t)$$

Each decoder step has a unique context vector, and the context vector for one decoder step is just **a weighted sum of all encoder hidden states**. In this way, the encoder has access to all input sequence states at each output step t, which removes the necessity to encode all information of the source sequence into a fixed-length vector, as the regular seq2seq model does:

$$c_t = \sum_{i=1}^{T} \alpha_{t,i} \mathbf{h}_i$$

Let's discuss this formula in more detail:

- c_t is the context vector for a decoder output step t out of T', the total output.
- h_i is the hidden state of encoder step i out of T total input steps.
- $\alpha_{t,i}$ is the scalar weight associated with h_i in the context of the current decoder step t.

Note that $\alpha_{t,i}$ is unique for both the encoder and decoder steps—that is, the input sequence states will have different weights depending on the current output step. For example, if the input and output sequences have lengths of 10, then the weights will be represented by a 10 × 10 matrix for a total of 100 weights. This means that the attention mechanism will focus the attention (get it?) of the decoder on different parts of the input sequence, depending on the current state of the output sequence. If $\alpha_{t,i}$ is large, then the decoder will pay a lot of attention to h_i at step t.

But how do we compute the weights $\alpha_{t,i}$? First, we should mention that the sum of all $\alpha_{t,i}$ for a decoder at step t is 1. We can implement this with a softmax operation on top of the attention mechanism:

$$\alpha_{t,i} = \frac{\exp(e_{t,i})}{\sum_{j=1}^{T} \exp(e_{t,j})}$$

Here, $e_{t,k}$ is an alignment model, which indicates how well the input sequence elements around position k match (or align with) the output at position t. This score (represented by the weight $\alpha_{t,i}$) is based on the previous decoder state s_{t-1} (we use s_{t-1} because we have not computed s_t yet), as well as the encoder state h_i:

$$e_{t,i} = a(s_{t-1}, h_i)$$

Here, a (and not alpha) is a differentiable function, which is trained with backpropagation together with the rest of the system. Different functions satisfy these requirements, but the authors of the paper chose the so-called **additive attention**, which combines s_{t-1} and h_i with the help of addition. It exists in two flavors:

$$e_{t,i} = a(s_{t-1}, h_i) = v^\mathsf{T} \tanh(W[h_i; s_{t-1}])$$
$$e_{t,i} = a(s_{t-1}, h_i) = v^\mathsf{T} \tanh(W_1 h_i + W_2 s_{t-1})$$

In the first formula, **W** is a weight matrix, applied over the concatenated vectors $\mathbf{s}_{t-1}$ and $\mathbf{h}_i$, and **v** is a weight vector. The second formula is similar, but this time we have separate fully connected layers (the weight matrices $\mathbf{W}_1$ and $\mathbf{W}_2$) and we sum $\mathbf{s}_{t-1}$ and $\mathbf{h}_i$. In both cases, the alignment model can be represented as a simple feed-forward network with one hidden layer.

Now that we know the formulas for $\mathbf{c}_t$ and $\alpha_{t,i}$, let's replace the latter in the former:

$$\mathbf{c}_t = \sum_{i=1}^{T} \alpha_{t,i} \mathbf{h}_i = \sum_{i=1}^{T} \frac{exp(e_{t,i})}{\sum_{j=1}^{T} exp(e_{t,j})} \mathbf{h}_i$$

As a conclusion, let's summarize the attention algorithm in a step-by-step manner as follows:

1. Feed the encoder with the input sequence and compute the set of hidden states $H = \{\mathbf{h}_1, \mathbf{h}_2, \ldots, \mathbf{h}_T\}$.

2. Compute the alignment scores $e_{t,i} = a(\mathbf{s}_{t-1}, \mathbf{h}_i)$, which use the decoder state from the preceding step $\mathbf{s}_{t-1}$. If $t = 1$, we'll use the last encoder state $\mathbf{h}_T$ as the initial hidden state.

3. Compute the weights $a_{t,i} = \text{softmax}(e_{t,i}/\mathbf{e}_t)$.

4. Compute the context vector $\mathbf{c}_t = \sum_{i=1}^{T} \alpha_{t,i} \mathbf{h}_i$.

5. Compute the hidden state $\mathbf{s}_t = \text{RNN}_{decoder}([\mathbf{s}_{t-1}; \mathbf{c}_t], y_{t-1})$, based on the concatenated vectors $\mathbf{s}_{t-1}$ and $\mathbf{c}_t$ and the previous decoder output y_{t-1}. At this point, we can compute the final output y_t. In the case where we need to classify the next word, we'll use the softmax output $y_t = \text{softmax}(\mathbf{W}_y \mathbf{s}_t)$, where $\mathbf{W}_y$ is a weight matrix.

6. Repeat steps 2–6 until the end of the sequence.

Next, we'll introduce a slightly improved attention mechanism called Luong attention.

Luong attention

Luong attention (see *Effective Approaches to Attention-based Neural Machine Translation* at `https://arxiv.org/abs/1508.04025`) introduces several improvements over Bahdanau attention. Most notably, the alignment scores e_t depend on the decoder hidden state s_t, as opposed to s_{t-1} in Bahdanau attention. To better understand this, let's compare the two algorithms:

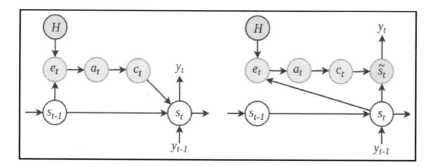

Left: Bahdanau attention: right: Luong attention

Let's go through a step-by-step execution of Luong attention:

1. Feed the encoder with the input sequence and compute the set of encoder hidden states $H = \{\mathbf{h}_1, \mathbf{h}_2, \ldots, \mathbf{h}_T\}$.

2. Compute the decoder hidden state $\mathbf{s}_t = \mathrm{RNN}_{decoder}(\mathbf{s}_{t-1}, y_{t-1})$ based on the previous decoder hidden state $\mathbf{s}_{t-1}$ and the previous decoder output y_{t-1} (not the context vector, though).

3. Compute the alignment scores $e_{t,i} = a(\mathbf{s}_t, \mathbf{h}_i)$, which use the decoder state from the current step $\mathbf{s}_t$. Besides additive attention, the Luong attention paper also proposes two types of **multiplicative attention**:
   - $e_{t,i} = \mathbf{s}_t^\mathsf{T} \mathbf{h}_i$: The basic dot product without any parameters. In this case, the vectors $\mathbf{s}$ and $\mathbf{h}$ need to have the same sizes.
   - $e_{t,i} = \mathbf{s}_t^\mathsf{T} \mathbf{W}_m \mathbf{h}_i$: Here, $\mathbf{W}_m$ is a trainable weight matrix of the attention layer.

   The multiplication of the vectors as an alignment score measurement has an intuitive explanation—as we mentioned in Chapter 1, *The Nuts and Bolts of Neural Networks*, the dot product acts as a similarity measure between vectors. Therefore, if the vectors are similar (that is, aligned), the result of the multiplication will be a large value and the attention will be focused on the current t,i relationship.

4. Compute the weights $a_{t,i} = \mathrm{softmax}(e_{t,i}/\mathbf{e}_t)$.

5. Compute the context vector $\mathbf{c}_t = \sum_{i=1}^{T} \alpha_{t,i} \mathbf{h}_i$.

6. Compute the vector $\tilde{\mathbf{s}}_t = \tanh(\mathbf{W}_c[\mathbf{c}_t; \mathbf{s}_t])$ based on the concatenated vectors $\mathbf{c}_t$ and $\mathbf{s}_t$. At this point, we can compute the final output y_t. In the case of classification, we'll use softmax $y_t = \mathrm{softmax}(\mathbf{W}_y \tilde{\mathbf{s}}_t)$, where $\mathbf{W}_y$ is a weight matrix.

7. Repeat steps 2–7 until the end of the sequence.

Next, let's discuss some more attention variants. We'll start with **hard** and **soft attention,** which relates to the way we compute the context vector c_t. So far, we've described soft attention, where c_i is a weighted sum of all hidden states of the input sequence. With hard attention, we still compute the weights $\alpha_{t,i}$, but we only take the hidden state h_{imax} with the maximum associated weight $\alpha_{t,imax}$. Then, the selected state h_{imax} serves as the context vector. At first, hard attention seems a little counter-intuitive—after all this effort to enable the decoder to have access to all input states, why limit it to a single state again? However, hard attention was first introduced in the context of image-recognition tasks, where the input sequence represents different regions of the same image. In such cases, it makes more sense to choose between multiple regions or a single region. Unlike soft attention, hard attention is a stochastic process, which is nondifferentiable. Therefore, the backward phase uses some tricks to work (this goes beyond the scope of this book).

Local attention represents a compromise between soft and hard attention. Whereas these mechanisms take into account either all input hidden vectors (global) or just a single input vector, local attention takes a window of vectors, surrounding a given input sequence location, and then applies soft attention over this window only. But how do we determine the center of the window p_t (known as the **aligned position**), based on the current output step t? The easiest way is to assume that the source and target sequences are roughly monotonically aligned—that is, to set $p_t = t$—following the logic that the input and output sequence positions relate to the same thing.

Next, we'll summarize what we have learned so far by introducing a general form of the attention mechanism.

General attention

Although we've discussed the attention mechanism in the context of NMT, it is a general deep-learning technique that can be applied to any seq2seq task. Let's assume that we are working with hard attention. In this case, we can think of the vector s_{t-1} as a **query** executed against a database of key-value pairs, where the **keys** are vectors and the hidden states h_i are the **values.** These are often abbreviated as **Q**, **K**, and **V**, and you can think of them as matrices of vectors. The keys **Q** and the values **V** of Luong and Bahdanau attention are the same vector—that is, these attention models are more like **Q/V**, rather than **Q/K/V**. The general attention mechanism uses all three components.

The following diagram illustrates this new general attention:

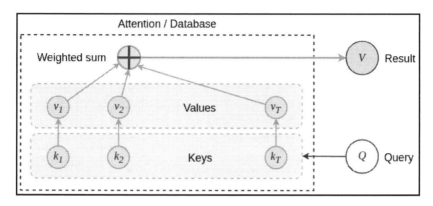

General attention

When we execute the query ($\mathbf{q} = \mathbf{s}_{t-1}$) against the database, we'll receive a single match—the key $\mathbf{k}_{imax}$ with the maximum weight $\alpha_{t,imax}$. Hidden behind this key is the vector $\mathbf{v}_{imax} = \mathbf{h}_{imax}$, which is the actual value we're interested in. But what about soft attention, where all values participate? We can think in the same query/key/value terms, but instead of a single value, the query results are all values with different weights. We can write a generalized attention formula (based on the context vector $\mathbf{c}_i$ formula) using the new notation:

$$\alpha_{\mathbf{q},\mathbf{k}_i} = \frac{\exp(e_{\mathbf{q},\mathbf{k}_i})}{\sum_j \exp(e_{\mathbf{q},\mathbf{k}_j})}$$

$$\text{Attention}(\mathbf{q}, \mathbf{K}, \mathbf{V}) = \sum_i \alpha_{\mathbf{q},\mathbf{k}_i} \mathbf{v}_{\mathbf{k}_i} = \sum_i \frac{\exp(e_{\mathbf{q},\mathbf{k}_i})}{\sum_j \exp(e_{\mathbf{q},\mathbf{k}_j})} \mathbf{v}_{\mathbf{k}_i}$$

In this generic attention, the queries, keys, and vectors of the database are not necessarily related in a sequential fashion. In other words, the database doesn't have to consist of the hidden RNN states at different steps, but could contain any kind of information instead. This concludes our introduction to the theory behind seq2seq models. We'll use this knowledge in the following section, where we'll implement a simple seq2seq NMT example.

Implementing seq2seq with attention

In this section, we'll use PyTorch 1.3.1 to implement a simple NMT example with the help of a seq2seq attention model. To clarify, we'll implement a seq2seq attention model, like the one we introduced in the *Introducing seq2seq models* section, and we'll extend it with Luong attention. The model encoder will take as input a text sequence (sentence) in one language and the decoder will output the corresponding sequence translated into another language.

We'll only show the most relevant parts of the code, but the full example is available at `https://github.com/PacktPublishing/Advanced-Deep-Learning-with-Python/tree/master/Chapter08/nmt_rnn_attention`. This example is partially based on the PyTorch tutorial at `https://github.com/pytorch/tutorials/blob/master/intermediate_source/seq2seq_translation_tutorial.py`.

Let's start with the training set. It consists of a large list of sentences in both French and English, stored in a text file. The `NMTDataset` class (a subclass of `torch.utils.data.Dataset`) implements the necessary data preprocessing. It creates a vocabulary with integer indexes of all possible words in the dataset. For the sake of simplicity, we won't use embedding vectors, and we'll feed the words to the network with their numerical representation. Also, we won't split the dataset into training and testing parts, as our goal is to demonstrate the work of the seq2seq model. The `NMTDataset` class outputs source-target tuple sentences, where each sentence is represented by a 1D tensor of indexes of the words in that sentence.

Implementing the encoder

Next, let's continue with implementing the encoder.

We'll start with the constructor:

```
class EncoderRNN(torch.nn.Module):
    def __init__(self, input_size, hidden_size):
        super(EncoderRNN, self).__init__()
        self.input_size = input_size
        self.hidden_size = hidden_size

        # Embedding for the input words
        self.embedding = torch.nn.Embedding(input_size, hidden_size)

        # The actual rnn sell
        self.rnn_cell = torch.nn.GRU(hidden_size, hidden_size)
```

The entry point is the `self.embedding` module. It will take the index of each word and it will return its assigned embedding vector. We will not use pretrained word vectors (such as GloVe), but nevertheless, the concept of embedding vectors is the same—it's just that we'll initialize them with random values and we'll train them along the way with the rest of the model. Then, we have the `torch.nn.GRU` RNN cell itself.

Next, let's implement the `EncoderRNN.forward` method (please bear in mind the indentation):

```
def forward(self, input, hidden):
    # Pass through the embedding
    embedded = self.embedding(input).view(1, 1, -1)
    output = embedded

    # Pass through the RNN
    output, hidden = self.rnn_cell(output, hidden)
    return output, hidden
```

It represents the processing of a sequence element. First, we obtain the `embedded` word vector and then we feed it to the RNN cell.

We'll also implement the `EncoderRNN.init_hidden` method, which creates an empty tensor with the same size as the hidden RNN state. This tensor serves as the first RNN hidden state at the beginning of the sequence (please bear in mind the indentation):

```
def init_hidden(self):
    return torch.zeros(1, 1, self.hidden_size, device=device)
```

Now that we've implemented the encoder, let's continue with the decoder implementation.

Implementing the decoder

Let's implement the `DecoderRNN` class—a basic decoder without attention. Again, we'll start with the constructor:

```
class DecoderRNN(torch.nn.Module):

    def __init__(self, hidden_size, output_size):
        super(DecoderRNN, self).__init__()
        self.hidden_size = hidden_size
        self.output_size = output_size

        # Embedding for the current input word
        self.embedding = torch.nn.Embedding(output_size, hidden_size)
```

```
# decoder cell
self.gru = torch.nn.GRU(hidden_size, hidden_size)

# Current output word
self.out = torch.nn.Linear(hidden_size, output_size)
self.log_softmax = torch.nn.LogSoftmax(dim=1)
```

It's similar to the encoder—we have the initial `self.embedding` word embedding and the `self.gru` GRU cell. We also have the fully connected `self.out` layer with `self.log_softmax` activation, which will output the predicted word in the sequence.

We'll continue with the `DecoderRNN.forward` method (please bear in mind the indentation):

```
def forward(self, input, hidden, _):
    # Pass through the embedding
    embedded = self.embedding(input).view(1, 1, -1)
    embedded = torch.nn.functional.relu(embedded)

    # Pass through the RNN cell
    output, hidden = self.rnn_cell(embedded, hidden)

    # Produce output word
    output = self.log_softmax(self.out(output[0]))
    return output, hidden, _
```

It starts with the `embedded` vector, which serves as input to the RNN cell. The module returns both its new `hidden` state and the `output` tensor, which represents the predicted word. The method accepts the void argument `_`, so it could match the interface of the attention decoder, which we'll implement in the next section.

Implementing the decoder with attention

Next, we'll implement the `AttnDecoderRNN` decoder with Luong attention. This also works in combination with `EncoderRNN`.

We'll start with the `AttnDecoderRNN.__init__` method:

```
class AttnDecoderRNN(torch.nn.Module):
    def __init__(self, hidden_size, output_size, max_length=MAX_LENGTH,
    dropout=0.1):
        super(AttnDecoderRNN, self).__init__()
        self.hidden_size = hidden_size
        self.output_size = output_size
        self.max_length = max_length
```

```
    # Embedding for the input word
    self.embedding = torch.nn.Embedding(self.output_size,
    self.hidden_size)

    self.dropout = torch.nn.Dropout(dropout)

    # Attention portion
    self.attn = torch.nn.Linear(in_features=self.hidden_size,
                            out_features=self.hidden_size)

    self.w_c = torch.nn.Linear(in_features=self.hidden_size * 2,
                            out_features=self.hidden_size)

    # RNN
    self.rnn_cell = torch.nn.GRU(input_size=self.hidden_size,
                            hidden_size=self.hidden_size)

    # Output word
    self.w_y = torch.nn.Linear(in_features=self.hidden_size,
                            out_features=self.output_size)
```

As usual, we have `self.embedding`, but this time, we'll also add `self.dropout` to prevent overfitting. The fully connected `self.attn` and `self.w_c` layers relate to the attention mechanism, and we'll learn how to use them when we look at the `AttnDecoderRNN.forward` method, which comes next. `AttnDecoderRNN.forward` implements the Luong attention algorithm we described in the *Seq2seq with attention* section. Let's start with the method declaration and parameter preprocessing:

```
def forward(self, input, hidden, encoder_outputs):
    embedded = self.embedding(input).view(1, 1, -1)
    embedded = self.dropout(embedded)
```

Next, we'll compute the current hidden state (`hidden` = s_t). Please bear in mind the indentation, as this code is still part of the `AttnDecoderRNN.forward` method:

```
rnn_out, hidden = self.rnn_cell(embedded, hidden)
```

Then, we'll compute the alignment scores (`alignment_scores` = $e_{t,i}$), following the multiplicative attention formula. Here, `torch.mm` is the matrix multiplication and `encoder_outputs` is the encoder outputs (surprise!):

```
alignment_scores = torch.mm(self.attn(hidden)[0], encoder_outputs.t())
```

Next, we'll compute softmax over the scores to produce the attention weights (`attn_weights` = $a_{t,i}$):

```
attn_weights = torch.nn.functional.softmax(alignment_scores, dim=1)
```

Then, we'll compute the context vector (`c_t` = c_i) following the attention formula:

```
c_t = torch.mm(attn_weights, encoder_outputs)
```

Next, we'll compute the modified state vector (`hidden_s_t` = $\tilde{s}_t$) by concatenating the current hidden state and the context vector:

```
hidden_s_t = torch.cat([hidden[0], c_t], dim=1)
hidden_s_t = torch.tanh(self.w_c(hidden_s_t))
```

Finally, we'll compute the next predicted word:

```
output = torch.nn.functional.log_softmax(self.w_y(hidden_s_t), dim=1)
```

We should note that `torch.nn.functional.log_softmax` applies the logarithm after a regular softmax. This activation function works in combination with the negative log-likelihood loss function `torch.nn.NLLLoss`.

Finally, the method returns `output`, `hidden`, and `attn_weights`. Later, we'll use `attn_weights` to visualize the attention between the input and output sentences (the method `AttnDecoderRNN.forward` ends here):

```
return output, hidden, attn_weights
```

Next, let's look at the training process.

Training and evaluation

Next, let's implement the `train` function. It's similar to other such functions that we've implemented in previous chapters; however, it takes into account the sequential nature of the input and the teacher forcing principle we described in the *Seq2eq with attention* section. For the sake of simplicity, we'll only train with a single sequence at a time (a mini batch of size 1).

First, we'll initiate the iteration over the training set, set up initial sequence tensors, and reset the gradients:

```
def train(encoder, decoder, loss_function, encoder_optimizer,
decoder_optimizer, data_loader, max_length=MAX_LENGTH):
    print_loss_total = 0

    # Iterate over the dataset
    for i, (input_tensor, target_tensor) in enumerate(data_loader):
        input_tensor = input_tensor.to(device).squeeze(0)
        target_tensor = target_tensor.to(device).squeeze(0)

        encoder_hidden = encoder.init_hidden()

        encoder_optimizer.zero_grad()
        decoder_optimizer.zero_grad()

        input_length = input_tensor.size(0)
        target_length = target_tensor.size(0)

        encoder_outputs = torch.zeros(max_length, encoder.hidden_size,
device=device)

        loss = torch.Tensor([0]).squeeze().to(device)
```

The encoder and decoder parameters are instances of `EncoderRNN` and `AttnDecoderRNN` (or `DecoderRNN`), `loss_function` represents the loss (in our case, `torch.nn.NLLLoss`), `encoder_optimizer` and `decoder_optimizer` (the names speak for themselves) are instances of `torch.optim.Adam`, and `data_loader` is a `torch.utils.data.DataLoader`, which wraps an instance of `NMTDataset`.

Next, we'll do the actual training:

```
with torch.set_grad_enabled(True):
    # Pass the sequence through the encoder and store the hidden states
    at each step
    for ei in range(input_length):
        encoder_output, encoder_hidden = encoder(
            input_tensor[ei], encoder_hidden)
        encoder_outputs[ei] = encoder_output[0, 0]

    # Initiate decoder with the GO_token
    decoder_input = torch.tensor([[GO_token]], device=device)

    # Initiate the decoder with the last encoder hidden state
    decoder_hidden = encoder_hidden
```

```
# Teacher forcing: Feed the target as the next input
for di in range(target_length):
    decoder_output, decoder_hidden, decoder_attention = decoder(
        decoder_input, decoder_hidden, encoder_outputs)
    loss += loss_function(decoder_output, target_tensor[di])
    decoder_input = target_tensor[di]   # Teacher forcing

loss.backward()

encoder_optimizer.step()
decoder_optimizer.step()
```

Let's discuss this in more detail:

- We feed the full sequence to the encoder and save the hidden states in the `encoder_outputs` list.
- We initiate the decoder sequence with `GO_token` as input.
- We use the decoder to generate new elements of the sequence. Following the teacher forcing principle, the `decoder` input at each step comes from the real target sequence `decoder_input = target_tensor[di]`.
- We train the encoder and decoder with `encoder_optimizer.step()` and `decoder_optimizer.step()`, respectively.

Similar to `train`, we have an `evaluate` function, which takes an input sequence and returns its translated counterpart and its accompanying attention scores. We won't include the full implementation here, but we'll focus on the encoder/decoder part. Instead of teacher forcing, the `decoder` input at each step is the output word of the previous step:

```
# Initiate the decoder with the last encoder hidden state
decoder_input = torch.tensor([[GO_token]], device=device)   # GO

# Initiate the decoder with the last encoder hidden state
decoder_hidden = encoder_hidden

decoded_words = []
decoder_attentions = torch.zeros(max_length, max_length)

# Generate the output sequence (opposite to teacher forcing)
for di in range(max_length):
    decoder_output, decoder_hidden, decoder_attention = decoder(
        decoder_input, decoder_hidden, encoder_outputs)
    decoder_attentions[di] = decoder_attention.data

    # Obtain the output word index with the highest probability
    _, topi = decoder_output.data.topk(1)
```

```
if topi.item() != EOS_token:
    decoded_words.append(dataset.output_lang.index2word[topi.item()])
else:
    break

# Use the latest output word as the next input
decoder_input = topi.squeeze().detach()
```

When we run the full program, it will display several example translations. It will also display a map of the attention scores between the elements of the input and output sequences, such as the following:

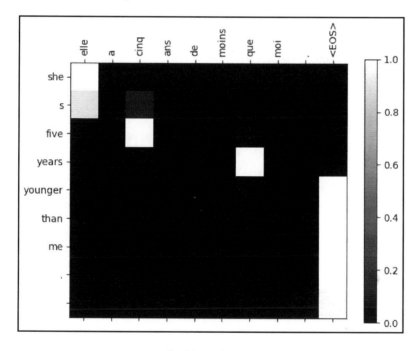

Translation attention scores

For example, we can see that the output word **she** focuses its attention to the input word **elle** (*she* in French). If we didn't have the attention mechanism and only relied on the last encoder hidden state to initiate the translation, the output could have been **She's five years younger than me** just as easily. Since the word **elle** is furthest away from the end of the sentence, it would have been hard to encode it within the last encoder hidden state alone.

In the next section, we'll leave the RNNs behind and we'll introduce the transformer—a seq2seq model, based solely on the attention mechanism.

Understanding transformers

We spent the better part of this chapter touting the advantages of the attention mechanism. But we still use attention in the context of RNNs—in that sense, it works as an addition on top of the core recurrent nature of these models. Since attention is so good, is there a way to use it on its own without the RNN part? It turns out that there is. The paper *Attention is all you need* (https://arxiv.org/abs/1706.03762) introduces a new architecture called **transformer** with encoder and decoder that relies solely on the attention mechanism. First, we'll focus our attention on the transformer attention (pun intended) mechanism.

The transformer attention

Before focusing on the entire model, let's take a look at how the transformer attention is implemented:

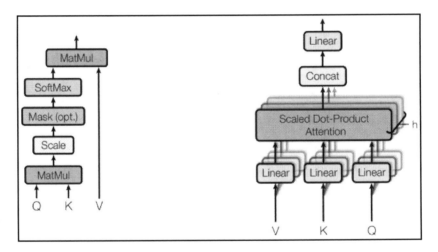

Left: Scaled dot product (multiplicative) attention: right: Multihead attention: source: https://arxiv.org/abs/1706.03762

The transformer uses dot product attention (the left-hand side diagram of the preceding diagram), which follows the general attention procedure we introduced in the *Seq2seq with attention* section (as we have already mentioned, it is not restricted to RNN models). We can define it with the following formula:

$$\text{Attention}(\mathbf{Q}, \mathbf{K}, \mathbf{V}) = \text{softmax}(\frac{\mathbf{Q}\mathbf{K}^{\mathsf{T}}}{\sqrt{d_k}})\mathbf{V}$$

In practice, we'll compute the attention function over a set of queries simultaneously, packed in a matrix **Q**. In this scenario, the keys **K**, the values **V**, and the result are also matrices. Let's discuss the steps of the formula in more detail:

1. Match the query **Q** and the database (keys **K**) with matrix multiplication to produce the alignment scores $\mathbf{QK}^\mathsf{T}$. Let's assume that we want to match m different queries to a database of n values and the query-key vector length is d_k. Then, we have the matrix $\mathbf{Q} \in \mathbb{R}^{m \times d_k}$ with one d_k-dimensional query per row for m total rows. Similarly, we have the matrix $\mathbf{K} \in \mathbb{R}^{n \times d_k}$ with one d_k-dimensional key per row for n total rows. Then, the output matrix will have $\mathbf{QK}^\mathsf{T} \in \mathbb{R}^{m \times n}$, where one row contains the alignment scores of a single query over all keys of the database:

$$
\mathbf{QK}^\mathsf{T} = \underbrace{\begin{bmatrix} q_{11} & q_{12} & \cdots & q_{1d_k} \\ q_{21} & q_{22} & \cdots & q_{2d_k} \\ \vdots & \vdots & \ddots & \vdots \\ q_{m1} & q_{m2} & \cdots & q_{md_k} \end{bmatrix}}_{\mathbf{Q}} \cdot \underbrace{\begin{bmatrix} k_{11} & k_{12} & \cdots & k_{1n} \\ k_{21} & k_{22} & \cdots & k_{2n} \\ \vdots & \vdots & \ddots & \vdots \\ k_{d_k1} & k_{d_k2} & \cdots & k_{d_kn} \end{bmatrix}}_{\mathbf{K}^\mathsf{T}} = \underbrace{\begin{bmatrix} e_{11} & e_{12} & \cdots & e_{1n} \\ e_{21} & e_{22} & \cdots & e_{2n} \\ \vdots & \vdots & \ddots & \vdots \\ e_{m1} & e_{m2} & \cdots & e_{mn} \end{bmatrix}}_{\mathbf{QK}^\mathsf{T}}
$$

In other words, we can match multiple queries against multiple database keys in a single matrix-matrix multiplication. In the context of NMT, we can compute the alignment scores of all words of the target sentence over all words of the source sentence in the same way.

2. Scale the alignment scores with $1/\sqrt{d_k}$, where d_k is the vector size of the key vectors in the matrix **K**, which is also equal to the size of the query vectors in **Q** (analogously, d_v is the vector size of the key vectors **V**). The authors of the paper suspect that for large values of d_k, the dot product grows large in magnitude and pushes the softmax in regions with extremely small gradients, which leads to the infamous vanishing gradients problem, hence the need to scale the results.

3. Compute the attention scores with the softmax operation along the rows of the matrix (we'll talk about the mask operation later):

$$
\mathrm{softmax}\left(\frac{\mathbf{QK}^\mathsf{T}}{\sqrt{d_k}}\right) = \begin{bmatrix} \mathrm{softmax}(e_{11}/\sqrt{d_k} & e_{12}/\sqrt{d_k} & \cdots & e_{1n}/\sqrt{d_k}) \\ \mathrm{softmax}(e_{21}/\sqrt{d_k} & e_{22}/\sqrt{d_k} & \cdots & e_{2n}/\sqrt{d_k}) \\ \vdots & \vdots & \ddots & \vdots \\ \mathrm{softmax}(e_{m1}/\sqrt{d_k} & e_{m2}/\sqrt{d_k} & \cdots & e_{mn}/\sqrt{d_k}) \end{bmatrix}
$$

4. Compute the final attention vector by multiplying the attention scores with the values $\mathbf{V}$:

$$\text{softmax}(\frac{\mathbf{QK}^\mathsf{T}}{\sqrt{d_k}})\mathbf{V} = \begin{bmatrix} \text{softmax}(e_{11}/\sqrt{d_k}) & e_{12}/\sqrt{d_k} & \cdots & e_{1n}/\sqrt{d_k} \\ \text{softmax}(e_{21}/\sqrt{d_k}) & e_{22}/\sqrt{d_k} & \cdots & e_{2n}/\sqrt{d_k} \\ \vdots & \vdots & \ddots & \vdots \\ \text{softmax}(e_{m1}/\sqrt{d_k}) & e_{m2}/\sqrt{d_k} & \cdots & e_{mn}/\sqrt{d_k} \end{bmatrix} \cdot \begin{bmatrix} v_{11} & v_{12} & \cdots & v_{1d_v} \\ v_{21} & v_{22} & \cdots & v_{2d_v} \\ \vdots & \vdots & \ddots & \vdots \\ v_{n1} & v_{m2} & \cdots & v_{nd_v} \end{bmatrix} = \mathbf{A} \in \mathbb{R}^{m \times d_v}$$

We can adapt this mechanism to work with both hard and soft attention.

The authors also propose **multihead attention** (see the right-hand side diagram of the preceding diagram). Instead of a single attention function with d_{model}-dimensional keys, we linearly project the keys, queries, and values h times to produce h different d_k-, d_k-, and d_v-dimensional projections of these values. Then, we apply separate parallel attention functions (or heads) over the newly created vectors, which yield a single d_v-dimensional output for each head. Finally, we concatenate the head outputs to produce the final attention result. Multihead attention allows each head to attend to different elements of the sequence. At the same time, the model combines the outputs of the heads in a single cohesive representation. More precisely, we can define this with the following formula:

$$\text{MultiHead}(\mathbf{Q}, \mathbf{K}, \mathbf{V}) = \text{Concat}(\text{head}_1, \text{head}_2, \ldots, \text{head}_h)\mathbf{W}^O$$
$$\text{where head}_i = \text{Attention}(\mathbf{QW}_i^Q, \mathbf{KW}_i^K, \mathbf{VW}_i^V)$$

Let's look at this in more detail, starting with the heads:

1. Each head receives the linearly projected versions of the initial $\mathbf{Q}$, $\mathbf{K}$, and $\mathbf{V}$. The projections are computed with the learnable weight matrices $\mathbf{W}_i^Q$, $\mathbf{W}_i^K$, and $\mathbf{W}_i^V$ respectively. Note that we have a separate set of weights for each component ($\mathbf{Q}$, $\mathbf{K}$, $\mathbf{V}$) and for each head i. To satisfy the transformation from d_{model} to and d_k and d_v, the dimensions of these matrices are $\mathbf{W}_i^Q \in \mathbb{R}^{d_{model} \times d_k}$, $\mathbf{W}_i^K \in \mathbb{R}^{d_{model} \times d_k}$, and $\mathbf{W}_i^V \in \mathbb{R}^{d_{model} \times d_v}$.

2. Once $\mathbf{Q}$, $\mathbf{K}$, and $\mathbf{V}$ are transformed, we can compute the attention of each head using the regular attention model we described at the beginning of this section.

3. The final attention result is the linear projection (the weight matrix $\mathbf{W}^O$ of learnable weights) over the concatenated head outputs head$_i$.

So far, we've demonstrated attention for different input and output sequences. For example, we've seen that in NMT each word of the translated sentence relates to the words of the source sentence. The transformer model also relies on **self-attention** (or intra-attention), where the query **Q** belongs to the same dataset as the keys **K** and vectors **V** of the query database. In other words, in self-attention, the source and the target are the same sequence (in our case, the same sentence). The benefit of self-attention is not immediately obvious, as there is no direct task to apply it to. On an intuitive level, it allows us to see the relationship between words of the same sequence. For example, the following diagram shows the multihead self-attention of the verb *making* (different colors represent different heads). Many of the attention heads attend to a distant dependency of *making*, completing the phrase *making ... more difficult*:

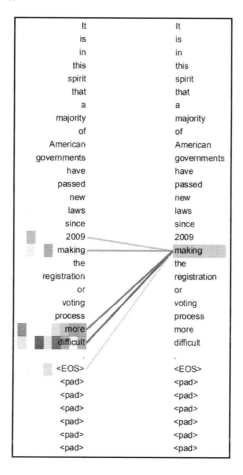

An example of multihead self-attention. Source: https://arxiv.org/abs/1706.03762

The transformer model uses self-attention as a replacement of the encoder/decoder RNNs, but more on that in the next section.

The transformer model

Now that we are familiar with multihead attention, let's focus on the full transformer model, starting with the following diagram:

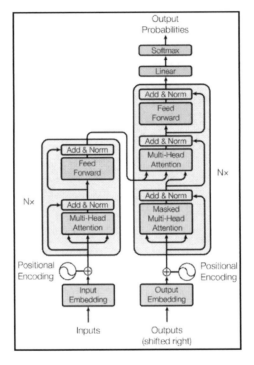

The transformer model architecture. The left-hand side shows the encoder and the right-hand side shows the decoder: source: https://arxiv.org/abs/1706.03762

It looks scary, but fret not—it's easier than it seems. We'll start with the encoder (the left-hand component of the preceding diagram):

- It begins with an input sequence of one-hot-encoded words, which are transformed into d_{model}-dimensional embedding vectors. The embedding vectors are further multiplied by $\sqrt{d_{model}}$.

- The transformer doesn't use RNNs, and therefore, it has to convey the positional information of each sequence element in some other way. We can do this explicitly by augmenting each embedding vector with positional encoding. In short, the positional encoding is a vector with the same length d_{model} as the embedding vector. The positional vector is added (elementwise) to the embedding vector and the result is propagated further in the encoder. The authors of the paper introduce the following function for each element i of the positional vector, when the current word has the position *pos* in the sequence:

$$PE(pos, 2i) = \sin\left(\frac{pos}{10000^{2i/d_{model}}}\right)$$

$$PE(pos, 2i+1) = \cos\left(\frac{pos}{10000^{2i/d_{model}}}\right)$$

Each dimension of the positional encoding corresponds to a sinusoid. The wavelengths form a geometric progression from 2π to $10000 \cdot 2\pi$. The authors hypothesize that this function would allow the model to easily learn to attend by relative positions, since, for any fixed offset k, PE_{pos+k} can be represented as a linear function of PE_{pos}.

- The rest of the encoder is composed of a stack of $N = 6$ identical blocks. Each block has two sublayers:
  - A multihead self-attention mechanism, like the one we described in the section titled *The transformer attention*. Since the self-attention mechanism works across the whole input sequence, the encoder is **bidirectional** by design. Some algorithms use only the encoder transformer part and are referred to as **transformer encoder**.
  - A simple, fully connected, feed-forward network, which is defined by the following formula:

$$FFN(x) = ReLU(\mathbf{W}_1 x + b_1)\mathbf{W}_2 + b_2$$

  The network is applied to each sequence element x separately. It uses the same set of parameters ($\mathbf{W}_1$, $\mathbf{W}_2$, b_1, and b_2) across different positions, but different parameters across the different encoder blocks.

Each sublayer (both the multihead attention and feed-forward network) has a residual connection around itself and ends with normalization over the sum of that connection and its own output and the residual connection. Therefore, the output of each sublayer is as follows:

$$\text{LayerNorm}(x + \text{SubLayer}(x))$$

The normalization technique is described in the paper *Layer Normalization* (https://arxiv.org/abs/1607.06450).

Next, let's look at the decoder, which is somewhat similar to the encoder:

- The input at step *t* is the decoder's own predicted output word at step *t-1*. The input word uses the same embedding vectors and positional encoding as the encoder.
- The decoder continues with a stack of *N* = 6 identical blocks, which are somewhat similar to the encoder blocks. Each block consists of three sublayers and each sublayer employs residual connections and normalization. The sublayers are:
  - A multihead self-attention mechanism. The encoder self-attention can attend to all elements of the sequence, regardless of whether they come before or after the target element. But the decoder has only a partially generated target sequence. Therefore, the self-attention here can only attend to the preceding sequence elements. This is implemented by **masking out** (setting to $-\infty$) all values in the input of the softmax, which correspond to illegal connections:

$$\text{mask}(\mathbf{QK}^\top) = \text{mask}\left(\begin{bmatrix} e_{11} & e_{12} & \cdots & e_{1n} \\ e_{21} & e_{22} & \cdots & e_{2n} \\ \vdots & \vdots & \ddots & \vdots \\ e_{m1} & e_{m2} & \cdots & e_{mn} \end{bmatrix}\right) = \begin{bmatrix} e_{11} & -\infty & -\infty & \cdots & -\infty \\ e_{21} & e_{22} & -\infty & \cdots & -\infty \\ e_{31} & e_{32} & e_{33} & \cdots & -\infty \\ \vdots & \vdots & \vdots & \ddots & \vdots \\ e_{m1} & e_{m2} & e_{m3} & \cdots & e_{mn} \end{bmatrix}$$

The masking makes the decoder **unidirectional** (unlike the bidirectional encoder). Algorithms that work with the decoder are referred to as **transformer decoder algorithms**.

- A regular attention mechanism, where the queries come from the previous decoder layer, and the keys and values come from the previous sublayer, which represents the processed decoder output at step *t-1*. This allows every position in the decoder to attend over all positions in the input sequence. This mimics the typical encoder-decoder attention mechanisms, which we discussed in the *Seq2seq with attention* section.

- A feed-forward network, which is similar to the one in the encoder.

- The decoder ends with a fully connected layer, followed by a softmax, which produces the most probable next word of the sentence.

The transformer uses dropout as a regularization technique. It adds dropout to the output of each sublayer before it is added to the sublayer input and normalized. It also applies dropout to the sums of the embeddings and the positional encodings in both the encoder and decoder stacks.

Finally, let's summarize the benefits of self-attention over the RNN attention models we discussed in the *Seq2seq with attention* section. The key advantage of the self-attention mechanism is the immediate access to all elements of the input sequence, as opposed to the bottleneck thought vector of the RNN models. Additionally—the following is a direct quote from the paper—a self-attention layer connects all positions with a constant number of sequentially executed operations, whereas a recurrent layer requires $O(n)$ sequential operations.

In terms of computational complexity, self-attention layers are faster than recurrent layers when the sequence length n is smaller than the representation dimensionality d, which is most often the case with sentence representations used by state-of-the-art models in machine translations, such as word-piece (see *Google's Neural Machine Translation System: Bridging the Gap between Human and Machine Translation* at https://arxiv.org/abs/1609.08144) and byte-pair (see *Neural Machine Translation of Rare Words with Subword Units* at https://arxiv.org/abs/1508.07909) representations. To improve computational performance for tasks involving very long sequences, self-attention could be restricted to considering only a neighborhood of size r in the input sequence centered around the respective output position.

This concludes our theoretical description of transformers. In the next section, we'll implement a transformer from scratch.

Implementing transformers

In this section, we'll implement the transformer model with the help of PyTorch 1.3.1. As the example is relatively complex, we'll simplify it by using a basic training dataset: we'll train the model to copy a randomly generated sequence of integer values—that is, the source and the target sequence are the same and the transformer will learn to replicate the input sequence as the output. We won't include the full source code, but you can find it at `https://github.com/PacktPublishing/Advanced-Deep-Learning-with-Python/tree/master/Chapter08/transformer.py`.

This example is based on `https://github.com/harvardnlp/annotated-transformer`. Let's also note that PyTorch 1.2 has introduced native transformer modules (the documentation is available at `https://pytorch.org/docs/master/nn.html#transformer-layers`). Still, in this section we'll implement the transformer from scratch to understand it better.

First, we'll start with the utility function `clone`, which takes an instance of `torch.nn.Module` and produces n identical deep copies of the same module (excluding the original source instance):

```
def clones(module: torch.nn.Module, n: int):
    return torch.nn.ModuleList([copy.deepcopy(module) for _ in range(n)])
```

With this short introduction, let's continue with the implementation of multihead attention.

Multihead attention

In this section, we'll implement multihead attention by following the definitions from the *The transformer attention* section. We'll start with the implementation of the regular scaled dot product attention:

```
def attention(query, key, value, mask=None, dropout=None):
    """Scaled Dot Product Attention"""
    d_k = query.size(-1)

    # 1) and 2) Compute the alignment scores with scaling
    scores = torch.matmul(query, key.transpose(-2, -1)) / math.sqrt(d_k)
    if mask is not None:
        scores = scores.masked_fill(mask == 0, -1e9)

    # 3) Compute the attention scores (softmax)
    p_attn = torch.nn.functional.softmax(scores, dim=-1)
```

```
if dropout is not None:
    p_attn = dropout(p_attn)

# 4) Apply the attention scores over the values
return torch.matmul(p_attn, value), p_attn
```

As a reminder, this function implements the formula $\text{Attention}(\mathbf{Q}, \mathbf{K}, \mathbf{V}) = \text{softmax}(\mathbf{Q}\mathbf{K}^{\mathsf{T}}/\sqrt{d_k})\mathbf{V}$, where $\mathbf{Q}$ = query, $\mathbf{K}$ = key, and $\mathbf{V}$ = value. If a mask is available, it will also be applied.

Next, we'll implement the multihead attention mechanism as `torch.nn.Module`. As a reminder, the implementation follows the following formula:

$$\text{MultiHead}(\mathbf{Q}, \mathbf{K}, \mathbf{V}) = \text{Concat}(\text{head}_1, \text{head}_2, \dots, \text{head}_h)\mathbf{W}^O$$
$$\text{where head}_i = \text{Attention}(\mathbf{Q}\mathbf{W}_i^Q, \mathbf{K}\mathbf{W}_i^K, \mathbf{V}\mathbf{W}_i^V)$$

We'll start with the __init__ method:

```
class MultiHeadedAttention(torch.nn.Module):
    def __init__(self, h, d_model, dropout=0.1):
        """
        :param h: number of heads
        :param d_model: query/key/value vector length
        """
        super(MultiHeadedAttention, self).__init__()
        assert d_model % h == 0
        # We assume d_v always equals d_k
        self.d_k = d_model // h
        self.h = h

        # Create 4 fully connected layers
        # 3 for the query/key/value projections
        # 1 to concatenate the outputs of all heads
        self.fc_layers = clones(torch.nn.Linear(d_model, d_model), 4)
        self.attn = None
        self.dropout = torch.nn.Dropout(p=dropout)
```

Note that we use the `clones` function to create four identical, fully connected `self.fc_layers`. We'll use three of them for the **Q/K/V** linear projections— $\mathbf{W}_i^Q, \mathbf{W}_i^K$, and $\mathbf{W}_i^V$. The fourth fully connected layer is to merge the concatenated results of the outputs of the different heads $\mathbf{W}^O$. We'll store the current attention results in the `self.attn` property.

Next, let's implement the `MultiHeadedAttention.forward` method (please bear in mind the indentation):

```
def forward(self, query, key, value, mask=None):
    if mask is not None:
        # Same mask applied to all h heads.
        mask = mask.unsqueeze(1)

    batch_samples = query.size(0)

    # 1) Do all the linear projections in batch from d_model => h x d_k
    projections = list()
    for l, x in zip(self.fc_layers, (query, key, value)):
        projections.append(
            l(x).view(batch_samples, -1, self.h, self.d_k).transpose(1, 2)
        )

    query, key, value = projections

    # 2) Apply attention on all the projected vectors in batch.
    x, self.attn = attention(query, key, value,
                             mask=mask,
                             dropout=self.dropout)

    # 3) "Concat" using a view and apply a final linear.
    x = x.transpose(1, 2).contiguous() \
        .view(batch_samples, -1, self.h * self.d_k)

    return self.fc_layers[-1](x)
```

We iterate over the **Q/K/V** vectors and their reference projection `self.fc_layers` and produce the **Q/K/V** `projections` with the following snippet:

```
l(x).view(batch_samples, -1, self.h, self.d_k).transpose(1, 2)
```

Then, we apply the regular attention over the projections using the `attention` function we first defined, and finally, we concatenate the outputs of multiple heads and return the results. Now that we've implemented multihead attention, let's continue by implementing the encoder.

Encoder

In this section, we'll implement the encoder, which is composed of several different subcomponents. Let's start with the main definition and then dive into more details:

```
class Encoder(torch.nn.Module):
    def __init__(self, block: EncoderBlock, N: int):
        super(Encoder, self).__init__()
        self.blocks = clones(block, N)
        self.norm = LayerNorm(block.size)

    def forward(self, x, mask):
        """Iterate over all blocks and normalize"""
        for layer in self.blocks:
            x = layer(x, mask)

        return self.norm(x)
```

It is fairly straightforward: the encoder is composed of `self.blocks`: N stacked instances of `EncoderBlock`, where each serves as input for the next. They are followed by `LayerNorm` normalization `self.norm` (we discussed these concepts in the *The transformer model* section). The `forward` method takes as input the data tensor `x` and an instance of `mask`, which blocks some of the input sequence elements. As we discussed in the *The transformer model* section, the mask is only relevant to the decoder part of the model, where the future elements of the sequence are not available yet. In the encoder, the mask exists only as a placeholder.

We'll omit the definition of `LayerNorm` (it's enough to know that it's a normalization at the end of the encoder) and we'll focus on `EncoderBlock` instead:

```
class EncoderBlock(torch.nn.Module):
    def __init__(self,
                 size: int,
                 self_attn: MultiHeadedAttention,
                 ffn: PositionwiseFFN,
                 dropout=0.1):
        super(EncoderBlock, self).__init__()
        self.self_attn = self_attn
        self.ffn = ffn

        # Create 2 sub-layer connections
        # 1 for the self-attention
        # 1 for the FFN
        self.sublayers = clones(SublayerConnection(size, dropout), 2)
        self.size = size
```

```
def forward(self, x, mask):
    x = self.sublayers[0](x, lambda x: self.self_attn(x, x, x, mask))
    return self.sublayers[1](x, self.ffn)
```

As a reminder, each encoder block consists of two sublayers (`self.sublayers` instantiated with the familiar `clones` function): a multihead self-attention `self_attn` (an instance of `MultiHeadedAttention`), followed by a simple fully connected network `ffn` (an instance of `PositionwiseFFN`). Each sublayer is wrapped by its residual connection, which is implemented with the `SublayerConnection` class:

```
class SublayerConnection(torch.nn.Module):
    def __init__(self, size, dropout):
        super(SublayerConnection, self).__init__()
        self.norm = LayerNorm(size)
        self.dropout = torch.nn.Dropout(dropout)

    def forward(self, x, sublayer):
        return x + self.dropout(sublayer(self.norm(x)))
```

The residual connection also includes normalization and dropout (according to the definition). As a reminder, it follows the formula $\mathrm{LayerNorm}(x + \mathrm{SubLayer}(x))$, but for code simplicity, the `self.norm` comes first rather than last. The `SublayerConnection.forward` phrase takes as input the data tensor x and `sublayer`, which is an instance of either `MultiHeadedAttention` or `PositionwiseFFN`. We can see this dynamic in the `EncoderBlock.forward` method.

The only component we haven't defined yet is `PositionwiseFFN`, which implements the formula $\mathrm{FFN}(x) = \mathrm{ReLU}(\mathbf{W}_1 x + b_1)\mathbf{W}_2 + b_2$. Let's add this missing piece:

```
class PositionwiseFFN(torch.nn.Module):
    def __init__(self, d_model: int, d_ff: int, dropout=0.1):
        super(PositionwiseFFN, self).__init__()
        self.w_1 = torch.nn.Linear(d_model, d_ff)
        self.w_2 = torch.nn.Linear(d_ff, d_model)
        self.dropout = torch.nn.Dropout(dropout)

    def forward(self, x):
        return
self.w_2(self.dropout(torch.nn.functional.relu(self.w_1(x))))
```

We have now implemented the encoder and all its building blocks. In the next section, we'll continue with the decoder definition.

Decoder

In this section, we'll implement the decoder. It follows a pattern that is very similar to the encoder:

```
class Decoder(torch.nn.Module):
    def __init__(self, block: DecoderBlock, N: int, vocab_size: int):
        super(Decoder, self).__init__()
        self.blocks = clones(block, N)
        self.norm = LayerNorm(block.size)
        self.projection = torch.nn.Linear(block.size, vocab_size)

    def forward(self, x, encoder_states, source_mask, target_mask):
        for layer in self.blocks:
            x = layer(x, encoder_states, source_mask, target_mask)

        x = self.norm(x)

        return torch.nn.functional.log_softmax(self.projection(x), dim=-1)
```

It consists of `self.blocks`: N instances of `DecoderBlock`, where the output of each block serves as input to the next. These are followed by the `self.norm` normalization (an instance of `LayerNorm`). Finally, to produce the most probable word, the decoder has an additional fully connected layer with softmax activation. Note that the `Decoder.forward` method takes an additional parameter `encoder_states`, which represents the attention vector of the encoder. The `encoder_states` are then passed to the `DecoderBlock` instances.

Next, let's implement the `DecoderBlock`:

```
class DecoderBlock(torch.nn.Module):
    def __init__(self,
                 size: int,
                 self_attn: MultiHeadedAttention,
                 encoder_attn: MultiHeadedAttention,
                 ffn: PositionwiseFFN,
                 dropout=0.1):
        super(DecoderBlock, self).__init__()
        self.size = size
        self.self_attn = self_attn
        self.encoder_attn = encoder_attn
        self.ffn = ffn

        # Create 3 sub-layer connections
        # 1 for the self-attention
        # 1 for the encoder attention
        # 1 for the FFN
```

```
        self.sublayers = clones(SublayerConnection(size, dropout), 3)

    def forward(self, x, encoder_states, source_mask, target_mask):
        x = self.sublayers[0](x, lambda x: self.self_attn(x, x, x,
target_mask))
        x = self.sublayers[1](x, lambda x: self.encoder_attn(x,
encoder_states, encoder_states, source_mask))
        return self.sublayers[2](x, self.ffn)
```

This is similar to `EncoderBlock`, but with one substantial difference: whereas `EncoderBlock` relies only on the self-attention mechanism, here we combine self-attention with the regular attention coming from the encoder. This is reflected in the `encoder_attn` module and later the `encoder_states` parameter of the `forward` method, as well as the additional `SublayerConnection` for the encoder attention values. We can see the combination of multiple attention mechanisms in the `DecoderBlock.forward` method. Note that `self.self_attn` uses x for both query/key/value, while `self.encoder_attn` uses x as a query and `encoder_states` for keys and values. In this way, the regular attention establishes the link between the encoder and the decoder.

This concludes the decoder implementation. We'll proceed with building the full transformer model in the next section.

Putting it all together

We'll continue with the main `EncoderDecoder` class:

```
class EncoderDecoder(torch.nn.Module):
    def __init__(self,
                 encoder: Encoder,
                 decoder: Decoder,
                 source_embeddings: torch.nn.Sequential,
                 target_embeddings: torch.nn.Sequential):
        super(EncoderDecoder, self).__init__()
        self.encoder = encoder
        self.decoder = decoder
        self.source_embeddings = source_embeddings
        self.target_embeddings = target_embeddings

    def forward(self, source, target, source_mask, target_mask):
        encoder_output = self.encoder(
            x=self.source_embeddings(source),
            mask=source_mask)

        return self.decoder(
```

```
            x=self.target_embeddings(target),
            encoder_states=encoder_output,
            source_mask=source_mask,
            target_mask=target_mask)
```

It combines the `Encoder`, `Decoder`, and `source_embeddings`/`target_embeddings`
(we'll focus on the embeddings later in this section). The `EncoderDecoder.forward`
method takes the source sequence and feeds it to `self.encoder`. Then,
`self.decoder` takes its input from the preceding output step
`x=self.target_embeddings(target)`, the encoder states
`encoder_states=encoder_output`, and the source and target masks. With these inputs,
it produces the predicted next element (word) of the sequence, which is also the return
value of the `forward` method.

Next, we'll implement the `build_model` function, which combines everything we've
implemented so far into one coherent model:

```python
def build_model(source_vocabulary: int,
                target_vocabulary: int,
                N=6, d_model=512, d_ff=2048, h=8, dropout=0.1):
    """Build the full transformer model"""
    c = copy.deepcopy
    attn = MultiHeadedAttention(h, d_model)
    ff = PositionwiseFFN(d_model, d_ff, dropout)
    position = PositionalEncoding(d_model, dropout)

    model = EncoderDecoder(
        encoder=Encoder(EncoderBlock(d_model, c(attn), c(ff), dropout), N),
        decoder=Decoder(DecoderBlock(d_model, c(attn), c(attn),c(ff),
                                dropout), N, target_vocabulary),
        source_embeddings=torch.nn.Sequential(
            Embeddings(d_model, source_vocabulary), c(position)),
        target_embeddings=torch.nn.Sequential(
            Embeddings(d_model, target_vocabulary), c(position)))

    # This was important from their code.
    # Initialize parameters with Glorot / fan_avg.
    for p in model.parameters():
        if p.dim() > 1:
            torch.nn.init.xavier_uniform_(p)

    return model
```

Besides the familiar `MultiHeadedAttention` and `PositionwiseFFN`, we also create the `position` variable (an instance of the `PositionalEncoding` class). This class implements the sinusoidal positional encoding we described in the *The transformer model* section (we won't include the full implementation here). Now let's focus on the `EncoderDecoder` instantiation: we are already familiar with the encoder and the decoder, so there are no surprises there. But the embeddings are a tad more interesting. The following code instantiates the source embeddings (but this is also valid for the target ones):

```
source_embeddings=torch.nn.Sequential(Embeddings(d_model,
source_vocabulary), c(position))
```

We can see that they are a sequential list of two components:

- An instance of the `Embeddings` class, which is simply a combination of `torch.nn.Embedding` further multiplied by $\sqrt{d_{model}}$ (we'll omit the class definition here)
- Positional encoding `c(position)`, which adds the positional sinusoidal data to the embedding vector

Once we have the input data preprocessed in this way, it can serve as input to the core part of the encoder/decoder.

This concludes our implementation of the transformer. Our goal with this example was to provide a supplement to the theoretical base of the sections called *The transformer attention* and *The transformer model*. Therefore, we have focused on the most relevant parts of the code and omitted a few *ordinary* code sections, chief among them the `RandomDataset` data generator for random numerical sequences and the `train_model` function, which implements the training. Nevertheless, I would encourage the reader to run through the full example step by step so that they can gain a better understanding of the way the transformer works.

In the next section, we'll talk about some of the state-of-the-art language models based on the attention mechanisms we have introduced so far.

Transformer language models

In Chapter 6, *Language Modeling*, we introduced several different language models (word2vec, GloVe, and fastText) that use the context of a word (its surrounding words) to create word vectors (embeddings). These models share some common properties:

- They are context-free (I know it contradicts the previous statement) because they create a single global word vector of each word based on all its occurrences in the training text. For example, *lead* can have completely different meanings in the phrases *lead the way* and *lead atom*, yet the model will try to embed both meanings in the same word vector.
- They are position-free because they don't take into account the order of the contextual words when training for the embedding vectors.

In contrast, it's possible to create transformer-based language models, which are both context- and position-dependent. These models will produce different word vectors for each unique context of the word, taking into account both the current context words and their positions. This leads to a conceptual difference between the classic and transformer-based models. Since a model such as word2vec creates static context- and position-free embedding vectors, we can discard the model and only use the vectors in subsequent downstream tasks. But the transformer model creates dynamic vectors based on the context, and therefore, we have to include it as part of the task pipeline.

In the following sections, we'll discuss some of the most recent transformer-based models.

Bidirectional encoder representations from transformers

The **bidirectional encoder representations from transformers (BERT)** (see *BERT: Pre-training of Deep Bidirectional Transformers for Language Understanding* at https://arxiv.org/abs/1810.04805) model has a very descriptive name. Let's look at some of the elements that are mentioned:

- Encoder representations: This model uses only the output of the multilayer encoder part of the transformer architecture we described in the *The transformer model* section.
- Bidirectional: The encoder has an inherent bidirectional nature.

To gain some perspective, let's denote the number of transformer blocks with L, the hidden size with H (previously denoted with d_{model}), and the number of self-attention heads with A. The authors of the paper experimented with two BERT configurations: $BERT_{BASE}$ ($L = 12$, $H = 768$, $A = 12$, total parameters = 110M) and $BERT_{LARGE}$ ($L = 24$, $H = 1024$, $A = 16$, total parameters = 340M).

To better understand the BERT framework, we'll start with the training, which has two steps:

1. **Pretraining**: The model is trained on unlabeled data over different pretraining tasks.
2. **Fine-tuning**: The model is initialized with the pretrained parameters and then all parameters are fine-tuned over the labeled dataset of the specific downstream task.

We can see the steps in the following diagram:

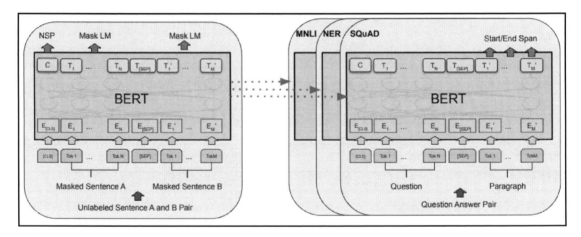

Left: Pretraining: Right: Fine-tuning Source: https://arxiv.org/abs/1810.04805

These diagrams will serve as references through the next sections, so stay tuned for more details. For now, it's enough for us to know that **Tok N** represents the one-hot-encoded input tokens, E represents the token embeddings, and T represents the model output vector.

Now that we have an overview of BERT, let's look at its components.

Input data representation

Before going into each training step, let's discuss the input and output data representations, which are shared by the two steps. Somewhat similar to fastText (see `Chapter 6`, *Language Modeling*), BERT uses a data-driven tokenization algorithm called WordPiece (`https://arxiv.org/abs/1609.08144`). This means that, instead of a vocabulary of full words, it creates a vocabulary of subword tokens in an iterative process until that vocabulary reaches a predetermined size (in the case of BERT, the size is 30,000 tokens). This approach has two main advantages:

- It allows us to control the size of the dictionary.
- It handles unknown words by assigning them to the closest existing dictionary subword token.

BERT can handle a variety of downstream tasks. To do so, the authors introduced a special-input data representation, which can unambiguously represent the following as a single-input sequence of tokens:

- A single sentence (for example, in classification tasks, such as sentiment analysis)
- A pair of sentences (for example, in question-answering problems)

Here, *sentence* not only refers to a linguistic sentence, but can mean any contiguous text of arbitrary length.

The model uses two special tokens:

- The first token of every sequence is always a special classification token (`[CLS]`). The hidden state corresponding to this token is used as the aggregate sequence representation for classification tasks. For example, if we want to apply sentiment analysis over the sequence, the output corresponding to the `[CLS]` input token will represent the sentiment (positive/negative) output of the model.
- Sentence pairs are packed together into a single sequence. The second special token (`[SEP]`) marks the boundary between the two input sentences (in the case that we have two). We further differentiate the sentences with the help of an additional learned segmentation embedding for every token indicating whether it belongs to sentence A or sentence B. Therefore, the input embeddings are the sum of the token embeddings, the segmentation embeddings, and the position embeddings. Here, the token and position embeddings serve the same purpose as they do in the regular transformer.

The following diagram displays the special tokens, as well as the input embeddings:

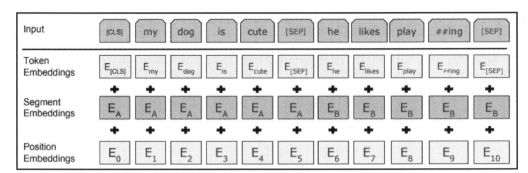

BERT input representation: the input embeddings are the sum of the token embeddings, the segmentation embeddings, and the position embeddings. Source: https://arxiv.org/abs/1810.04805

Now that we know how the input is processed, let's look at the pretraining step.

Pretraining

The pretraining step is illustrated on the left-hand side of the diagram in the *Bidirectional encoder representations from transformers* section. The authors of the paper trained the BERT model using two unsupervised training tasks: **masked language modeling** (**MLM**) and **next sentence prediction** (**NSP**).

We'll start with MLM, where the model is presented with an input sequence and its goal is to predict a missing word in that sequence. In this case, BERT acts as a **denoising autoencoder** in the sense that it tries to reconstruct its intentionally corrupted input. MLM is similar in nature to the CBOW objective of the word2vec model (see `Chapter 6`, *Language Modeling*). To solve this task, the BERT encoder output is extended with a fully connected layer with softmax activation to produce the most probable word, given the input sequence. Each input sequence is modified by randomly masking 15% (according to the paper) of the WordPiece tokens. To better understand this, we'll use an example from the paper itself: assuming that the unlabeled sentence is *my dog is hairy*, and that, during the random masking procedure, we chose the fourth token (which corresponds to `hairy`), our masking procedure can be further illustrated by the following points:

- **80% of the time**: Replace the word with the `[MASK]` token—for example, *my dog is hairy* → *my dog is* `[MASK]`.
- **10% of the time**: Replace the word with a random word—for example, *my dog is hairy* → *my dog is apple*.

- **10% of the time**: Keep the word unchanged *my dog is hairy* → *my dog is hairy*. The purpose of this is to bias the representation toward the actual observed word.

> Because the model is bidirectional, the [MASK] token can appear at any position in the input sequence. At the same time, the model will use the full sequence to predict the missing word. This is opposed to unidirectional autoregressive models (we'll discuss these in the following sections), which always try to predict the next word from all preceding words, thereby avoiding the need to have [MASK] tokens.

There are two main reasons why we need this 80/10/10 distribution:

- The [MASK] token creates a mismatch between pretraining and fine-tuning (we'll discuss this in the next section), since it only appears in the former but not in the latter—that is, the fine-tuning task will present the model with input sequences without the [MASK] token. Yet, the model was pretrained to expect sequences with [MASK], which might lead to undefined behavior.
- BERT assumes that the predicted tokens are independent of each other. To understand this, let's imagine that the model tries to reconstruct the input sequence *I went* [MASK] *with my* [MASK]. BERT can predict the sentence *I went cycling with my bicycle*, which is a valid sentence. But because the model does not relate the two masked words, nothing prevents it from predicting *I went swimming with my bicycle*, which is not valid.

With the 80/10/10 distribution, the transformer encoder does not know which words it will be asked to predict or which have been replaced by random words, so it is forced to keep a distributional contextual representation of every input token. Additionally, because random replacement only occurs for 1.5% of all tokens (that is, 10% of 15%), this does not seem to harm the model's language-understanding ability.

One disadvantage of MLM is that, because the model only predicts 15% of the words in each batch, it might converge more slowly than pretraining models that use all words.

Next, let's continue with NSP. The authors argue that many important downstream tasks, such as **question answering (QA)** and **natural language inference (NLI)**, are based on understanding the relationship between two sentences, which is not directly captured by language modeling.

Natural language inference determines whether a sentence, which represents a **hypothesis**, is either true (entailment), false (contradiction), or undetermined (neutral) given another sentence, called a **premise**. The following table shows some examples:

Premise	Hypothesis	Label
I am running	I am sleeping	contradiction
I am running	I am listening to music	neutral
I am running	I am training	entailment

In order to train a model that understands sentence relationships, we pretrain for a next-sentence prediction task that can be trivially generated from any monolingual corpus. Specifically, each input sequence consists of a starting `[CLS]` token, followed by two concatenated sentences, A and B, which are separated by the `[SEP]` token (see the diagram in the *Bidirectional encoder representations from transformers* section). When choosing the sentences A and B for each pretraining example, 50% of the time, B is the actual next sentence that follows A (labeled as `IsNext`), and 50% of the time, it is a random sentence from the corpus (labeled as `NotNext`). As we mentioned, the model outputs the `IsNext/NotNext` labels on the `[CLS]` corresponding input.

The NSP task is illustrated using the following example:

- `[CLS]` *the man went to* `[MASK]` *store* `[SEP]` *he bought a gallon* `[MASK]` *milk [SEP]* with the label `IsNext`.
- `[CLS]` *the man* `[MASK]` *to the store* `[SEP]` *penguins* `[MASK]` *are flight ##less birds* `[SEP]` with the label `NotNext`. Note the use of the *##less* token, which is the result of the WordPiece tokenization algorithm.

Next, let's look at the fine-tuning step.

Fine-tuning

The fine-tuning task follows the pretraining task, and apart from the input preprocessing, the two steps are very similar. Instead of creating a masked sequence, we simply feed the BERT model with the task-specific unmodified input and output and fine-tune all the parameters in an end-to-end fashion. Therefore, the model that we use in the fine-tuning phase is the same model that we'll use in the actual production environment.

The following diagram shows how to solve several different types of task with BERT:

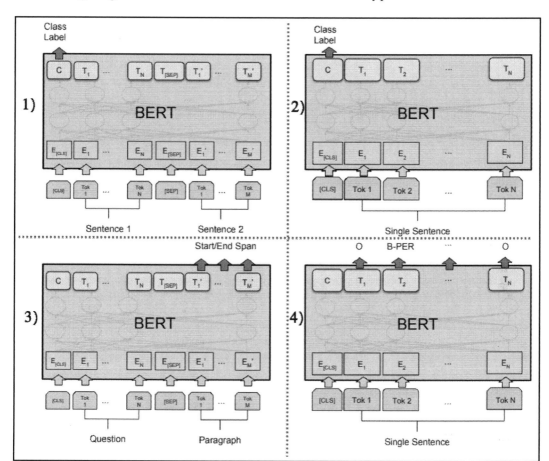

BERT applications for different tasks: source: https://arxiv.org/abs/1810.04805

Let's discuss them:

- The top-left scenario illustrates how to use **BERT** for sentence-pair classification tasks, such as NLI. In short, we feed the model with two concatenated sentences and only look at the [CLS] token output classification, which will output the model result. For example, in an NLI task, the goal is to predict whether the second sentence is an entailment, a contradiction, or neutral with respect to the first one.

- The top-right scenario illustrates how to use **BERT** for single-sentence classification tasks, such as sentiment analysis. This is very similar to the sentence-pair classification.

- The bottom-left scenario illustrates how to use **BERT** on the **Stanford Question Answering Dataset** (**SQuAD** v1.1, `https://rajpurkar.github.io/SQuAD-explorer/explore/1.1/dev/`). Given that sequence A is a question and sequence B is a passage from Wikipedia, which contains the answer, the goal is to predict the text span (start and end) of the answer within this passage. We introduce two new vectors: a start vector $S \in \mathbb{R}^H$ and an end vector $E \in \mathbb{R}^H$, where H is the hidden size of the model. The probability of each word i as being the start (or end) of the answer span is computed as a dot product between its output vector T_i and S (or E), followed by a softmax over all the words of the sequence B: $P_i = \frac{e^{S \cdot T_i}}{\sum_j e^{S \cdot T_j}}$. The score of a candidate span starting from position i and spanning to j is computed as $S \cdot T_i + E \cdot T_j$. The output candidate is the one with the maximum score, where $j \geq i$.

- The bottom-right scenario illustrates how to use **BERT** for **named entity recognition** (**NER**), where each input token is classified as some type of entity.

This concludes our section dedicated to the BERT model. As a reminder, it is based on the transformer encoder. In the next section, we'll discuss transformer decoder models.

Transformer-XL

In this section, we'll talk about an improvement over the vanilla transformer, called transformer-XL, where XL stands for extra long (see *Transformer-XL: Attentive Language Models Beyond a Fixed-Length Context* at `https://arxiv.org/abs/1901.02860`). To understand the need to improve the regular transformer, let's discuss some of its limitations, one of which comes from the nature of the transformer itself. An RNN-based model has the (at least theoretical) ability to convey information about sequences of arbitrary length, because the internal RNN state is adjusted based on all previous inputs. But the transformer's self-attention doesn't have such a recurrent component, and is restricted entirely within the bounds of the current input sequence. If we had infinite memory and computation, a simple solution would be to process the entire context sequence. But in practice, we have limited resources, and so we split the entire text into smaller segments and train the model only within each segment, as image **(a)** in the following diagram shows:

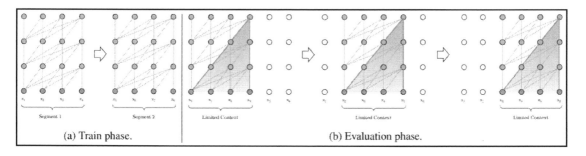

(a) Train phase.   (b) Evaluation phase.

Illustration of the training (a) and evaluation (b) of a regular transformer with an input sequence of length 4: note the use of the unidirectional transformer decoder. Source: https://arxiv.org/abs/1901.02860

The horizontal axis represents the input sequence $[x_1,..., x_4]$ and the vertical axis represents the stacked decoder blocks. Note that element x_i can only attend to the elements $x_{i \leq j}$. That's because transformer-XL is based on the transformer decoder (and doesn't include the encoder), unlike BERT, which is based on the encoder. Therefore, the transformer-XL decoder is not the same as the decoder in the *full* encoder-decoder transformer, because it doesn't have access to the encoder state, as the regular decoder does. In that sense, the transformer-XL decoder is very similar to a general transformer encoder, with the exception that it's unidirectional, because of the input sequence mask. Transformer-XL is an example of an **autoregressive model**.

As the preceding diagram demonstrates, the largest possible dependency length is upper-bounded by the segment length, and although the attention mechanism helps prevent vanishing gradients by allowing immediate access to all elements of the sequence, the transformer cannot fully exploit this advantage, because of the limited input segment. Furthermore, the text is usually split by selecting a consecutive chunk of symbols without respecting the sentence or any other semantic boundary, which the authors of the paper refer to as context fragmentation. To quote the paper itself, the model lacks the contextual information needed to well predict the first few symbols, leading to inefficient optimization and inferior performance.

Another issue of the vanilla transformer is manifested during evaluation, as shown on the right-hand side of the preceding diagram. At each step, the model takes the full sequence as input, but only makes a single prediction. To predict the next output, the transformer is shifted right with a single position, yet the new segment (which is the same as the last segment, except for the last value) has to be processed from scratch over the full input sequence.

Now that we've identified some problems with the transformer model, let's look at how to solve them.

Segment-level recurrence with state reuse

Transformer-XL introduces a recurrence relationship in the transformer model. During training, the model caches its state for the current segment, and when it processes the next segment, it has access to that cached (but fixed) value, as we can see in the following diagram:

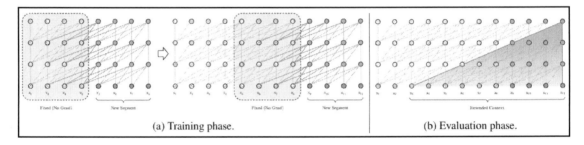

(a) Training phase.   (b) Evaluation phase.

Illustration of the training (a) and evaluation (b) of transformer-XL with an input sequence length of 4. Source: https://arxiv.org/abs/1901.02860

During training, the gradient is not propagated through the cached segment. Let's formalize this concept (we'll use the notation from the paper, which might differ slightly from the previous notations in this chapter). We'll denote two consecutive segments of length L with $s_\tau = [x_{\tau,1}, \ldots, x_{\tau,L}]$ and $s_{\tau+1} = [x_{\tau+1,1}, \ldots, x_{\tau+1,L}]$ and the nth block hidden state of the τth segment with $\mathbf{h}_\tau^n \in \mathbb{R}^{L \times d}$, where d is the hidden dimension (equivalent to d_{model}). To clarify, $\mathbf{h}_\tau^n$ is a matrix with L rows, where each row contains the d-dimensional self-attention vector of each element of the input sequence. Then, the nth layer hidden state of the $\tau+1$th segment is produced by going through the following steps:

$$\tilde{\mathbf{h}}_{\tau+1}^{n-1} = [\text{SG}(\mathbf{h}_\tau^{n-1}) \circ \mathbf{h}_{\tau+1}^{n-1}]$$
$$\mathbf{Q}_{\tau+1}^n, \mathbf{K}_{\tau+1}^n, \mathbf{V}_{\tau+1}^n = \mathbf{h}_{\tau+1}^{n-1} \mathbf{W}_Q^\mathsf{T}, \tilde{\mathbf{h}}_{\tau+1}^{n-1} \mathbf{W}_K^\mathsf{T}, \tilde{\mathbf{h}}_{\tau+1}^{n-1} \mathbf{W}_V^\mathsf{T}$$
$$\mathbf{h}_{\tau+1}^n = \text{Transformer-Layer}(\mathbf{Q}_{\tau+1}^n, \mathbf{K}_{\tau+1}^n, \mathbf{V}_{\tau+1}^n)$$

Here, $SG(\cdot)$ refers to the stop gradient, $\mathbf{W}_\cdot$ refers to the model parameters (previously denoted with $\mathbf{W}^*$), and $[\mathbf{h}_\tau^{n-1} \circ \mathbf{h}_{\tau+1}^{n-1}] \in \mathbb{R}^{2L \times d}$ refers to the concatenation of the two hidden sequences along the length dimension. To clarify, the concatenated hidden sequences is a matrix with $2L$ rows, where each row contains the d-dimensional self-attention vector of one element of the combined input sequences τ and τ+1. The paper does a great job of explaining the intricacies of the preceding formulas, so the following explanation contains some direct quotes. Compared to the standard transformer, the critical difference lies in that the key $\mathbf{K}_{\tau+1}^n$ and value $\mathbf{V}_{\tau+1}^n$ are conditioned on the extended context $\tilde{\mathbf{h}}_{\tau+1}^{n-1}$, and so $\mathbf{h}_\tau^{n-1}$ is cached from the previous segment (shown with the green paths in the preceding diagram). With this recurrence mechanism applied to every two consecutive segments of a corpus, it essentially creates a segment-level recurrence in the hidden states. As a result, the effective context that is utilized can go way beyond just two segments. However, note that the recurrent dependency between $\mathbf{h}_{\tau+1}^n$ and $\mathbf{h}_\tau^{n-1}$ shifts one layer downward per segment. Consequently, the largest possible dependency length grows linearly with respect to the number of layers as well as the segment length—that is, $O(N \times L)$, as visualized by the shaded area of the preceding diagram.

Besides achieving extra-long context and resolving fragmentation, another benefit that comes with the recurrence scheme is significantly faster evaluation. Specifically, during evaluation, the representations from the previous segments can be reused instead of being computed from scratch, as in the case of the vanilla model.

Finally, note that the recurrence scheme does not need to be restricted to only the previous segment. In theory, we can cache as many previous segments as the GPU memory allows and reuse all of them as the extra context when processing the current segment.

The recurrence scheme will require a new way to encode the positions of the sequence elements. Let's look at this topic next.

Relative positional encodings

The vanilla transformer input is augmented with sinusoidal positional encodings (see the *The transformer model* section), which are relevant only within the current segment. The following formula shows how to schematically compute the states $\mathbf{h}_\tau$ and $\mathbf{h}_{\tau+1}$ with the current positional encodings:

$$\mathbf{h}_{\tau+1} = f(\mathbf{h}_\tau, \mathbf{E}_{s_{\tau+1}} + \mathbf{U}_{1:L})$$
$$\mathbf{h}_\tau = f(\mathbf{h}_{\tau-1}, \mathbf{E}_{s_\tau} + \mathbf{U}_{1:L})$$

Here, $\mathbf{E}_{s_\tau} \in \mathbb{R}^{L \times d}$ is the word-embedding sequence of s_τ, and f is the transformation function. We can see that we use the same positional encoding $\mathbf{U}_{1:L}$ for both $\mathbf{E}_{s_\tau}$ and $\mathbf{E}_{s_{\tau+1}}$. Because of this, the model cannot distinguish between the positions of two elements of the same position within the different sequences $x_{\tau,j}$ and $x_{\tau+1,j}$. To avoid this, the authors of the paper propose a new type of **relative** positional encoding scheme. They made the observation that when a query vector (or matrix of queries) $\mathbf{Q}_{\tau,i}$ attends to key vectors $\mathbf{K}_{\tau,j\leq i}$, it does not need to know the absolute position of each key vector to identify the temporal order of the segment. Instead, it is enough to know the relative distance between each key vector $\mathbf{K}_{\tau,j}$ and itself $\mathbf{Q}_{\tau,i}$—that is $i-j$.

The proposed solution is to create a set of relative positional encodings $\mathbf{R} \in \mathbb{R}^{L_{max} \times d}$, where each cell of the ith row indicates the relative distance between the ith element and the rest of the elements of the sequence. $\mathbf{R}$ uses the same sinusoidal formula as before, but this time, with relative instead of absolute positions. This relative distance is injected dynamically (as opposed to being part of the input preprocessing), which makes it possible for the query vector to distinguish between the positions of $x_{\tau,j}$ and $x_{\tau+1,j}$. To understand this, let's start with the product absolute position attention formula from the *The transformer attention* section, which can be decomposed as follows:

$$A_{i,j}^{abs} = \underbrace{\mathbf{E}_{x_i}^{\mathsf{T}} \mathbf{W}_Q^{\mathsf{T}} \mathbf{W}_K \mathbf{E}_{x_j}}_{(1)} + \underbrace{\mathbf{E}_{x_i}^{\mathsf{T}} \mathbf{W}_Q^{\mathsf{T}} \mathbf{W}_K \mathbf{U}_j}_{(2)}$$

$$+ \underbrace{\mathbf{U}_i^{\mathsf{T}} \mathbf{W}_Q^{\mathsf{T}} \mathbf{W}_K \mathbf{E}_{x_j}}_{(3)} + \underbrace{\mathbf{U}_i^{\mathsf{T}} \mathbf{W}_Q^{\mathsf{T}} \mathbf{W}_K \mathbf{U}_j}_{(4)}$$

Let's discuss the components of this formula:

1. Indicates how much word i attends to word j, regardless of their current position (content-based addressing)—for example, how much the word *tire* relates to the word *car*.
2. Reflects how much word i attends to the word in position j, regardless of what that word is (content-dependent positional bias)—for example, if the word i is *cream*, we may want to check the probability that word $j = i - 1$ is *ice*.
3. This step is the opposite of step 2.
4. Indicates how much a word in position i should attend to a word in position j, regardless of what the two words are (global-positioning bias)—for example, this value could be low for positions that are far apart.

In transformer-XL, this formula is modified to include the relative positional embeddings:

$$\mathbf{A}_{i,j}^{rel} = \underbrace{\mathbf{E}_{x_i}^{\mathsf{T}} \mathbf{W}_Q^{\mathsf{T}} \mathbf{W}_{K,E} \mathbf{E}_{x_j}}_{(1)} + \underbrace{\mathbf{E}_{x_i}^{\mathsf{T}} \mathbf{W}_Q^{\mathsf{T}} \mathbf{W}_{K,R} \mathbf{R}_{i-j}}_{(2)}$$
$$+ \underbrace{u^{\mathsf{T}} \mathbf{W}_{K,E} \mathbf{E}_{x_j}}_{(3)} + \underbrace{v^{\mathsf{T}} \mathbf{W}_{K,R} \mathbf{R}_{i-j}}_{(4)}$$

Let's outline the changes with respect to the absolute position formula:

- Replace all appearances of the absolute positional embedding U_j for computing key vectors in terms (2) and (4) with its relative counterpart R_{i-j}.
- Replace the query $U_i^{\mathsf{T}} \mathbf{W}_Q^{\mathsf{T}}$ in term (3) with a trainable parameter $u \in \mathbb{R}^d$. The reasoning behind this is that the query vector is the same for all query positions; therefore, the attentive bias toward different words should remain the same regardless of the query position. Similarly, a trainable parameter $v \in \mathbb{R}^d$ substitutes $U_i^{\mathsf{T}} \mathbf{W}_Q^{\mathsf{T}}$ in term (4).
- Separate $\mathbf{W}_K$ into two weight matrices $\mathbf{W}_{K,E}$ and $\mathbf{W}_{K,R}$ to produce separate content-based and position-based key vectors.

To recap, the segment-level recurrence and relative positional encodings are the main improvements of transformer-XL over the vanilla transformer. In the next section, we'll look at yet another improvement of transformer-XL.

XLNet

The authors note that bidirectional models with denoising autoencoding pretraining (such as BERT) achieve better performance compared to unidirectional autoregressive models (such as transformer-XL). But as we mentioned in the *Pretraining* subsection of the *Bidirectional encoder representations from transformers* section, the [MASK] token introduces a discrepancy between the pretraining and fine-tuning steps. To overcome these limitations, the authors of transformer-XL propose XLNet (see *XLNet: Generalized Autoregressive Pretraining for Language Understanding* at https://arxiv.org/abs/1906.08237): a generalized **autoregressive** pretraining mechanism that enables learning bidirectional contexts by maximizing the expected likelihood over all permutations of the factorization order. To clarify, XLNet builds upon the transformer decoder model of transformer-XL and introduces a smart permutation-based mechanism for bidirectional context flow within the autoregressive pretraining step.

The following diagram illustrates how the model processes the same input sequence with different factorization orders. Specifically, it shows a transformer decoder with two stacked blocks and segment-level recurrence (the **mem** fields):

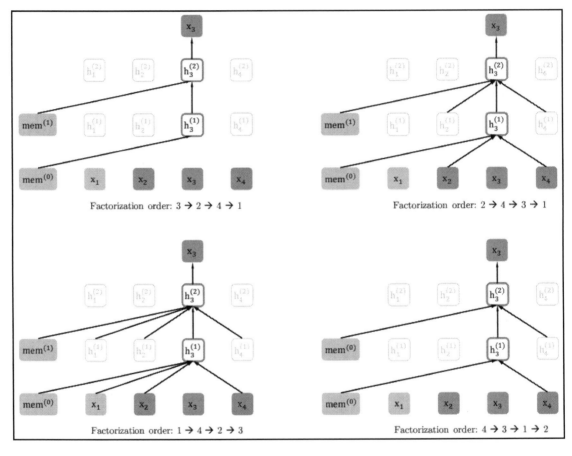

Predicting x_3 over the same input sequence with four different factorization orders. Source: https://arxiv.org/abs/1906.08237

There are $T!$ different orders to perform a valid autoregressive factorization over a sequence of length T. Let's assume that we have an input sequence of $[x_1, x_2, x_3, x_4]$ with length 4. The diagram shows four of the possible $4! = 24$ factorization orders of that sequence (starting clockwise from the top-left corner): $[x_3, x_2, x_4, x_1]$, $[x_2, x_4, x_3, x_1]$, $[x_4, x_3, x_1, x_2]$, and $[x_1, x_4, x_2, x_3]$. Remember that the autoregressive model allows the current element to attend only to the preceding elements of the sequence. Therefore, under normal circumstances, x_3 would be able to attend only to x_1 and x_2. But the XLNet algorithm trains the model not only with the regular sequence, but also with different factorization orders of that sequence. Therefore, the model will *see* all four factorization orders as well as the original input. For example, with $[x_3, x_2, x_4, x_1]$, x_3 will not be able to attend to any of the other elements, because it's the first one. Alternatively, with $[x_2, x_4, x_3, x_1]$, x_3 will be able to attend to x_2 and x_4. Under the previous circumstances, x_4 would have been inaccessible. The black arrows in the diagram indicate the elements that x_3 can attend to, depending on the factorization order (the unavailable elements have no arrows).

But how can this work, and what is the point of the training when the sequence will lose its meaning if it's not in its natural order? To answer this, let's remember that the transformer has no implicit recurrent mechanism, and instead, we convey the position of the elements with the explicit positional encodings. Let's also remember that in the regular transformer decoder, we use the self-attention mask to limit the access to the sequence elements following the current one. When we feed a sequence with another factorization order, say $[x_2, x_4, x_3, x_1]$, the elements of the sequence will maintain their original positional encoding and the transformer will not lose their correct order. In fact, the input is still the original sequence $[x_1, x_2, x_3, x_4]$, but with an **altered attention mask** to provide access only to elements x_2 and x_4.

To formalize this concept, let's introduce some notations: $\mathcal{Z}_T$ is the set of all possible permutations of the length-T index sequence $[1, 2, \ldots, T]$; $\mathbf{z} \in \mathcal{Z}_T$ is one permutation of ; is the tth element of that permutation; $\mathbf{z}_{<t}$ are the first $t-1$ elements of that permutation, and $P_\theta(x_{z_t} | \mathbf{x}_{\mathbf{z}<t})$ is the probability distribution of the next word x_{z_t}, given the current permutation $\mathbf{x}_{\mathbf{z}<t}$ (the autoregressive task, which is the output of the model), where θ are the model parameters. Then, the permutation language modeling objective is as follows:

$$\min_\theta \mathbb{E}_{\mathbf{z} \sim \mathcal{Z}_T} \left[\sum_{t=1}^{T} \log P_\theta(x_{z_t} | \mathbf{x}_{\mathbf{z}<t}) \right]$$

It samples different factorization orders of the input sequence one at a time and attempts to maximize the probability p_θ—that is, to increase the chance of the model to predict the correct word. The parameters θ are shared across all factorization orders; therefore, the model will be able to see every possible element $x_i \neq x_t$, thereby emulating bidirectional context. At the same time, this is still an autoregressive function, which doesn't need [MASK] tokens.

We need one more piece to fully utilize the permutation-based pretraining. We'll start by defining the probability distribution of the next word X_{z_t}, given the current permutation $\mathbf{x}_{\mathbf{z}<t}$ (the autoregressive task, which is the output of the model) $P_\theta(X_{z_t}|\mathbf{x}_{\mathbf{z}<t})$, which is simply the softmax output of the model:

$$P_\theta(X_{z_t} = x|\mathbf{x}_{\mathbf{z}<t}) = \frac{\exp(e(x)^\mathsf{T} h_\theta(\mathbf{x}_{\mathbf{z}<t}))}{\sum_{x'} \exp(e(x')^\mathsf{T} h_\theta(\mathbf{x}_{\mathbf{z}<t}))}$$

Here, $e(x)$ acts as the query and $h_\theta(\mathbf{x}_{\mathbf{z}<t})$ is the hidden representation produced by the transformer after the proper masking, which acts as the key-value database.

Next, let's assume that we have two factorization orders $\mathbf{z}^{(1)} = [x_3, x_2, x_4, x_1]$ and $\mathbf{z}^{(2)} = [x_3, x_2, x_1, x_4]$, where the first two elements are the same and the second two are swapped. Let's also assume that $t = 3$—that is, the model has to predict the third element of the sequence. Since $\mathbf{z}^{(1)}_{<2} = \mathbf{z}^{(2)}_{<2}$, we can see that $h_\theta(\mathbf{x}_{\mathbf{z}<t})$ will be the same in both cases. Therefore, $P^{(1)}_\theta(X_{z_t}|\mathbf{x}_{\mathbf{z}^{(1)}<t}) = P^{(2)}_\theta(X_{z_t}|\mathbf{x}_{\mathbf{z}^{(2)}<t})$. But this is not a valid result, because in the first case, the model should predict x_4 and in the second, x_1. Let's remember that although we predict x_1 and x_4 in position 3, they still maintain their original positional encodings. Therefore, we can alter the current formula to include the positional information for the predicted element (which will be different for x_1 and x_4), but exclude the actual word. In other words, we can modify the task of the model from *predict the next word* to *predict the next word, given that we know its position*. In this way, the formula for the two-sample factorization orders will be different. The modified formula is as follows:

$$P_\theta(X_{z_t} = x|\mathbf{x}_{\mathbf{z}<t},) = \frac{\exp(e(x)^\mathsf{T} g_\theta(\mathbf{x}_{\mathbf{z}<t}, z_t))}{\sum_{x'} \exp(e(x')^\mathsf{T} g_\theta(\mathbf{x}_{\mathbf{z}<t}, z_t))}$$

Here, g_θ is the new transformer function, which also includes the positional information z_t. The authors of the paper propose a special mechanism called two-stream self-attention to solve this. As the name suggests, it consists of two combined attention mechanisms:

- Content representation $h_\theta(\mathbf{x}_{\mathbf{z}<t})$, which is the attention mechanism we are already familiar with. This representation encodes both the context and the content x_{z_t} itself.
- Query representation $g_\theta(\mathbf{x}_{\mathbf{z}<t}, z_t)$, which only has access to the contextual information $x_{\mathbf{z}<t}$ and the position z_t, but not the content x_{z_t}, as we mentioned previously.

I would encourage you to check the original paper for more details. In the next section, we'll implement a basic example of a transformer language model.

Generating text with a transformer language model

In this section, we'll implement a basic text-generation example with the help of the `transformers` 2.1.1 library (https://huggingface.co/transformers/), released by Hugging Face. This is a well-maintained and popular open source package that implements different transformer language models, including BERT, transformer-XL, XLNet, OpenAI GPT, GPT-2, and others. We'll use a pretrained transformer-XL model to generate new text based on an initial input sequence. The goal is to give you a brief taste of the library:

1. Let's start with the imports:

```
import torch
from transformers import TransfoXLLMHeadModel, TransfoXLTokenizer
```

The `TransfoXLLMHeadModel` and `TransfoXLTokenizer` phrases are the implementations of the transformer-XL language model and its corresponding tokenizer.

2. Next, we'll initialize the device and instantiate the `model` and the `tokenizer`. Note that we'll use the `transfo-xl-wt103` pretrained set of parameters, available in the library:

```
device = torch.device("cuda:0" if torch.cuda.is_available() else
"cpu")

# Instantiate pre-trained model-specific tokenizer and the model
itself
```

```
tokenizer = TransfoXLTokenizer.from_pretrained('transfo-xl-wt103')
model = TransfoXLLMHeadModel.from_pretrained('transfo-xl-
wt103').to(device)
```

3. Then, we'll specify the initial sequence, tokenize it, and turn it into a model-compatible input `tokens_tensor`, which contains a list of tokens:

```
text = "The company was founded in"
tokens_tensor = \
    torch.tensor(tokenizer.encode(text)) \
        .unsqueeze(0) \
        .to(device)
```

4. Next, we'll use this token to initiate a loop, where the model will generate new tokens of the sequence:

```
mems = None   # recurrence mechanism

predicted_tokens = list()
for i in range(50):   # stop at 50 predicted tokens
    # Generate predictions
    predictions, mems = model(tokens_tensor, mems=mems)

    # Get most probable word index
    predicted_index = torch.topk(predictions[0, -1, :], 1)[1]

    # Extract the word from the index
    predicted_token = tokenizer.decode(predicted_index)

    # break if [EOS] reached
    if predicted_token == tokenizer.eos_token:
        break

    # Store the current token
    predicted_tokens.append(predicted_token)

    # Append new token to the existing sequence
    tokens_tensor = torch.cat((tokens_tensor,
predicted_index.unsqueeze(1)), dim=1)
```

We start the loop with the initial sequence of tokens `tokens_tensor`. The model uses this to generate the `predictions` (a softmax over all tokens of the vocabulary) and `mems` (a variable that stores the previous hidden decoder state for the recurrence relation). We extract the index of the most probable word `predicted_index` and we convert it to a vocabulary token `predicted_token`. Then, we append it to the existing `tokens_tensor` and initiate the loop again with the new sequence. The loop ends either after 50 tokens or when the special `[EOS]` token is reached.

5. Finally, we'll display the result:

    ```
    print('Initial sequence: ' + text)
    print('Predicted output: ' + " ".join(predicted_tokens))
    ```

    The output of the program is as follows:

    ```
    Initial sequence: The company was founded in
    Predicted output: the United States .
    ```

With this example, we conclude a long chapter about attention models.

Summary

In this chapter, we focused on seq2seq models and the attention mechanism. First, we discussed and implemented a regular recurrent encoder-decoder seq2seq model and learned how to complement it with the attention mechanism. Then, we talked about and implemented a purely attention-based type of model called a **transformer**. We also defined multihead attention in their context. Next, we discussed transformer language models (such as BERT, transformerXL, and XLNet). Finally, we implemented a simple text-generation example using the `transformers` library.

This chapter concludes our series of chapters with a focus on natural language processing. In the next chapter, we'll talk about some new trends in deep learning that aren't fully matured yet but hold great potential for the future.

Section 4: A Look to the Future

4

In this section, we'll discuss some recent DL techniques that have not reached widespread adoption yet, but are nevertheless promising.

This section contains the following chapters:

- Chapter 9, *Emerging Neural Network Designs*
- Chapter 10, *Meta Learning*
- Chapter 11, *Deep Learning for Autonomous Vehicles*

9
Emerging Neural Network Designs

In this chapter, we'll look at some emerging **Neural Network (NN)** designs. They haven't reached maturity yet, but hold potential for the future because they try to address fundamental limitations in existing DL algorithms. If one day any of these technologies prove successful and useful for practical applications, we might get one step closer to artificial general intelligence.

One thing that we need to bear in mind is the nature of structured data. So far in this book, we've focused on processing either images or text—in other words, unstructured data. This is not a coincidence, because NNs excel in the seemingly complex task of finding structure in combinations of pixels or text sequences. On the other hand, ML algorithms, such as gradient boosted trees or random forests, seem to perform on a par with, or better than, NNs when it comes to structured data, such as social-network graphs or brain connections. In this chapter, we'll introduce graph NNs to deal with arbitrary structured graphs.

Another NN limitation manifests itself with **Recurrent Networks (RNNs)**. In theory, these are one of the most powerful NN models because they are Turing-complete, which means that an RNN can theoretically solve any computational problem. This is often not the case in practice. RNNs (even **Long Short-Term Memory (LSTM)**) can struggle to carry information over extended periods of time. One possible solution is to extend the RNN with an external addressable memory. We'll look at how to do this in this chapter.

The topics in this chapter are not detached from the rest of the topics in this book. In fact, we'll see that the new network architectures that we'll look at are based on many of the algorithms that we've already covered. These include convolutions, RNNs, and attention models, as well as others.

This chapter will cover the following topics:

- Introducing graph NNs
- Introducing memory-augmented NNs

Introducing Graph NNs

Before learning about **graph NNs** (**GNNs**), let's look at why we need graph networks in the first place. We'll start by defining a graph, which is a set of objects (also known as **nodes** or **vertices**) where some pairs of objects have connections (or **edges**) between them.

 In this section, we'll use several survey papers as resources, most notably *A Comprehensive Survey on Graph Neural Networks* (https://arxiv.org/abs/1901.00596), which contains some quotes and images.

A graph has the following properties:

- We'll represent the graph as $G = (V, E)$, where V is the set of nodes and E is the set of edges.
- The expression $e_{i,j} = (v_i, v_j) \in E$ describes an edge between two nodes, $v_i, v_j \in V$.
- An adjacency matrix, $\mathbf{A} \in \mathbb{R}^{n \times n}$, where n is the number of graph nodes. This is written as $a_{ij} = 1$ if an edge $e_{i,j} = (v_i, v_j)$ exists and $a_{ij} = 0$ if it doesn't.
- Graphs can be **directed** when the edges have a direction and **undirected** when they don't. The adjacency matrix of an undirected graph is symmetric—that is $\mathbf{A} = \mathbf{A}^\mathsf{T}$. The adjacency matrix of a directed graph is asymmetric—that is $\mathbf{A} \neq \mathbf{A}^\mathsf{T}$.
- Graphs can be **cyclic** or **acyclic**. As the name suggests, a cyclic graph contains at least one cycle, which is a non-empty path of nodes where only the first and the last node are the same. Acyclic graphs don't contain cycles.
- Both graph edges and nodes can have associated attributes, known as feature vectors. We'll denote the d-dimensional feature vector of node v with $\mathbf{x}_v \in \mathbb{R}^d$. If a graph has n nodes, we can represent them as a matrix $\mathbf{X} \in \mathbb{R}^{n \times d}$. Analogously, each edge attribute is a c-dimensional feature vector, expressed as $\mathbf{x}_{v,u}^e \in \mathbb{R}^c$, where v and u are nodes. We can represent the set of edge attributes of a graph as a matrix $\mathbf{X}^e \in \mathbb{R}^{n \times c}$.

The following diagram shows a directed graph with five nodes and its corresponding adjacency matrix:

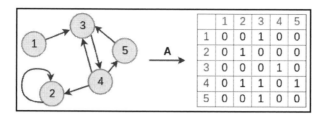

Directed graph with five nodes and its corresponding $\mathbf{A} \in \mathbb{R}^{5 \times 5}$ adjacency matrix

A graph is a versatile data structure that lends itself well to the way data is organized in many real-world scenarios. The following is a nonexhaustive list of examples:

- We can use graphs to represent users in a social network (nodes) and their groups of friends (edges). In fact, this is what Facebook does with their social graph (*The Anatomy of the Facebook Social Graph*, https://arxiv.org/abs/1111.4503).
- We can represent a molecule as a graph, where the nodes are atoms and the edges are the chemical bonds between them.
- We can represent a street network (a classic example) as a graph, where the streets are edges and their intersections are nodes.
- In online commerce, we can represent both users and items as nodes and the relationships between them as edges.

Next, let's discuss the types of task we can solve with graphs. They fall broadly into three categories:

- **Node-focused**: Classification and regression of individual nodes. For example, in the famous Zachary's karate club problem (https://en.wikipedia.org/wiki/Zachary%27s_karate_club) we have a number of karate club members (nodes) and the friendships between them (edges). Initially, the club has a single instructor and all the members train as a group under that instructor. Later, the club splits into two groups with two separate instructors. Assuming that all but one club member opts to join one of the two groups, the goal is to determine which group will choose the last undecided member (classification), given its set of friendships with other members.

- **Edge-focused**: Classification and regression of individual edges of the graph. For example, we can predict how likely it is that two people in a social network know each other. In other words, the task is to determine whether an edge exists between two graph nodes.
- **Graph-focused**: Classification and regression of full graphs. For example, given a molecule represented as a graph, we can predict whether the molecule is toxic.

Next, let's outline the main training frameworks of GNNs:

- **Supervised**: All training data is labeled. We can apply supervised learning at node, edge, and graph level.
- **Unsupervised**: The goal here is to learn some form of graph embedding—for example, using autoencoders (we'll discuss this scenario later in the chapter). We can apply unsupervised learning at node, edge, and graph level.
- **Semi-supervised**: This is usually applied at node level, where some graph nodes are labeled and some aren't. Semi-supervised learning is especially suited for graphs because we can make the simple (but often true) assumption that neighboring nodes are likely to have the same labels. For example, say that we have two neighboring connected nodes. One of them contains an image of a car and the other contains an image of a truck. Let's assume that the truck node is labeled as a vehicle while the car node is unlabeled. We can safely assume that the car node is also a vehicle because of its proximity to another vehicle node (the truck). There are multiple ways we can utilize this graph property in GNNs. We'll outline two of them (they are not mutually exclusive):
    - Use this property implicitly by feeding the adjacency matrix of the graph as input to the network. The network will do its magic and hopefully infer that neighboring nodes are likely to have the same labels, thereby increasing the accuracy of the predictions thanks to the additional information. Most GNNs we'll discuss in this chapter use this mechanism.
    - **Label propagation**, where we can use labeled nodes as a seed for assigning labels to unlabeled ones based on their proximity to the labeled. We can do this in an iterative way as far as convergence by going through the following steps:
        1. Start with the seed labels.
        2. For all graph nodes (except the seed), assign a label based on the labels of their neighboring nodes. This step creates a new label configuration for the whole graph, where some of the nodes might need a new label, based on the modified neighbors' labels.

3. Stop label propagation if a convergence criterion is met; otherwise, repeat step 2.

We'll use this short introduction to graphs as a base for the next few sections, where we'll discuss various types of graph-focused NN model. The GNN arena is relatively new, and there is no outright perfect model resembling **convolutional networks** (**CNNs**) in computer vision. Instead, we have different models with various properties. Most of them fall into a few general categories, and there are attempts to create a framework that is generic enough to combine them all. This book doesn't aim to invent new models or model taxonomies but; instead, we'll introduce you to some existing ones.

Recurrent GNNs

We'll start this section by looking at **graph neural networks** (**GraphNNs**; see *The Graph Neural Network Model*, https://ieeexplore.ieee.org/document/4700287). Although the authors of the paper abbreviated the model to GNN, we'll refer to it with the GraphNN acronym to avoid conflict with the GNN abbreviation, which is reserved for the general class of graph networks. This is one of the first GNN models to be proposed. It extends existing NNs to process graph-structured data. In the same way that we used the context of a word (that is, its surrounding words) to create embedding vectors (Chapter 6, *Language Modeling*), we can use the neighboring graph nodes of a node to do the same. GraphNNs aim to create an *s*-dimensional vector state $\mathbf{h}_v \in \mathbb{R}^s$ of a node *v* based on the neighborhood of that node. In a similar way to language modeling, the vector state can serve as the input for other tasks, such as node classification.

The state of a node is updated by exchanging neighborhood information recurrently until a stable equilibrium is reached. Let's denote the set of neighborhood nodes *v* with $\mathcal{N}(v)$ and a single node of that neighborhood with *u*. The hidden state of a node is recurrently updated using the following formula:

$$\mathbf{h}_v^{(t)} = \sum_{u \in \mathcal{N}(v)} f\left(\mathbf{x}_v, \mathbf{x}^{\mathbf{e}}_{(u,v)}, \mathbf{x}_u, \mathbf{h}_u^{(t-1)}\right)$$

Here, f is a parametric function (for example, a **feed-forward NN (FFNN)**) and each state $\mathbf{h}_v^{(0)}$ is initialized randomly. The parametric function f takes as inputs the feature vector $\mathbf{x}_v$ of v, the feature vector $\mathbf{x}_u$ of its neighbor u, the feature vector $\mathbf{x}_{v,u}^e$ of the edge connecting u and v, and the state vector $\mathbf{h}_u^{(t-1)}$ of u at step t-1. In other words, f uses all known information about the neighborhood of v. The expression $\mathbf{h}_v^{(t)}$ is a sum of the f applied over all neighboring nodes, which allows GraphNN to be independent of the number of neighbors and their ordering. The function f is the same (that is, has the same weights) for all steps of the process.

Note that we have an iterative (or recurrent) process, where the states at step t are based on the number of steps up to t-1, as follows:

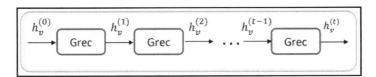

The recurrent process of updating the feature vector states: the **Grec** recurrent layer is the same (that is, has the same weights) for all steps: Source: https://arxiv.org/abs/1901.00596

The process continues until a stable equilibrium is reached. For this to work, the function f must be a contraction mapping. Let's clarify this: when applied to any two points (or values) A and B, a contraction mapping function f satisfies the condition $|f(A) - f(B)| \leq \gamma |A - B|$, where γ is a scalar value and $0 \leq \gamma < 1$. In other words, the contraction mapping shrinks the distance between two points after mapping. This ensures that the system will converge (exponentially quickly) to the equilibrium state vector $\mathbf{h}_v$ for any initial value $\mathbf{h}_v^{(0)}$. We can modify an NN to be a contracting function, but this goes beyond the scope of this book.

Now that we have the hidden state, we can use it for tasks such as node classification. We can express this with the following formula:

$$o_v = g(\mathbf{x}_v, \mathbf{h}_v)$$

In this equation, $\mathbf{h}_v$ is the state once an equilibrium is reached and g is a parametric function—for example, a fully connected layer with softmax activation for classification tasks.

Next, let's look at how to train the GraphNN, given a set of training labels t_i for some or all graph nodes and a mini-batch of size m. To train the GraphNN, go through the following steps:

1. Compute $\mathbf{h}_v$ and o_v for all m nodes, following the recurrent process we just described.
2. Compute the cost function (t_i is the label of node i):

$$J = \sum_{i=1}^{m}(t_i - o_i)$$

3. Propagate the cost backward. Note that alternating the node state update of step 1 with the gradient propagation of the current step allows GraphNN to process cyclic graphs.
4. Update the weights of the combined network $g(f)$.

GraphNN has several limitations, one of which is that computing the equilibrium state vector $\mathbf{h}_v$ is not efficient. Furthermore, as we mentioned previously in this section, GraphNN uses the same parameters (weights) to update $\mathbf{h}_v$ over all steps t. In contrast, other NN models can use multiple stacked layers with different sets of weights, which makes it possible for us to capture the hierarchical structure of the data. It also allows us to compute $\mathbf{h}_v$ in a single forward pass. Finally, it's worth mentioning that, although computing $\mathbf{h}_v$ is a recurrent process, GraphNN isn't a recurrent network.

The **Gated Graph NN** model (**GGNN**, https://arxiv.org/abs/1511.05493) tries to overcome these limitations with the help of **Gated Recurrent Unit** cells (or **GRU**; for more information, see Chapter 7, *Understanding Recurrent Networks*) as a recurrent function. We can define GGNN as the following:

$$\mathbf{h}_v^{(t)} = \text{GRU}(\mathbf{h}_v^{(t-1)}, \sum_{u \in \mathcal{N}(v)} \mathbf{W}\mathbf{h}_u^{(t)})$$

In the preceding formula, $\mathbf{h}_v^{(0)} = \mathbf{x}_v$. To clarify, GGNN updates the state based on its neighboring states $\mathbf{h}_u^{(t)}$ of the same step t and its previous hidden state $\mathbf{h}_v^{(t-1)}$.

From a historical perspective, GraphNNs were one of the first GNN models. But as we mentioned, they have some limitations. In the next section, we'll discuss Convolutional Graph Networks, which are a more recent development.

Convolutional Graph Networks

Convolutional Graph Networks (ConvGNN) use a stack of special graph convolutional layers (Gconv*) to perform a convolution over the nodes of a graph when updating the state vectors. In a similar way to GraphNNs, the graph convolution takes the neighbors of a node and produces its vector representation $\mathbf{h}_v$. But whereas GraphNN uses the same layer (that is, the same set of weights) over all steps t of the computation of $\mathbf{h}_v^{(t)}$, ConvGNN uses different layers at every step. The difference between the two approaches is illustrated in the following diagram:

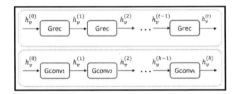

Top: GraphNN uses the same Grec recurrent layer over all steps t: Bottom: GCN uses a different Gconv. layer for each step: Source: https://arxiv.org/abs/1901.00596

With ConvGNN, the number of steps t is defined by the depth of the network. Although we will discuss this from a somewhat different perspective, ConvGNN behaves as a regular FFNN, but with graph convolutions. By stacking multiple layers, the final hidden representation of each node receives messages from a further neighborhood, as we can see in the following diagram:

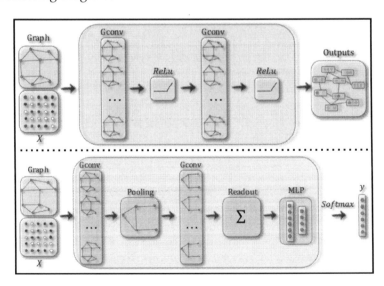

Top: Node-level classification GraphCN: Bottom: Graph-level classification GraphCN. Source: https://arxiv.org/abs/1901.00596

The diagram shows two scenarios:

- Node-level (top), where the output of each convolutional layer (including the last) is a vector for each node of the graph. We can perform node-level operations over these vectors.

- Graph-level (bottom), which alternates graph convolutions and pooling operations and ends with a readout layer, followed by several fully connected layers that summarize the whole graph to produce a single output.

Now that we have a high-level overview of ConvGNN, in the following section, we'll discuss graph convolutions (and after that, we'll talk about the readout and pooling layers).

Spectral-based convolutions

There are various types of graph convolutions (check out *A Comprehensive Survey on Graph Neural Networks*), but in this section, we'll discuss the algorithm from *Semi-Supervised Classification with Graph Convolutional Networks* (https://arxiv.org/abs/1609.02907). We'll denote this convolution with GCN to avoid confusion with the general ConvGNN notation, which refers to graph convolutional networks in general. GCN is a representative of the so-called **spectral-based** category of ConvGNNs. These algorithms define graph convolutions by introducing filters from the perspective of graph-signal processing, where the graph convolutional operation is interpreted as removing noises from graph signals.

In the *Graph neural network* section, we defined the hidden node state $\mathbf{h}_v^{(t)}$ and noted that $\mathbf{h}_v^{(0)} = \mathbf{x}_v$ in the case of GGNN. Let's extend this notation by stacking the hidden vector states of all nodes in the graph in a matrix $\mathbf{H} \in \mathbb{R}^{n \times d}$, where n is the total number of nodes in the graph and d is the size of the feature vectors. Each row of the matrix represents the hidden state of a single node. Then, we can define the generic formula for a single GCN layer at step $l+1$ as the following:

$$\mathbf{H}^{(l+1)} = f(\mathbf{H}^{(l)}, \mathbf{A})$$

Here, $\mathbf{A}$ is the adjacency matrix, f is a nonlinear activation, such as ReLU, and $\mathbf{H}^{(0)} = \mathbf{X}$ (the feature vector matrix). Since $\mathbf{h}_v^{(0)}$ and $\mathbf{x}_v$ have the same size, $\mathbf{H}^{(0)}$ has the same dimensions as the node feature matrix $\mathbf{X}$ (see the *Graph neural networks* section). However, $\mathbf{H}^{(l)} \in \mathbb{R}^{n \times z}$, where z is the size of the hidden state vector $\mathbf{h}_v^{(l)}$ and is not necessarily the same as the initial d.

Let's continue with a simplified but concrete version of the GCN:

$$f(\mathbf{H}^{(l)}, \mathbf{A}) = \sigma(\mathbf{A}\mathbf{H}^{(l)}\mathbf{W}^{(l)})$$

Here, $\mathbf{W}^{(l)} \in \mathbb{R}^{z_l \times z_{l+1}}$ is a weight matrix and σ is the sigmoid function. Since the adjacency matrix $\mathbf{A}$ represents the graph in matrix form, we can compute the output of the layer in a single operation. The $\mathbf{A}\mathbf{H}^{(l)}$ operation allows each node to receive input from its neighboring nodes (it also allows GCN to work with both directed and undirected graphs). Let's see how this works with an example. We'll use the five-node graph that we introduced in the *Graph neural networks* section. For the sake of readability, we'll assign a one-dimensional vector hidden state $\mathbf{h}_v$ for each node with a value equal to the node number $[\mathbf{h}_1^{(l)} = 1, \mathbf{h}_2^{(l)} = 2, \mathbf{h}_3^{(l)} = 3, \mathbf{h}_4^{(l)} = 4, \mathbf{h}_5^{(l)} = 5]$. Then we can compute the example with the following formula:

$$\mathbf{A}\mathbf{H}^{(l)} = \begin{bmatrix} 0 & 0 & 1 & 0 & 0 \\ 0 & 1 & 0 & 0 & 0 \\ 0 & 0 & 0 & 1 & 0 \\ 0 & 1 & 1 & 0 & 1 \\ 0 & 0 & 1 & 0 & 0 \end{bmatrix} \cdot \begin{bmatrix} 1 \\ 2 \\ 3 \\ 4 \\ 5 \end{bmatrix} = \begin{bmatrix} 0*1+0*2+1*3+0*4+0*5 \\ 0*1+1*2+0*3+0*4+0*5 \\ 0*1+0*2+0*3+1*4+0*5 \\ 0*1+1*2+1*3+0*4+1*5 \\ 0*1+0*2+1*3+0*4+0*5 \end{bmatrix} = \begin{bmatrix} 3 \\ 2 \\ 4 \\ 10 \\ 3 \end{bmatrix}$$

We can see how $\mathbf{h}_4^{(l)} = 10$ because it receives input from nodes 2, 3, and 5. If $\mathbf{h}_v$ had more dimensions, then each cell of the output vector would be a sum of the corresponding cells of the state vectors of the input nodes:

$$\mathbf{h}_v^{(l+1)} = \begin{bmatrix} a_{v,1}\mathbf{h}_{1,1}^{(l)} + a_{v,2}\mathbf{h}_{2,1}^{(l)} + \ldots + a_{v,n}\mathbf{h}_{z,1}^{(l)} \\ a_{v,1}\mathbf{h}_{1,2}^{(l)} + a_{v,2}\mathbf{h}_{2,2}^{(l)} + \ldots + a_{v,n}\mathbf{h}_{z,2}^{(l)} \\ \ldots \\ a_{v,1}\mathbf{h}_{1,n}^{(l)} + a_{v,2}\mathbf{h}_{2,n}^{(l)} + \ldots + a_{v,n}\mathbf{h}_{z,n}^{(l)} \end{bmatrix}$$

Here, $a_{v,i}$ are the cells of the adjacency matrix.

Although this solution is elegant, it has two limitations:

- Not all nodes receive input from their own previous state. In the preceding example, only node 2 takes input from itself because it has a loop edge (this is the edge that connects the node to itself). The solution to this problem is to artificially create loop edges for all nodes by setting all values along the main diagonal of the adjacency matrix to ones: $\hat{\mathbf{A}} = \mathbf{A} + \mathbf{I}$. In this equation, $\mathbf{I}$ is the identity matrix, which has ones along the main diagonal and zeros in all other cells.

- Since **A** is not normalized, the state vectors of nodes with a large number of neighbors will change their scale in a different way compared to nodes with a smaller number of neighbors. We can see this in the preceding example, where $h_4^{(l)} = 10$ is larger compared to the other nodes because node 4 has 3 nodes in its neighborhood. The solution to this problem is to normalize the adjacency matrix in such a way that the sum of all elements in one row is equal to 1: $a_{v,1} + a_{v,2} + \ldots + a_{v,n} = 1$. We can achieve this by multiplying **A** by the inverse degree matrix $\mathbf{D}^{-1}$. The degree matrix **D** is a diagonal matrix (that is, all other elements except the main diagonal are zeros) that contains information about the degree of each node. We refer to the number of neighbors of a node as a degree of that node. For example, the degree matrix of our example graph is the following:

$$\mathbf{D} = \begin{bmatrix} 1 & 0 & 0 & 0 & 0 \\ 0 & 1 & 0 & 0 & 0 \\ 0 & 0 & 1 & 0 & 0 \\ 0 & 0 & 0 & 3 & 0 \\ 0 & 0 & 0 & 0 & 1 \end{bmatrix}$$

Therefore, $\mathbf{D}^{-1}\mathbf{A}$ becomes the following:

$$\mathbf{D}^{-1}\mathbf{A} = \begin{bmatrix} 1 & 0 & 0 & 0 & 0 \\ 0 & 1 & 0 & 0 & 0 \\ 0 & 0 & 1 & 0 & 0 \\ 0 & 0 & 0 & \frac{1}{3} & 0 \\ 0 & 0 & 0 & 0 & 1 \end{bmatrix} \cdot \begin{bmatrix} 0 & 0 & 1 & 0 & 0 \\ 0 & 1 & 0 & 0 & 0 \\ 0 & 0 & 0 & 1 & 0 \\ 0 & 1 & 1 & 0 & 1 \\ 0 & 0 & 1 & 0 & 0 \end{bmatrix} = \begin{bmatrix} 0 & 0 & 1 & 0 & 0 \\ 0 & 1 & 0 & 0 & 0 \\ 0 & 0 & 0 & 1 & 0 \\ 0 & \frac{1}{3} & \frac{1}{3} & 0 & \frac{1}{3} \\ 0 & 0 & 1 & 0 & 0 \end{bmatrix}$$

This mechanism assigns the same weight to each of the neighboring nodes. In practice, the authors of the paper discovered that using the symmetric normalization $\mathbf{D}^{-\frac{1}{2}}\mathbf{A}\mathbf{D}^{-\frac{1}{2}}$ works better.

After we incorporate these two improvements, the final form of the GCN formula can be written as follows:

$$f(\mathbf{H}^{(l)}, \mathbf{A}) = \sigma(\hat{\mathbf{D}}^{-\frac{1}{2}} \hat{\mathbf{A}} \hat{\mathbf{D}}^{-\frac{1}{2}} \mathbf{H}^{(l)} \mathbf{W}^{(l)})$$

Note that the GCN we just described includes only the immediate neighborhood of the node as the context. Each stacked layer effectively increases the receptive field of the node beyond its immediate neighbors by 1. The receptive field of the second layer of a ConvGNN includes the immediate neighbors, the receptive field of the second layer includes the nodes that are two hops away from the current node, and so on.

In the next section, we'll look at the second major category of graph convolution operations, called spatial-based convolutions.

Spatial-based convolutions with attention

The second ConvGNN category is spatial-based methods, which take inspiration from the computer vision convolution (Chapter 2, *Understanding Convolutional Networks*). We can think of an image as a graph, where each pixel is a node, directly connected to its neighboring pixels (the left-hand image in the following diagram). For example, if we use 3 × 3 as a filter, the neighborhood of each pixel consists of eight pixels. In the image convolution, this 3 × 3 weighted filter is applied over the 3 × 3 patch and the result is a weighted sum of the intensities of all nine pixels. Similarly, the spatial-based graph convolution convolves the representation of the central node with the representations of its neighbors to derive an updated representation for the central node, as illustrated in the right-hand image in the following diagram:

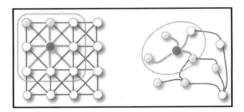

Left: 2D convolution over a pixel grid: Right: Spatial graph convolution. Source: https://arxiv.org/abs/1901.00596

The generic spatial-based convolution is somewhat similar to the GCN in the sense that both operations rely on graph neighbors. The GCN uses the inverse degree matrix to assign weights to each neighbor. Spatial convolutions use the convolution filter for the same purpose. The main difference between the two is that in the case of GCNs, the weights are fixed and normalized, whereas the filter weights of the spatial convolution are learnable and not normalized. In some sense, we can think of the GCN as a spatial-based approach as well.

We'll continue this section with a specific type of spatial-based model called the **Graph Attention Network (GAT)** (for more information, go to https://arxiv.org/abs/1710.10903), which implements graph convolutions with a special graph self-attention layer. Instead of learning a convolutional filter or using the averaged adjacency matrix as a GCN, GAT uses the attention scores of the self-attention mechanism to assign weights to each of the neighboring nodes. The GAT layer is the main building block of graph attention networks, which consist of multiple stacked GAT layers. As with GCN, each additional layer increases the receptive field of the target node.

Similar to GCN, the GAT layer takes as input a set of node feature vectors $\mathbf{H}^{(l)} \in \mathbb{R}^{n \times z_l}$ and outputs a different set of feature vectors $\mathbf{H}^{(l+1)} \in \mathbb{R}^{n \times z_{l+1}}$, not necessarily of the same cardinality. Following the procedure we outlined in Chapter 8, *Sequence-to-Sequence Models and Attention*, the operation starts by computing the alignment scores between the feature vectors $\mathbf{h}_i^{(l)}$ and $\mathbf{h}_j^{(l)}$ of each two nodes of the neighborhood:

$$e_{ij} = f_a(\mathbf{W}^{(l)}\mathbf{h}_i, \mathbf{W}^{(l)}\mathbf{h}_j)$$

Here, $\mathbf{W}^{(l)} \in \mathbb{R}^{z_{l+1} \times z_l}$ is a weight matrix that transforms the input vectors to the cardinality of the output vectors and provides the necessary learnable parameters. The f_a expression is a simple FFN with a single layer and LeakyReLU activation, which is parameterized by a weight vector $\mathbf{a} \in \mathbb{R}^{2z_{l+1}}$ and implements the additive attention mechanism:

$$f_a = \text{LeakyReLU}(\mathbf{a}^\top[\mathbf{W}^{(l)}\mathbf{h}_i, \mathbf{W}^{(l)}\mathbf{h}_j])$$

Here, $[\mathbf{W}^{(l)}\mathbf{h}_i, \mathbf{W}^{(l)}\mathbf{h}_j]$ represents concatenation. If we don't impose any restrictions, each node will be able to attend to all other nodes of the graph, regardless of their proximity to the target node; however, we're only interested in the neighboring nodes. The authors of GAT propose to solve this by using masked attention, where the mask covers all nodes that are not immediate neighbors of the target node. We'll denote the immediate neighbors of node i with $\mathcal{N}_i$.

Next, we compute attention scores by using softmax. The following are the generic formula and the formula with f_a (applied only over the immediate neighbors):

$$\alpha_{i,j} = \text{softmax}(e_{i,j}) = \frac{\exp(e_{i,j})}{\sum_{k \in \mathcal{N}_i} \exp(e_{i,k})}$$

$$\alpha_{i,j} = \frac{\exp(\text{LeakyReLU}(\mathbf{a}^\top[\mathbf{W}^{(l)}\mathbf{h}_i, \mathbf{W}^{(l)}\mathbf{h}_j]))}{\sum_{k \in \mathcal{N}_i} \exp(\text{LeakyReLU}(\mathbf{a}^\top[\mathbf{W}^{(l)}\mathbf{h}_i, \mathbf{W}^{(l)}\mathbf{h}_k]))}$$

Once we have the attention scores, we can use them to compute the final output feature vector of each node (we referred to this as the context vector in Chapter 8, *Sequence-to-Sequence Models and Attention*), which is a weighted combination of the input feature vectors of all neighbors:

$$\mathbf{h}_i^{(l+1)} = \sigma\left(\sum_{j \in \mathcal{N}_i} \alpha_{i,j} \mathbf{W}\mathbf{h}_j^{(l)}\right)$$

Here, σ is the sigmoid function. The authors of the paper also found multihead attention to be beneficial to the performance of the model:

$$\mathbf{h}_i^{(l+1)} = \text{Concat}_{k=1}^{K}(\sigma(\sum_{j \in \mathcal{N}_i} \alpha_{i,j}^k \mathbf{W}^{(l)(k)} \mathbf{h}_j^{(l)}))$$

Here, k is the index of each head (for a total of K heads), $\alpha_{i,j}^k$ are the attention scores for each attention head, and $\mathbf{W}^{(l)(k)}$ is the weight matrix of each attention head. Since $\mathbf{h}_i^{(l+1)}$ is a result of concatenation, its cardinality will be $k \times z_{l+1}$. Because of this, concatenation is not possible in the final attention layer of the network. To solve this, the authors of the paper suggest that you should average the outputs of the attention heads in the final layer (denoted with index L):

$$\mathbf{h}_i^{(L)} = \sigma(\frac{1}{K} \sum_{k=1}^{K} \sum_{j \in \mathcal{N}_i} \alpha_{i,j}^k \mathbf{W}^{(L-1)(k)} \mathbf{h}_j^{(L-1)})$$

The following diagram shows a comparison between regular and multihead attention in the GAT context. In the left image, we can see the regular attention mechanism, applied between two nodes and i and j. In the right image, we can see the multihead attention with $k = 3$ heads of node 1 with its neighborhood. The aggregated features are either concatenated (for all hidden GAT layers) or averaged (for the final GAT layer):

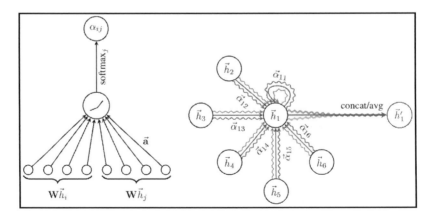

Left: Regular attention over two nodes: Right: Multihead attention of node 1 with its neighborhood. Source: https://arxiv.org/abs/1710.10903

Once we have the output of the final GAT layer, we can use it as input to the next task-specific layers. For example, this could be a fully connected layer with softmax activation for node classification.

Before we conclude this section devoted to ConvGNNs, let's discuss two final components that we haven't addressed yet. The first is the readout layer that we introduced in the graph-level classification example at the beginning of the *Convolutional Graph Networks* section. It takes as input all the node states of the last graph convolutional layer $\mathbf{H}^{(L)}$ and outputs a single vector that summarizes the whole graph. We can define it formally as the following:

$$\mathbf{h}_G = R(\mathbf{h}_v^{(L)}, v \in G)$$

Here, G represents the set of graph nodes and R is the readout function. There are various ways to implement it, but the simplest is to take the element-wise sum or mean of all node states.

The next (and final) ConvGNN component we'll look at is the pooling operation. Once again, there are various ways to use this, but one of the simplest is to use the same max/average pooling operations as we did in the computer vision convolutions:

$$\mathbf{h}_G = \mathrm{mean/max/sum}(\mathbf{h}_1^{(l)}, \mathbf{h}_2^{(l)}, \ldots, \mathbf{h}_p^{(l)})$$

Here, p indicates the size of the pooling window. If the pooling window contains the whole graph, the pooling becomes similar to the readout.

This concludes our discussion about ConvGNNs. In the next section, we'll discuss graph autoencoders, which provide a way to generate new graphs.

Graph autoencoders

Let's have a quick recap of autoencoders, which we first introduced in `Chapter 5`, *Generative Models*. An **autoencoder** is an FFN that tries to reproduce its input (more accurately, it tries to learn an identity function, $h_{w,w'}(x) = x$). We can think of the autoencoder as a virtual composition of two components—the **encoder**, which maps the input data to the network's internal latent feature space (represented as vector z), and the **decoder**, which tries to reconstruct the input from the network's internal data representation. We can train the autoencoder in an unsupervised way by minimizing a loss function (known as a **reconstruction error)**, which measures the distance between the original input and its reconstruction.

Graph autoencoders (**GAE**) are similar to autoencoders, with the distinction that the encoder maps the graph nodes into the autoencoder latent feature space and then the decoder tries to reconstruct specific graph features from it. In this section, we'll discuss a GAE variant, introduced in *Variational Graph Auto-Encoders* (`https://arxiv.org/abs/1611.07308`), which also outlines the variational version of GAE (**VGAE**). The following diagram shows an example GAE:

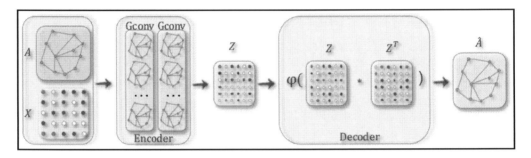

An example of graph autoencoder. Source: https://arxiv.org/abs/1901.00596

The encoder is a GCN model that we defined in the *Spectral-based convolutions* section to compute a network embedding $\mathbf{Z} \in \mathbb{R}^{n \times d}$ for graph nodes, where the embedding for each of the n total nodes is a d-dimensional vector $\mathbf{z}$. It takes as input the adjacency matrix $\mathbf{A}$ and the set of node feature vectors $\mathbf{X}$ (like the other GNN models we discussed in this chapter). The encoder is represented by the following formula:

$$\mathbf{Z} = \mathrm{GCN}_{enc}(\mathbf{X}, \mathbf{A}) = \mathrm{Gconv}(f(\mathrm{Gconv}(\mathbf{A}, \mathbf{X}; \mathbf{W}_1)); \mathbf{W}_2)$$

Here, $\mathbf{W}_1$ and $\mathbf{W}_2$ are the learnable parameters (weights) of the two GCN graph convolutions, and f is a nonlinear activation function, like ReLU. The authors of the paper use two graph convolutional layers, although the proposed algorithm can work for any number of layers.

The decoder tries to reconstruct the graph adjacency matrix $\hat{\mathbf{A}}$:

$$\hat{\mathbf{A}} = \sigma(\mathbf{Z}\mathbf{Z}^{\mathsf{T}})$$

Here, σ is the sigmoid function. It first computes the dot (or inner) product between $\mathbf{Z}$ and its transpose: $\mathbf{zz}^\mathsf{T}$. To clarify, this operation computes a dot product of the vector embedding z_i of each node i and the vector embedding z_j of every other node j of the graph, as shown in the following example:

$$
\mathbf{zz}^\mathsf{T} =
\begin{bmatrix}
z_{11} & z_{12} & \cdots & z_{1d} \\
z_{21} & z_{22} & \cdots & z_{2d} \\
\vdots & \vdots & \ddots & \vdots \\
z_{n1} & z_{n2} & \cdots & z_{nd}
\end{bmatrix}
\cdot
\begin{bmatrix}
z_{11} & z_{21} & \cdots & z_{n1} \\
z_{12} & z_{22} & \cdots & z_{n2} \\
\vdots & \vdots & \ddots & \vdots \\
z_{1d} & z_{2d} & \cdots & z_{nd}
\end{bmatrix}
=
\begin{bmatrix}
d_{11} & d_{12} & \cdots & d_{1n} \\
d_{21} & d_{22} & \cdots & d_{2n} \\
\vdots & \vdots & \ddots & \vdots \\
d_{n1} & d_{n2} & \cdots & d_{nn}
\end{bmatrix}
$$

As we mentioned in Chapter 1, *The Nuts and Bolts of Neural Networks*, we can think of the dot product as a similarity measure between vectors. Therefore, $\mathbf{zz}^\mathsf{T}$ measures the distance between every possible pair of nodes. These distances serve as a base for the reconstruction effort. After this, the decoder applies a nonlinear activation function and proceeds to reconstruct the graph adjacency matrix. We can train the GAE by minimizing the discrepancy between the real reconstructed adjacency matrices.

Next, let's focus on **Variational Graph Autoencoders** (VGAE). Much like the **Variational Autoencoders** (VAE) we discussed in Chapter 5, *Generative Models*, the VGAE is a generative model that can generate new graphs (more specifically, new adjacency matrices). To understand this, let's start with a short recap of VAEs. Unlike regular autoencoders, the VAE bottleneck layer won't directly output latent state vectors. Instead, it will output two vectors, which describe the **mean** μ and the **variance** σ of the distribution of the latent vector **z**. We'll use them to sample a random vector ε with the same dimensions as **z** from a Gaussian distribution. More specifically, we'll shift ε by the latent distribution's mean μ and scale it by the latent distribution's variance σ:

$$
\mathbf{z} = \mu + \sigma \odot \varepsilon
$$

This technique is known as the **reparameterization** trick, and it allows the random vector to have the same mean and variance as the original dataset.

We can think of VGAE as a combination of GAE and VAE in the sense that it works with graph inputs (such as GAE) and follows the same principles to generate new data (like VAE). First, let's focus on the encoder, which is split into two paths:

$$
\mu = \mathrm{GCN}_\mu(\mathbf{X}, \mathbf{A}) = \tilde{\mathbf{A}}\mathrm{ReLU}(\tilde{\mathbf{A}}\mathbf{X}\mathbf{W_0})\mathbf{W}_\mu
$$
$$
\sigma = \mathrm{GCN}_\sigma(\mathbf{X}, \mathbf{A}) = \tilde{\mathbf{A}}\mathrm{ReLU}(\tilde{\mathbf{A}}\mathbf{X}\mathbf{W_0})\mathbf{W}_\sigma
$$

Here, the weights $\mathbf{W}_0$ are shared between the paths, $\tilde{\mathbf{A}}$ is the symmetrically normalized adjacency matrix, $\boldsymbol{\mu}$ is the matrix of mean vectors $\boldsymbol{\mu}_i$, and $\boldsymbol{\sigma}$ is the matrix of variances σ_i of each graph node. Then, the encoder inference step for the full graph is defined as the inner product of the latent representations of all graph nodes i:

$$q_\varphi(\mathbf{Z}|\mathbf{X},\mathbf{A}) = \prod_{i=1}^{n} q_\varphi(\mathbf{z}_i|\mathbf{X},\mathbf{A})$$

In this formula, n is the number of nodes in the graph and $q_\varphi(\mathbf{z}_i|\mathbf{X},\mathbf{A})$ represents the encoder approximation of the real probability distribution $p(\mathbf{z}_i|\mathbf{X},\mathbf{A})$, where φ is the network parameters (here, we have preserved the notation of `Chapter 5`, *Generative Models*). The approximation is a Gaussian distribution with node-specific mean μ_i and diagonal covariance values σ_i^2:

$$q_\varphi(\mathbf{z}_i|\mathbf{X},\mathbf{A}) = \mathcal{N}(\mathbf{z}_i|\mu_i, diag(\sigma_i^2))$$

Next, we define the generative step, which creates the new adjacency matrix. It is an inner product of the random latent vectors:

$$p_\theta(\mathbf{A}|\mathbf{Z}) = \prod_{i=1}^{n}\prod_{j=1}^{n} p_\theta(\mathbf{A}_{i,j}|\mathbf{z}_i,\mathbf{z}_j)$$

Here, $\mathbf{A}_{i,j}$ indicates whether an edge exists between two nodes i and j, and $p_\theta(\mathbf{A}_{i,j}|\mathbf{z}_i,\mathbf{z}_j)$ represents the decoder approximation of the real probability $p(\mathbf{A}_{i,j}|\mathbf{z}_i,\mathbf{z}_j)$. We can train the VGAE using the already familiar VAE cost:

$$L(\theta,\varphi;\mathbf{X}) = -D_{KL}(q_\varphi(\mathbf{Z}|\mathbf{X},\mathbf{A})\|p_\theta(\mathbf{Z})) + E_{q_\varphi(\mathbf{Z}|\mathbf{X},\mathbf{A})}[\log(p_\theta(\mathbf{A}|\mathbf{Z}))]$$

Here, the first term is the Kullback–Leibler divergence and the second is the reconstruction cost.

This concludes our description of GAE and VGAE. In the next section, we'll discuss yet another graph-learning paradigm, which makes it possible to mix structured and unstructured data as network inputs.

Neural graph learning

In this section, we'll describe the **Neural Graph Learning** paradigm (**NGL**) (for more information, see *Neural Graph Learning: Training Neural Networks Using Graphs* at `https://storage.googleapis.com/pub-tools-public-publication-data/pdf/bbd774a3c6f13f05bf754e09aa45e7aa6faa08a8.pdf`), which makes it possible to augment training based on unstructured data with structured signals. More specifically, we'll discuss the **neural structured learning** framework (**NSL**) (for more information, go to `https://www.tensorflow.org/neural_structured_learning/`), which is based on TensorFlow 2.0 and implements these principles.

To understand how NGL works, we'll use the CORA dataset (`https://relational.fit.cvut.cz/dataset/CORA`), which consists of 2,708 scientific publications classified into 1 of 7 classes (this is the unstructured part of the dataset). The number of unique words in all publications (that is, the vocabulary) in the dataset is 1,433. Each publication is described as a single **multihot** encoded vector. This is a vector of size 1,433 (the same as the vocabulary), where the cell values are either 0 or 1. If a publication contains the i-th word of the vocabulary, then the ith cell of the one-hot encoded vector of that publication is set to 1. If the word is not present in the publication, the cell is set to 0. This mechanism preserves information about the words present in an article, but not information about their order. The dataset also contains a directed graph of 5,429 citations, where the nodes are publications and the edges between them indicate whether publication v cites publication u (this is the structured part of the dataset).

Next, let's focus on NGL itself, starting with the following diagram:

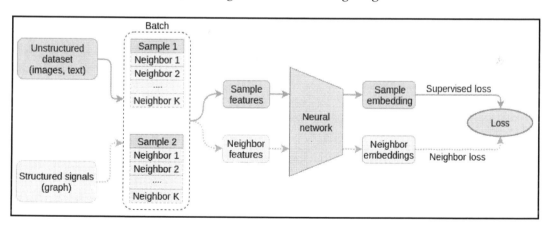

The NGL framework: green solid lines show the unstructured input data flow: yellow dashed lines show the structured signals data flow: Inspired by: https://www.tensorflow.org/neural_structured_learning/framework

It acts as a kind of wrapper over the regular NN training framework, and it can be applied over any type of network, including FFN and RNN. For example, we can have a regular FFN, which takes as input the multihot encoded publication vector and tries to classify it to one of the 7 classes, using softmax output, as illustrated in the preceding diagram with green uninterrupted lines. NGL allows us to extend this network with structured data, offered by the citations, as illustrated by the yellow dashed lines.

Let's look at how this works. We start with the assumption that neighboring nodes in the graph are somewhat similar. We can transfer this assumption to the NN domain by saying that the embedding vector produced by the NN (the embedding is the output of the last hidden layer) of sample *i* should be somewhat similar to the embedding of sample *j*, provided that the two samples are neighbors in the associated graph. In our example, we can assume that the embedding vector of publication *i* should be similar to the embedding of publication *j*, provided that one of them cites the other (that is, they are neighbors in the graph of citations). In practice, we can implement this with the following steps:

1. Start with a dataset that contains both unstructured data (multihot-encoded publications) and structured data (the graph of citations).
2. Build special types of composite training samples (organized in batches), where each composite sample consists of a single regular input sample (one multihot-encoded publication) and *K* of its neighboring samples (the multihot-encoded publications that cite or are cited by the initial sample).
3. Feed the composite sample to the NN and produce embeddings for both the initial sample and its neighbors. Although the preceding diagram shows the two paths running in parallel, this is not the case. The diagram aims to illustrate that the network processes both the central sample and its neighbors, but the actual NN is not privy to this arrangement—it just takes all of the multihot-encoded inputs as part of a single batch and processes them. Instead, the NSL portion on top of the regular NN differentiates the two components.
4. Compute a special type of composite loss function composed of two parts: regular supervised loss and regularization neighbor loss, which uses a metric to measure the distance between the initial sample embedding and the embedding of its neighbors. The neighbor loss is the mechanism that allows us to augment unstructured training data with structured signals. The composite loss is defined as follows:

$$J_\theta = \frac{1}{n} [\underbrace{\sum_{i=1}^{n} \mathcal{L}_s(f_\theta(x_i), t_i)}_{\text{Supervised cost}} + \alpha \underbrace{\sum_{i=1}^{n} \sum_{x_j \in \mathcal{N}(x_i)} w_{ij} \mathcal{D}(f_\theta(x_i), f_\theta(x_j))]}_{\text{Neighbor cost}}$$

This formula has the following features:

- n is the number of composite samples in the mini-batch.
- $\mathcal{L}_s$ is the supervised loss function.
- f_θ is the NN function with weights θ.
- α is a scalar parameter that determines the relative weight between the two loss components.
- $\mathcal{N}(x_i)$ is the set of graph neighbors of sample x_i. Note that the neighbor loss iterates over all neighbors of all nodes of the graph (two sums).
- w_{ij} is the weight of the graph edge between samples i and j. If the task doesn't have a notion of weights, we can assume that all weights are 1.
- $\mathcal{D}$ is the distance metric between the embedding vectors of samples i and j.

Because of the regularization nature of the neighbor loss, NGL is also referred to as **graph regularization**.

5. Propagate the error backward and update the network weights θ.

Now that we have an overview of graph regularization, let's implement it.

Implementing graph regularization

In this section, we'll implement graph regularization over the Cora dataset with the help of the NSL framework. This example is based on the tutorial available at `https://www.tensorflow.org/neural_structured_learning/tutorials/graph_keras_mlp_cora`. Before we proceed with the implementation, we have to satisfy some prerequisites. First, we need TensorFlow 2.0 and the `neural-structured-learning` 1.1.0 package (available via `pip`).

Once we satisfy these requirements, we can proceed with the implementation:

1. We'll start with the package imports:

```
import neural_structured_learning as nsl
import tensorflow as tf
```

2. We'll continue with some constant parameters of the program (hopefully the constant names and the comments speak for themselves):

```
# Cora dataset path
TRAIN_DATA_PATH = 'data/train_merged_examples.tfr'
TEST_DATA_PATH = 'data/test_examples.tfr'
# Constants used to identify neighbor features in the input.
```

```
NBR_FEATURE_PREFIX = 'NL_nbr_'
NBR_WEIGHT_SUFFIX = '_weight'
# Dataset parameters
NUM_CLASSES = 7
MAX_SEQ_LENGTH = 1433
# Number of neighbors to consider in the composite loss function
NUM_NEIGHBORS = 1
# Training parameters
BATCH_SIZE = 128
```

The files under `TRAIN_DATA_PATH` and `TEST_DATA_PATH` contain the Cora dataset and labels, preprocessed in a TensorFlow-friendly format.

3. Next, let's load the dataset. This process is implemented by using two functions: `make_dataset`, which builds the whole dataset, and `parse_example`, which parses a single composite sample (`make_dataset` uses `parse_example` internally). We'll start with `make_dataset`:

```
def make_dataset(file_path: str, training=False) ->
tf.data.TFRecordDataset:
    dataset = tf.data.TFRecordDataset([file_path])
    if training:
        dataset = dataset.shuffle(10000)
    dataset = dataset.map(parse_example).batch(BATCH_SIZE)

    return dataset
```

Note that `dataset.map(parse_example)` internally applies `parse_example` over all samples of the dataset. Let's continue with the definition of `parse_example`, starting from the declaration:

```
def parse_example(example_proto: tf.train.Example) -> tuple:
```

The function creates the `feature_spec` dictionary that represents a kind of template for a single composite sample, which is later filled with actual data from the dataset. First, we fill `feature_spec` with the placeholder instances of `tf.io.FixedLenFeature` for 'words', which represents a multihot-encoded publication, and 'label', which represents the class of the publication (please bear in mind the indentation as this code is still part of `parse_example`):

```
feature_spec = {
    'words':
        tf.io.FixedLenFeature(shape=[MAX_SEQ_LENGTH],
                              dtype=tf.int64,
                              default_value=tf.constant(
                                  value=0,
```

```
                                        dtype=tf.int64,
                                        shape=[MAX_SEQ_LENGTH])),
                'label':
                    tf.io.FixedLenFeature((), tf.int64, default_value=-1),
        }
```

Then, we iterate over the first NUM_NEIGHBORS neighbors and add their multihot vectors and edge weights to feature_spec under the nbr_feature_key and nbr_weight_key keys respectively:

```
        for i in range(NUM_NEIGHBORS):
            nbr_feature_key = '{}{}_{}'.format(NBR_FEATURE_PREFIX, i,
    'words')
            nbr_weight_key = '{}{}{}'.format(NBR_FEATURE_PREFIX, i,
    NBR_WEIGHT_SUFFIX)
            feature_spec[nbr_feature_key] = tf.io.FixedLenFeature(
                shape=[MAX_SEQ_LENGTH],
                dtype=tf.int64,
                default_value=tf.constant(
                    value=0, dtype=tf.int64, shape=[MAX_SEQ_LENGTH]))

            feature_spec[nbr_weight_key] = tf.io.FixedLenFeature(
                shape=[1], dtype=tf.float32,
    default_value=tf.constant([0.0]))

        features = tf.io.parse_single_example(example_proto,
    feature_spec)

        labels = features.pop('label')
        return features, labels
```

Note that we populate the template with a real sample from the dataset with the following code snippet:

```
        features = tf.io.parse_single_example(example_proto,
    feature_spec)
```

4. Now, we can instantiate the training and testing datasets:

```
    train_dataset = make_dataset(TRAIN_DATA_PATH, training=True)
    test_dataset = make_dataset(TEST_DATA_PATH)
```

5. Next, let's implement the model, which is a simple FFN with two hidden layers and softmax as output. The model takes the multihot-encoded publication vector as input and outputs the publication class. It is independent of NSL and can be trained, in a simple supervised way, as a classification:

```python
def build_model(dropout_rate):
    """Creates a sequential multi-layer perceptron model."""
    return tf.keras.Sequential([
        # one-hot encoded input.
        tf.keras.layers.InputLayer(
            input_shape=(MAX_SEQ_LENGTH,), name='words'),

        # 2 fully connected layers + dropout
        tf.keras.layers.Dense(64, activation='relu'),
        tf.keras.layers.Dropout(dropout_rate),
        tf.keras.layers.Dense(64, activation='relu'),
        tf.keras.layers.Dropout(dropout_rate),

        # Softmax output
        tf.keras.layers.Dense(NUM_CLASSES, activation='softmax')
    ])
```

6. Next, let's instantiate the model:

```python
model = build_model(dropout_rate=0.5)
```

7. We have all the ingredients that we need to use graph regularization. We'll start by wrapping the `model` with the NSL wrapper:

```python
graph_reg_config = nsl.configs.make_graph_reg_config(
    max_neighbors=NUM_NEIGHBORS,
    multiplier=0.1,
    distance_type=nsl.configs.DistanceType.L2,
    sum_over_axis=-1)
graph_reg_model = nsl.keras.GraphRegularization(model,
                                        graph_reg_config)
```

We instantiate the `graph_reg_config` object (an instance of `nsl.configs.GraphRegConfig`) with the graph regularization parameters: `max_neighbors=NUM_NEIGHBORS` is the number of neighbors to use, `multiplier=0.1` is equivalent to the parameter α of the composite loss we introduced in the *Neural structured learning* section, and `distance_type=nsl.configs.DistanceType.L2` is the distance metric between the neighboring node embeddings.

8. Next, we can build a training framework and initiate the training for 100 epochs:

```
graph_reg_model.compile(
    optimizer='adam',
    loss='sparse_categorical_crossentropy',
    metrics=['accuracy'])

# run eagerly to prevent epoch warnings
graph_reg_model.run_eagerly = True

graph_reg_model.fit(train_dataset, epochs=100, verbose=1)
```

9. Once the training is done, we can run the trained model over the test dataset:

```
eval_results = dict(
    zip(graph_reg_model.metrics_names,
        graph_reg_model.evaluate(test_dataset)))
print('Evaluation accuracy: {}'.format(eval_results['accuracy']))
print('Evaluation loss: {}'.format(eval_results['loss']))
```

If everything goes alright, the output of the program should be:

```
Evaluation accuracy: 0.8137432336807251
Evaluation loss: 1.1235489577054978
```

This concludes our discussion about GNN. As we mentioned, there are various types of GNNs, and we only included a small set here. If you are interested in learning more, I suggest that you refer to the survey paper we introduced at the beginning of the section or check out the following curated list of GNN-related papers at https://github.com/thunlp/GNNPapers.

In the next section, we'll discuss a new type of NN that uses external memory to store information.

Introducing memory-augmented NNs

We've already seen the concept of memory (albeit in a strange form) in NNs—for example, the LSTM cell can add or delete information on its hidden cell state with the help of the input and the forget gates. Another example is the attention mechanism, where the set of vectors that represent the encoded source sequence can be viewed as external memory that is written to by the encoder and read from by the decoder. But this ability comes with some limitations. For one, the encoder can only write to a single memory location, which is the current element of the sequence. It also cannot update previously written vectors. On the other hand, the decoder can only read from the database, but cannot write to it.

In this section, we'll take the concept of memory one step further and look at **Memory-Augmented NNs (MANNs)**, which resolve these limitations. This is a new class of algorithm and is still in its early stages, unlike the more mainstream types of NN, such as convolutional and RNNs, which have been around for decades. The first MANN network we'll discuss is the neural Turing machine.

Neural Turing machines

The concept of MANNs was first introduced with the concept of the **neural Turing machine (NTM)** (for more information, go to `https://arxiv.org/abs/1410.5401`). The NTM has two components:

- A NN controller.
- An external memory, represented as a matrix $\mathbf{M} \in \mathbb{R}^{n \times d}$. The matrix contains n rows of d-dimensional vectors.

The following diagram provides an overview of the NTM architecture:

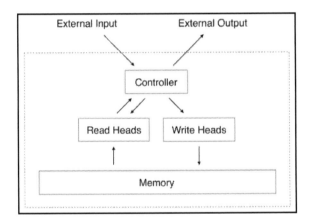

NTM Source: https://arxiv.org/abs/1410.5401

An NTM works in a sequential fashion (like an RNN), where the controller takes input vectors and produces output vectors in response. It also reads and writes to memory with the help of multiple parallel read/write heads.

Let's focus on the reading operation, which is very similar to the attention mechanism we looked at in `Chapter 8`, *Sequence-to-Sequence Models and Attention*. A read head always reads the full memory matrix, but it does so by attending to different memory vectors with different intensities. To do this, the read head emits an *n*-dimensional vector $\mathbf{w}_t^r$ (at step *t*) with the following constraints:

$$\sum_{i=1}^{n} w_t^r(i) = 1, \quad 0 \le w_t^r(i) \le 1$$

The $\mathbf{w}_t^r$ implements an attention mechanism, where each cell *i* of the vector indicates the weight of the *i*th memory vector (that is, the *i*th row of the matrix **M**) in forming the output. The output of a read operation at step *t* is a *d*-dimensional vector $\mathbf{r}_t$, defined as the weighted sum of all memory vectors:

$$\mathbf{r}_t \leftarrow \sum_{i=1}^{n} w_t^r(i)\mathbf{M}_t(i)$$

This operation is similar to the soft attention mechanism we discussed in `Chapter 8`, *Sequence-to-Sequence Models and Attention*. Soft attention (unlike hard attention) is differentiable, and this also true of this operation. In this way, the whole NTM (controller and memory) is a single differentiable system, which makes it possible to train it with gradient descent and backpropagation.

Next, let's focus on the writing operation, which is composed of two steps: **erase** followed by an **add**. The write head emits the same type of attention vector $\mathbf{w}_t^w$ as the reading heads. It also emits another **erase** vector $\mathbf{e}_t \in \mathbb{R}^d$, whose values are all within the (0, 1) range. We can define the erase operation at step *t* over a single row *i* of the memory as a function of these two vectors and the memory state at step *t-1*, $\mathbf{M}_{t-1}$:

$$\tilde{\mathbf{M}}_t(i) \leftarrow \mathbf{M}_{t-1}(i)[\mathbf{1} - w_t^w(i)\mathbf{e}_t]$$

Here, **1** is a *d*-dimensional vector of ones and the multiplication between $\mathbf{M}_{t-1}(i)$ and the erase component is element-based. According to this formula, a memory location can be erased only if both the weight $w_t^w(i)$ and $\mathbf{e}_t$ are nonzero. This mechanism can work with multiple attention heads writing in an arbitrary order, because multiplication is commutative.

The erase operation is followed by the add operation. The write head produces an **add** vector $\mathbf{a}_t \in \mathbb{R}^d$, which is added to the memory after the erase to produce the final memory state at step t:

$$\mathbf{M}_t(i) \leftarrow \tilde{\mathbf{M}}_t(i) + w_t^w(i)\mathbf{a}_t$$

We are now familiar with read and write operations, but we still don't know how to produce attention vectors $\mathbf{w}_t$ (we'll omit the superscript index, because the following descriptions apply for both read and write heads). NTM uses two complementary addressing mechanisms to do this: content-based and location-based.

We'll start with content-based addressing, where each head (both reading and writing) emits a key vector $\mathbf{k}_t \in \mathbb{R}^d$. This vector is compared to each memory vector $\mathbf{M}_t(i)$ using the similarity measure $K[\mathbf{k}_t, \mathbf{M}_t(i)]$. The NTM authors propose using cosine similarity, defined as follows:

$$K[\mathbf{k}_t, \mathbf{M}_t(i)] = \frac{\mathbf{k}_t \cdot \mathbf{M}_t(i)}{|\mathbf{k}_t| \cdot |\mathbf{M}_t(i)|}$$

Then, we define a single cell of the content-based addressing vector as a softmax over the similarity results of all memory vectors:

$$w_t^c(i) \leftarrow \frac{\exp(\beta_t K[\mathbf{k}_t, \mathbf{M}_t(i)])}{\sum_{j=1}^n \exp(\beta_t K[\mathbf{k}_t, \mathbf{M}_t(j)])}$$

Here, β_t is a scalar value key strength, which widens or narrows the scope of the focus. For small values of β_t, the attention will diffuse over all memory vectors, and for large β_t, the attention will focus only on the most similar memory vectors.

The authors of NTM argue that in some problems, content-based attention is not enough, because the content of a variable can be arbitrary but its address has to be recognizable. They cite arithmetic problems as one such problem: two variables, x and y, can take on any two values, but the procedure $f(x, y) = x \times y$ should still be defined. A controller for this task could take the values of the variables x and y, store them in different addresses, then retrieve them and perform a multiplication algorithm. In this case, the variables are addressed by location, not by content, which brings us to the location-based addressing mechanism. It works with both random-access memory jumps and simple iterations across locations. It does this by shifting the attention weights one step forward or backward.

For example, if the current weighting focuses entirely on a single location, a rotation of 1 would shift the focus to the next location. A negative shift would move the weighting in the opposite direction.

Content and location addressing work in combination, as shown in the following diagram:

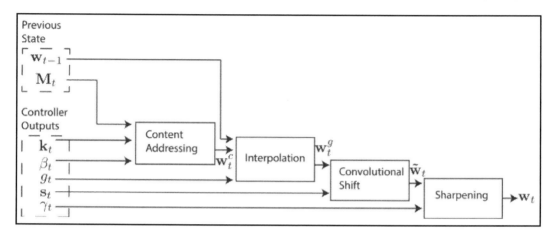

Flow diagram of the addressing mechanism. Source: https://arxiv.org/abs/1410.5401

Let's see how it works step by step:

1. Content addressing produces the content addressing vector $\mathbf{w}_t^c$, based on the memory $\mathbf{M}_t$, the key vector $\mathbf{k}_t$, and the key strength β_t.
2. **Interpolation** is the first of three steps in the location addressing mechanism, and it comes before the actual weight shifting. Each head (read or write) emits a scalar **interpolation gate** g_t in the (0, 1) range. The g_t dictates whether to preserve the weight $\mathbf{w}_{t-1}$ produced by the head at step *t-1* or replace it with the content-based weight $\mathbf{w}_t^c$ of the current step *t*. The interpolation is defined as follows:

$$\mathbf{w}_t^g \leftarrow g_t \mathbf{w}_t^c + (1 - g_t)\mathbf{w}_{t-1}$$

If $g_t = 0$, then we'll preserve the previous addressing vector completely. Alternatively, if $g_t = 1$, we'll only use the content-based addressing vector.

3. The next step is the **convolutional shift**, which takes interpolation attention $\mathbf{w}_t^g$ and determines how to shift it. Let's assume that the head attention can shift forward (+1), backward (-1), or stay the same (0). Each head emits a shift weighting s_t that defines a normalized distribution over the allowed shifts. In this case, s_t will have three elements, which indicate the degree to which shifts of -1, 0, and 1 are performed. If we assume that the memory vector indices are 0-based (from 0 to n-1), then we can define the rotation of $\mathbf{w}_t^g$ by s_t as a circular convolution:

$$\tilde{w}_t(i) \leftarrow \sum_{j=0}^{n-1} w_t^g(j) s_t(i-j)$$

Note that, although we iterate over all memory indices, s_t will have nonzero values only at the allowed positions.

4. The final addressing step is the **sharpening** step. One side, effect of the ability to simultaneously shift with different degrees over multiple directions is that the attention might blur. For example, let's say that we shift forward (+1) with a probability of 0.6, shift backward (-1) with a probability of 0.2, and don't shift (0) with a probability of 0.2. When we apply the shifting, the original focused attention will blur between the three locations. To solve this, the authors of NTM suggest that you modify each head to emit another scalar $\gamma_t \geq 1$, which will sharpen the final results using the following formula:

$$w_t(i) \leftarrow \frac{\tilde{w}_t(i)^{\gamma_t}}{\sum_{j=0}^{n-1} \tilde{w}_t(j)^{\gamma_t}}$$

Now that we know how addressing works, let's focus on the controller, where we can use either RNN (for example, LSTM) or FFN. The authors of NTM argue that an LSTM controller has internal memory, which is complementary to the external memory and also allows the controller to mix information from multiple time steps. However, in the context of NTM, an FFN controller can mimic an RNN one by reading and writing at the same memory location at every step. Additionally, the FFN is more transparent because its read/write pattern is easier to interpret than the internal RNN state.

The authors of the paper illustrate how NTM works with several tasks, one of which is a copy operation where the NTM has to replicate the input sequence as output. The task illustrates the model's ability to store and access information over long periods of time. The input sequence has a random length between 1 and 20. Each element of the sequence is a vector with eight binary elements (representing a single byte). First, the model takes the input sequence step by step until a special delimiter is reached. Then, it starts to generate the output sequence. No additional inputs are presented during the generation phase to ensure that the model can generate the entire sequence without intermediate assistance. The authors compare the performance of NTM- and LSTM-based models and note that NTM converges faster during training and can replicate longer sequences compared to LSTM. Based on these results, and after examining the interactions of the controller and the memory, they conclude that NTM doesn't simply memorize the input sequence; instead, it learns a type of copy algorithm. We can describe the sequence of operations for the algorithm with the following pseudocode:

```
initialize: move head to start location
while input delimiter not seen do
    receive input vector
    write input to head location
    increment head location by 1
end while
return head to start location
while true do
    read output vector from head location
    emit output
    increment head location by 1
end while
```

The NTM model learns a form of copy algorithm: source: https://arxiv.org/abs/1410.5401

Next, let's focus on the copy algorithm from the perspective of the interaction between the controller and the memory, as illustrated in the following image:

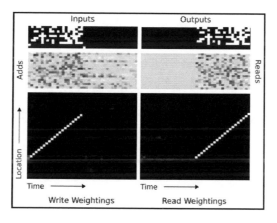

The controller/memory interaction during the copy algorithm: Source: https://arxiv.org/abs/1410.5401

The left column shows the input phase. The top-left image represents the input sequence of 8-bit binary vectors, the middle-left image represents the vectors added to the memory, and the bottom-left image represents the memory write attention weights at each step. The right column shows the output phase. The top-right image represents the generated output sequence of 8-bit binary vectors, the middle-right image represents the vectors read from the memory, and the bottom-right image represents the memory-read attention weights at each step. The bottom images illustrate incremental shifts of the head locations during write and read operations. Note that attention weights are clearly focused on a single memory location. At the same time, the input and output sequences read from the same location at each time step and the read vectors are equivalent to the write vectors. This indicates that each element of the input sequence is stored in a single memory location.

Before we conclude this section, let's mention that the authors of NTM have released an improved memory network architecture called a **Differential Neural Computer (DNC)** (for more information, see *Hybrid computing using a neural network with dynamic external memory,* at `https://www.nature.com/articles/nature20101`). The DNC introduces several improvements over NTM:

- The model only uses content-based addressing (as opposed to content and location in NTM).
- The model uses dynamic memory allocation by maintaining a list of available memory locations by adding locations to, and removing them from, a linked list (this is still differentiable). This mechanism allows the model to write new data only at locations that are marked as free.
- The model uses temporal memory linkage by maintaining information about the order of the memory locations that the controller writes to, which allows it to store sequential data at different memory locations.

This concludes our description of the NTM architecture. In the next section, we'll discuss an improvement to NTM introduced in the *One-shot Learning with Memory-Augmented Neural Networks* paper (`https://arxiv.org/abs/1605.06065`). We'll denote the improved architecture with MANN* to avoid confusion with the MANN acronym, which references the general class of memory networks.

MANN*

The MANN* read operation is very similar to the NTM read operation, with the exception that it doesn't include the key strength parameter β_t. On the other hand, MANN* introduces a new content-based write addressing mechanism called **Least Recently Used Access (LRUA)** as a replacement for the combined content/location NTM addressing mechanism. The LRUA write operation writes to either the least-used memory location or the most recently used one. There are two reasons for implementing this: to preserve recently stored information by writing new memories to the most rarely-used locations, and by writing new data to the last used location, the new information serves as a kind of update to the previously written state. But how does the model know which of the two options to use? The MANN* addressing mechanism interpolates between the two options by introducing a vector of usage weights $\mathbf{w}_t^u \in \mathbb{R}^d$. These weights are updated at each time step by adding the usage weights $\mathbf{w}_{t-1}^u$ at step *t-1* with the current read and write attention weights:

$$\mathbf{w}_t^u \leftarrow \gamma \mathbf{w}_{t-1}^u + \mathbf{w}_t^r + \mathbf{w}_t^w$$

Here, the scalar γ is a decay parameter, which determines the balance between the two components of the equation. MANN* also introduces the least recently used weights vector $\mathbf{w}_t^{lu}$, where each element of the vector is defined as follows:

$$w_t^{lu}(i) = \begin{cases} 0 & \text{if } w_t^u(i) > m(\mathbf{w}_t^u, n) \\ 1 & \text{if } w_t^u(i) \le m(\mathbf{w}_t^u, n) \end{cases}$$

Here, $m(\mathbf{w}_t^u, n)$ is the *n*th smallest element of the vector $\mathbf{w}_t$ and *n* is equal to the number of memory reads. At this point, we can compute the write weights, which are an interpolation between the read weights and the least-recently used weights at step *t-1*:

$$\mathbf{w}_t^w \leftarrow \sigma(\alpha)\mathbf{w}_{t-1}^r + (1 - \sigma(\alpha))\mathbf{w}_{t-1}^{lu}$$

Here, σ is the sigmoid function and α is a learnable scalar parameter, which indicates how to balance between the 2 input weights. Now, we can write new data to the memory, which is done in 2 steps: the first is for computing the least recently used location using the weights $\mathbf{w}_{t-1}^u$. The second step is the actual writing:

$$\mathbf{M}_t(i) \leftarrow \mathbf{M}_{t-1}(i) + w_t^w(i)\mathbf{k}_t$$

Here, $\mathbf{k}_t$ is the key vector we defined when we discussed NTM.

The MANN* paper goes into a bit more detail (compared to the original NTM paper) about the way the controller interacts with the input data and the read/write heads. The authors of the paper noted that their best performing models use LSTM (see `Chapter 7`, *Understanding Recurrent Networks*) controllers. So the following is how the LSTM controller plugs into the MANN* system:

- The controller inputs at step *t* are the concatenated vectors $[\mathbf{x}_t, \mathbf{y}_{t-1}]$, where $\mathbf{x}_t$ is the input data and $\mathbf{y}_{t-1}$ is the system's output at step *t-1*. In classification tasks, the outputs $\mathbf{y}_t$ are one-hot encoded class representations.
- The controller outputs at step *t* are the concatenated $\mathbf{o}_t = [\mathbf{h}_t, \mathbf{r}_t]$, where $\mathbf{h}_t$ is the LSTM cell hidden state and $\mathbf{r}_t$ is a result of the read operation. For classification tasks, we can use $\mathbf{o}_t$ as an input for a fully connected layer with softmax output, resulting in the expression $\mathbf{y}_t = \mathrm{softmax}(\mathbf{W}_o\mathbf{o}_t)$, where $\mathbf{W}_o$ is the fully connected layer weights.
- The key vector $\mathbf{k}_t$, which serves as a base for the attention weights of the read/write operations, is the LSTM cell state $\mathbf{c}_t$.

This concludes our discussion of MANNs and, indeed, the chapter.

Summary

In this chapter, we covered two categories of emerging NN models—GNNs and MANNs. We started with a short introduction to graphs and then we looked at several different types of GNN, including GraphNN, graph convolutional networks, graph attention networks, and graph autoencoders. We concluded the graph section by looking at the NGL and we implemented an NGL example using the TensorFlow-based NSL framework. Then we focused on memory-augmented networks, where we looked at the NTM and MANN* architectures.

In the next chapter, we'll look at the emerging field of meta learning, which involves making ML algorithms learn to learn.

10
Meta Learning

In Chapter 9, *Emerging Neural Network Designs*, we introduced new **neural network** (**NN**) architectures to tackle some of the limitations of existing **deep learning** (**DL**) algorithms. We discussed graph neural networks that are used to process structured data, represented as graphs. We also introduced memory augmented neural networks, which allow networks to use external memory. In this chapter, we'll look at how to improve DL algorithms by giving them the ability to learn more information using fewer training samples.

Let's illustrate this problem with an example. Imagine that a person has never seen a certain type of object, say a car (I know—highly unlikely). They will only need to see a car once to be able to recognize other cars as well. But this is not the case with DL algorithms. A DNN needs a lot of training samples (and sometimes data augmentation as well), to be able to recognize a certain class of object. Even the relatively small CIFAR-10 (https://www.cs.toronto.edu/~kriz/cifar.html) dataset contains 50,000 training images for only 10 classes of objects, the equivalent of 5,000 images per class.

Meta learning, also referred to as learning to learn, allows **machine learning** (**ML**) algorithms to leverage and channel knowledge, gained over multiple training tasks, to improve its training efficiency over a new task. Hopefully, in this way, the algorithm will require fewer training samples to learn the new task. The ability to train with fewer samples has two advantages: reduced training time and good performance when there is not enough training data. In that regard, the goals of meta learning are similar to the transfer learning mechanism that we introduced in Chapter 2, *Understanding Convolutional Networks*. In fact, we can think of transfer learning as a meta learning algorithm. But there are multiple approaches to meta learning. In this chapter, we'll discuss some of them.

This chapter will cover the following topics:

- Introduction to meta learning
- Metric-based meta learning
- Optimization-based meta learning

Introduction to meta learning

As we mentioned in the introduction, the goal of meta learning is to allow an ML algorithm (in our case, NN) to learn from relatively fewer training samples compared to standard supervised training. Some meta learning algorithms try to achieve this goal by finding a mapping between their existing knowledge of the domain of a well-known task to the domain of a new task. Other algorithms are simply designed from scratch to learn from fewer training samples. Yet another category of algorithms introduce new optimization training techniques, designed specifically with meta learning in mind. But before we discuss these topics, let's introduce some basic meta learning paradigms. In a standard ML supervised learning task, we aim to minimize the cost function $J(\theta)$ across a training dataset D by updating the model parameters θ (network weights, in the case of NNs). As we mentioned in the introduction, in meta learning we usually work with multiple datasets. Therefore, in a meta learning scenario, we can extend this definition by saying that we aim to minimize $J(\theta)$ over a distribution of these datasets $P(D)$:

$$\theta^* = \arg\min_{\theta} \mathbb{E}_{D \sim P(D)}[J_\theta(D)]$$

Here, θ^* is the optimal model parameters and $J_\theta(D)$ is the cost function, which now depends on the current dataset as well as the model parameters. In other words, the goal is to find model parameters θ^* such that the expected value (as described in Chapter 1, *The Nuts and Bolts of Neural Networks*, in the *Random variables and probability distributions* section) of the cost across all datasets $\mathbb{E}_{D \sim P(D)}[J_\theta(D)]$ is minimized. We can think of this scenario as training over a single dataset whose training samples are themselves datasets.

Next, let's continue by expanding the expression *fewer training samples* that we used in the introduction. In supervised training, we can refer to this scenario of scarce training data as **k-shot learning**, where k can be 0, 1, 2, and so on. Let's assume that our training dataset consists of labeled samples distributed among n classes. In k-shot learning, we have k labeled training samples for each of the n classes (the total number of labeled samples is $n \times k$). We refer to this dataset as the **support set**, and we'll denote it with S. We also have a **query set** Q, which contains unlabeled samples that belong to one of the n classes. Our goal is to correctly classify the samples of the query set. There are three types of k-shot learning: zero-shot, one-shot, and few-shot. Let's start with zero-shot learning.

Zero-shot learning

We'll begin with zero-shot learning ($k = 0$), where we know that a particular class exists, but we don't have any labeled samples of that class (that is, there is no support set). At first, this sounds impossible—how can we classify something we have never seen before? But in meta learning, this is not exactly the case. Recall that we leverage knowledge of previously learned tasks (let's denote them with a) over the task at hand (b). In that regard, zero-shot learning is a form of transfer learning. To understand how this works, let's imagine that a person has never seen an elephant (another highly unlikely example), yet they have to recognize one when they see a picture of it (new task b). However, the person has read in a book that the elephant is large, gray, has four legs, large ears, and a trunk (previous task a). Given this description, they'll easily recognize an elephant when they see it. In this example, the person applied their knowledge from the domain of a previously learned task (reading a book) to the domain of the new task (image classification).

In the context of ML, these features can be encoded as nonhuman readable embedding vectors. We can replicate the elephant recognition example in the NN realm by using language-modeling techniques, such as word2vec or transformers to encode a context-based embedding vector of the word *elephant*. We can also use a convolutional network (CNN) to produce an embedding vector $\mathbf{h}_b$ of an image of an elephant. Let's look at how to implement this step by step:

1. Apply encoders f and g (NNs) over labeled and unlabeled samples a and b to produce embeddings $\mathbf{h}_a$ and $\mathbf{h}_b$ respectively.
2. Use a mapping function to transform $\mathbf{h}_b$ to the vector space of the embeddings $\mathbf{h}_{a^*}$ of the known samples. The mapping function could be an NN as well. Furthermore, the encoders and the mapping could be combined in a single model and learned jointly.

3. Once we have the transformed representation of the query sample, we can compare it to all representations h_a^* using a similarity measure (for example, cosine similarity). We then assume that the query sample's class is the same as the class of the support sample most closely related to the query. The following diagram illustrates this scenario:

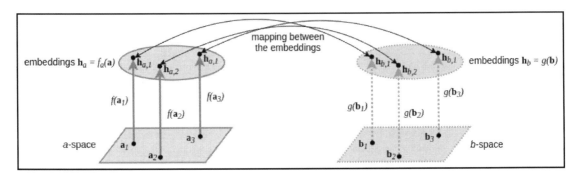

Zero-shot learning is possible thanks to transfer learning. Inspired by Chapter 15 of http://www.deeplearningbook.org/

Let's formalize the zero-shot learning scenario. In a traditional classification task with a single dataset, the NN represents the conditional probability $P_\theta(y|x)$, where y is the label of input sample x and θ is the model parameters. In meta learning, x and y belong to the traditional dataset, but we introduce a random variable T that describes the new task we're interested in. In our example, x would be the context (surrounding words) of the word *elephant*, and the label y is a one-hot encoding of the class elephant. On the other hand, T will be an image we're interested in; therefore, the meta learning model represents a new conditional probability $P_\theta(y|x, T)$. The zero-shot scenario we just described is part of so-called metric-based meta learning (we'll see more examples of this later in the chapter). For now, let's move on to one-shot learning.

One-shot learning

In this section, we'll be looking at **one-shot learning** ($k = 1$) and its generalization **few-shot learning** ($k > 1$). In this case, the support set is not empty and we have one or more labeled samples of each class. This is an advantage over the zero-shot scenario because we can rely on labeled samples from the same domain instead of using a mapping from the labeled samples of another domain. Therefore, we have a single encoder f and no need for additional mapping.

An example of a one-shot learning task is a company's facial recognition system. This system should be able to recognize the identity of an employee based on a single photo. It should be possible to add new employees with a single photo as well. Let's note that in this scenario, adding a new employee is equivalent to adding a new class that has already been seen (the photo itself), but which is otherwise unknown. This is in contrast to zero-shot learning, where we had unseen, but known classes. A naive way to solve this task is with a classification **feed-forward network** (**FFN**), which takes the photo as input and ends with a softmax output, where each class represents one employee. This system will have two major disadvantages. First, every time we add a new employee, we have to retrain the whole model using the full dataset of employees. And second, we need multiple images per employee to train the model.

 The following description is based on the method introduced in *Matching Networks for One Shot Learning* (https://arxiv.org/abs/1606.04080). The paper has two major contributions: a novel one-shot training procedure and a special network architecture. In this section, we'll discuss the training procedure and we'll describe the network architecture in the *Matching networks* section.

We can also solve this task within the one-shot learning framework. The first thing we'll need is a pretrained network that can produce embedding vectors of the employee images. We'll assume that the pretraining allows the network to produce a sufficiently unique embedding **h** for each photo. We'll also store all employee photos in some external database. For performance reasons, we can apply the network to all photos and then store the embedding of each image as well. Let's focus on the use case where the system has to identify an existing employee when he or she tries to authenticate with a new photo. We'll use the network to produce an embedding of that photo and then we'll compare it to the embeddings in the database. We'll identify the employee by taking the database embedding that most closely matches the embedding of the current photo.

Next, let's look at the use case when a new employee is added to the system. Here, we'll simply take a photo of that employee and store it in the database. In this way, every time the employee tries to authenticate, their current photo will be compared to the initial one (along with all other photos). In this way, we have added a new class (the employee) without any changes to the network. We can think of the employee photo/identification database as a support set $S = \{ (\mathbf{x}_1, y_1), (\mathbf{x}_2, y_2), \ldots, (\mathbf{x}_n, y_n) \}$. The goal of the task is to map this support set to a classifier $c_S(\hat{\mathbf{x}})$, which outputs a probability distribution over the labels $\hat{y}$, given a previously unseen query sample $\hat{\mathbf{x}}$. In our case, the $(\hat{\mathbf{x}}, \hat{y})$ pairs represent new employees (that is, new query samples and new classes) that were not part of the system before.

In other words, we want to be able to predict never before seen classes with the help of the existing support set. We'll define the mapping $S \to c_S(\hat{x})$ as a conditional probability $P_\theta(\hat{y}|\hat{x}, S)$, implemented by a neural network with weights θ. Additionally, we can also plug a new support set S' into the same network, which would lead to a new probability distribution $P_\theta(\hat{y}|\hat{x}, S')$. In this way, we can condition the outputs over the new training data without changing the network weights θ.

Now that we are familiar with k-shot learning, let's look at how to train an algorithm with few-shot datasets.

Meta-training and meta-testing

The scenarios we described in the *Zero-shot learning* and *One-shot learning* sections are referred to as **meta-testing phases**. In this phase, we leverage the knowledge of a pretrained network and apply it to predict previously unseen labels with the help of only a small support set (or no support set at all). We also have a **meta-training phase**, where we train a network from scratch in a few-shot context. The authors of *Matching Networks for One Shot Learning* introduce a meta-training algorithm that closely matches the meta-testing. This is necessary so that we can train the model under the same conditions that we expect it to work in the testing phase. Since we train the network from scratch, the training set (denoted with **D**) is not a few-shot dataset, and instead contains a sufficient number of labeled examples of each class. Nevertheless, the training process simulates a few-shot dataset.

Here's how it works:

1. Sample a set of labels $L \sim T$, where T is the set of all labels in D. To clarify, L contains only part of all labels T. In this way, the training mimics the testing when the model sees just a couple of samples. For example, adding a new employee to the facial recognition system requires a single image and a label.
2. Sample a support set $S^L \sim D$, where the labels of all samples in S^L are only part of L $y_{S^L} \in L$. The support set contains k samples of each label.
3. Sample a training batch $B^L \sim D$, where $y_{B^L} \in L$ (the same as the support set). The combination of S^L and B^L represents one training **episode**. We can think of the episode as a separate learning **task** with its corresponding dataset. Alternatively, in supervised learning, one episode is simply a single training sample.

4. Optimize the network weights over the episode. The network represents the probability $P_\theta(\hat{y}|\hat{x}, S)$ and uses both S^L and B^L as inputs. To clarify, the set B^L consists of the $(\hat{x}, \hat{y})$ tuples, conditioned on the support set S^L. This is the "meta" part of the training process, because the model learns to learn from a support set to minimize the loss over the full batch. The model uses the following cross-entropy objective:

$$\theta = \arg\max_\theta E_{L\sim T}\left[E_{S^L\sim D, B^L\sim D}\left[\sum_{(\mathbf{x},y)\in B^L}\log P_\theta(y|\mathbf{x}, S^L)\right]\right]$$

Here, $E_{L\sim T}$ and $E_{S^L\sim D, B^L\sim D}$ reflect the sampling of labels and examples respectively. Let's compare this to the same task, but in a classic supervised learning scenario. In this case, we sample mini batches B from the dataset D and there is no support set. The sampling is random and doesn't depend on the labels. Then, the preceding formula would transform to the following:

$$\theta = \arg\max_\theta E_{B\sim D}\left[\sum_{(\mathbf{x},y)\in B}\log P_\theta(y|\mathbf{x})\right]$$

Meta learning algorithms can be classified into three main categories: metric-based, model-based, and optimization-based. In this chapter, we'll focus on the metric- and optimization-based approaches (excluding model-based). Model-based meta learning algorithms don't impose any restrictions on the type of ML algorithm that implements the probability $P_\theta(\hat{y}|\hat{x}, S)$. That is, there is no requirement for encoder and mapping functions. Instead, they rely on network architectures specifically adapted to work with a small number of labeled samples. You may recall that in Chapter 9, *Emerging Neural Network Designs*, we introduced one such model when we looked at the *One-shot Learning with Memory-Augmented Neural Networks* paper(https://arxiv.org/abs/1605.06065). As the name suggests, the paper demonstrates the use of memory-augmented neural networks in a one-shot learning framework. Since we have already discussed the network architecture, and the training process is similar to the one we described in this section, we won't include another model-based example in this chapter.

Now that we've introduced the basics of meta learning, in the following section we'll focus on metric-based learning algorithms.

Metric-based meta learning

We mentioned a metric-based approach when we discussed the one-shot scenario in the *Introduction to meta learning* section, but this approach applies to *k*-shot learning in general. The idea is to measure the similarity between the unlabeled query sample $\hat{\mathbf{x}}$ and all other samples $\mathbf{x}$ of the support set. Using these similarity scores, we can compute a probability distribution $\hat{y}$. The following formula reflects this mechanism:

$$P(\hat{y}|\hat{\mathbf{x}}, S) = \sum_{i=1}^{|S|} \alpha(\hat{\mathbf{x}}, \mathbf{x}_i) y_i$$

Here, α is the similarity measure between the query samples and $|S|$ is the size of the support set with n classes and k samples of each class. To clarify, the label of the query sample is simply a linear combination of all samples of the support set. The classes of the samples with higher similarities will have higher contributions to the distribution of the label of the query sample. We can implement α as a clustering algorithm (for example, *k*-nearest neighbors) or an attention model (as we'll see later in the upcoming section). In the case of zero-shot learning, this process has two formal steps: compute sample embeddings and then compute the similarity between the embeddings. But the preceding formula is a generalized combination of the two steps, and computes the similarity directly from the query samples (although internally, the steps could still be separate). The two-step metric-based learning (including the encoders *f* and *g*) is illustrated in the following diagram:

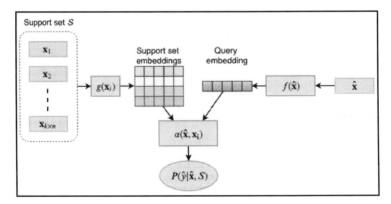

Generic metric-based learning algorithm

In the next few sections, we'll discuss some of the more popular metric meta-learning algorithms.

Matching networks for one-shot learning

We already discussed the training procedure that was introduced alongside matching networks in the *Introduction to meta learning* section. Now, let's focus on the actual model, starting with the similarity measure, which we outlined in the *Metric-based meta learning* section. One way to implement this is with cosine similarity (denoted with c), followed by softmax:

$$\alpha(\hat{\mathbf{x}}, \mathbf{x}_i) = \frac{\exp(c(f(\hat{\mathbf{x}}), g(\mathbf{x}_i)))}{\sum_j \exp(c(f(\hat{\mathbf{x}}), g(\mathbf{x}_j)))}$$

Here, f and g are encoders of the samples of the new task and the support set respectively (as we discussed, it's possible that f and g are the same function). The encoders could be CNNs for image inputs or word embeddings, such as word2vec in the case of natural language processing tasks. This formula is very similar to the attention mechanism that we introduced in `Chapter 8`, *Sequence-to-Sequence Models and Attention*.

With the current definition, the encoder g only encodes one support sample at a time, independently of the other samples of the support set. However, it's possible that the embeddings $g(\mathbf{x}_i)$ and $g(\mathbf{x}_j)$ of two samples i and j are very close in the embedding feature space, but that the two samples have different labels. The authors of the paper propose modifying g to take the whole support set S as additional input: $g(\mathbf{x}_i, S)$. In this way, the encoder could condition the embedding vector of $\mathbf{x}_i$ on S and avoid this problem. We can apply similar logic to the encoder f as well. The paper refers to new embedding functions as **full context embeddings**.

Let's look at how to implement full context embeddings over f. First, we'll introduce a new function $f'(\hat{\mathbf{x}})$, which is similar to the old encoder (before including S as input)—that is, f' could be a CNN or word-embedding model, which creates sample embedding, independently of the support set. The result of $f'(\hat{\mathbf{x}})$ will serve as the input for the full embedding function $f(f'(\hat{\mathbf{x}}), S)$. We'll treat the support set as a sequence, which allows us to embed it using long short-term memory (LSTM). Because of this, computing the embedding vector is a sequential process of multiple steps.

However, S is a set, which implies that the order of samples in the sequence is not relevant. To reflect this, the algorithm also uses a special attention mechanism over the elements of the support set. In this way, the embedding function can attend to all previous elements of the sequence, regardless of their order.

Let's see how one step of the encoder works:

1. $\hat{\mathbf{h}}_t, \mathbf{c}_t = \mathrm{LSTM}(f'(\hat{\mathbf{x}}), [\mathbf{h}_{t-1}, \mathbf{r}_{t-1}], \mathbf{c}_{t-1})$, where t is the current element of the input sequence, $\hat{\mathbf{h}}_t$ is an intermediate hidden state, $\mathbf{h}_{t-1}$ is the hidden state at step t-1, and $\mathbf{c}_{t-1}$ is the cell state. The attention mechanism is implemented with a vector $\mathbf{r}_{t-1}$, which is concatenated to the hidden state $\mathbf{h}_{t-1}$.

2. $\mathbf{h}_t = \hat{\mathbf{h}}_t + f'(\hat{\mathbf{x}})$, where $\mathbf{h}_t$ is the final hidden state at step t.

3. $\mathbf{r}_{t-1} = \sum_{i=1}^{|S|} \alpha(\mathbf{h}_{t-1}, g(\mathbf{x}_i)) g(\mathbf{x}_i)$, where $|S|$ is the size of the support set, g is an embedding function for the support set, and α is a similarity measure, which is defined as multiplicative attention, followed by a softmax:

$$\alpha(\mathbf{h}_{t-1}, g(\mathbf{x}_i)) = \mathrm{softmax}(\mathbf{h}_{t-1}^{\mathsf{T}} g(\mathbf{x}_i))$$

The process continues for T steps (T is a parameter). We can summarize it with the following formula:

$$f(\hat{\mathbf{x}}, S) = \mathrm{attnLSTM}(f'(\hat{\mathbf{x}}), g(S), T)$$

Next, let's focus on the full context embeddings of g. Like f, we'll introduce a new function, $g'(\mathbf{x}_i)$, which is similar to the old encoder (before including S as input). The authors propose to use a bidirectional LSTM encoder, defined as follows:

$$g(\mathbf{x}_i, S) = \overrightarrow{\mathbf{h}}_i + \overleftarrow{\mathbf{h}}_i + g'(\mathbf{x}_i)$$

Here, $\overrightarrow{\mathbf{h}}_i$ and $\overleftarrow{\mathbf{h}}_i$ are the cell hidden states in both directions. We can define them as follows:

$$\overrightarrow{\mathbf{h}}_i, \overrightarrow{\mathbf{c}}_i = \mathrm{LSTM}(g'(\mathbf{x}_i), \overrightarrow{\mathbf{h}}_{i-1}, \overrightarrow{\mathbf{c}}_{i-1})$$
$$\overleftarrow{\mathbf{h}}_i, \overleftarrow{\mathbf{c}}_i = \mathrm{LSTM}(g'(\mathbf{x}_i), \overleftarrow{\mathbf{h}}_{i+1}, \overleftarrow{\mathbf{c}}_{i+1})$$

In the next section, we'll discuss another metric-based learning approach called Siamese networks.

Siamese networks

In this section, we'll discuss the *Siamese Neural Networks for One-shot Image Recognition* paper (`https://www.cs.cmu.edu/~rsalakhu/papers/oneshot1.pdf`). A Siamese network is a system of two identical base networks, as illustrated in the following diagram:

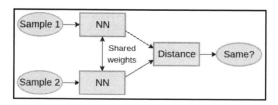

Siamese networks

The two networks are identical in the sense that they share the same architecture and the same parameters (weights). Each network is fed a single input sample and the last hidden layer produces an embedding vector of that sample. The two embeddings are fed to a distance measure. The distance is further processed to produce the final output of the system, which is binary and represents a verification of whether the two samples are from the same class. The distance measure itself is differentiable, which allows us to train the networks as a single system. The authors of the paper recommend using *L1* distance:

$$L1 = |f_\theta(\mathbf{x}_i) - f_\theta(\mathbf{x}_j)|$$

Here, f_θ is the base network. Using Siamese networks in a one-shot learning scenario follows the same general idea we described in the *Meta-training and meta-testing* section, but in this case, the task is simplified because we always have only two classes (same or not same), regardless of the actual number of classes in the dataset. In the meta-training phase, we train the system with a large labeled dataset. We do this by generating samples of image pairs and binary labels with either the same or a different class. In the meta-testing phase, we have a single query sample and a support set. We then create multiple pairs of images, where each pair contains the query sample and a single sample of the support set. We have as many image pairs as the size of the support set. Then, we feed all pairs to the Siamese system and we pick the pair with the smallest distance. The class of the query image is determined by the class of the support sample of that pair.

Implementing Siamese networks

In this section, we'll use Keras to implement a simple example of Siamese networks, which will verify whether two MNIST images are from the same class or not. It is partially based on `https://github.com/keras-team/keras/blob/master/examples/mnist_siamese.py`.

Let's look at how to do this step by step:

1. We'll start with the import statements:

   ```
   import random

   import numpy as np
   import tensorflow as tf
   ```

2. Next, we'll implement the `create_pairs` function to create the train/test dataset (both for training and testing):

   ```
   def create_pairs(inputs: np.ndarray, labels: np.ndarray):
       num_classes = 10

       digit_indices = [np.where(labels == i)[0] for i in
   range(num_classes)]
       pairs = list()
       labels = list()
       n = min([len(digit_indices[d]) for d in range(num_classes)]) -
   1

       for d in range(num_classes):
           for i in range(n):
               z1, z2 = digit_indices[d][i], digit_indices[d][i + 1]
               pairs += [[inputs[z1], inputs[z2]]]
               inc = random.randrange(1, num_classes)
               dn = (d + inc) % num_classes
               z1, z2 = digit_indices[d][i], digit_indices[dn][i]
               pairs += [[inputs[z1], inputs[z2]]]
               labels += [1, 0]

       return np.array(pairs), np.array(labels, dtype=np.float32)
   ```

   Each dataset sample consists of an input pair of two MNIST images and a binary label, which indicates whether they are from the same class. The function creates an equal number of true/false samples distributed over all classes (digits).

3. Next, let's implement the `create_base_network` function, which defines one branch of the Siamese network:

```
def create_base_network():
    return tf.keras.models.Sequential([
        tf.keras.layers.Flatten(),
        tf.keras.layers.Dense(128, activation='relu'),
        tf.keras.layers.Dropout(0.1),
        tf.keras.layers.Dense(128, activation='relu'),
        tf.keras.layers.Dropout(0.1),
        tf.keras.layers.Dense(64, activation='relu'),
    ])
```

The branch represents the base network that starts from the input and goes to the last hidden layer, before the distance measure. We'll use a simple NN of three fully connected layers.

4. Next, let's build the whole training system, starting from the MNIST dataset:

```
(x_train, y_train), (x_test, y_test) =
tf.keras.datasets.mnist.load_data()
x_train = x_train.astype(np.float32)
x_test = x_test.astype(np.float32)
x_train /= 255
x_test /= 255
input_shape = x_train.shape[1:]
```

5. We'll use the raw dataset to create the actual train and test verification datasets:

```
train_pairs, tr_labels = create_pairs(x_train, y_train)
test_pairs, test_labels = create_pairs(x_test, y_test)
```

6. Then, we'll build the base portion of the Siamese network:

```
base_network = create_base_network()
```

The `base_network` object is shared between the two forks of the Siamese system. In this way, we ensure that the weights are the same in the two branches.

7. Next, let's create the two branches:

```
# Create first half of the siamese system
input_a = tf.keras.layers.Input(shape=input_shape)

# Note how we reuse the base_network in both halfs
encoder_a = base_network(input_a)

# Create the second half of the siamese system
input_b = tf.keras.layers.Input(shape=input_shape)
encoder_b = base_network(input_b)
```

8. Next, we'll create the L1 distance, which uses the outputs of `encoder_a` and `encoder_b`. It is implemented as a `tf.keras.layers.Lambda` layer:

```
l1_dist = tf.keras.layers.Lambda(
    lambda embeddings: tf.keras.backend.abs(embeddings[0] -
embeddings[1])) \
    ([encoder_a, encoder_b])
```

9. Then, we'll create the final fully connected layer, which takes the output of the distance and compresses it to a single sigmoid output:

```
flattened_weighted_distance = tf.keras.layers.Dense(1,
activation='sigmoid') \
    (l1_dist)
```

10. Finally, we can build the model and initiate the training for 20 epochs:

```
# Build the model
model = tf.keras.models.Model([input_a, input_b],
flattened_weighted_distance)

# Train
model.compile(loss='binary_crossentropy',
              optimizer=tf.keras.optimizers.Adam(),
              metrics=['accuracy'])

model.fit([train_pairs[:, 0], train_pairs[:, 1]], tr_labels,
          batch_size=128,
          epochs=20,
          validation_data=([test_pairs[:, 0], test_pairs[:, 1]],
test_labels))
```

If everything goes alright, the model will achieve around 98% accuracy.

Next, we'll discuss yet another metric learning method called prototypical networks.

Prototypical networks

In a few short learning scenarios, it would be very easy for a high-capacity model (an NN with many layers and parameters) to overfit. Prototypical networks (as discussed in the *Prototypical Networks for Few-shot Learning* paper, `https://arxiv.org/abs/1703.05175`) address this issue by computing a special prototype vector of each label, which is based on all samples of that label. The same prototypical network computes an embedding of the query samples as well. Then, we measure the distance between the query embedding and the prototypes and assign the query class accordingly (more details on this later in the section).

Prototypical networks work for both zero-shot and few-shot learning, as illustrated in the following diagram:

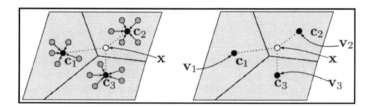

Left: Few-shot learning: Right: Zero-shot learning. Source: https://arxiv.org/abs/1703.05175

Let's start with the few-shot learning scenario, where the prototype vector c_k of each class k is computed as the element-wise mean value of all samples of that class:

$$c_k = \frac{1}{|S_k|} \sum_{(\mathbf{x}_i, y_i) \in S_k} f_\theta(\mathbf{x}_i)$$

Here, $|S_k|$ is the number of samples in the support set of class k and f_θ is the prototypical network with parameters θ. In the zero-shot learning scenario, the prototype is computed as follows:

$$c_k = g_\vartheta(\mathbf{v}_k)$$

Here, $\mathbf{v}_k$ is a metadata vector, which gives a high-level description of the label, and g_ϑ is the embedding function (encoder) of that vector. The metadata vectors could be given in advance or computed.

Each new query sample is classified as a softmax over the distance between the sample embedding and all prototypes:

$$P_\theta(\hat{y} = k | \hat{\mathbf{x}}) = \frac{\exp(-d(f_\theta(\hat{\mathbf{x}}), \mathbf{c}_k))}{\sum_{k'} \exp(-d(f_\theta(\hat{\mathbf{x}}), \mathbf{c}_{k'}))}$$

Here, d is a distance measure (for example, the linear Euclidean distance).

Now that we have an overview of the main idea behind prototype networks, let's focus on how to train them (the procedure is similar to the training we outlined in the *Introduction to meta learning* section).

Before we start, we'll introduce some notations:

- D is the few-shot training set.
- D_k is the training samples of D of class k.
- T is the total number of classes in the dataset.
- $L \sim T$ is the subset of labels, selected for each training episode.
- N_S is the number of support samples per class per episode.
- N_Q is the number of query samples per episode.

The algorithm starts with the training set D and outputs the result of the cost function J. Let's look at how it works step by step:

1. Sample a set of labels $L \sim T$.

2. For each class k in L, do the following:
    1. Sample support set $S_k \sim D_k$, where $|S_k| = N_s$.
    2. Sample query set $Q_k \sim D_k$, $Q_k \setminus S_k$, where $|Q_k| = N_q$.
    3. Compute the class prototype from the support set:

$$c_k = \frac{1}{|S_k|} \sum_{(\mathbf{x}_i, y_i) \in S_k} f_\theta(\mathbf{x}_i)$$

3. Initialize the cost function $J(\theta) = 0$.
4. For each class k in L, do the following:
    1. For each query sample $(\hat{\mathbf{x}}, \hat{y}) \in Q_k$, update the cost function as follows:

$$J(\theta) \rightarrow J(\theta) + \frac{1}{|L|N_Q} [d(f_\theta(\hat{\mathbf{x}}), c_k) + \log \sum_{k'} \exp(-d(f_\theta(\hat{\mathbf{x}}), c_{k'}))]$$

Intuitively, the first component (in the square braces) minimizes the distance between the query and its corresponding prototype of the same class. The second term maximizes the sum of the distance between the query and the prototypes of the other classes.

The authors of the paper demonstrated their work on the Omniglot dataset (https://github.com/brendenlake/omniglot), which contains 1,623 images of handwritten characters collected from 50 alphabets. There are 20 examples associated with each character, where each example is drawn by a different human subject. The goal is to classify a new character as one of the 1,623 classes. They trained prototypical networks using Euclidean distance, one-shot, and five-shot scenarios, and training episodes with 60 classes and 5 query points per class. The following screenshot shows a *t*-SNE (https://lvdmaaten.github.io/tsne/) visualization of the embeddings of a subset of similar (but not the same) characters of the same alphabet, learned by the prototypical network.

Even though the visualized characters are minor variations of each other, the network is able to cluster the hand-drawn characters closely around the class prototypes. Several misclassified characters are highlighted in rectangles, along with arrows pointing to the correct prototype:

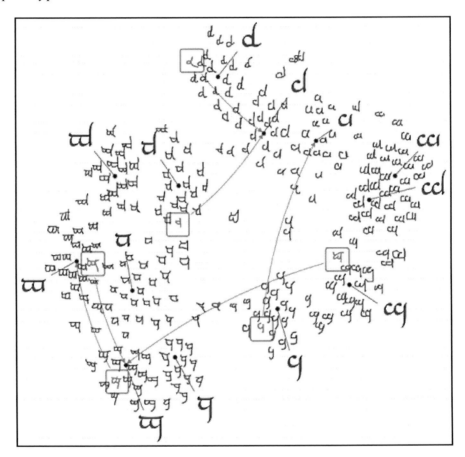

A *t*-SNE visualization of the embeddings of a subset of similar characters. learned by the network: source: https://arxiv.org/abs/1703.05175

This concludes our description of prototypical networks and metric-based meta learning as well. Next, we'll focus on model-based methods.

Optimization-based learning

So far, we have discussed metric-based learning, which uses a special similarity measure (which is hard to overfit) to adapt the representational power of NNs with the ability to learn from datasets with few training samples. Alternatively, model-based approaches rely on improved network architectures (for example, memory augmented networks) to solve the same issue. In this section, we'll discuss optimization-based approaches, which adjust the training framework to adapt to the few-shot learning requirements. More specifically, we'll focus on a particular algorithm called **model-agnostic meta learning** (MAML; *Model-Agnostic Meta-Learning for Fast Adaptation of Deep Networks*, `https://arxiv.org/abs/1703.03400`). As the name suggests, MAML can be applied over any learning problem and model that is trained with gradient descent.

To quote the original paper:

> *The key idea underlying our method is to train the model's initial parameters such that the model has maximal performance on a new task after the parameters have been updated through one or more gradient steps computed with a small amount of data from that new task.*
>
> *...*
>
> *The process of training a model's parameters such that a few gradient steps, or even a single gradient step, can produce good results on a new task can be viewed from a feature learning standpoint as building an internal representation that is broadly suitable for many tasks. If the internal representation is suitable to many tasks, simply fine-tuning the parameters slightly (e.g. by primarily modifying the top layer weights in a feedforward model) can produce good results. In effect, our procedure optimizes for models that are easy and fast to fine-tune, allowing the adaptation to happen in the right space for fast learning. From a dynamical systems standpoint, our learning process can be viewed as maximizing the sensitivity of the loss functions of new tasks with respect to the parameters: when the sensitivity is high, small local changes to the parameters can lead to large improvements in the task loss.*
>
> *The primary contribution of this work is a simple model and task-agnostic algorithm for meta-learning that trains a model's parameters such that a small number of gradient updates will lead to fast learning on a new task. We demonstrate the algorithm on different model types, including fully connected and convolutional networks, and in several distinct domains, including few-shot regression, image classification, and reinforcement learning. Our evaluation shows that our meta-learning algorithm compares favorably to state-of-the-art one-shot learning methods designed specifically for supervised classification, while using fewer parameters, but that it can also be readily applied to regression and can accelerate reinforcement learning in the presence of task variability, substantially outperforming direct pretraining as initialization.*

To understand MAML, we'll introduce some paper-specific notations (some of them overlap with notations from the preceding sections, but I prefer to preserve the originals from the paper):

- We'll denote the model (neural network) with f_θ, which maps inputs $\mathbf{x}$ to outputs $\mathbf{a}$.
- We'll denote the full training set with $\mathcal{D}$ (equivalent to the dataset D). Similar to the meta-training of the *Meta-training and meta-testing* section, we sample tasks $\mathcal{T}$ (equivalent to episodes) from $\mathcal{D}$ during training. This process is defined as a distribution over tasks $p(\mathcal{T})$.
- We'll denote one task (an episode) with $\mathcal{T} = \{\mathcal{L}(\mathbf{x}_1, \mathbf{a}_1, \ldots, \mathbf{x}_H, \mathbf{a}_H), q(\mathbf{x}_1), q(\mathbf{x}_{t+1}|\mathbf{x}_t, \mathbf{a}_t), H\}$. It is defined by a loss function $\mathcal{L}(\mathbf{x}_1, \mathbf{a}_1, \ldots, \mathbf{x}_H, \mathbf{a}_H)$ (equivalent to the loss J), a distribution over the initial observations $q(\mathbf{x}_1)$, a transition distribution $q(\mathbf{x}_{t+1}|\mathbf{x}_t, \mathbf{a}_t)$, and length H.

To understand some components of the MAML task definition, let's note that besides supervised problems, MAML can be applied to **reinforcement learning** (**RL**) tasks as well. In the RL framework, we have an environment and an agent, which continuously interact with each other. At each step, the agent takes an action (from a number of possible actions) and the environment provides it with feedback. The feedback consists of a reward (which could be negative) and the new state of the environment after the agent's action. Then the agent takes a new action, and so on, as illustrated in the following diagram:

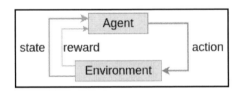

The RL framework

Many real-world tasks can be represented as RL problems, including games, where the agent is the player and the environment is the game universe.

We can view task $\mathcal{T}$ in both supervised and RL contexts. With a supervised task, we have labeled training samples $(\mathbf{x}_i, \mathbf{a}_i)$ in no particular order. But in an RL context, we can view the inputs $\mathbf{x}$ as the environment state and the outputs $\mathbf{a}$ as the agent's action. In this scenario, the task is sequential—state $\mathbf{x}_1$ leads to action $\mathbf{a}_1$, which in turn leads to state $\mathbf{x}_2$, and so on. The initial state of the environment is denoted as $q(\mathbf{x}_1)$. This means that $q(\mathbf{x}_{t+1}|\mathbf{x}_t, \mathbf{a}_t)$ is the probability of a new environment state $\mathbf{x}_{t+1}$, given the previous state $\mathbf{x}_t$ and the agent's action $\mathbf{a}_t$. The loss $\mathcal{L}$ can be viewed in both contexts as well: a misclassification loss in the supervised scenario and a cost function (the one that provides rewards) in the RL scenario.

Now that we're familiar with the notation, let's focus on the MAML algorithm. To understand how it works, we'll look at another quote from the original paper:

> *We propose a method that can learn the parameters of any standard model via meta-learning in such a way as to prepare that model for fast adaptation. The intuition behind this approach is that some internal representations are more transferable than others. For example, a neural network might learn internal features that are broadly applicable to all tasks in $p(\mathcal{T})$, rather than a single individual task. How can we encourage the emergence of such general-purpose representations? We take an explicit approach to this problem: since the model will be fine-tuned using a gradient-based learning rule on a new task, we will aim to learn a model in such a way that this gradient-based learning rule can make rapid progress on new tasks drawn from $p(\mathcal{T})$, without overfitting. In effect, we will aim to find model parameters that are sensitive to changes in the task, such that small changes in the parameters will produce large improvements on the loss function of any task drawn from $p(\mathcal{T})$, when altered in the direction of the gradient of that loss.*

After all this suspense, let's check the MAML algorithm, illustrated by the following pseudocode:

Require: $p(\mathcal{T})$: distribution over tasks
Require: α, β: step size hyperparameters
1: randomly initialize θ
2: **while** not done **do**
3:     Sample batch of tasks $\mathcal{T}_i \sim p(\mathcal{T})$
4:     **for all** $\mathcal{T}_i$ **do**
5:         Evaluate $\nabla_\theta \mathcal{L}_{\mathcal{T}_i}(f_\theta)$ with respect to K examples
6:         Compute adapted parameters with gradient descent: $\theta_i' = \theta - \alpha \nabla_\theta \mathcal{L}_{\mathcal{T}_i}(f_\theta)$
7:     **end for**
8:     Update $\theta \leftarrow \theta - \beta \nabla_\theta \sum_{\mathcal{T}_i \sim p(\mathcal{T})} \mathcal{L}_{\mathcal{T}_i}(f_{\theta_i'})$
9: **end while**

The MAML algorithm: source: https://arxiv.org/abs/1703.03400

The algorithm has an outer (line 2) and an inner loop (line 4). We'll start with the inner loop, which iterates over a number of tasks, sampled from the task distribution $\tau_i \sim p(\tau)$. Let's focus on a single loop iteration, which handles a single task $\mathcal{T}_i$ with $|S_i|$ training samples, where S_i is the support set of the task. The training samples are processed as batches in the following steps (lines 4 through 7 in the preceding screenshot):

1. Propagate the samples through the model and compute the loss $\mathcal{L}_{\mathcal{T}_i}(f_\theta)$.
2. Compute the error gradient $\nabla_\theta \mathcal{L}_{\mathcal{T}_i}(f_\theta)$ with respect to the initial parameters θ.
3. Propagate the gradient backward and compute the updated model parameters $\theta_i' = \theta - \alpha \nabla_\theta \mathcal{L}_{\mathcal{T}_i}(f_\theta)$, where α is the learning rate. Note that the parameters θ_i' are auxiliary and are specific for each task. To clarify, whenever the inner loop starts a new iteration for a new task $\mathcal{T}_{i+1}$, the model always starts with the same initial parameters θ. At the same time, each task stores its updated weights as an additional variable θ_i' without actually modifying the initial parameters θ (we'll update the original model in the outer loop).
4. We can perform such gradient updates multiple times over the same task. Think of it as training over multiple batches, implemented with an additional nested loop in the inner loop. In this scenario, the algorithm starts each iteration i with the weights θ_{i-1}' of the last iteration and not with the initial parameters θ, as shown in the following formula:

$$\theta_{i,0}' = \theta$$
$$\theta_{i,1}' = \theta_{i,0}' - \alpha \nabla_\theta \mathcal{L}_{\mathcal{T}_i}(f_{\theta_{i,0}'})$$
$$\theta_{i,2}' = \theta_{i,1}' - \alpha \nabla_\theta \mathcal{L}_{\mathcal{T}_i}(f_{\theta_{i,1}'})$$
$$\cdots$$
$$\theta_{i,p}' = \theta_{i,p-1}' - \alpha \nabla_\theta \mathcal{L}_{\mathcal{T}_i}(f_{\theta_{i,p-1}'})$$

In the case of multiple iterations, only the latest weights $\theta_{i,p}'$ are preserved.

Only after the inner loop is done can we proceed to update the initial parameters θ of the original model, based on the feedback of all tasks $\mathcal{T}_i$. To understand why this is necessary, let's take a look at the following diagram:

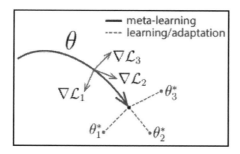

MAML that optimizes for parameters θ that can quickly adapt to new tasks: source: https://arxiv.org/abs/1703.03400

It shows the error gradients of three tasks $\{\nabla\mathcal{L}_1, \nabla\mathcal{L}_2, \nabla\mathcal{L}_3\}$ along the global error gradient. Let's assume that, instead of an inner/outer loop mechanism, we iterate sequentially over each task and simply update the original model parameters θ after each mini batch. We can see that the gradients of the different loss functions would push the model in completely different directions; for example, the error gradient of task 2 will contradict the gradient of task 1. MAML solves this problem by aggregating (but not applying) the updated weights for each task from the inner loop (the auxiliary parameters θ'_i). Then, we can compute the outer loop cost function (referred to as the meta-objective), combining the updated weights of all tasks all at once (this is a meta optimization across all tasks):

$$\min_{\theta} \sum_{T_i \sim p(T)} \mathcal{L}_{T_i}(f_{\theta'_i}) = \min_{\theta} \sum_{T_i \sim p(T)} \mathcal{L}_{T_i}(f_{\theta - \alpha \nabla_\theta \mathcal{L}_{T_i}(f_\theta)})$$

We use the following formula for the weight update of the main model parameters:

$$\theta \leftarrow \theta - \beta \nabla_\theta \sum_{T_i \sim p(T)} \mathcal{L}_{T_i}(f_{\theta'_i})$$

Here, β is the learning rate. The outer loop tasks T_i (line 8 of the MAML pseudocode program) are not the same as the ones from the inner loop (line 3). We can think of inner loop tasks as the training set and the tasks of the outer loop as the validation set. Note that we use task-specific parameters θ'_i to compute the losses, but we compute the loss gradient with respect to the initial parameters θ. To clarify, this means that we backpropagate through the outer loop and the inner loop as well. This is referred to as a second-order gradient, because we compute a gradient over the gradient (second derivative). This makes it possible to learn parameter that can generalize over a task even after a number of updates.

One disadvantage of MAML is that backpropagation through the full computational graph (the outer loop and inner loop) is computationally expensive. In addition, because of the large number of backpropagation steps, it can suffer from vanishing or exploding gradients. To better understand this, let's assume that we have a single task T_i (we'll omit it from the formulas); we perform a single gradient step (one inner loop iteration) for that task, and the inner loop's updated parameters are θ'. That is, we change the notation of the loss function from $\mathcal{L}_{T_i}(f(\theta'_{i,0}))$ to $\mathcal{L}(\theta')$. Then, the parameter update rule of the outer loop becomes the following:

$$\theta \leftarrow \theta - \beta \nabla_\theta \mathcal{L}(\theta')$$
$$\theta \leftarrow \theta - \beta \nabla_\theta \mathcal{L}(\theta - \alpha \nabla_\theta \mathcal{L}(\theta))$$

We can compute the gradient of the loss with respect to the initial parameters θ with the help of the chain rule (see Chapter 1, *The Nuts and Bolts Of Neural Networks*):

$$\nabla_\theta \mathcal{L}(\theta') = (\nabla_{\theta'} \mathcal{L}(\theta')) . (\nabla_\theta \theta')$$
$$= (\nabla_{\theta'} \mathcal{L}(\theta')) . (\nabla_\theta (\theta - \alpha \nabla_\theta \mathcal{L}(\theta)))$$

We can see that the formula includes second-degree derivative $\nabla_\theta(\theta - \alpha \nabla_\theta \mathcal{L}(\theta))$. The authors of MAML have proposed the so-called **first-order MAML (FOMAML)**, which simply ignores the term $\alpha \nabla_\theta \mathcal{L}(\theta)$. With this, we have $\nabla_\theta(\theta) = 1$ and the FOMAML gradient becomes:

$$\nabla_\theta \mathcal{L}(\theta') = \nabla_{\theta'} \mathcal{L}(\theta')$$

This simplified formula excludes the computationally expensive second-order gradient.

So far, we have looked at the generic MAML algorithm, which applies for both supervised and RL settings. Next, let's focus on the supervised version. Let's recall that in the supervised case, each task is a list of unrelated input/label pairs and the episode length H is 1. We can see the MAML algorithm for few-shot supervised learning in the following pseudocode (it's similar to the generic algorithm):

Require: $p(\mathcal{T})$: distribution over tasks
Require: α, β: step size hyperparameters
1: randomly initialize θ
2: **while** not done **do**
3:     Sample batch of tasks $\mathcal{T}_i \sim p(\mathcal{T})$
4:     **for all** $\mathcal{T}_i$ **do**
5:         Sample K datapoints $\mathcal{D} = \{\mathbf{x}^{(j)}, \mathbf{y}^{(j)}\}$ from $\mathcal{T}_i$
6:         Evaluate $\nabla_\theta \mathcal{L}_{\mathcal{T}_i}(f_\theta)$ using $\mathcal{D}$ and $\mathcal{L}_{\mathcal{T}_i}$ in Equation (2) or (3)
7:         Compute adapted parameters with gradient descent: $\theta'_i = \theta - \alpha \nabla_\theta \mathcal{L}_{\mathcal{T}_i}(f_\theta)$
8:         Sample datapoints $\mathcal{D}'_i = \{\mathbf{x}^{(j)}, \mathbf{y}^{(j)}\}$ from $\mathcal{T}_i$ for the meta-update
9:     **end for**
10:    Update $\theta \leftarrow \theta - \beta \nabla_\theta \sum_{\mathcal{T}_i \sim p(\mathcal{T})} \mathcal{L}_{\mathcal{T}_i}(f_{\theta'_i})$ using each $\mathcal{D}'_i$ and $\mathcal{L}_{\mathcal{T}_i}$ in Equation 2 or 3
11: **end while**

MAML for few-shot supervised learning: source: https://arxiv.org/abs/1703.03400

In the preceding code, equations 2 and 3 both refer to cross-entropy losses for classification tasks or mean square errors for regression tasks, $\mathcal{D}$ refers to the inner loop training set, and $\mathcal{D}'$ refers to the validation set of the outer loop.

Finally, let's discuss the RL scenario, as illustrated by the following pseudocode:

Require: $p(\mathcal{T})$: distribution over tasks
Require: α, β: step size hyperparameters
1: randomly initialize θ
2: **while** not done **do**
3:     Sample batch of tasks $\mathcal{T}_i \sim p(\mathcal{T})$
4:     **for all** $\mathcal{T}_i$ **do**
5:         Sample K trajectories $\mathcal{D} = \{(\mathbf{x}_1, \mathbf{a}_1, ...\mathbf{x}_H)\}$ using f_θ in $\mathcal{T}_i$
6:         Evaluate $\nabla_\theta \mathcal{L}_{\mathcal{T}_i}(f_\theta)$ using $\mathcal{D}$ and $\mathcal{L}_{\mathcal{T}_i}$ in Equation 4
7:         Compute adapted parameters with gradient descent: $\theta'_i = \theta - \alpha \nabla_\theta \mathcal{L}_{\mathcal{T}_i}(f_\theta)$
8:         Sample trajectories $\mathcal{D}'_i = \{(\mathbf{x}_1, \mathbf{a}_1, ...\mathbf{x}_H)\}$ using $f_{\theta'_i}$ in $\mathcal{T}_i$
9:     **end for**
10:    Update $\theta \leftarrow \theta - \beta \nabla_\theta \sum_{\mathcal{T}_i \sim p(\mathcal{T})} \mathcal{L}_{\mathcal{T}_i}(f_{\theta'_i})$ using each $\mathcal{D}'_i$ and $\mathcal{L}_{\mathcal{T}_i}$ in Equation 4
11: **end while**

MAML for few-shot reinforcement learning: source: https://arxiv.org/abs/1703.03400

Each sample $\mathcal{D} = \{(x_1, a_1, \ldots, x_H, a_1)\}$ represents a trajectory of one game episode, where the environment presents the agent with its current state x_t at step t. In turn, the agent (NN) samples use **policy** f_θ to map states x_t to a distribution over actions $a_i = f_\theta(x_i)$. The model uses a special type of loss function, which aims to train the network to maximize rewards over all steps of the episode.

Summary

In this chapter, we looked at the field of meta learning, which can be described as learning to learn. We started with an introduction to meta learning. More specifically, we talked about zero-shot and few-shot learning, as well as meta training and meta testing. Then, we focused on several metric-based learning approaches. We looked at matching networks, implemented an example of a Siamese network, and we introduced prototypical networks. Next, we focused on optimization-based learning, where we introduced the MAML algorithm.

In the next chapter, we'll learn about an exciting topic: automated vehicles.

11
Deep Learning for Autonomous Vehicles

Let's think about how **autonomous vehicles** (**AVs**) will affect our lives. For one thing, instead of focusing our attention on driving, we'll be able to do something else during our trip. Catering to the needs of such travelers could probably spawn a whole industry in itself. But that's just an added bonus. If we can be more productive or just relax during our travels, it is likely that we'll start traveling more, not to mention the benefits for people with limited ability to drive themselves. Making such an essential and basic commodity as transportation more accessible has the potential to transform our lives. And that's just the effect on us as individuals—AVs can have profound effects on the economy too, starting from delivery services to just-in-time manufacturing. In short, making AVs work is a very high-stakes game. No wonder, then, that in recent years the research in this area has moved from the academic world to the real economy. Companies from Waymo, Uber, and NVIDIA to virtually all major vehicle manufacturers are rushing to develop AVs.

However, we are not there just yet. One of the reasons for this is that self-driving is a complex task, composed of multiple subproblems, each a major task in its own right. To navigate successfully, the vehicle's program needs an accurate 3D model of the environment. The way to construct such a model is to combine the signals coming from multiple sensors. Once we have the model, we still need to solve the actual driving task. Think about the many unexpected and unique situations a driver has to overcome without crashing. But even if we create a driving policy, it needs to be accurate almost 100% of the time. Say that our AV will successfully stop at 99 out of 100 red traffic lights. 99% accuracy is a great success for any other **machine learning** (**ML**) task; not so for autonomous driving, where even a single mistake can lead to a crash.

In this chapter, we'll explore the applications of deep learning in AVs. We'll look at how to use deep networks to help the vehicle make sense of its surrounding environment. We'll also see how to use them in actually controlling the vehicle.

This chapter will cover the following topics:

- Introduction to AVs
- Components of an AV system
- Introduction to 3D data processing
- Imitation driving policy
- Driving policy with ChauffeurNet

Introduction to AVs

We'll start this section with a brief history of AV research (which started surprisingly long ago). We'll also try to define the different levels of AV automation according to the **Society of Automotive Engineers** (SAE).

Brief history of AV research

The first serious attempts to implement self-driving cars began in the 1980s in Europe and the USA. Since the mid 2000s, progress has rapidly accelerated. The first major effort in the area was the Eureka Prometheus Project (https://en.wikipedia.org/wiki/Eureka_Prometheus_Project), which lasted from 1987 to 1995. It culminated in 1995, when an autonomous Mercedes-Benz S-Class took a 1,600 km trip from Munich to Copenhagen and back using computer vision. At some points, the car achieved speeds of up to 175 km/h on the German Autobahn (fun fact: some sections of the Autobahn don't have speed restrictions). The car was able to overtake other cars on its own. The average distance between human interventions was 9 km, and at one point it drove 158 km without interventions.

In 1989, Dean Pomerleau from Carnegie Mellon University published *ALVINN: An Autonomous Land Vehicle in a Neural Network* (https://papers.nips.cc/paper/95-alvinn-an-autonomous-land-vehicle-in-a-neural-network.pdf), a pioneering paper on the use of neural networks for AVs. This work is especially interesting, as it applied many of the topics we've discussed in this book in AVs 30 years ago. Let's look at the most important properties of ALVINN:

- It uses a simple neural network to decide the steering angle of a vehicle (it doesn't control the acceleration and the brakes).
- The network is fully connected with one input layer, one hidden layer, and one output layer.

- The input consists of the following:
  - A 30×32 single-color image (they used the blue channel from an RGB image) from a forward-facing camera mounted on the vehicle.
  - An 8×32 image from a laser range finder. This is simply a grid, where each cell contains the distance to the nearest obstacle covered by that cell in the field of view.
  - One scalar input, which indicates the road intensity—that is, whether the road is lighter or darker than the nonroad in the image from the camera. This values comes recursively from the network output.
- A single fully connected hidden layer with 29 neurons.
- A fully connected output layer with 46 neurons. The curvature of the road is represented by 45 of those neurons in a way that resembles one-hot encoding—that is, if the middle neuron has the highest activation, then the road is straight. Conversely, the left and right neurons represent increasing road curvature. The final output unit indicates the road intensity.
- The network was trained for 40 epochs on a dataset of 1,200 images:

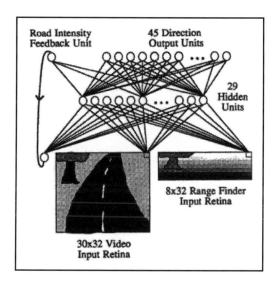

The network architecture of ALVINN. Source: The ALVINN paper

Next, let's take a look at the more recent timeline of (mostly) commercial AV progress:

- The DARPA Grand Challenge (https://en.wikipedia.org/wiki/DARPA_Grand_Challenge) was organized in 2004, 2005, and 2007. In the first year, the participating teams' AVs had to navigate a 240 km route in the Mojave Desert. The best-performing AV managed just 11.78 km of that route, before getting hung up on a rock. In 2005, the teams had to overcome a 212 km off-road course in California and Nevada. This time, five vehicles managed to drive the whole route. The 2007 challenge was to navigate a mock urban environment, built in an air force base. The total route length was 89 km and the participants had to obey the traffic rules. Six vehicles finished the whole course.

- In 2009, Google started developing self-driving technology. This effort led to the creation of Alphabet's (Google's parent company) subsidiary Waymo (https://waymo.com/). In December 2018, they launched the first commercial on-demand ride-hailing service with AVs in Phoenix, Arizona. In October 2019, Waymo announced the start of the first truly driverless cars as part of their robotaxi service (previously, a safety driver had always been present).

- Mobileye (https://www.mobileye.com/) uses deep neural networks to provide driver-assistance systems (for example, lane-keeping assistance). The company has developed a series of **system-on-chip** (**SOC**) devices, specifically optimized to run neural networks with low energy consumption, required for automotive use. Its products are used by many of the major vehicle manufacturers. In 2017, Mobileye was acquired by Intel for $15.3 billion. Since then, BMW, Intel, Fiat-Chrysler, SAIC, Volkswagen, NIO, and the automotive supplier Delphi (now Aptiv) have cooperated on the joint development of self-driving technology. In the first three quarters of 2019, the total sales of Mobileye were $822 million, compared to $358 million in all four quarters of 2016.

- In 2016, General Motors acquired Cruise Automation (https://getcruise.com/), a developer of self-driving technology, for more than $500 million (the exact figure is unknown). Since then, Cruise Automation has tested and demonstrated multiple AV prototypes, driving in San Francisco. In October 2018, it was announced that Honda will also participate in the venture by investing $750 million in return for a 5.7% stake. In May 2019, Cruise secured $1.15 billion additional investment from a group of new and existing investors.

- In 2017, Ford Motor Co. acquired majority ownership of the self-driving startup Argo AI. In 2019, Volkswagen announced that it will invest $2.6 billion in Argo AI as part of a larger deal with Ford. Volkswagen would contribute $1 billion in funding and its $1.6 billion Autonomous Intelligence Driving subsidiary with more than 150 employees, based in Munich.

Levels of automation

When we talk about AVs, we usually imagine fully driverless vehicles. But in reality, we have cars that require a driver, but still provide some automated features.

The SAE has developed a scale of six levels of automation:

- **Level 0**: The driver handles the steering, acceleration, and braking of the vehicle. The features at this level can only provide warnings and immediate assistance to the driver's actions. Examples of features of this level include the following:
    - A lane-departure warning simply warns the driver when the vehicle has crossed one of the lane markings.
    - A blind-spot warning warns the driver when another vehicle is located in the blind spot area of the car (the area immediately left or right of the rear end of the vehicle).

- **Level 1**: Features that provide either steering or acceleration/braking assistance to the driver. The most popular of these features in vehicles today are the following:
    - **Lane-keeping assist (LKA)**: The vehicle can detect the lane markings and use the steering to keep itself centered in the lane.
    - **Adaptive cruise control (ACC)**: The vehicle can detect other vehicles and use brakes and acceleration to maintain a preset speed or reduce it, depending on the circumstances.
    - **Automatic emergency braking (AEB)**: The vehicle can stop automatically if it detects an obstacle and the driver doesn't react.

- **Level 2**: Features that provide both steering and brake/acceleration assistance to the driver. One such feature is a combination of LKA and adaptive cruise control. At this level, the car can return control to the driver without advance warning at any moment. Therefore, he or she has to maintain a constant focus on the road situation. For example, if the lane markings suddenly disappear, the LKA system can prompt the driver to take control of the steering immediately.

- **Level 3**: This is the first level where we can talk about real autonomy. It is similar to level 2 in the sense that the car can drive itself under certain limited conditions and can prompt the driver to take control; however, this is guaranteed to happen in advance with sufficient time to allow an inattentive person to familiarize themselves with the road conditions. For example, say that the car drives itself on the highway, but the cloud-connected navigation obtains information about construction works on the road ahead. The driver will be prompted to take control well in advance of reaching the construction area.

- **Level 4**: Vehicles at level 4 are fully autonomous in a wider range of situations, compared to level 3. For example, a locally geofenced (that is, limited to a certain region) taxi service could be at level 4. There is no requirement for the driver to take control. Instead, if the vehicle goes outside this region, it should be able to safely abort the trip.
- **Level 5**: Full autonomy under all circumstances. The steering wheel is optional.

All commercially available vehicles today have features at level 2 at most (even Tesla's Autopilot). The only exception (according to the manufacturer) is the 2018 Audi A8, which has a level 3 feature called AI Traffic Jam Pilot. The system takes charge of driving at speeds up to 60 km/h on multilane roads with a physical barrier between the two directions of traffic. The driver can be prompted to take control with 10 seconds of advance warning. This feature was demonstrated during the launch of the vehicle, but as of the writing of this chapter, Audi cites regulatory limitations and doesn't include it in all markets. I have no information on where (or if) this feature is available.

In the next section, we'll look at the components that make up an AV system.

Components of an AV system

In this section, we'll outline two types of AV system from a software architecture perspective. The first type uses sequential architecture with multiple components, as illustrated in the following diagram:

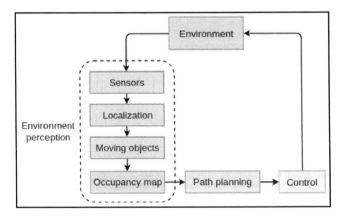

The components of an AV system

The system resembles the reinforcement-learning framework we briefly discussed in `Chapter 10`, *Meta Learning*. We have a feedback loop where the environment (either the physical world or a simulation) provides the agent (vehicle) with its current state. In turn, the agent decides on its new trajectory, the environment reacts to it, and so on. Let's start with the environment-perception subsystem, which has the following modules (we'll discuss them in more detail in the following sections):

- **Sensors:** Physical devices, such as cameras and radars.
- **Localization:** Determines the exact position of the vehicle (with centimeter accuracy) within a high-definition map.
- **Moving object detection and tracking:** Detects and tracks other traffic participants, such as vehicles and pedestrians.

The output of the perception system combines the data from its various modules to produce a **middle-level** virtual representation of the surrounding environment. This representation is usually a top-down (birds-eye) 2D view of the environment, referred to as the **occupancy map**. The following screenshot shows an example occupancy map of the ChauffeurNet system, which we'll discuss later in the chapter. It includes road surfaces (white and yellow lines), traffic lights (red lines), and other vehicles (white rectangles). The image is best viewed in color:

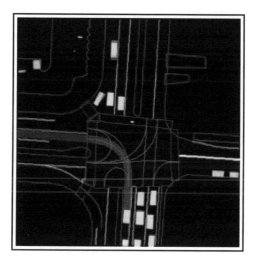

Occupancy map of ChauffeurNet. Source: https://arxiv.org/abs/1812.03079

The occupancy map serves as input for the **path-planning** module, which uses it to determine the future trajectory of the vehicle. The **control** module takes the desired trajectory and translates it to low-level control inputs to the vehicle.

The middle-level representation approach has several advantages. Firstly, it is well-suited for the functions of the path-planning and control modules. Also, instead of using the sensor data to create the top-down image, we can produce it with a simulator. In this way, it will be easier to collect training data, as we won't have to drive a real car. Even more important is that we'll be able to simulate situations that rarely occur in the real world. For example, our AV has to avoid crashes at any cost, yet real-world training data will have very few, if any, crashes. If we only use real sensor data, one of the most important driving situations will be severely underrepresented.

The second type of AV system uses a single end-to-end component, which takes the raw sensor data as input and produces driving policy in the form of steering controls, as shown in the following diagram:

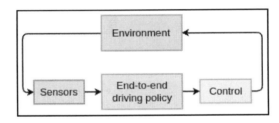

End-to-end AV system

In fact, we already mentioned an end-to-end system when we discussed ALVINN (in the *Brief history of AV research* section). Next, we'll focus on the different modules of the sequential system. We'll cover the end-to-end system in more detail later in the chapter.

Environment perception

For any automation feature to work, the vehicle needs a good perception of its surrounding environment. The environment-perception system has to identify the exact position, distance, and direction of moving objects, such as pedestrians, cyclists, and other vehicles. Additionally, it has to create a precise mapping of the road surface and the exact position of the vehicle on that surface and in the environment as a whole. Let's discuss the hardware and software components that help the AV create this virtual model of the environment.

Sensing

The key to building a good environment model is the vehicle sensors. The following is a list of the most important sensors:

- **Camera**: Its images are used to detect the road surface, lane markings, pedestrians, cyclists, other vehicles, and so on. An important camera property in the automotive context (besides the resolution) is the field of view. It measures how much of the observable world the camera sees at any given moment. For example, with a 180° field of view, it can see everything in front of it and nothing behind. With a 360° field of view, it can see everything in front of it and everything behind the vehicle (full observation). The following different types of camera systems exist:

    - **Mono camera**: Uses a single forward-facing camera, usually mounted on the top of the windshield. Most automation features rely on this type of camera to work. A typical field of view for the mono camera is 125°.

    - **Stereo camera**: A system of two forward-facing cameras, slightly removed from each other. The distance between the cameras allows them to capture the same picture from a slightly different angle and combine them into a 3D image (in the same way we use our eyes). A stereo system can measure the distance to some of the objects in the image, while a mono camera relies only on heuristics to do this.

    - **360° surrounding view of the environment**: some vehicles have a system of four cameras (front, back, left, and right).

    - **Night vision camera**: a system, where the vehicle includes a special type of headlight, which emits light in the infrared spectrum in addition to its regular function. The light is recorded from infrared cameras, which can display an enhanced image to the driver and detect obstacles during the night.

- **Radar**: A system that uses a transmitter to emit electromagnetic waves (in the radio or microwave spectrum) in different directions. When the waves reach an object, they are usually reflected, some of them in the direction of the radar itself. The radar can detect them with a special receiver antenna. Since we know that radio waves travel at the speed of light, we can calculate the distance to the reflected object by measuring how much time has passed between emitting and receiving the signal. We can also calculate the speed of an object (for example, another vehicle) by measuring the difference between the frequencies of the outgoing and incoming waves (Doppler effect). The "image" of the radar is noisier, narrower, and with lower resolution, compared to a camera image. For example, a long-range radar can detect objects at a distance of 160 m, but in a narrow 12° field of view. The radar can detect other vehicles and pedestrians, but it won't be able to detect the road surface or lane markings. It is usually used for ACC and AEB, while the LKA system uses a camera. Most vehicles have one or two front-facing radars and, on rare occasions, a rear-facing radar.
- **Lidar (light detection and ranging)**: This sensor is somewhat similar to radar, but instead of radio waves, it emits laser beams in the near-infrared spectrum. Because of this, one emitted pulse can accurately measure the distance to a single point. Lidar emits multiple signals very fast in a pattern, which creates a 3D point cloud of the environment (the sensor can rotate very fast). The following is a diagram of how a vehicle would see the world with a lidar:

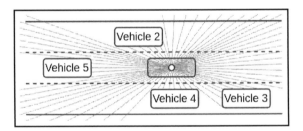

A diagram of how a vehicle sees the world through lidar

- **Sonar (sound navigation ranging)**: This sensor emits pulses of ultrasonic waves and maps the environment by listening to the echos of the waves, reflected by the surrounding objects. Sonar is inexpensive compared to radar, but has a limited effective range of detection. Because of this, they are usually used in parking assistance features.

The data from multiple sensors can be merged into a single environment model with a process called **sensor fusion**. Sensor fusion is usually implemented using Kalman filters (https://en.wikipedia.org/wiki/Kalman_filter).

Localization

Localization is the process of determining the exact position of the vehicle on the map. Why is this important? Companies such as HERE (https://www.here.com/) specialize in creating extremely accurate road maps, where the entire area of the road surface is known to within a few centimeters. These maps could also include information about static objects of interest, such as lane markings, traffic signs, traffic lights, speed restrictions, zebra crossings, speed bumps, and so on. Therefore, if we know the exact position of the vehicle on the road, it won't be hard to calculate the optimal trajectory.

One obvious solution is to use GPS; however, GPS can be accurate to within 1-2 meters under perfect conditions. In areas with high-rise buildings or mountains, the accuracy can suffer because the GPS receiver won't be able to get a signal from a sufficient number of satellites. One way to solve this problem is with **simultaneous localization and mapping (SLAM)** algorithms. These algorithms are beyond the scope of this book, but I encourage you to do your own research on the topic.

Moving object detection and tracking

We now have an idea of what sensors the vehicle uses, and we have briefly mentioned the importance of knowing its exact location on the map. With this knowledge, the vehicle could theoretically navigate to its destination by simply following a breadcrumb trail of fine-grained points. However, the task of autonomous driving isn't that simple, because the environment is dynamic, as it includes moving objects such as vehicles, pedestrians, cyclists, and so on. An autonomous vehicle must constantly know the positions of the moving objects and track them as it plans its trajectory. This is one area where we can apply deep-learning algorithms to the raw sensor data. First, we'll do this for the camera. In Chapter 5, *Object Detection and Image Segmentation*, we discussed how to use **convolutional networks (CNNs)** in two advanced vision tasks—object detection and semantic segmentation.

To recap, object detection creates a bounding box around different classes of objects detected in the image. Semantic segmentation assigns a class label to every pixel of the image. We can use segmentation to detect the exact shape of the road surface and the lane markings on the camera image. We can use object detection to classify and localize the moving objects of interest in the environment; however, we have already covered these topics in Chapter 5, *Object Detection and Image Segmentation*. In this chapter, we'll focus on the lidar sensor and we'll discuss how to apply CNNs over the 3D point cloud this sensor produces.

Now that we've outlined the perception subsystem components, in the next section, we'll introduce the path planning subsystem.

Path planning

Path planning (or driving policy) is the process of calculating the vehicle trajectory and speed. Although we might have an accurate map and exact location of the vehicle, we still need to keep in mind the dynamics of the environment. The car is surrounded by other moving vehicles, pedestrians, traffic lights, and so on. What happens if the vehicle in front stops suddenly? Or if it's moving too slow? Our AV has to make the decision to overtake and then execute the maneuver. This is an area where ML and DL in particular can be especially useful, and we'll discuss two ways to implement these in this chapter. More specifically, we'll discuss using an imitation driving policy in an end-to-end learning system, as well as a driving policy algorithm called ChauffeurNet, which was developed by Waymo.

One obstacle in AV research is that building an AV and obtaining the necessary permits to test it is very expensive and time-consuming. Thankfully, we can still train our algorithms with the help of AV simulators.

Some of the most popular simulators are the following:

- Microsoft AirSim, built on the Unreal Engine (`https://github.com/Microsoft/AirSim/`)
- CARLA, built on the Unreal Engine (`https://github.com/carla-simulator/carla`)
- Udacity's Self-Driving Car Simulator, built with Unity (`https://github.com/udacity/self-driving-car-sim`)
- OpenAI Gym's `CarRacing-v0` environment (we'll see an example of this in the *Imitation driving policy* section)

This concludes our description of the components of an AV system. Next, we'll discuss how to process 3D spatial data.

Introduction to 3D data processing

The lidar produces a point cloud—a set of data points in a three-dimensional space. Remember that the lidar emits laser beams. A beam reflecting off of a surface and returning to the receiver generates a single data point of the point cloud. If we assume that the lidar device is the center of the coordinate system and each laser beam is a vector, then a point is defined by the vector's direction and magnitude. Therefore, the point cloud is an **unordered set** of vectors. Alternatively, we can define the points by their Cartesian coordinates $\mathbb{R}^3$ in space, as illustrated in the left side of the following diagram. In this case, the point cloud is a set of vectors $\{\mathbf{p}_i | i = 1, \ldots, n\}$, where each vector $\mathbf{p}_i = [x_i, y_i, z_i]$ contains the three coordinates of the point. For the sake of clarity, each point is represented as a cube:

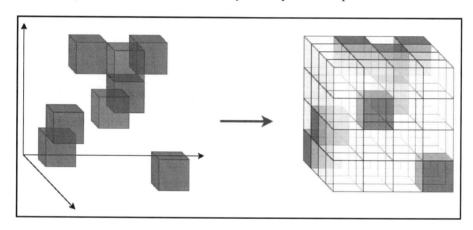

Left: Points (represented as cubes) in the 3D space: Right: A 3D grid of voxels

Next, let's focus on the input data format for neural networks, and specifically CNNs. A 2D color image is represented as a tensor with three slices (one for each channel) and each slice is a matrix (2D grid) composed of pixels. The CNN uses 2D convolutions (see Chapter 2, *Understanding Convolutional Networks*). Intuitively, we might think that we can use a similar 3D grid of **voxels** (a voxel is a 3D pixel) for 3D point clouds, as illustrated in the right image of the preceding diagram. Assuming the point cloud points have no color, we can represent the grid as a 3D tensor and use it as input to a CNN with 3D convolutions.

However, if we take a closer look at this 3D grid, we can see that it is sparse. For example, in the preceding diagram, we have a point cloud with 8 points, but the grid contains 4 x 4 x 4 = 64 cells. In this simple case, we increase the memory footprint of the data eightfold, but in the real world the conditions, could be even worse. In this section, we'll introduce PointNet (see *PointNet: Deep Learning on Point Sets for 3D Classification and Segmentation*, https://arxiv.org/abs/1612.00593), which provides a solution to this problem.

PointNet takes as input the set of point cloud vectors $\mathbf{p}_i$, rather than their 3D grid representation. To understand its architecture, we'll start with the properties of the set of point cloud vectors that led to the network design (the following bullets contain quotes from the original paper):

- **Unordered**: Unlike pixel arrays in images or voxel arrays in 3D grids, a point cloud is a set of points without a specific order. Therefore, a network that consumes N 3D point sets needs to be invariant to $N!$ permutations of the input set in data-feeding order.

- **Interaction among points**: Similar to the pixels of an image, the distance between 3D points can indicate the level of relation among them—that is, it's more likely that nearby points are part of the same object, compared to distant ones. Therefore, the model needs to be able to capture local structures from nearby points and the combinatorial interactions among local structures.

- **Invariance under transformations**: As a geometric object, the learned representation of the point set should be invariant to certain transformations. For example, rotating and translating points all together should not modify the global point cloud category, nor the segmentation of the points.

Now that we know these prerequisites, let's see how PointNet addresses them. We'll start with the network architecture and then we'll discuss its components in more detail:

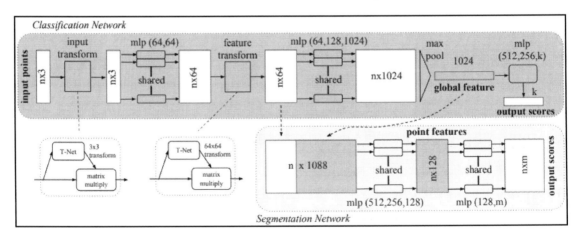

PointNet architecture. Source: https://arxiv.org/abs/1612.00593

PointNet is a **multilayer perceptron** (**MLP**). This is a feed-forward network that consists only of fully connected layers (and max pooling, but more on that later). As we mentioned, the set of input point cloud vectors $\mathbf{p}_i$ is represented as an $n \times 3$ tensor. It is important to note that the network (up until the max pooling layer) is **shared** among all points of the set. That is, although the input size is $n \times 3$, we can think of PointNet as applying the same network n times over n input vectors of size 1×3. In other words, the network weights are shared among all points of the point cloud. This sequential arrangement also allows for an arbitrary number of input points.

The input passes through the input transform (we'll look at this in more detail later), which outputs another $n \times 3$ tensor, where each of the n points is defined by three components (similar to the input tensor). This tensor is fed to an upsampling fully connected layer, which encodes each point to a 64-dimensional vector for $n \times 64$ output. The network continues with another transformation, similar to the input transform. The result is then gradually upsampled with 64, then 128, and finally 1,024 fully connected layers to produce the final $n \times 1024$ output. This tensor serves as input to a max pooling layer, which takes the maximum element of the same location among all n points and produces a 1,024-dimensional output vector. This vector is an aggregated representation of the whole set of points.

But why use max pooling in the first place? Remember that max pooling is a symmetric operation—that is, it will produce the same output regardless of the order of the inputs. At the same time, the set of points is unordered as well. Using max pooling ensures that the network will produce the same result regardless of the order of the points. The authors of the paper chose max pooling over other symmetric functions, such as average pooling and sum, because max pooling demonstrated the highest accuracy in the benchmark datasets.

After the max pooling, the network splits into two networks, depending on the type of task (see the preceding diagram):

- **Classification**: The 1024D aggregate vector serves as input to several fully connected layers, which end with k-way softmax, where k is the number of classes. This is a standard classification pipeline.
- **Segmentation**: This assigns a class to each point of the set. An extension of the classification net, this task requires a combination of local and global knowledge. As the diagram illustrates, we concatenate each of the n 64D intermediate point representations with the global 1024D vector for a combined $n \times 1088$ tensor. Like the initial segment of the network, this path is also shared among all points. The vector of each point is downsampled to 128D with a series (1088 to 512, then to 256, and finally, to 128) fully connected layers. The final fully connected layer has m units (one for each class) and softmax activation.

So far, we have explicitly addressed the unordered nature of the input data with the max pooling operation, but we still have to address the invariance and interaction among points. This is where the input and feature transforms will help. Let's start with the input transform (in the preceding diagram, this is T-net). T-net is an MLP, which is similar to the full PointNet (it is referred to as a mini-PointNet), as illustrated in the following diagram:

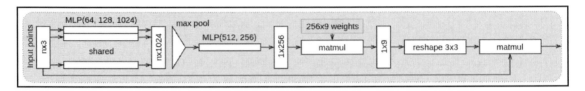

Input (and feature) transform T-nets

The input transform T-net takes as input the $n \times 3$ set of points (the same input as the full network). Like the full PointNet, T-net is shared among all points. First, the input is upsampled to $n \times 1024$ with 64-, then 128-, and finally, 1024-unit fully connected layers. The upsampled output is fed to a max pooling operation, which outputs 1×1024 vector. Then, the vector is downsampled to 1×256 using two 512- and 256-unit fully connected layers. The 1×256 vector is multiplied by a 256×9 matrix of global (shared) learnable weights. The result is reshaped as a 3×3 matrix, which is multiplied by the original input point $\mathbf{p}_i$ over all points to produce the final $n \times 3$ output tensor. The intermediate 3×3 matrix acts as a type of learnable affine transformation matrix over the set of points. In this way, the points are normalized into a familiar perspective with respect to the network—that is, the network becomes invariant under transformations. The second T-net (feature transform) is almost identical to the first, with the exception that the input tensor is $n \times 64$, which results in a 64×64 matrix.

Although the global max pooling layer ensures that the network is not influenced by the order of the data, it has another disadvantage, because it creates a single representation of the whole input set of points; however, these points might belong to different objects (for example, vehicles and pedestrians). In situations like this, the global aggregation could be problematic. To solve this, the authors of PointNet introduced PointNet++ (see *PointNet++: Deep Hierarchical Feature Learning on Point Sets in a Metric Space* at https://arxiv.org/abs/1706.02413), which is a hierarchical neural network that applies PointNet recursively on a nested partitioning of the input point set.

In this section, we looked at 3D data processing in the context of the AV environment-perception system. In the next section, we'll shift our attention to the path-planning system with an imitation driving policy.

Imitation driving policy

In the *Components of an AV system* section, we outlined several modules that were necessary for a self-driving system. In this section, we'll look at how to implement one of them—the driving policy—with the help of DL. One way to do this is with RL, where the car is the agent and the environment is, well, the environment. Another popular approach is **imitation learning**, where the model (network) learns to imitate the actions of an expert (human). Let's look at the properties of imitation learning in the AV scenario:

- We'll use a type of imitation learning, known as **behavioral cloning**. This simply means that we'll train our network in a supervised way. Alternatively, we could use imitation learning in a reinforcement learning (RL) scenario, which is known as inverse RL.

- The output of the network is the driving policy, represented by the desired steering angle and/or acceleration or braking. For example, we can have one regression output neuron for the steering angle and one neuron for acceleration or braking (as we cannot have both at the same time).

- The network input can be either of the following:
    - Raw sensor data for end-to-end systems—for example, an image from the forward-facing camera. AV systems, where a single model uses raw sensor inputs and outputs a driving policy, are referred to as **end-to-end**.
    - Middle-level environment representation for sequential composite systems.

- We'll create the training dataset with the help of an expert. We'll let the expert drive the vehicle manually, either in the real world or in a simulator. At each step of the journey, we'll record the following:
    - The current state of the environment. This could be the raw sensor data or the top-down view representation. We'll use the current state as input for the model.
    - The actions of the expert in the current state of the environment (steering angle and braking/acceleration). This will be the target data for the network. During training, we'll simply minimize the error between the network predictions and the driver actions using the familiar gradient descent. In this way, we'll teach the network to imitate the driver.

The behavioral cloning scenario is illustrated in the following diagram:

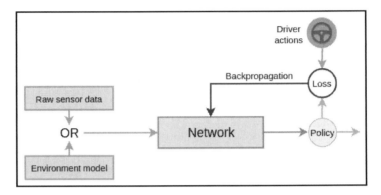

Behavioral cloning scenario

As we have already mentioned, ALVINN (from the *Brief history of AV research* section) is a behavioral cloning end-to-end system. More recently, the paper *End to End Learning for Self-Driving Cars* (https://arxiv.org/abs/1604.07316) introduced a similar system, which uses a CNN with five convolutional layers instead of a fully connected network. In their experiment, the images of a forward-facing camera on the vehicle are fed as input to the CNN. The output of the CNN is a single scalar value, which represents the desired steering angle of the car. The network doesn't control acceleration and braking. To build the training dataset, the authors of the paper collected about 72 hours of real-world driving videos. During the evaluation, the car was able to drive itself 98% of the time in a suburban area (excluding making lane changes and turns from one road to another). Additionally, it managed to drive without intervention for 16 km on a multilane divided highway. In the following section, we'll implement something fun—a behavioral cloning example with PyTorch.

Behavioral cloning with PyTorch

In this section, we'll implement a behavioral cloning example with PyTorch 1.3.1. To help us with this task, we'll use OpenAI Gym (https://gym.openai.com/), which is an open source toolkit for the development and comparison of reinforcement learning algorithms. It allows us to teach **agents** to undertake various tasks, such as walking or playing games such as Pong, Pinball, some other Atari games, and even Doom.

We can install it with `pip`:

```
pip install gym[box2d]
```

In this example, we'll use the `CarRacing-v0` OpenAI Gym environment, as shown in the following screenshot:

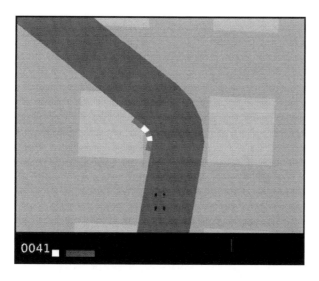

In the CarRacing-v0 environment. the agent is a racing car: a birds-eye view is used the whole time

 This example contains multiple Python files. In this section, we'll mention the most important parts. The full source code is at https://github.com/PacktPublishing/Advanced-Deep-Learning-with-Python/tree/master/Chapter11/imitation_learning.

The goal is for the red racing car (referred to as the agent) to drive around the track as quickly as it can without sliding off of the road surface. We can control the car using four actions: accelerate, brake, turn left, and turn right. The input for each action is continuous—for example, we can specify full throttle with the value 1.0 and half throttle with the value 0.5 (the same goes for the other controls).

For the sake of simplicity, we'll assume that we can only specify two discrete action values: 0 for no action and 1 for full action. Since, originally, this was an RL environment, the agent will receive an award at each step as it progresses along the track; however, we'll not use it, since the agent will learn directly from our actions. We'll perform the following steps:

1. Create a training dataset by driving the car around the track ourselves (we'll control it with the keyboard arrows). In other words, we'll be the expert that the agent tries to imitate. At every step of the episode, we'll record the current game frame (state) and the currently pressed keys, and we'll store them in a file. The full code for this step is available at `https://github.com/PacktPublishing/ Advanced-Deep-Learning-with-Python/blob/master/Chapter11/imitation_ learning/keyboard_agent.py`. All you have to do is run the file and the game will start. As you play, the episodes will be recorded (once every five episodes) in the `imitation_learning/data/data.gzip` file. If you want to start over, you can simply delete it. You can exit the game by pressing *Escape* and pause the game using the *Spacebar*. You can also start a new episode by pressing *Enter*. In this case, the current episode will be discarded and its sequence will not be stored. We suggest that you play at least 20 episodes for a sufficient size of the training dataset. It would be good to use the brake more often because otherwise, the dataset will become too imbalanced. In normal play, acceleration is used much more frequently than the brake or the steering. Alternatively, if you don't want to play, the GitHub repository already includes an existing data file.

2. The agent is represented by a CNN. We'll train it in a supervised manner using the dataset we just generated. The input will be a single game frame and the output will be a combination of steering direction and brake/acceleration. The target (labels) will be the action recorded for the human operator. If you want to omit this step, the repository already has a trained PyTorch network located at `https://github.com/PacktPublishing/Advanced-Deep-Learning-with-Python/ tree/master/Chapter11/imitation_learning/data/model.pt`.

3. Let the CNN agent play by using the network output to determine the next action to send to the environment. You can do this by simply running the `https://github.com/PacktPublishing/Advanced-Deep-Learning-with- Python/blob/master/Chapter11/imitation_learning/nn_agent.py` file. If you haven't performed any of the previous two steps, this file will use the existing agent.

With that introduction, let's continue by preparing the training dataset.

Generating the training dataset

In this section, we'll look at how to generate a training dataset and load it as an instance of PyTorch's `torch.utils.data.DataLoader` class. We'll highlight the most relevant parts of the code, but the full source code is located at `https://github.com/PacktPublishing/ Advanced-Deep-Learning-with-Python/blob/master/Chapter11/imitation_learning/ train.py`.

We'll create the training dataset in several steps:

1. The `read_data` function reads `imitation_learning/data/data.gzip` in two `numpy` arrays: one for the game frames and the other for the keyboard combinations associated with them.

2. The environment accepts actions, composed of a three-element array, where the following are true:
   - The first element has a value in the range `[-1, 1]` and represents the steering angle (–1 for right, 1 for left).
   - The second element is in the `[0, 1]` range and represents the throttle.
   - The third element is in the `[0, 1]` range and represents the brake power.

3. We'll use the seven most common key combinations: `[0, 0, 0]` for no action (the car is coasting), `[0, 1, 0]` for acceleration, `[0, 0, 1]` for brake, `[-1, 0, 0]` for left, `[-1, 0, 1]` for a combination of left and brake, `[1, 0, 0]` for right, and `[1, 0, 1]` for the right and brake combination. We have deliberately prevented the simultaneous use of acceleration and left or right, as the car becomes very unstable. The rest of the combinations are implausible.
   The `read_data` phrase will convert these arrays to a single class label from 0 to 6. In this way, we'll simply solve a classification problem with seven classes.

4. The `read_data` function will also balance the dataset. As we mentioned, acceleration is the most common key combination, while some of the others, such as brake, are the rarest. Therefore, we'll remove some of the acceleration samples and we'll multiply some of the braking (and left/right + brake). However, the author did this in a heuristic way by trying multiple combinations of deletion/multiplication ratios and selected the ones that work best. If you record your own dataset, your driving style may differ, and you may want to modify these ratios.

Once we have the `numpy` arrays of the training samples, we'll use the `create_datasets` function to convert them to `torch.utils.data.DataLoader` instances. These classes simply allow us to extract the data in mini batches and apply data augmentation.

But first, let's implement the `data_transform` list of transformations, which modify the image before feeding it to the network. The full implementation is available at `https://github.com/PacktPublishing/Advanced-Deep-Learning-with-Python/blob/master/Chapter11/imitation_learning/util.py`. We'll convert the image to grayscale, normalize the color values in the `[0, 1]` range, and crop the bottom part of the frame (the black rectangle, which shows the rewards and other information). The implementation is as follows:

```
data_transform = torchvision.transforms.Compose([
    torchvision.transforms.ToPILImage(),
    torchvision.transforms.Grayscale(1),
    torchvision.transforms.Pad((12, 12, 12, 0)),
    torchvision.transforms.CenterCrop(84),
    torchvision.transforms.ToTensor(),
    torchvision.transforms.Normalize((0,), (1,)),
])
```

Next, let's shift our attention back to the `create_datasets` function. We'll start with the declaration:

```
def create_datasets():
```

Then, we'll implement the `TensorDatasetTransforms` helper class to be able to apply the `data_transform` transformations over the input image. The implementation is as follows (please bear in mind the indentation, as this code is still part of the `create_datasets` function):

```
class TensorDatasetTransforms(torch.utils.data.TensorDataset):
    def __init__(self, x, y):
        super().__init__(x, y)

    def __getitem__(self, index):
        tensor = data_transform(self.tensors[0][index])
        return (tensor,) + tuple(t[index] for t in self.tensors[1:])
```

Next, we'll read the previously generated dataset in full:

```
x, y = read_data()
x = np.moveaxis(x, 3, 1)  # channel first (torch requirement)
```

Then, we'll create the training and validation data loaders (`train_loader` and `val_loader`). Finally, we'll return them as the result of the `create_datasets` function:

```
# train dataset
x_train = x[:int(len(x) * TRAIN_VAL_SPLIT)]
y_train = y[:int(len(y) * TRAIN_VAL_SPLIT)]

train_set = TensorDatasetTransforms(torch.tensor(x_train),
torch.tensor(y_train))

train_loader = torch.utils.data.DataLoader(train_set,
batch_size=BATCH_SIZE,
                                       shuffle=True, num_workers=2)

# test dataset
x_val, y_val = x[int(len(x_train)):], y[int(len(y_train)):]

val_set = TensorDatasetTransforms(torch.tensor(x_val),
torch.tensor(y_val))

val_loader = torch.utils.data.DataLoader(val_set,
batch_size=BATCH_SIZE,
                                       shuffle=False, num_workers=2)

return train_loader, val_loader
```

Next, let's focus on the agent NN architecture.

Implementing the agent neural network

The agent is represented by a CNN with the following properties:

- A single-input 84 × 84 slice.
- Three convolutional layers with striding for downsampling.
- ELU activations.
- Two fully connected layers.
- Seven output neurons (one for each neuron).
- Batch normalization and dropout, applied after each layer (even the convolutional) to prevent overfitting. Overfitting in this task is particularly exaggerated because we cannot use any meaningful data augmentation techniques. For example, say that we randomly flipped the image horizontally. In this case, we would have to also alter the label to reverse the steering value. Therefore, we'll rely on regularization as much as we can.

The following code block shows the network implementation:

```
def build_network():
    return torch.nn.Sequential(
        torch.nn.Conv2d(1, 32, 8, 4),
        torch.nn.BatchNorm2d(32),
        torch.nn.ELU(),
        torch.nn.Dropout2d(0.5),
        torch.nn.Conv2d(32, 64, 4, 2),
        torch.nn.BatchNorm2d(64),
        torch.nn.ELU(),
        torch.nn.Dropout2d(0.5),
        torch.nn.Conv2d(64, 64, 3, 1),
        torch.nn.ELU(),
        torch.nn.Flatten(),
        torch.nn.BatchNorm1d(64 * 7 * 7),
        torch.nn.Dropout(),
        torch.nn.Linear(64 * 7 * 7, 120),
        torch.nn.ELU(),
        torch.nn.BatchNorm1d(120),
        torch.nn.Dropout(),
        torch.nn.Linear(120, len(available_actions)),
    )
```

Having implemented the training dataset and the agent, we can proceed with the training.

Training

We'll implement the training itself with the help of the `train` function, which takes the network and the `cuda` device as parameters. We'll use cross-entropy loss and the Adam optimizer (the usual combination for classification tasks). The function simply iterates `EPOCHS` times and calls the `train_epoch` and `test` functions for each epoch. The following is the implementation:

```
def train(model: torch.nn.Module, device: torch.device):
    loss_function = torch.nn.CrossEntropyLoss()

    optimizer = torch.optim.Adam(model.parameters())

    train_loader, val_order = create_datasets()  # read datasets

    # train
    for epoch in range(EPOCHS):
        print('Epoch {}/{}'.format(epoch + 1, EPOCHS))

        train_epoch(model, device, loss_function, optimizer, train_loader)
```

```
    test(model, device, loss_function, val_order)

    # save model
    model_path = os.path.join(DATA_DIR, MODEL_FILE)
    torch.save(model.state_dict(), model_path)
```

Then, we'll implement the `train_epoch` for a single epoch training. This function iterates over all mini batches and performs forward and backward passes for each one. The following is the implementation:

```
def train_epoch(model, device, loss_function, optimizer, data_loader):
    model.train() # set model to training mode
    current_loss, current_acc = 0.0, 0.0

    for i, (inputs, labels) in enumerate(data_loader):
        inputs, labels = inputs.to(device), labels.to(device) # send to
device

        optimizer.zero_grad() # zero the parameter gradients
        with torch.set_grad_enabled(True):
            outputs = model(inputs) # forward
            _, predictions = torch.max(outputs, 1)
            loss = loss_function(outputs, labels)

            loss.backward() # backward
            optimizer.step()

        current_loss += loss.item() * inputs.size(0) # statistics
        current_acc += torch.sum(predictions == labels.data)

    total_loss = current_loss / len(data_loader.dataset)
    total_acc = current_acc / len(data_loader.dataset)

    print('Train Loss: {:.4f}; Accuracy: {:.4f}'.format(total_loss,
total_acc))
```

The `train_epoch` and `test` functions are similar to the ones we implemented for the transfer learning code example in Chapter 2, *Understanding Convolutional Networks*. To avoid repetition, we won't implement the `test` function here, although it's available in the GitHub repository.

We'll run the training for around 100 epochs, but you can shorten this to 20 or 30 epochs for rapid experiments. One epoch usually takes less than a minute using the default training set. Now that we are familiar with the training, let's see how to use the agent NN to drive the race car in our simulated environment.

Letting the agent drive

We'll start by implementing the `nn_agent_drive` function, which allows the agent to play the game (defined in `https://github.com/PacktPublishing/Advanced-Deep-Learning-with-Python/blob/master/Chapter11/imitation_learning/nn_agent.py`).
The function will start the `env` environment with an initial state (game frame). We'll use it as an input to the network. Then, we'll convert the softmax network output from one-hot encoding to an array-based action and we'll send it to the environment to make the next step. We'll repeat these steps until the episode ends. The `nn_agent_drive` function also allows the user to exit by pressing *Escape*. Note that we still use the same `data_transform` transformations as we did for the training.

First, we'll implement the initialization part, which binds the *Esc* key and initializes the environment:

```
def nn_agent_drive(model: torch.nn.Module, device: torch.device):
    env = gym.make('CarRacing-v0')

    global human_wants_exit  # use ESC to exit
    human_wants_exit = False

    def key_press(key, mod):
        """Capture ESC key"""
        global human_wants_exit
        if key == 0xff1b:  # escape
            human_wants_exit = True

    state = env.reset()  # initialize environment
    env.unwrapped.viewer.window.on_key_press = key_press
```

Next, we'll implement the main loop, where the agent (vehicle) takes an `action`, the environment returns the new `state`, and so on. This dynamic is reflected in the infinite `while` loop (please mind the indentation, as this code is still part of `nn_agent_play`):

```
while 1:
    env.render()

    state = np.moveaxis(state, 2, 0) # channel first image
    state = torch.from_numpy(np.flip(state, axis=0).copy()) # np to
tensor
    state = data_transform(state).unsqueeze(0) # apply transformations
    state = state.to(device) # add additional dimension

    with torch.set_grad_enabled(False): # forward
        outputs = model(state)

    normalized = torch.nn.functional.softmax(outputs, dim=1)

    # translate from net output to env action
    max_action = np.argmax(normalized.cpu().numpy()[0])
    action = available_actions[max_action]
    action[2] = 0.3 if action[2] != 0 else 0 # adjust brake power

    state, _, terminal, _ = env.step(action) # one step

    if terminal:
        state = env.reset()

    if human_wants_exit:
        env.close()
        return
```

We now have all the ingredients to run the program, which we will do in the following section.

Putting it all together

Finally, we can run the whole thing. The full code for this is available at `https://github.com/PacktPublishing/Advanced-Deep-Learning-with-Python/blob/master/Chapter11/imitation_learning/main.py`.

The following snippet builds and restores (if available) the network, runs the training, and evaluates the network:

```
# create cuda device
dev = torch.device("cuda:0" if torch.cuda.is_available() else "cpu")

# create the network
model = build_network()

# if true, try to restore the network from the data file
restore = False
if restore:
    model_path = os.path.join(DATA_DIR, MODEL_FILE)
    model.load_state_dict(torch.load(model_path))

# set the model to evaluation (and not training) mode
model.eval()

# transfer to the gpu
model = model.to(dev)

# train
train(model, dev)

# agent play
nn_agent_drive(model, dev)
```

Although we cannot show the agent in action here, you can easily see it in action by following the instructions in this section. Still, we can say that it learns well and is able to make full laps of the racing track on a regular basis (but not always). Interestingly, the network's driving style strongly resembles the style of the operator who generated the dataset. The example also goes to show that we shouldn't underestimate supervised learning. We were able to create a decently performing agent with a small dataset, and in a relatively short training time.

With this, we conclude our imitation learning example. Next, we'll discuss a much more sophisticated driving policy algorithm called ChauffeurNet.

Driving policy with ChauffeurNet

In this section, we'll discuss a recent paper called *ChauffeurNet: Learning to Drive by Imitating the Best and Synthesizing the Worst* (`https://arxiv.org/abs/1812.03079`). It was released in December 2018 by Waymo, one of the leaders in the field of AV. Let's look at some of the properties of the ChaffeurNet model:

- It is a combination of two interconnected networks. The first is a CNN called FeatureNet, which extracts features from the environment. These features are fed as inputs to a second, recurrent network called AgentRNN, which determines the driving policy.
- It uses imitation supervised learning in a similar way to the algorithms we described in the *Imitation driving policy* section. The training set is generated based on records of real-world driving episodes. ChauffeurNet can handle complex driving situations, such as lane changes, traffic lights, traffic signs, changing from one street to another, and so on.

 This paper is published by Waymo on arxiv.org and is used here for referential purposes only. Waymo and arxiv.org are not affiliated, and do not endorse this book, or the authors.

We'll start our discussion about ChauffeurNet with the input and output data representations.

Input and output representations

The end-to-end approach feeds raw sensor data (for example, camera images) to the ML algorithm (NN), which in turn produces the driving policy (steering angle and acceleration). In contrast, ChauffeurNet uses the middle-level input and output that we introduced in the *Components of an AV system* section. Let's look at the input to the ML algorithm first. This is a series of top-down (birds-eye) view 400 × 400 images, similar to the images of the `CarRacing-v0` environment, but much more complex. One moment of time *t* is represented by multiple images, where each one contains different elements of the environment.

We can see an example of a ChauffeurNet input/output combination in the following image:

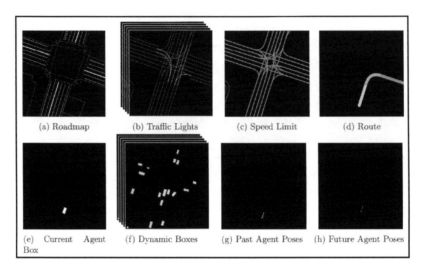

ChauffeurNet inputs. Source: https://arxiv.org/abs/1812.03079

Let's look at the input elements ((a) through (g)) in alphabetical order:

- (a) is a precise representation of the road map. It is an RGB image, which uses different colors to represent various road features, such as lanes, cross-walks, traffic signs, and curbs.
- (b) is a temporal sequence of grayscale images of the traffic lights. Unlike the features of (a), the traffic lights are dynamic—that is, they can be green, red, or yellow at different times. In order to properly convey their dynamics, the algorithm uses a series of images, displaying the state of the traffic lights for each lane at each of the past T_{scene} seconds up to the current moment. The color of the lines in each image represents the state of each traffic light, where the brightest color is red, intermediate is for yellow, and the darkest is green or unknown.
- (c) is a grayscale image with the known speed limit for each lane. Different color intensities represent different speed limits.
- (d) is the intended route between the start and the destination. Think of it as the directions generated by Google Maps.
- (e) is a grayscale image that represents the current location of the agent (displayed as a white box).

- (f) is a temporal sequence of grayscale images that represents the dynamic elements of the environment (displayed as boxes). These could be other vehicles, pedestrians, or cyclists. As these objects change locations over time, the algorithm conveys their trajectories with a series of snapshot images, representing their positions over the last T_{scene} seconds. This works in the same way as the traffic lights (b).
- (g) is a single grayscale image for the agent trajectory of the past T_{pose} seconds until the current moment. The agent locations are displayed as a series of points on the image. Note that we display them in a single image, and not with a temporal sequence like the other dynamic elements. The agent at moment t is represented in the same top-down environment with the properties $\mathbf{P}_t, \theta_t, s_t$, where $\mathbf{P}_t = (x_t, y_t)$ is the coordinates, θ_t is the orientation (or heading), and s_t is the speed.
- (h) is the algorithm middle-level output: the agent's future trajectory, represented as a series of points. These points carry the same meaning as the past trajectory (g). The future location output at time *t+1* is generated by using the past trajectory (g) up to the current moment *t*. We'll denote ChauffeurNet as:

$$\mathbf{p}_{t+\delta t} = \text{ChauffeurNet}(I, \mathbf{p}_t)$$

Here, *I* is all the preceding input images, $\mathbf{p}_t$ is the agent position at time *t*, and δt is a 0.2 s time delta. The value of δt is arbitrary, chosen by the authors of the paper. Once we have $t+\delta t$, we can add it to the past trajectory (g) and we can use it to generate the next location at step $t+2\delta t$ in a recurrent manner. The newly generated trajectory is fed to the control module of the vehicle, which tries its best to execute it via the vehicle controls (steering, acceleration, and brakes).

As we mentioned in the *Components of an AV system* section, this middle-level input representation allows us to use different sources of training data with ease. It can be generated from real-world driving with a fusion of the vehicle sensor inputs (such as cameras and lidar) and mapping data (such as streets, traffic lights, traffic signs, and so on). But we can also generate images of the same format with a simulated environment. The same applies to the middle-level output, where the control module can be attached to various types of physical vehicles or to a simulated vehicle. Using a simulation makes it possible to learn from situations that occur rarely in the real world, such as emergency braking or even crashes. To help the agent learn about such situations, the authors of the paper explicitly synthesized multiple rare scenarios using simulations.

Now that we are familiar with the data representation, let's shift our focus to the model's core components.

Model architecture

The following diagram illustrates the ChauffeurNet model architecture:

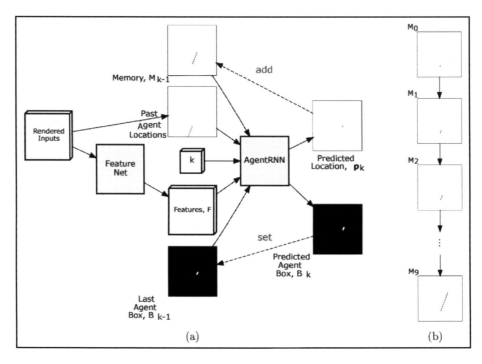

(a) ChauffeurNet architecture and (b) the memory updates over the iterations Source: https://arxiv.org/abs/1812.03079

First, we have FeatureNet (in the preceding diagram, this is marked by (a)). This is a CNN with residual connections, whose inputs are the top-down images we looked at in the *Input and output representations* section. The output of FeatureNet is a feature vector *F* which represents the synthesized network's understanding of the current environment. This vector serves as one of the inputs to the recurrent network AgentRNN, which predicts successive points in the driving trajectory iteratively. Let's say that we want to predict the next point of the agent's trajectory at step *k*. In this case, AgentRNN has the following outputs:

- $\mathbf{p}_k$ is the predicted next point of the driving trajectory at that step. As we can see from the diagram, the output of AgentRNN is actually a heatmap with the same dimensions as the input images. It represents a probability distribution $P_k(x, y)$ over the spatial coordinates, which indicates the probability of the next waypoint over each cell (pixel) of the heatmap. We use the `arg-max` operation to obtain the coarse pose prediction $\mathbf{p}_k$ from this heatmap.

- B_k is the predicted bounding box of the agent at step k. Like the waypoint output, B_k is a heatmap, but, here, each cell uses sigmoid activation and represents the probability that the agent occupies that particular pixel.
- There are also two additional outputs that are not displayed in the diagram: θ_k for the heading (or orientation) of the agent and s_k for the desired speed.

ChauffeurNet also includes an additive memory, denoted by M (in the preceding diagram, this is marked by (b)). M is the single-channel input image (g) that we defined in the *Input and output representations* section. It represents the waypoint predictions ($\mathbf{p}_k, \mathbf{p}_{k-1}, \ldots, \mathbf{p}_0$) of the past steps k. The current waypoint $\mathbf{p}_k$ is added to the memory at each step, as displayed in the preceding diagram.

The outputs $\mathbf{p}_k$ and B_k are fed back recursively as inputs to AgentRNN for the next step $k+1$. The formula for the AgentRNN output is as follows:

$$\mathbf{p}_{k+1}, B_{k+1} = \text{AgentRNN}(k+1, F, M_k, B_k)$$

Next, let's check how ChauffeurNet integrates within the sequential AV pipeline:

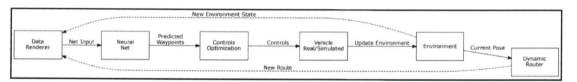

ChauffeurNet within the full end-to-end driving pipeline. Source: https://arxiv.org/abs/1812.03079

The system resembles the feedback loop that we introduced in the *Components of an AV system* section. Let's look at its components:

- **Data Renderer**: Receives input from both the environment and the dynamic router. Its role is to transform these signals into the top-down input images we defined in the *Input and output representations* section.
- **Dynamic Router**: Provides the intended route, which is dynamically updated, based on whether the agent was able to reach the previous target coordinates. Think of it as a navigation system, where you input a destination and it provides you with a route to the target. You start navigating this route and, if you stray from it, the system will calculate a new route dynamically based on your current location and your destination.

- **Neural Net**: The ChauffeurNet module, which outputs the desired future trajectory.
- **Controls Optimization**: Receives the future trajectory and translates it into low-level control signals that drive the vehicle.

ChauffeurNet is a rather complex system, so let's now look at how to train it.

Training

ChauffeurNet was trained with 30 million expert driving examples using imitation supervised learning. The model inputs are the top-down images we defined in the *Input and output representations* section, as illustrated in the following flattened (aggregated) input image:

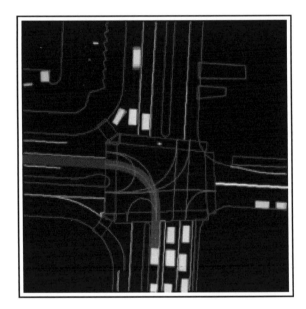

The image is best viewed in color. Source: https://arxiv.org/abs/1812.03079

Next, let's look at the components of the ChauffeurNet training process:

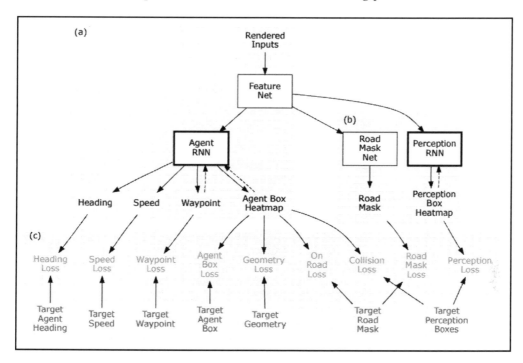

ChauffeurNet training components: (a) the model itself. (b) the additional networks. and (c) the losses. Source: https://arxiv.org/abs/1812.03079

We are already familiar with the ChauffeurNet model itself (marked as (a) in the preceding image). Let's focus on the two additional networks involved in the process (marked as (b) in the preceding image):

- **Road Mask Net**: Outputs a segmentation mask with the exact area of the road surface over the current input images. To better understand this, the following image illustrates a target road mask (left) and the network's predicted road mask (right):

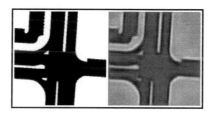

Source: https://arxiv.org/abs/1812.03079

- **PerceptionRNN**: Outputs a segmentation mask with the predicted future locations of every other dynamic object in the environment (vehicles, cyclists, pedestrians, and so on). The output of PerceptionRNN is illustrated in the following diagram, which shows the predicted location of other vehicles (the light rectangles):

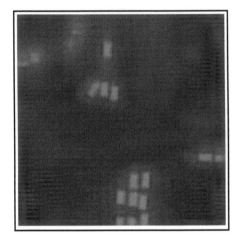

Source: https://arxiv.org/abs/1812.03079

These networks don't participate in the final vehicle control and are used only during training. The goal behind their use is that the FeatureNet network will learn better representations if it receives feedback from the tree tasks (AgentRNN, Road Mask Net, and PerceptionRNN), compared to simply getting feedback from AgentRNN.

Now, let's focus on the various loss functions (the bottom section (c) of the ChauffeurNet schema). We'll start with the imitation losses, which reflect how the model prediction of the future agent position differs from the human expert ground truth. The following list shows the AgentRNN outputs with their corresponding loss functions:

- A probability distribution $P_k(x, y)$ over the spatial coordinates of the predicted waypoint $\mathbf{p}_k$. We'll train this component with the following loss:

$$J_p = \mathcal{H}(P_k, P_k^{gt})$$

Here, $\mathcal{H}$ is the cross-entropy loss, P_k is the predicted distribution, and P_k^{gt} is the ground truth distribution.

- A heatmap of the agent bounding box B_k. We can train it with the following loss (applied along the cells of the heatmap):

$$J_B = \frac{1}{WH} \sum_x \sum_y \mathcal{H}(B_k(x,y), B_k^{gt}(x,y))$$

Here, W and H are the input image dimensions, $B_k(x,y)$ is the predicted heatmap, and $B_k^{gt}(x,y)$ is the ground truth heatmap.

- The heading (orientation) of the agent θ_k with the following loss:

$$J_\theta = |\theta_k - \theta_k^{gt}|$$

Here, θ_k is the predicted orientation and θ_k^{gt} is the ground truth orientation.

The authors of the paper also introduce past motion dropout. We can best explain this by citing the paper:

During training, the model is provided the past motion history as one of the inputs (image (g) of the schema in section Input and output representations). Since the past motion history during training is from an expert demonstration, the net can learn to "cheat" by just extrapolating from the past rather than finding the underlying causes of the behavior. During closed-loop inference, this breaks down because the past history is from the net's own past predictions. For example, such a trained net may learn to only stop for a stop sign if it sees a deceleration in the past history, and will therefore never stop for a stop sign during closed-loop inference. To address this, we introduce a dropout on the past pose history, where for 50% of the examples, we keep only the current position (u_0, v_0) of the agent in the past agent poses channel of the input data. This forces the net to look at other cues in the environment to explain the future motion profile in the training example.

They also observed that the imitation learning approach works well when the driving situation does not differ significantly from the expert driving training data. However, the agent has to be prepared for many driving situations that are not part of the training, such as collisions. If the agent only relies on the training data, it will have to learn about collisions implicitly, which is not easy. To solve this problem, the paper proposes explicit loss functions for the most important situations. These include the following:

- **Waypoint loss**: The error between the ground truth and the predicted agent future position p_k.
- **Speed loss**: The error between the ground truth and the predicted agent future speed s_k.
- **Heading loss**: The error between the ground truth and the predicted agent future direction θ_k.
- **Agent-box loss**: The error between the ground truth and the predicted agent bounding box B_k.
- **Geometry loss**: Force the agent to explicitly follow the target trajectory, independent of the speed profile.
- **On-road loss**: Force the agent to navigate only over the road surface area and avoid the nonroad areas of the environment. This loss will increase if the predicted bounding box of the agent overlaps with the nonroad area of the image, predicted by the road mask network.
- **Collision loss**: Explicitly force the agent to avoid collisions. This loss will increase if the agent's predicted bounding box overlaps with the bounding boxes of any of the other dynamic objects of the environment.

ChauffeurNet performed well in various real-world driving situations. You can see some of the results at https://medium.com/waymo/learning-to-drive-beyond-pure-imitation-465499f8bcb2.

Summary

In this chapter, we explored the applications of deep learning in AVs. We started with a brief historical overview of AV research and we discussed the different levels of autonomy. Then we described the components of the AV system and identified when it's appropriate to use DL techniques. Next, we looked at 3D-data processing and PointNet. Then we introduced the topic of implementing driving policies using behavioral cloning, and we implemented an imitation learning example with PyTorch. Finally, we looked at Waymo's ChauffeurNet system.

This chapter concludes our book. I hope you enjoyed the read!

Other Books You May Enjoy

If you enjoyed this book, you may be interested in these other books by Packt:

Hands-On Deep Learning Architectures with Python
Yuxi (Hayden) Liu, Saransh Mehta

ISBN: 978-1-78899-808-6

- Implement CNNs, RNNs, and other commonly used architectures with Python
- Explore architectures such as VGGNet, AlexNet, and GoogLeNet
- Build deep learning architectures for AI applications such as face and image recognition, fraud detection, and many more
- Understand the architectures and applications of Boltzmann machines and autoencoders with concrete examples
- Master artificial intelligence and neural network concepts and apply them to your architecture
- Understand deep learning architectures for mobile and embedded systems

Hands-On Deep Learning Algorithms with Python
Sudharsan Ravichandiran

ISBN: 978-1-78934-415-8

- Implement basic-to-advanced deep learning algorithms
- Master the mathematics behind deep learning algorithms
- Become familiar with gradient descent and its variants, such as AMSGrad, AdaDelta, Adam, and Nadam
- Implement recurrent networks, such as RNN, LSTM, GRU, and seq2seq models
- Understand how machines interpret images using CNN and capsule networks
- Implement different types of generative adversarial network, such as CGAN, CycleGAN, and StackGAN
- Explore various types of autoencoder, such as Sparse autoencoders, DAE, CAE, and VAE

Leave a review - let other readers know what you think

Please share your thoughts on this book with others by leaving a review on the site that you bought it from. If you purchased the book from Amazon, please leave us an honest review on this book's Amazon page. This is vital so that other potential readers can see and use your unbiased opinion to make purchasing decisions, we can understand what our customers think about our products, and our authors can see your feedback on the title that they have worked with Packt to create. It will only take a few minutes of your time, but is valuable to other potential customers, our authors, and Packt. Thank you!

Index

C

D

E

F

one-stage detection methods 148
OpenAI Gym
  reference link 418
optimization-based learning 393, 394, 395, 396,
  397, 398, 399, 400

P

padding 69
parametric ReLU (PReLU) 43
path-planning module 408
Perceptual Losses, for Real-Time Style Transfer
  and Super-Resolution
  reference link 224
Picasso problem 137
PointNet 415
pooling operations 69
principal component analysis (PCA) 248
probability density function (PDF) 23
probability distributions 22, 23, 25, 26, 27
probability mass function (PMF) 23
probability
  about 16, 17
  conditional probability 20
  empirical 17
  theoretical 17
prototypical networks 389, 390, 391, 392
PyTorch 1.3.1 92
PyTorch
  Faster R-CNN, implementing with 163, 164, 165
  Mask R-CNN, implementing with 172, 173, 174
  reference link 12
  transfer learning, implementing 92, 93, 94, 96,
    97
  used, for behavioral cloning implementation 418

Q

query set 377
question answering (QA) 323

R

random variables
  about 22, 23
  continuous 22
  discrete 22
  properties 24, 25

receptive fields 66
reconstruction error 178, 355
reconstruction loss 180
rectified linear unit (ReLU)
  about 41, 42
  exponential linear units (ELU) 43
  leaky ReLU 42
  parametric ReLU (PReLU) 43
recurrent GNNs 345, 346, 347
recurrent neural networks (RNNs)
  about 251, 252, 253, 254
  backpropagation through time 258, 259, 260,
    261
  gradients, exploding 262, 264
  gradients, vanishing 262, 264
  implementing 256, 257, 258
  many-to-many direct 255
  many-to-many indirect 255
  many-to-one 255
  one-to-many 255
  one-to-one 255
  parameters 252
  training 256, 257, 258
Region of Interest (RoI) 161
Region Proposal Network (RPN) 148
region proposal network (RPN) 159, 160
regions of interest (RoI) 148
regular backpropagation 84
regularization 87
reinforcement learning (RL) 394
reparameterization 357
reparameterization trick 181
residual blocks
  implementing 111, 112, 113, 115, 117
residual networks 108, 109
ResNets 108

S

sample point 18
sample space 18
scalars 10
scaled exponential linear units (SELU) 44
scikit-learn
  reference link 243
segmentation 415

Made in the USA
Coppell, TX
22 May 2021